City of Suspects

Amigos los tres.

PABLO PICCATO

City of Suspects

CRIME IN MEXICO CITY, 1900–1931

Duke University Press

Durham and London

2001

Printed in the United States of America on acid-free paper ♾
Designed by C. H. Westmoreland
Typeset in Carter & Cohn Galliard by Tseng Information Systems, Inc.
Library of Congress Cataloging-in-Publication Data appear on the last printed page of this book.

Portions of chapters one and two were published in *Anuario de Estudios Urbanos,* and parts of chapter three are reprinted from *Mexican Studies–Estudios Mexicanos* 11, no. 2 (Summer 1995): 203–41, by permission of the Regents of the University of California.

Frontispiece art: Luis Chávez and friends, "Friends the three of them," ca. 1924. *Courtesy Tribunal Superior de Justicia del Distruto Federal.*

para Xóchitl, Catalina y Aída

Contents

Acknowledgments

I owe this book to the effort of many people. Xóchitl Medina read the following pages and improved everything about them. She and my daughters helped me see the reason to do it, so this book is theirs. The University of Texas at Austin was the place where it began as a dissertation submitted in 1997. I thank first Jonathan C. Brown, my adviser, and the teachers (Susan Deans-Smith, Richard Graham, Alan Knight, Sandra Lauderdale-Graham, Naomi Lindstrom, and Mauricio Tenorio) and fellow students (Catherine Nolan, Daniel Hayworth, Mark Macleod, Joseph Ridout, Michael Snodgrass, Pamela Voekel, and Elliott Young) who made comments to papers or ideas that became part of this book and encouraged me beyond their duty. To many I am indebted for their advice, interest, and generosity during the research and writing process of the book: Félix Alonso, Carlos Aguirre, Jaime del Arenal, Silvia Arrom, Edward Beatty, Tito Bracamontes, Fanny Cabrejo, Gabriela Cano, Brian Connaughton, Ana Gamboa de Trejo, Renato González Mello, Matt Gutmann, Carlos Illades, Timothy Kessler, Herbert Klein, John Lear, Steve Lewis, Javier Macgregor, Salvador Martínez Martínez, Jose Humberto Medina González, Kevin Middlebrook, Alisa Newman, Marcela Noguez, Juan Ortiz, Ricardo Pérez Montfort, David Parker, Cecilia Piccato, Antonio Piccato, Josué Ramírez, Ariel Rodríguez Kuri, Cristina Sacristán, Richard Snyder, Alejandro Tortolero, Eric Van Young, Heather Williams, Justin Wolfe, and René Zenteno. Robert Buffington generously read the entire manuscript and, as Seth Fein, made invaluable comments. Credit for the mistakes is entirely mine.

I am indebted to the staffs of the Benson Latin American Collection at the University of Texas at Austin, the Archivo Histórico de la Ciudad de México, the Archivo Histórico de la Secretaría de Salud, the Archivo Porfirio Díaz, the Centro de Estudios de Historia de México Condumex, and particularly to Héctor Madrid at the Archivo General de la Nación, and Abelardo Sánchez Rojas and José Angel García at the Judicial Archives of the Reclusorio Sur in Mexico City. Without the trust and professionalism of the latter two this book would not exist. Material support came from the University of Texas at Austin, the Center for U.S.-Mexican Studies of the University of California, San Diego, the Consejo Nacional para la Ciencia y la Tecnología, the Instituto Nacional de Estudios Históricos de la Revolución Mexicana, and the Institute of Latin American and Iberian Studies and the Department of History at Columbia University. More material and spiritual support came from Ana Rodríguez, the Medina González family in Mexico City, and from Mary Helen Quinn and Anne Dibble in Austin.

Introduction

This book is about criminals and their victims in Mexico City at the beginning of the twentieth century. Crime was then, as it is now, a central problem for the inhabitants of Mexico's capital. Understanding and preventing it was a key aspect of the interactions between the state and all social groups. Its causes and consequences affected many parts of everyday life. A history of crime is, therefore, a history of the city and its inhabitants.

Since the difficult years that followed independence from Spain in 1821, violence and crime marked the nation's growth. Insurgency and the royalist reaction devastated the economy of the country. There followed years of instability, military uprisings, civil wars (leading to the Reforma War, 1857–1861), foreign invasions (most importantly by the United States, in 1847, and France, 1861–1867), and multiple constitutional experiments oscillating between liberal federalism and conservative centralism. Independence also brought forth uncontrollable banditry around highways and uncertainty regarding the survival of judicial institutions. Things clearly began to change with the 1867 restoration of the 1857 Constitution, the passing of civil and criminal codes in the early 1870s, and Porfirio Díaz's ascension to the presidency in 1876. The Porfirian regime (1876–1911) managed to control banditry and political dissent, guarantee the interests of foreign investors, and enforce liberal legislation on property, with the resulting dispossession of large numbers of peasants and the accumulation of wealth by national elites. Both facts contributed to renewed population growth in the capital and rising crime rates (see appendix, table 1) despite the state's activism vis-à-vis social reform through the strengthening of police, penalties, and prisons.[1]

The 1910 centennial celebration of independence, centered on Mexico City, seemed to demonstrate in the eyes of the world the civilization and stability achieved by the country. But the neat scheme of science and order set forth by the late Porfirian ruling group could not avoid a revolution. In that year, Francisco I. Madero issued a call to arms after Díaz persisted in imposing his own reelection. What began as a democratic rebellion triggered an uprising fueled by Madero's vague promise of justice—interpreted both as the restitution of lands to communities and as a penal and judicial reform. Throughout the country, political conflict turned into social revolution had a high economic cost and meant the loss of nearly a million lives. Although the parties of the civil war did not give Mexico City great strategic significance, beginning in 1913 its population nonetheless suffered the consequences of conflict. In February, President Madero was overthrown by a military coup and the following months were characterized by street battles, military occupation, heightened immigration, hunger, and lawlessness. Collective forms of violence and offenses against property became, it seemed, more frequent than ever. After 1917, a new regime began to reconstitute the mechanisms of political control and rebuild the economy. Political stability, achieved in the 1930s, crystallized into a single-party political system with strong popular support based on corporative organizations and remarkable accomplishments in the spheres of education and public health—at least in comparison with the rest of Latin America—but less concerned about punishment. Despite the widespread violence of the revolutionary decade and continuing population growth, the frequency of crime in Mexico City decreased after 1916, establishing a trend that would last until the 1990s.

The paradox posed by decreasing crime rates and declining state interest in penitentiary repression needs to be observed as a local, multilayered historical phenomenon. Thus the present study is about class and the negotiations and resistance that characterized the relations between social groups and between citizens and the state. Throughout the early decades of the twentieth century, the better-off considered criminality to be the social issue of greatest concern. They perceived crime to be more intense and dangerous after 1900 than in any previous era in the capital's history, and thus a challenge to their project of social order and material progress—two ideals that defined a modern nation. Criminologists, the police, and the judiciary set out to identify criminals and isolate them from decent citizens. In the process, they made suspects of those who seemed to depart from "modern" customs.

For the majority of the city's inhabitants, in contrast, crime was an integral part of everyday life. It disrupted the trust and hierarchies that structured interactions in neighborhoods, at home, and at work. Yet victims, their relatives, and neighbors relied on the active participation of their communities to guarantee order rather than the judicial and penal institutions designed for that purpose. They knew that transgressions had their reasons—defense of honor motivated violence, economic need prompted theft—and that the criminal justice system catered mainly to the needs and fears of the upper classes, so they had to keep a mindful eye on everyone around. Thus, the proud capital became a city of suspects, where criminality was explained as a regrettable aspect of urban growth, and the urban poor bore the weight of punishment as well as victimization.

A social construct, crime is a relational category, incarnated in the suspicion of the police, judges, and the law itself toward the urban poor, and the latter's distrust toward state ideologies and practices with respect to crime. These actors defined crime in divergent ways. What authorities saw as embezzlement, for example, workers might regard as a fair retribution. Likewise, retail practices that merchants and the law deemed legitimate triggered the indignation of consumers. But if considered as merely the product of contested social interactions, "crime" can turn into a vague, all-encompassing category. The following pages stress the singularity of each case and the precise behavior that constituted an offense in the eyes of the public. The analysis will focus on the most common types of predatory offenses, that is, battery and theft. In addition, violence against women, although less frequently reported, will prove to be central to understanding the gendered workings of violence and honor in general.[2] The goal is not to narrate the famous cases that captured the imagination of the press, but to reconstruct the texture of crime as experienced in everyday life by those who formed the majority of offenders and victims.[3] Their view of transgression and punishment was imprinted by institutions and state action, but they also resisted and negotiated crime and punishment, shaping them into a complex reality.

This study places those relations against the dynamic of historical change. Growing crime rates during the Porfiriato resulted from the coincidence of a period of intense economic and social transformation and authoritarian methods of punishment that stressed the isolation of offenders from society and the centralization of punishment. After the Revolution, the meaning of crime and the identity of criminals became less of a biological problem and more of an issue of social justice and political legitimacy. Elite ideologies and state penal strategies frame this historical perspective. The question "Who is a criminal?" was at the heart of positivist criminology—the dominating outlook among academics interested in crime in the late nineteenth century. Internationally renowned authors, such as the Italian criminal anthropologist Cesare Lombroso, the French environmental criminologist Gabriel Tarde, and their Mexican counterparts, believed that physiognomic, psychological, and cultural traits distinguished criminals from the rest of the population. Drawing from this scientific credo, the police and the press treated criminals as a clearly identifiable social group. In doing so, criminology and penology unified "crime," constructing it as an urban, modern phenomenon. In the past, banditry, drunkenness, and petty urban theft had been understood and dealt with as distinct phenomena. This idea of a "criminal class" lumped together in one scientific net diverse transgressions and suspects. "Crime" became identified with urban criminality, as Mexico City seemed the breeding ground of all modern social pathologies. This suspicion justified the professionalization of the police and judiciary, and the hegemony of penitentiary regulations over other strategies to deal with transgressions. Lawlessness itself confirmed the diagnosis: districts characterized by marginality, squalor, and danger grew around the city's central spaces while the frequency of crime increased during the first decade of the twentieth century.

Such evidence suggested a weakness in modernization. The colonial regime had combined with some degree of success crime prevention strategies based on traditional communal structures with an array of institutions and codes, most of them legislated from Spain, including the Real Audiencia del Crimen, the Acordada tribunal, and the Inquisition. To this confusing legacy, parts of which remained in effect after Independence, national governments added the liberal tenets of the 1812 Cádiz Constitution and several constitutions after 1824. During most of the nineteenth century, crime was tackled by multiple agents: local authorities, city councils, the army, civic militias, the Tribunal de Vagos. Although some states attempted a codification of penal laws as early as the 1830s (in Veracruz), Mexico City remained a haphazard combination of old policing methods at the local level and unpredictable national politics that were often at odds with those of the city council. The arrangement persisted thanks largely to stagnated population growth in the capital and a decaying economy nationwide.[4]

In the wake of the triumph against imperialists in 1867, liberals enacted a penal code for the Federal District in 1871 and began to professionalize and unify the police in the capital. The late Porfiriato was marked by the coincidence of growing urban disorder and a federal state strong enough to invoke scientific methods in its fight against crime. This coincidence is best expressed by 1890s reforms to the 1871 Code, new penitentiary legislation, and, most visibly, the 1900 inauguration of the federal penitentiary in San Lázaro. Thus started the most aggressive era of authoritarian punishment in the country's history.

During the years of the Revolution, however, judicial and penal institutions lost the respect they used to inspire. Soldiers harassed policemen, prisoners escaped jail, and judges lost their jobs, leaving behind scores of cases without adjudication. Although some revolutionary factions voiced the need to reform the penal system, continuity along the former ideological and institutional lines began to be reestablished shortly after the end of the conflict. In 1915, revolutionary leader Venustiano Carranza took control of city government and vigorously applied Porfirian methods such as collective arrests of suspects and their transportation to penal colonies. But crime did not disappear. The widespread presence of guns, the threatening multiplication of automobiles, and the appearance of organized gangs of robbers made urban criminality more complex and difficult to control. In the 1920s, under presidents Alvaro Obregón and Plutarco Elías Calles, new welfare policies increasingly took the place of overt repression, while theories about "readaptation" began to gain acceptance over positivist strategies of isolation.

In the realm of penal legislation, this translated into an uneasy encounter of positivist criminology, classical penology (represented by the 1871 Penal Code and most of the legal profession), and radical views about the causes of social ills (espoused by many among the new political elite). Such a combination was first reflected by a new penal code for the Federal District decreed in 1929, opposed by many because of its doctrinaire use of positivist criminology, and then by the 1931 Penal Code, which combined old and new penal ideas with the revolutionary impulse of social reform. The new legislation marks the end of the period discussed in this book, as it coincides with the political consolidation of the postrevolutionary regime and a new institutional framework for police and penal institutions.

Within a narrow periodization defined by institutional change, this book sets crime against more stable everyday practices of the urban population. Facing rapid social change, urban communities (neighborhoods, tenements, extended families) set out to consolidate the social networks of reciprocity that made possible everyday survival.[5] They dealt with crime by appealing to the offenders' sense of shame and by negotiating potentially violent conflicts. Crime for them was more than abstract "social pathologies." As a result of the unified idea of crime forged by criminologists, many men and women had been punished out of suspicion rather than actual offenses. For the victims of actual crimes and their communities, however, criminals were simply those who committed crimes—whether they were forced to do so by circumstances or because of their shamelessness. They deserved to be punished, but their singularity could not be denied. Rather than a collective threat against society, criminals were people who looked much like their victims. In order to explore these neglected perspectives, this study deals with the practices and narratives constructed around specific offenses.[6]

A NOTE ON SOURCES

Crime is also what documents preserve. The evasive nature of the brief and tense interactions that we lump together under the word "crime" becomes more puzzling when stored in judicial records. As in Akira Kurosawa's film *Rashomon,* each participant has a perspective, but the truth does not belong to anyone. Mexican suspects, victims, and witnesses knew that judges were sometimes unfair, and that guilt was often determined by prejudice, rather than by the impact of testimonies. This does not render judicial accounts useless but does turn them into composite statements about individual morality, social relationships, and the meaning of crime and justice.

A critical view of penal institutions and their subjects requires a suitable reading of the documents they generated. The archive of the Federal District Higher Court (Tribunal Superior de Justicia del Distrito Federal) holds court records in individual case files organized by court and the accused's name. Along with published reports on some jury trials, these files provide information about the workings of the judicial system and register the narratives produced by victims and the accused. In selecting the files to be used in this study (209 of them, out of uncatalogued, dusty, and unmarked bundles stored in the basement of the South Penitentiary court building in San Mateo Xalpa, Distrito Federal), I tried to obtain a sample resembling the information provided by statistics on the most frequent type of crimes and their changing frequency during the period. Thus, 95 cases correspond to the years 1900–1909, 67 to 1910–1920 and 47 to 1921–1930. Of these trials, 121 dealt with battery, homicide, and other offenses against persons, 24 with sexual offenses, 66 with crimes against property, and 12 with offenses against the state (some trials dealt with more than one offense).

Records began with an affidavit written at the police station, in which victim and accused described the events, and sometimes included a statement by the arresting officer and additional witnesses. The officer in charge at the station then sent the case to the public prosecution (Ministerio Público), the suspects to jail, and the wounded to the Juárez Hospital. In the hours or days after the arrest, participants were questioned again by a judge, who directed the investigation thereafter, usually summoning more witnesses. Trial files also contain records of the appointments of defense lawyers and the identity and antecedents of suspects (picture, anatomical description, and list of previous entrances in jail). After all evidence was entered, the prosecution and the defense wrote their conclusions, usually brief. Finally, the judge summarized the case, listed the applicable chapters of the penal code, determined guilt or innocence and, if necessary, the length of the sentence. In serious offenses, such as homicide and rape, a jury decided guilt or innocence. The records also included notices about the accused's appeal of the arrest or sentence or their request to post bond.

Judicial documents hold contentious versions of events, but they also recover voices that are usually silent in historical accounts. These two functions conflict at times because the narratives presented by actors had precise intentions—to which factual truth was often subordinated. Suspects sought to elude responsibility or to place the blame on someone else. Victims wanted to provide a convincing account of the events, to secure punishment for their adversaries, and to avoid becoming suspects themselves. The scholar's reading of these statements inadvertently forces regularities and rationality onto the remnants of exceptional and chaotic moments in the lives of actors. In using them I tried to remain aware of that and to be careful in building a connection between individual cases and social practices. The problems faced by anthropologists (the false certainties of objectivism and the narrative biases of informants) provide a sobering point of reference for the cultural historian who uses judicial sources.[7]

Yet, I must confess my overarching trust in accused and victims' statements. They can be believed because they wanted their statements to achieve an obvious goal (punishment, freedom). Their claims to truth may be suspect even today, but they referred to socialized norms about veracity and justifications of individual behavior. They addressed, perhaps in an indirect way but with no less soundness, the paradoxes of transgression and justice.

A NOTE ON HISTORIOGRAPHY

In a useful reversal of common sense, the historiography that this book engages has placed punishment before crime. The social history of modern Western societies of the last decades has indeed benefited from new research on the role of institutions of punishment within the process of national states adapting themselves to the demands of industrial capitalism. Punishment, these studies maintain, became central pieces in the construction of productive working classes and a more penetrating state authority.[8] Historical works on crime itself add important nuances, frequently overlooked, to the model of class and social control: crime follows its own rhythms, independent of punishment and generally within a multisecular decreasing trend in the modern era.[9] Studies of social control in Latin America have made valuable contributions that complement studies on punishment. Recent works on Brazil, Argentina, Peru, and Mexico stress the specific historical circumstances in which the ruling groups imported European and North American strategies of control during the late nineteenth century. The regional elite's discourse of progress and economic expansion revolved around the racial and cultural "regeneration" of the population and the top-down creation of new citizens through immigration and miscegenation, and included fighting backwardness and lack of discipline with hygiene, criminology, and penology. Criminality became a favorite theme of social reform because the scientific discipline built around it provided plausible explanations of popular vices, and penitentiary institutions gave authorities a suitable instrument to regenerate the people. The distinction between criminal and citizen became, according to Robert Buffington, "the fundamental dichotomy within modern Mexican society."[10]

In a parallel path, other scholars have uncovered the contested nature of power and social control and brought attention to multiple actors who challenge the foundations of class, gender, and political rule behind capitalist modernization. As a result, it is no longer possible to assume social compliance to the technologies of power—even in the most industrialized countries—and the "overcalculated" Foucaldian view of punishment.[11] In Latin America, the historiographical emphasis on popular agency emerged as a revision of elite-centered interpretations of the region's history. Studies of peasant resistance to capitalism, for example, have demonstrated that the traditional narratives of national history fail to account for local politics and for the efforts of people and communities to survive the onslaught of conquest and colonial acculturation.[12] The accent on resistance has also increased historians' interest in groups that appeared marginal in previous accounts. Bandits, slaves, the urban plebes, and women were proved to possess historical agency and now share the place of male salaried workers and politicians in historical accounts.[13]

The present volume visits the common ground of these two seemingly conflicting research agendas. Caution is required, however, to deal with the distortions from both sides. Resistance, first, threatens to become the central theme in the historical experience of the lower classes, and hegemony, however vaguely defined, the defining trait of multifaceted class and political relationships. The result, according to William Taylor, is a dichotomy in which rulers and subjects are neatly divided. Popular resistance comes to the forefront, while state actions and institutions are moved "into the background." As Gilbert Joseph notes for the study of banditry, the power/rebellion dichotomy poses the danger of neglecting popular practices that were not expressed in clear political terms.[14] To put it in the terms of the present study, criminals not only resisted domination when they broke the law, they also established specific relations with state officials and their own communities.

An artificial division between the study of power and that of disorder is bound to yield partial results. Studies of social control in Latin America tend to analyze strategies and discourses as part of the region's intellectual history, thus embracing (with retrospective reservations) the narrative of order and progress developed by positivist elites and the alleged impact of state-building policies on the life of the lower classes. According to this argument, for example, everything that happened to the penal system in

Mexico since 1900 was an advance toward modernization and the rationalization of punishment.[15] Yet, even in those countries that received massive numbers of European immigrants, results did not satisfy the expectations of social engineers. Danger in the streets and low productivity at work were common images in contemporary accounts of social change in Latin American cities at the turn of the century. Recent studies of the national and regional impact of social policies suggest instead that social engineering should be judged in the context of the negotiation between the interests of reformers and those of the "reformed" population—in other words, as a political process rather than pure exercise of power.[16]

The case of Mexico City shows the limits of a narrow focus on the institutional side of punishment and deviance. In his chapter of *México, su evolución social,* the great synthesis of Porfirian achievements published in 1900, Miguel Macedo spelled out the importance of punishment: "The punitive function of the state . . . is certainly one of the basic elements of social order."[17] Following this lead, historians have construed crime control as a chapter of the successful Porfirian drive to attract foreign investors. The Mexico City penitentiary, therefore, expressed the entrance of modern technologies of power into Mexico.[18] But crime resulted from a more complex and historically stable set of causes and conditions. Colonial domination in a multiethnic society had already established the contradictions between penal institutions and community reactions to crime. Industrialization and newly emerged class divides had deep effects, beyond the reach of the institutional looking glass, on a city with an already long tradition of artisanal work, commerce, and unemployment.[19]

What questions are to be asked in a more comprehensive attempt? The sociology of crime, concerned with explanation and policy making, offers useful reference points for a historical approach. The notion that deviance means the transgression of universal values or an imbalance of the social body is challenged by empirical research. "Criminals," sociologists argue, undertake a consistent pattern of law-breaking behavior because they are immersed in a social environment that privileges and legitimizes that behavior. Ample evidence is cited to the effect that people associated with criminals are more likely to break the law, and that criminals are often associated with certain cultural traits—such as tattoos, slang, and drinking. Culture, however, poses dangerous temptations. The observations cited above become less useful when reified into the rigid yet popular category of "subculture"—an isolated and stable set of values that ascribes deviance to an identifiable group.[20] Explaining crime thus becomes an ethnographic exercise.

As an alternative, interpretations that focus on the labeling of certain groups as criminal explain the emergence and continuity of deviant behaviors as the product of the decision by society, or rather by its ruling groups, to define petty offenders as criminals and thus pressure them into repeated law breaking. The social practices that stigmatize offenders have the effect of breaking all other connections with the community and perpetuating deviance as a social role. The question, therefore, is no longer "Who is a criminal?" but "Who defines him or her?"[21] An exclusive stress on labeling, however, might return us to the starting point: since crime is "produced" by the state, all that there is left to study is the penal institutions, while actual criminal practices can be neglected as anecdotal.

This book addresses these questions but weaves them in a wider historical frame. It moves beyond the history of punishment into the cultural history of a city and its inhabitants. In doing so, its ambition is to tie together historiographical strands that have studied elite social engineering and popular resistance as parallel, isolated phenomena. By looking at both crime and punishment as cultural products, this book seeks to restore the political meaning of everyday social interactions and conflicts with the state. The stress on the local level of justice and the individuality of victims and offenders runs counter to the grand generalizations about crime and punishment, yet reveals the centrality of both aspects of Mexico City life. Crossing the revolutionary divide, the study hopes to challenge the fundamental chronological and conceptual axes (ancien regime/revolution, elite/popular) of Mexican political historiography. The result describes a city marked by suspicion: criminology and repressive state strategies created suspects out of the urban poor; these in turn resisted and negotiated their status vis-à-vis their communities and authorities, whom they also mistrusted. However tense and complex, these relations defined crime in their place and time.

I

THE CONTEXT

Turn-of-the-century Mexico City contained all the symbols of nationalism and many remarkable examples of colonial architecture. By the end of the first century of national life, it was the locus of progress and the capital of Porfirio Díaz's long-lasting regime. Railroads, tramways, paved and illuminated streets, broad avenues, parks, new residential areas, and high buildings appeared as distinctive signs of material progress. Improvements in the design and use of urban space were based on the understanding that the rich and poor were not to mingle: a rational division between the safe and beautiful areas of the modern city and the dangerous and unhealthy marginal zones. Urban design also meant social reform: the state and the wealthy classes wanted to translate the city's physical evolution into a new culture among its inhabitants.

The elites' idea of renewal faced the challenge of a growing and untamed population. The urban lower classes, so distant from the aspirations of wealth and comfort associated with progress, used the city in their own way, defying the class-structured organization of the capital. As tensions arose around the use of the streets and other public areas, the government relied on the police and penal institutions to instill a sense of appropriate conduct in the people. Criminal behavior (whether a genuine transgression of social norms, or simply a violation of the many laws and regulations generated during the period) acquired a different meaning in the context of the dispute over the use of the city. Crime, however, was not the only way in which people defied the Utopia of Porfirian rulers. A host of practices in the streets (vending, begging, drinking, or merely walking) also subverted the ideal social map.

The next pages will weave a counterpoint between the elite model of the city and its defiance by the urban poor. Chapters 1 and 2 will describe how the ideal city hoped and failed to impose its strict divisions of urban space, as the connection between the appropriation of urban space and the criminalization of lower-class uses remained a long-lasting feature of the capital. The projects and policies aimed at building a modern capital for the benefit of a minority of its inhabitants will be contrasted with the consequences of late-nineteenth-century growth on the city's physical infrastructure and, more importantly, on the everyday life of the lower class. After an outline of the ideal city designed by Porfirian rulers, chapter 1 will describe the demographic and technological changes that caused the model to fail and the city to expand at an unprecedented rate. This will be followed by a probe into everyday practices and living conditions in the marginal city—the city that grew around and across the Porfirian ideal city. Authorities' attempt to reform behaviors deemed to be a threat to progress, the urban policies that sought to preserve the social geography of the city and the collective reactions to those policies will be the theme of chapter 2. Urban communities, in their various and often coterminous forms, appear in these chapters as central actors in this story of conflict about the rules and spaces of city life.

Criminology was the new science called to account for the negative sides of modernization, but also to provide recipes to improve society. Chapter 3 will examine the scientific discourse that was inspired by and tried to tame urban growth. Mexican criminology directed the fascination of educated males toward the marginal spaces of the ideal city: peripheral neighborhoods, crowded homes, nightly disorder. Explaining crime was one way to dispel that fascination—but one with significant implications for the design of state policies.

In sum, the following section looks at the cultural articulation of demographic and spatial growth under an authoritarian regime. This description of a disputed city questions the Porfirians' contention that their projects of urban renewal went unchallenged and ultimately succeeded. While the urban poor used the city in ways that contradicted those projects, elite perceptions of "dangerous" areas identified poverty with criminality. As a result, officials increasingly relied on punishment to impose their social ideas, while the urban poor identified the police and judicial system with the interests of the wealthy. Crime itself was produced at this juncture of fear and neglect.

1

The Modern City

Our views of Porfirian Mexico City are heavily influenced by the grandeur of the buildings and avenues and the elegance of *colonias* built during that period. It is easy to share the nostalgia for *los tiempos de don Porfirio,* an era when Mexican society seemed as peaceful and well organized as the walkways under the shady trees of the Paseo de la Reforma. The following pages, however, contend that such images of civilization were only the precarious result of a negotiation between the regime's projects of urban modernization and the everyday practices of the majority of the urban population.

THE IDEAL CITY

The changes that swept early-twentieth-century Mexico City began nearly forty years earlier, during Emperor Maximilian's attempt to turn Mexico into a modern European nation, and accelerated in the late Porfiriato. The ideal city of the 1910 centennial celebration of independence epitomized the unifying myths of progress and nationhood. The colonial center of the city, the Zócalo or *Plaza Mayor,* extended its stately architecture westward along Avenida Juárez to the Alameda park and then southwest along the elegant Paseo de la Reforma to its terminus at Chapultepec Castle, the presidential residence (see fig. 1). The Alameda was part of the colonial design of the city

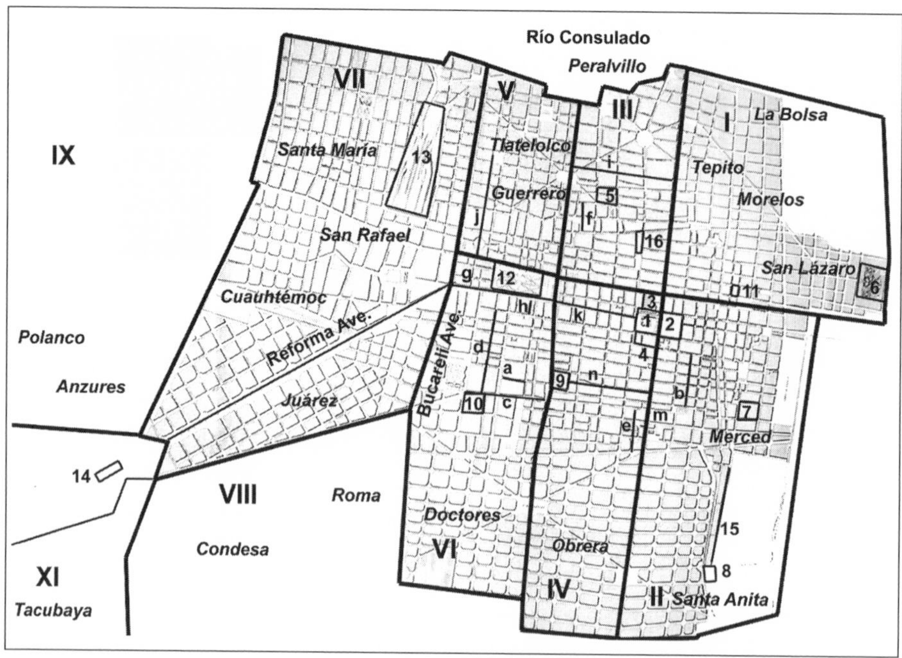

1. Mexico City: Colonias, Barrios, Police Districts. Sites Mentioned: 1. Zócalo; 2. National Palace; 3. Cathedral; 4. City Council; 5. Lagunilla Market; 6. Federal Penitentiary; 7. La Merced Market; 8. Jamaica Market; 9. Plaza de las Vizcaínas; 10. Belem Jail; 11. Plaza Mixcalco; 12. Alameda; 13. Central Railroad Station; 14. Chapultepec Castle; 15. La Viga Canal; 16. Plaza Santo Domingo. Streets: a. Delicias; b. Las Cruces; c. Arcos de Belén Ave.; d. Revillagigedo; e. Cuahtemoctzin; f. Amargura; g. Juárez Ave.; h. Tarasquillo; i. Libertad; j. Héroes; k. Plateros; m. San Antonio Abad; n. Regina.

and became an upper-class place of leisure during the nineteenth century. The Paseo de la Reforma's wide design and execution followed the aesthetic and urbanistic ideas that had transformed Paris and other European capitals since the 1850s. This was the axis of a less visible modification of urban territory that resulted in the displacement of indigenous communities from valuable lands. Of all the cycles of change that Mexico City had experienced after the sixteenth century, the one that peaked during the late Porfiriato was perhaps the most disruptive because it combined population growth, land dispossession, and heightened cultural conflict.[1]

Porfirian urban design corresponded with a drive to reorganize society within the city. Around the Paseo de la Reforma, private companies were licensed by city authorities to develop upper- and middle-class residential areas or colonias, such as Juárez, Cuauhtémoc, Roma, and Condesa. Officials protected the development of these colonias, and often ordered the elimination of undeserving or ill-looking buildings. Designers and builders had a clear idea of the social meaning of modernization: the poor had to be displaced from the elegant quarters, while city services were to be concentrated only in the well-kept districts. This strategy meant a clear departure from the multiclass dwellings in the city center dating back to colonial times. Porfirian investors, often closely associated with city officials, bought and partitioned lands for the wealthiest classes in privileged areas, while reserving other zones for working-class homeowners, thus working together to preserve the spatial separation between classes. Separating customers according to their socioeconomic status would create a stronger real estate market.[2]

Hygiene and security, both symbolically achieved with the inauguration of great drainage works and the San Lázaro penitentiary in 1900, were requisites for the stability of the colonized city. In order to protect the integrity of new upper-class neighborhoods, municipal and health authorities planned the growth of industries and working-class neighborhoods away from upper-class suburbs. The Consejo Superior de Salubridad (Public Health Council) defined in 1897 a "zone which has the goal of maintaining certain types of industries at a distance from the only avenue of the capital," that is, the Paseo de la Reforma.[3] The residential developments would expand from the axis Zócalo-Alameda-Reforma toward the west and southwest. The east was discarded because of its proximity to the Texcoco lake, its lower ground level, and unfavorable ecological conditions. The designers of the new penitentiary located it on the eastern San Lázaro plains, in order to send the prisoners' "miasma" away from the center.[4] On the margins of the central city, authorities and developers had to deal with the existence of popular residential areas: lower-class colonias and old barrios. Although barrios had always existed close to the center, their poverty had preserved what Andrés Lira calls a "social distance" from the modern city. For lower-class developments, urbanization did not mean access to drainage, electricity, and pavement as it did for more affluent colonias and the protected environment of the central area.[5]

Life in the wealthiest colonias followed European bourgeois models of privacy and autonomy. City planners and developers shared the tacit premise that business, leisure, and work should be clearly separated, and that men and women had unmistakably different roles in public and domestic environments. The new colonias organized the living accommodations of the upper classes in single-house lots equipped with all the amenities of modern life, including electricity, drainage, running water, and telephones. Thanks to these services, the inhabitants of the house did not have to rely on old-fashioned methods of satisfying their daily needs, such as manually bringing water to the household or dumping human waste in the street. The ideal of an autonomous residence drew well-to-do families away from downtown, which had become increasingly oriented toward commercial use. An enhanced, city-wide transportation system sought to facilitate the movement of people from the new residence areas to their workplaces.[6]

The separation of public and private spaces and activities was also the guiding principle for official action regarding people's demeanor. Private behavior in public spaces had always been a concern for authorities in Mexico City. *Policía y buen gobierno* defined the authorities' intervention since colonial times, encompassing not only police issues but also the upkeep of streets and the control of collective meetings. Like its counterparts in the seventeenth century and the Bourbon period, the Porfirian City Council ordered *pulquerías* (stores selling pulque, a fermented beverage made from the sap of the maguey) and *cantinas* to conceal customers from the eye of pedestrians, and withdrew permission from restaurants to place chairs and tables on the sidewalks. The state even regulated the clothes worn by pedestrians: Indians (defined by their use of white trousers and shirts instead of dark suits) were required to wear dark trousers. Repeated publications of this prohibition, in the 1890s and then during Francisco I. Madero's presidency, suggest the futility of the attempt and reveal municipal authorities' belief that indigenous people were not culturally prepared to use the city.[7]

These attempts to divide the use of the city were far from perfect, and the reality of urban life never accommodated itself to the Porfirian ideal. Instead of working as autonomous, suburban households (as their architects conceived them), upper-class mansions reproduced the dynamics of the *casco de hacienda,* where servants and workers were an extension of the patriarchal family. Masters and domestic workers formed an intimate association that was not easily opened to public authority. Isidro Esqueda, for example, escaped a violent and, in his view, unjustified attempt at arrest by a drunken policeman by seeking refuge inside the home of his boss, Lic. José Raz Guzmán, who later detained the policeman himself.[8] Lic. Raz Guzmán had good reasons to act: wealthy residences needed the mediation of servants and sellers to obtain access to many basic products and services.

The functional divisions of urban space could not resist the erosion of everyday life precisely because the design of the upper-class, "civilized" city left outside, unplanned, the very factors of its survival. The elegant new colonias around the Paseo de la Reforma, as well as the older aristocratic homes downtown, needed labor and supplies, often from distant places. The Eighth District, for example, lacked a single produce market in 1904.[9] Conversely, workers had to leave their homes to satisfy many needs of everyday life: to drink, eat, socialize, or simply earn a living through petty commerce in the streets. These needs and a distinctive conception of urban space impelled the urban poor to blur the artificial borders between a modern city, where public and private functions were clearly separated, and another city, where elite models of behavior seemed less important. A tension thus emerged between the hierarchical and rigid map of the capital imagined by the Porfirian elites and the ambiguous, often not articulated, horizontal view of those who spent most of their time on the streets. Before looking into that tension, however, we must ask what prevented Mexico City from becoming the model capital that its rulers imagined.

POPULATION, TRANSPORTATION, AND THE FAILURE OF THE MODEL

The Porfirian regime failed to consolidate its ideal capital because the constant arrival of migrants and the development of new means of transportation, both expected to facilitate progress, instead weakened social divisions and undermined the authorities' control over public spaces.

Population growth posed an unexpected problem to planners and administrators even before it was clearly expressed by the census.[10] Population counts reveal the unprecedented rate of this growth during the late Porfiriato. Since 1895, date of the first national census, the population of Mexico City had not only grown at a faster pace than the national total, but also faster than other cities in the country. While nineteenth-century estimates placed its population around 200,000, in 1895 Mexico City had 329,774 inhabitants, and by 1921 it had grown to 615,327 (see appendix, table 5). Internal migration was the main cause of urban growth. In 1900, more than half of Mexico City's inhabitants were born in other states. In 1910, more than a quarter of the total number of migrants in the entire country lived in the Federal District.[11] Large numbers of migrants reached the capital and established themselves in diverse dwellings and occupations.

Despite the rural origin of most migrants, Mexico City's population was not what we can call a "traditional" society. Literacy figures, for example, show that the capital's population was more educated than the national average at the end of the Porfiriato, and continued to be so during the following decades. While in 1900 the nation's literacy rate was 18 percent, in the Federal District it was 45 percent. In 1930 the percentages were 39 and 75, respectively.[12] Although schooling was more accessible in the capital, many migrants came already educated. In 1895, the largest age group in Mexico City were those between 21 and 30 years old, accounting for 40 percent of the city's total population. Meanwhile, the largest population group in the country as a whole comprised children aged 10 or less, representing 30 percent of the national population.[13] People came to the capital searching for jobs, but they did not necessarily lack education, a degree of status, or familiarity with urban life.

Migration to Mexico City also distinguished itself from that to other areas of the country in that the sex ratio favored women. In 1895, men were 50 percent of the national population, compared to 46 percent in Mexico City. The disparity grew until men represented less than 45 percent of the capital's population in 1930.[14] This contrasted with the rapidly developing northern regions of the country, where the tendency was the opposite. According to François-Xavier Guerra, the sex imbalance of certain regions during the Porfiriato partly explains revolutionary mobilization: men outnumbered women by up to 10 percent in the mining areas of the north and in parts of the state of Morelos—both foci of the Revolution. Male predominance was a sign, in Guerra's view, of modernization and social change, thus fueling political participation.[15] This view coincides with contemporaneous revolutionary interpretations of Mexico City as a territory of conservatism, decadence, and lack of masculinity. In 1914, veteran opposition writer Heriberto Frías stated that

> the Porfirian dictatorship, sanctioned and supported by the rich, the military and the clergy, systematically tried to abolish the virility of the middle class,

particularly in the Federal District, where employees and professionals formed a corrupted Court living in a state of serfdom caused by atavisms and the environment.[16]

This view of the capital as a "retrograde" and conservative city seems to be supported by the absence of a massive (and male) popular revolt. Recent scholarship, however, has argued that women's participation in the Revolution was more important than traditionally acknowledged, and that Mexico City's lower-class women in particular were visibly active in urban politics in 1915, when the civil war hit the capital in full force and scarcity and inflation triggered food riots.[17]

Mexico City offered the conditions for women to explore work opportunities beyond their traditional gender roles. Census data for working women show a sharp contrast between national figures and those for Mexico City: while in 1900 women were only 17 percent of the national employed population, in Mexico City they were almost half. This did not mean, however, that women invaded customarily male areas of work. Certain jobs seemed to attract female labor more than others. According to the 1895 census, the trades favored by women were those of needlework (5,505 women and no men listed by the census), cigar making (1,709 women and no men), domestic work (25,129 women and 8,883 men), laundry (5,673 women and 112 men), and concierge work (1,431 women and 994 men). Taken together, these categories made up 50 percent of the employed female population.[18] For many of these women, living in the capital meant not only leaving behind their hometowns but also a domestic environment.

In sum, turn-of-the-century Mexico City was dominated by young newcomers, more educated than the norm and with a strong presence of women in certain areas of economic activity. By contrast with more developed metropoles, industrial jobs did not employ large numbers of people in Mexico City; only 1 percent of employed men in the city in 1895 worked in industry, while 11 percent were listed as *comerciantes* (employed in commerce) and 7 percent as domestic workers.[19] Moving to the capital did not necessarily translate into better living conditions, although it opened the possibility of access to better-paying jobs.

Along with demographic growth, modernization brought new means of transportation. It became easier for travelers to reach the capital and for its inhabitants to move within it. The development of railroads, cast in a countrywide network whose lines converged in Mexico City, allowed artisans of modest income and poor migrants to make one-day trips from nearby towns. Compared to the traditional canoes and ox carts that in the 1880s still transported much of the foodstuffs needed in the capital, trains brought products from regions beyond the valley. Soon, railroads replaced canals and roads as the principal means of communication between the city and the surrounding towns. In response to the sudden ease of reaching the capital from the interior, crowds who did not behave or dress according to "civilized" foreign models poured onto the city streets. Railroad stations bustled with outsiders, particularly during national holidays or religious occasions, such as the December 12 celebration of the Virgin of Guadalupe, which brought many pilgrims of rural appearance. Regardless of origin, visitors crowded the streets, drinking and eating and creating a bonanza for merchants and a headache for the police.[20]

New means of transportation, particularly tramways, enhanced people's mobility within the city. In addition to the private and rented coaches, which provided transportation for "people of medium and great wealth," *tranvías* made commuting faster and affordable, and brought the center of the city closer to the suburbs. In 1903, most tramways were pulled by mules, although there were electric units as well. By 1920, there were 345 kilometers of tramway lines with 370 passenger cars, all owned by the Compañía de Tranvías de México. Tramways were cheap enough to be used by working-class people on a daily basis and occasionally by the poorest residents.[21] They became an important element of the urban poor's everyday life. For the characters in Angel de Campo's novel *La Rumba,* the tramway was much more than the daily means of transportation. Remedios, a seamstress, commuted to work on the tramway and made it the setting for her romantic life. Horse-driven cabs continued to be a common sight at the turn of the century, as well as ox carts, mules, and hand-pulled carts. Starting in the 1910s, automobiles added to the intricacy of transportation, with greater speed and different rules governing their movement.[22]

The impact of these new means of transportation on the popular perception of the capital was twofold. First, tramways, trains, and automobiles were commonly identified with the worst, more aggressive aspects of modernization. Walking in the middle of the street became a dangerous "rural" habit in this city. Accidents were common. Echoing public concern, the penny press called tramway drivers *mataristas* (from the verb *matar*—

to kill), instead of *motoristas.* The impunity of car and tramway drivers was a central consequence of urban progress from the point of view of lower-class pedestrians: the street became a threatening environment, where the victims were poor and the guilty were protected by their companies and judicial corruption. Thus, drivers who ran over pedestrians were often surrounded by witnesses and spontaneously brought to the police.[23] Modern transit created a world of movement that was both attractive and dangerous. Beggars wheedled in train stations, boys peddled on tramways, theft was common at both sites, and journalists even described a special kind of professional thief who targeted unaware passengers.[24]

Danger expressed the conflicts over the use of urban space. Traffic was one of the preferred contexts of the struggle between "traditional" and "modern" behaviors. The use of the street for fast transportation competed with its use as a place for commerce and sociability. The city council sought to teach coach drivers to keep to their right and pedestrians to move along, reminding them "that it is forbidden to stop on the street forming groups that obstruct the circulation of vehicles and animals." The prohibition was, again, merely a description: vendors set up their booths in the middle of the streets, blocking traffic despite the inspectors' threats; pedestrians stood in the middle of the sidewalks blocking circulation, particularly at corners and outside theaters, forming groups instead of lines.[25]

The second consequence of technological change was a transformed understanding of the city. Modern transportation widened the city. Tramway lines reached as far as San Angel and linked different areas of the city with downtown destinations—the Zócalo and Avenida Plateros—but also with the gambling houses in Tacubaya and other "dangerous" quarters of the city. In 1882, poet Manuel Gutiérrez Nájera used the tramway as the vehicle of an imaginary exploration into passengers' lives. He already saw a different city than that of pre-tramway days: "The wagon takes me to unknown worlds and virgin regions. No, Mexico City does not start at the National Palace, nor does it end at Reforma Avenue. I give you my word that the city is much bigger. It is a great turtle that extends its dislocated legs toward the four cardinal points. Those legs are dirty and hairy. The City Council, with fatherly care, paints them with mud every month."[26] As the city expanded, society became more complex and mobile, and the impression of an ordered, stable cosmopolitan city was broken down by the daily movement of its variegated population.

The last factor for the failure of the ideal city of the Porfiriato was the Revolution. Beginning in 1913, the civil war took its toil on the population of the capital, not only in terms of casualties, but also through scarcity, lawlessness, and increased migration into the city. With the revolutionary armies arrived unruly characters like Manuel González, soldier of a general Gil, who was sent to the penitentiary in 1916 "for hunting doves with a bow and arrow" in the colonia Roma.[27] No longer the picturesque innocents portrayed by nineteenth-century chroniclers, the multitude of dangerous *extranjeros* (foreigners) frightened neighbors of the colonia de la Bolsa and often left behind unidentified corpses.[28] Threatened by the initial radicalism of revolutionary leaders, those who had benefited from Porfirian modernization left the city and their luxurious homes for exile.

After the civil war, however, the old and the new elite reconciled and continued urban development along the basic lines established during Díaz's regime. After 1920, the capital slowly began to improve its image again. Elegant colonias near Chapultepec park, such as Polanco and Anzures, became the residence of choice for the new politicians and businessmen. Sanitation and expansion of new developments recovered their fast pace by the end of the decade based, as in prerevolutionary times, on the harmony of developers' interests and urban policies. The area of the city tripled in ten years. Cars came to dominate traffic, and by 1928 animal-drawn vehicles were prohibited, as officials resumed their attack against the practices of the urban poor.[29] Despite the political changes brought about by the Revolution, the majority of the urban population still distrusted authority and challenged the social divides of the city, and life in the streets continued to be a transaction between the old and the new.

THE IMPACT OF MODERNIZATION ON EVERYDAY LIFE

What did the Porfirian redesign of the city mean for the urban poor? This question is at the center of any attempt to explain the relationship between modernization and crime. The urban poor lived in conditions that could not be reconciled with bourgeois models; they had to cope with overcrowding, displacement, and the authoritarian policies of the regime. They also had to meet with the disapproval of observers such as *El Imparcial*, which in 1902 declared that

> a sizable part of the population, precisely that which does not have the best personal hygiene, lives in the narrow rooms that the capital's buildings offer to the poorer classes. Those tenement houses . . . show the most surprising spectacle of human overcrowding one could imagine. Only medieval "Ghettos," those typical neighborhoods in which the Jews were confined, could resemble the narrowness, slovenliness and filth of these dwellings.[30]

The description implied that overcrowding and filth made necessary the lower classes' geographical and even cultural isolation, as they challenged bourgeois notions of civility and undermined the class and gender divides intended to structure urban life.

In the old barrios near the urban center and in many of the newly developed lower class colonias, people lived in *vecindades*—one- or two-story tenements that lacked the clear spatial autonomy of modern homes. Several families lived in single- or double-room apartments with a single door that opened into a narrow hallway. Tenants shared sanitary services and the use of the hallway for cleaning or cooking. There were no strong reasons for owners to improve these arrangements. In the colonia de la Bolsa, where most tenants could not provide a guarantor, rents were established on a short-term basis at relatively high rates. Landlords did not enter vecindades, much less maintain them, and carried out their deals with tenants on the street.[31] According to *Nueva Era,* policemen did not dare enter either, because vecindades were not welcoming places: dogs were loose and aggressive, clothes hung in the middle of the hallway, and neighbors saw any government representative as an intruder. On the other hand *vendedores ambulantes* (peddlers) entered vecindades at will, contributing to frequent thefts in tenants' apartments. The housing deficit explained these problems. According to the 1902 *El Imparcial* report, nothing decent could be leased for less than fifty pesos a month; houses renting for less than twenty pesos were "troglodyte dwellings."[32] For lower-class households, vecindades were simply the only option.

Public dormitories or inns, called *mesones,* offered an alternative for individuals. They provided a roof for the night in exchange for a daily, low-cost ticket. This suited the economic conditions of those who lacked a stable income, such as ambulantes or beggars. Although ostensibly designed for travelers, mesones became the permanent address of many poor *capitalinos* who were ready to endure the crowding. Sleeping space on the floor (which men, women, and children shared) could become the object of bloody disputes. Felipe Toledo was arrested in 1907 because he stuck a pencil four centimeters into Amador Rodríguez's chest. Rodríguez had stepped on Toledo while looking for an opening at a mesón in the Plaza de las Vizcaínas.[33] Although required to provide showers, conditions were less than hygienic, especially as demand grew. In 1918, the Beneficencia Pública dormitory received 54,750 people. On an average day in 1920, 91 men, 19 women, and 8 children used one public dormitory.[34] Mesones and vecindades inspired Porfirian writers' allegations of sexual promiscuity among the poor: immorality was the only possible consequence of what they saw and endured in those places.[35] Such claims are difficult to document, but one clear outcome of overcrowding and lack of housing was the urban poor's need to carry out many of the activities associated with the private realm in public places.

A widespread problem of popular dwellings, perhaps the main reason its occupants spent most of the day in the streets, was the absence of running water and sewers. Collective toilets in vecindades emptied into sewers or the street through open channels that ran down the middle of hallways.[36] This stimulated the development of *baños públicos* (public baths), an important institution in the lives of the inhabitants of the city and one that further mixed intimate needs and social life. At these facilities, men and women could take a shower and do laundry for a small fee. In the 1880s, baños públicos were the largest constructions on the Paseo de la Reforma, near the Alameda. Swimming pools were also crowded on hot days, especially on Saint John the Baptist's day. Attendance at these facilities was high: in 1914, during the month of April, 5,434 men and 5,267 women used the Baños de la Lagunilla, administered by the Beneficencia Pública.[37]

Other, less pleasing practices prompted by the lack of hygienic facilities at lower-class dwellings further offended the sensibility of upper-class observers. Urinating and defecating in the streets was a matter-of-fact practice for poor men, women, and children. This problem had concerned authorities since the Bourbon period. Although public urinals were available in several sites around the city, arrests were still common after the Revolution for "having bowel movements on the public road."[38] Establishing public toilets was necessary, declared a physician in 1892, since the only available alternative were pulquerías, where "there is the custom of having barrels or buckets used to contain the urine of any individual who wants to use them."[39] The problem became more evident in the recently paved streets near theaters and restaurants where, at night, people left "large pools of urine" and feces. The city council, however, found it difficult to punish even its own employees: "What can the policemen do," asked a report, "if they have to stay eight hours on their corner, or the coach drivers, who often spend the whole day in the street, or the street merchants or, in sum, anyone who walks the city and who is far from his home, when they face an urgent need [*alguna necesidad*]?"[40] For lower-class men and particularly for women, neither their dwellings nor public facilities offered a "decent" solution to their daily bodily needs. Their only option was to ignore the dictates of urbanity, endure the shame, and risk punishment.[41]

Lastly, the scarcity of potable water in their homes drove people to the street in order to satiate their thirst. Men and women of all ages had to use public fountains, buy flavored water (*aguas frescas*) at street booths, or patronize pulquerías. Many houses lacked wells or were distant from water pipes, although drinking water was less of a concern for the colonias west of the center, where springs from Chapultepec provided abundant and good-quality water. Thirst led people to the streets, where alcoholic beverages were at the center of social life. Migrants were lured by the anonymity of the city and came to enjoy the deregulated, secularized use of alcohol.[42] Pulque consumption had a particularly slow rhythm, but other low-alcohol beverages like *tepache* (fermented pineapple juice) and *infusiones* (teas with alcohol) also allowed customers to spend hours in pulquerías, cantinas or cheap restaurants. Despite specific official regulations, a profuse decoration made the stay in these establishments more comfortable. Clients spent time fraternizing, eating, or simply moving from one outlet to another, starting sometimes in the morning and continuing throughout the day. José Dolores Méndez, accused of raping María Guadalupe Rodríguez, described how he invited her to several cantinas, where they began drinking lemonade and concluded with twelve glasses of *rompope* (eggnog). They ended up in a hotel where, according to her accusation, he tried to force himself on her.[43]

Control of alcohol in public places became more difficult as the number of outlets continued to grow throughout the period. Up to 1871, the sale of pulque was officially restricted to the Calle del Aguila, two blocks north of the Alameda, but by the end of the century pulquerías had surpassed any precedent in terms of quantity and extension. As the city expanded, new pulquerías emerged in the outskirts of the city, with new buildings and colorful mural paintings. According to official records, in 1902 there were 2,423 alcohol outlets in the capital, including cantinas, pulquerías, and smaller establishments. The greatest concentration of these was in the blocks east of the Zócalo. Of a total of 924 pulquerías in the city, 170 existed inside an area around the center where they were formally prohibited.[44] City authorities sought to prevent crime and disturbances associated with alcohol consumption by limiting the operating hours of cantinas and pulquerías, prohibiting gambling and music on their premises, and banning the sale of alcohol during festivities. Alcohol became the rationale for further official control of people's movements. Since pulque was subject to a tax when it entered the city, even pedestrians carrying as little as two liters were arrested by the police. Policemen dragged dozens of sleeping drunkards (*borrachos tirados*) from the streets to police stations. In most cases, they were summarily fined and released the next morning.[45]

Finding a comprehensive solution to the problem of alcoholism proved difficult, in part because of the strong economic interests connected to the pulque business in Mexico City. Growing demand and increasing state supervision led to quarrels between cantinas and pulquerías, which had to meet municipal licensing requirements, and the numerous informal outlets such as *tendajones* (small stores) and *puestos* (street booths), which sold alcohol without a license, especially at night when legal outlets were forced to close. Owners of small cantinas and pulquerías accused authorities of enforcing regulations in favor of the monopolistic Compañía Expendedora de Pulques and the proprietors of elegant outlets downtown. The Compañía, whose property included haciendas, railroads, and urban real estate, had powerful partners who were also senior public officials, such as Pablo Macedo—brother of jurist and criminologist Miguel, and high-ranking official in the Díaz government and the city council. After Díaz's demise, many of the small sellers' grievances against the Compañía became public and the new governments were, at least rhetorically, more willing to act upon the fears of alcoholism as a social problem.[46]

Street commerce, another long-standing source of tension between authorities and city dwellers, reinforced the street life associated with alcohol. Since most of the city's inhabitants spent their days and nights outside, a great variety of exchanges occurred in all areas of the city. Many enterprising citizens saw street commerce as a ready, if risky, source of income, for which it was worth confronting the authorities' penchant for control of the streets. A multitude of services were offered: scribes (*escribanos,* also called *evangelistas*), barbers, dentists, phonograph operators, and musicians exercised their trades on the sidewalks, with or without official authorization. Women cooked and sold food (chopping beef, making tortillas, fixing *tacos*) in the middle of narrow streets, especially around markets like La Merced.[47]

What these trades lacked in stability they offered in flexibility and freedom of movement. Small vegetable or candy vendors would acquire their daily stock at La Merced market or the *embarcaderos* (docks where canoes brought in produce from the countryside across Lake Texcoco), walk the streets or take a place on a sidewalk, and work until the sun set or their merchandise was gone. Forty-five-year-old María Magdalena Gutiérrez walked every day from the Jamaica market to the Fourth District to peddle vegetables. She spoke Nahuatl and some Spanish, and used to live in Lerma, state of Mexico, where she made tortillas; but, she informed a social worker in 1931, "after she saw that the selling of vegetables could be more profitable, she turned to that activity and moved to the capital," where she was able to earn approximately one peso per day. She would wake up very early every day, buy the "lettuce, green peas, artichokes, etc.," sell them in the street, and return home by foot. She was arrested on the suspicion of being a beggar while more than two kilometers away from home.[48]

Peddlers like María Magdalena fought a constant battle against authorities to occupy those areas of the city where customers and money were accessible. Indian sellers coming to the capital to sell their own produce were common since colonial times. In the perception of early-twentieth-century authorities, however, she represented a serious source of disorder, no longer a "natural" element of the city's landscape but an agent of social conflict, struggling for space against established merchants and respectable neighbors. The 1900 census classified only 334 persons as street peddlers, but many testimonies strongly suggest much larger numbers. In 1894, merchants of the Calle del Empedradillo, near the cathedral, complained about the "plague" of ambulantes in that street and the reluctance of the police to take strong measures against them. As the city council conceded, municipal regulations could not be easily enforced due to the negligence of the police, who refused to take strong measures against ambulantes.[49]

Disputes between established merchants and ambulantes over access to customers were rife. Many sellers stationed themselves outside the markets, offering the same products available inside, which they had acquired early in the morning at lower prices. The key to success was finding the right spot. Food vendors outside La Merced market complained to the city council that if they were displaced to a different zone with less circulation of customers—as city authorities intended—their livelihood would be destroyed.[50] Police agents and inspectors made peddlers' lives harder by demanding either the official permit (which most of them lacked and could cost thirteen cents a day for a square meter of a downtown sidewalk) or a bribe.[51] Ambulantes were particularly troublesome for the group of affluent merchants and urban reformers who sought to establish control over downtown streets and turn them into a modern business district. They pressured for more stringent enforcement in the streets near the center but were less concerned about populous spots, such as the Plaza de Santo Domingo.[52] After all, the Zócalo was one of the showpieces of the ideal city, while Santo Domingo, only three blocks to the north, already belonged to the margins.

Other types of exchanges challenged the social divisions of urban geography. The immediate need for cash drove people downtown to pawn their possessions. The city council had to authorize pawn shops in other areas of the city in order to prevent the long lines and agglomerations formed around the Monte de Piedad building, but it did not allow private entrepreneurs to offer lower rates than the Monte de Piedad.[53] Theft was another reason for some people to enter the wealthy areas of the capital. Reports of pick-pockets in such places as the cathedral inflamed concerns about crime in general and supported the demands for harsh treatment of petty thieves. It was common practice for some thieves to enter a store, grab a piece of fine silk from the counter and try to outrun clerks and policemen.[54] Even though thieves were fewer than ambulantes, they also participated in the disruption of the social geography of the capital.

Certainly more visible than thieves, beggars became the focus of upper-class struggles to "recover" public spaces. In 1897, influential hygienist Dr. Eduardo Liceaga proposed that beggars be sent to jail instead of to the overcrowded asylum. *El Imparcial* supported the idea, since it would prevent "those immoral scenes that contradict our culture."[55] In 1916, *El Universal* complained that beggars were aggressive, showing "sickening sores, with reprehensible impudence" and threatening to infect pedestrians. Their places should not be the streets, but "the farthest corner of hospitals."[56] In 1917, Julio Anaya was arrested near La Merced and sent to the penitentiary because he was begging "and to that end [according to the police] he pierced the skin of his neck with a needle."[57] But it was the location of beggars rather than their begging style that dictated official intervention. Like vendors and thieves, beggars gravitated toward the central, more crowded areas of the capital. Police inspectors reported to the city council in 1895 that beggars came from surrounding neighborhoods or villages, particularly during religious celebrations. Their presence was rare in suburban districts, like the Seventh and Eighth.[58] In 1930, *El Universal* published a map of the zone of "greatest concentration of beggars." The area stretched from Las Cruces to Guerrero Streets, and from Arcos de Belem Avenue to República de Panamá Street. This overlapped with the central downtown streets, the cosmopolitan zone around the Alameda and Zócalo.[59]

Peddling, stealing, begging, and drinking were certainly not the only reasons for the urban poor to appropriate the spaces of the wealthy city, but they were the most visible. Laboring at workshops, upper-class houses, government offices, or stores, inhabitants of the marginal city moved daily into the central city, filling the streets with their presence. The city could not work without this movement across social boundaries. Yet, city authorities sought to control and channel the dynamics of urban life. They tried to teach the urban lower classes how to use their own city. This dominating pretense, rather than material improvements, characterized the Porfirian version of the modern capital.

2

The Policed City

As early twentieth-century urban authorities, merchants, and developers tried to organize the city according to their interests, they turned to the police to punish the public behaviors that did not conform to those goals. The urban poor, on the other hand, developed a skeptical view of order. They used the city in different ways, walking across the social boundaries, challenging the authority of the police, and even subverting the official dictates about street nomenclature.

Conflict was the distinctive feature of the late Porfirian city. Thieves, drunkards, and beggars became the target of several official campaigns to "clean up" the city. Perhaps the harshest campaigns took place in 1908–10 under Porfirio Díaz's iron hand, and subsequently in 1917–19 when Venustiano Carranza sought to consolidate revolutionary legitimacy using ancien régime methods.[1] These policies were the most aggressive example of official attitudes toward the urban lower classes. They emerged in the context of the dispute between different notions about the use and structure of the city. But it was not a one-sided fight: city inhabitants challenged authorities' skewed distribution of resources, which favored upper-class colonias and the center over the rest of the city. Issues of health, policing, and street nomenclature reveal contesting perceptions of urban space and illustrate how the unintended consequences of modernization subverted the Porfirian model of a cosmopolitan capital.

BOUNDARIES

The internal and external boundaries of Mexico City became particularly unstable during the Porfiriato. Since the early colonial period, ethnic stratification had defined an area of Spanish population around the political and religious center of the *Plaza Mayor.* The *traza* or outline of the central city displaced the indigenous inhabitants of Tlatelolco and Tenochtitlan to the edges of the lake that surrounded the city. According to Andrés Lira, from those early moments on, the areas of Spanish and indigenous occupancy moved and overlapped constantly. The tension these movements imposed on the "social distance" reached its peak in the second half of the nineteenth century.[2] Areas of lower-class housing, characterized by overcrowded tenements near the downtown and squatters' shacks in the outskirts of the city, surrounded the center in a crescent moon whose curve embraced the Zócalo and Alameda, closer east of the National Palace and farther away at its extremes. The moon's farthest points were the colonia Guerrero in the northwest and the Belem jail in the southwest. Its territory included the colonias Morelos and la Bolsa, located north and northeast of the old barrio Tepito, and the colonia Obrera.

The barrios of older, lower-class housing near the center presented obvious problems. Many of them had been established in pre-Hispanic times, some still preserving indigenous habits and language, but others were the result of the recent increases in population density. According to *El Imparcial,* real estate speculation, the centralization of services and commerce, and the price of tramway fares forced "our poor classes to cram like canned sardines into the small rooms available."[3] Many run-down vecindades, pulquerías, and dangerous streets were located just behind the National Palace. American visitor Eaton Smith noted that, as a consequence, the Zócalo "is rather the lounging-place for the lower classes, as the Alameda is for the upper."[4] After the Revolution, lower-class neighborhoods close to downtown remained a world of poverty and disease. In the early 1920s, sanitary authorities considered the area north of the Plaza de la Constitución as an "endemic" zone of typhus, whose inhabitants had to be "*desinsectizados*" to prevent new outbreaks of the disease.[5]

The contrast was also stark in the poorer suburbs, where traditional rural ways coexisted with the newest aspects of modernization. In the Seventh and Eighth districts, unkempt open spaces prompted the city council to order the fencing of empty lots near "inhabited zones."[6] Still open to the surrounding countryside, these areas showed the unfinished transition to urban life. Dogs, horses, donkeys, pigs, cattle, and chicken were everywhere and created sanitation problems: in December 1900, the bodies of seven hundred animals were picked up and incinerated.[7] In Mixcoac, south of Chapultepec, well-to-do neighbors complained about a forty-three-room tenement house and the corresponding animals, which they considered a focus of disease and crime and an insult to nearby residences. To the east, farther away from the ideal city, Smith explored barrios San Lázaro, Santa Anita, La Soledad, and La Palma, a "rather slummy part of the town," in the southeastern limit of the Second District. Situated next to Lake Texcoco, the area suffered the worst effects of dusty winds and flooding.[8]

The external limits of the capital lost their ordering function during the Porfiriato, as the capital expanded its area almost fivefold and railroads reached the heart of the capital.[9] Several gates (*garitas*) had been placed at the outskirts of the city to control the traffic of merchandise brought in by carts. By the turn of the twentieth century, however, the gates were rapidly becoming obsolete: officials still collected fees on pulque and other products but their fiscal importance had been reduced by increasing railroad traffic, and they no longer marked the city's outer limits. City authorities during the Porfiriato could not monitor the influx of travelers entering through the garitas or checking into mesones, as had been the practice since the colonial period.[10] The Revolution exhibited the loss of control over the external boundaries of the city. Zapatista insurgents from Morelos acquired weapons, money, and information in the capital, and carried them through the southern hills of the valley with relative ease, although on a small scale. The entrance of Zapata's army in November 1914 was the symbolic culmination of this silent invasion.[11]

In the 1880s, the separation between recently arrived "outsiders" (*fuereños*) and city dwellers seemed clear to everyone because both groups had distinctive clothes and manners. As the city grew and trains brought anonymous multitudes, fuereños became harder to discern.[12] For many

2. Panoramic view of barrio Tepito and its church, ca. 1930. Source: Fototeca Nacional, Fondo Casasola, 92766. © INAH.

capitalinos, the modernization of transportation meant a wider urban space, but also one plagued by anonymity and danger.

The crescent moon, therefore, posed a threat to the security of the modern city. Certain barrios and lower-class colonias were identified by *gente decente* as places of criminality and vice. To the north in the Third District, barrio Tepito and colonia de la Bolsa, known for their role in the traffic of stolen goods, were also territories of crime (see fig. 2.). An *El Imparcial* reporter depicted colonia de la Bolsa as "the cradle of crime." He described his excursion to the colonia as though it were a journey into the unknown: "As an explorer seeking the source of rivers by sailing against the stream, I followed the complex network of small streets that are the bridges sending evil from la Bolsa to invade the city." Once there "a crowd of horrible and strange figures . . . emerged before my terrified eyes, beholding that dark world where people seem to come from generations of criminals."[13] The barrio of Tepito was also feared as a thieves' lair. Eaton Smith was told that the "Thieves Market" was the place where stolen merchandise could be sold three months after the theft, without fear of prosecution. The visitor thought this an exaggeration, "at least nowadays under the strong hand of Díaz."[14] To the southeast and south of the center, mainly within the Second and Fourth Districts, La Merced market and Cuauhtemotzín Street (an area of prostitution) were seen as foci of danger. An 1895 guide for visitors, suggestively entitled *México y sus alrededores. Guía para los viajeros escrita por un Mexicano. Cuidado con los rateros* [Mexico and its Surroundings: A Guide for Travelers written by a Mexican: Beware of the Thieves], warned that La Merced is "famous because of the quantity of thieves who are there."[15] Around Belem Jail, in the Sixth District, a motley world of prisoners' relatives, witnesses and victims attending court, policemen, jury trial audiences, vendors, and scribes reminded observers of the large population involved in the business of crime and punishment.

Alcohol consumption defined these areas. In a survey ordered by the city council in 1902, the Second District had the greatest number of alcohol outlets (534 of a total of 2,423 in the whole city). Together with the First District and the Third District, they encompassed more than half of the pulquerías (484 of a total of 924) in all eight districts.[16]

A closer look at information in the judicial database about criminals' addresses and the locations of crimes seems to reinforce this perception. The data, based on a sample and not normalized to population figures, show certain areas as having a greater frequency of crimes: colonias Doctores, Guerrero, and Morelos and the barrios east of the Zócalo make up 60 percent of the cases in the database. The addresses of suspects suggestively correspond to the bad image of certain colonias: 99 suspects of the 248 for whom information is available lived in San Lázaro, Merced, Esperanza, Tepito, and, again, Doctores and Morelos.

The image proves less convincing when population data (available for police districts but not colonias) is used to normalize crime data. Rates per 100,000 inhabitants from judicial sources, presented in the form of indices in table 6 in the appendix, are not conclusive about the endemic character of crime in certain areas. Only the Fourth District had a consistently higher index of committals and suspects' addresses than did the city as a whole—but only in the rates based on a direct compilation from judicial and administrative sources, in the second, third, and fourth columns. Few suspects lived in the Eighth District, containing the elegant Condesa and Roma colonias, although arrests were more common there—suggesting greater police concern about security in those areas. The feared Second and Third Districts, however, are not clearly prominent except in the rates obtained from the 1917–18 campaign against *rateros.* The results from this campaign, discussed in chapter 7, present an image more like the perceptions described in the previous paragraphs: more of the suspected rateros lived in the Second, Third, and Fourth Districts, while the Seventh and Eighth Districts had low indices. This, I argue, was the product of police notions about the profile of criminals rather than the committal of specific crimes.

The lack of police in these poor areas furthered the elite sense of "dangerous" territories within the city. Despite the even distribution of crime relative to population throughout the city, authorities' deployment of urban services, including policing, favored the more affluent neighborhoods. These administrative decisions provoked reactions from the inhabitants of lower-class neighborhoods and often grew into political disputes over the uses of the urban space and the right to security. The city council was in charge of making urban expansion official. It had to "receive" a colonia before granting it the benefits of infrastructure. The city council approved the transfer of property in *Colonias* Roma, Condesa, Juárez, San Rafael, Santa María, and Guerrero, in lands that had formerly belonged to haciendas, and ensured that their developers provided all the services offered to proprietors. Other areas seemed to be ignored. In 1903, for example, neighbors of colonia de la Bolsa asked for pavement and street lighting, but the city council denied their request on the grounds that the partitioning (or *fraccionamiento*) of the lands had not been officially approved. After a political struggle with the governor of the Federal District, the city council finally accepted the neighbors' petition, although pavement was to take time, and security remained a problem. The inhabitants of colonia Obrera were involved in a similar dispute.[17]

Business needs weighed heavily on these decisions because the city council was usually elected from a group of influential citizens who had economic interests at stake. The results were pragmatic policies that concentrated limited resources on the embellishment of the modern city, rather than on the expansion of all services.[18] Street cleaning and hygiene were targeted only insofar as visible results could be achieved without great expense—particularly in downtown and upper-class areas "frequented by foreigners." Cleanliness, in this perspective, meant prohibiting paintings on the façades of buildings "that obviously defy good taste and are painted against the rules of art"—a clear reference to pulquerías' tradition of covering their exteriors with colorful murals. The police were in charge of enforcing the fines established for noncompliance.[19]

Social conflict over the uses and hierarchies of urban space also developed with regard to public health. In 1901, the Public Health Council indicated that a typhus epidemic had originated in the lower-class suburbs. According to the council, these zones could not be sanitized unless enough police were available to compel their inhabitants to clean up garbage and feces. Resources, concluded the council, were insufficient to attend to both the city's suburbs and center.[20] In the same year, neighbors of the First and Second Districts challenged the council to do something about the filthy Plazuela of Mixcalco:

> With all respect, we the subscribers inform you that we are suffering typhus, pneumonia, and many other diseases whose exact name we do not know because we are ignorant of the science of medicine . . . because of the harmful hygiene produced by the public dumpsite that is the plaza known as Mixcalco, located in front of our homes; we are invaded by a serious catastrophe of illnesses that are killing us with the electric violence of lightning.[21]

Although the subscribers were asking for street cleaning, the city government saw the problem as one of morals. Authorities focused their reform attempts on changing the habits of the lower classes—a cheaper strategy than sanitation. Doctors denounced and prohibited practices such as spitting that they considered unhealthy and that were associated with pulque consumption and blamed for the spread of tuberculosis. The disease was responsible for the death of 2,013 people in 1901. Inhabitants of tenement houses were advised to defecate in "portable buckets," which would be provided and collected every night by authorities. However, in 1907 the service was still not reliable in areas such as Tacubaya. The lack of piped drainage, running water, and garbage collection had caused typhus among the approximately one hundred inhabitants of a tenement house in the Second District, but several visits by inspectors between 1902 and 1906 only served to document worsening conditions. Vecindades, however, could not be closed outright, nor remodeled with public money, and landlords were rarely mentioned as responsible for these situations. The dissipation, untidiness, and alcoholism of the Mexican urban poor were easier to blame.[22]

THE POLICE AS AN INSTRUMENT OF SOCIAL REFORM

It is in the context of this fragmented urban space, made both of disdain and discord, that the Mexico City police need to be comprehended. Policemen were often caught in the contradiction of serving a project of modernization and responding to the demands of the urban population from which they came.

For the governor and the city council, the police were the best weapon of social reform. From their perspective, penal sanctions and police pressure were the means to instill good behavior in the inhabitants of the city. A handwritten note, casually attached to papers concerning traffic regulations discussed at the city council in 1904, portrays this faith in the beneficial effects of policing. The author of the note, probably a council member, divided pedestrians between "cultivated persons" and "idem illiterate." The first group was to be taught about traffic rules through newspaper advertisements and signs; the second, by "insistent warnings, reprimands, constant admonishment by the police and penal sanction."[23] Rather than a plan, this was a factual statement whose ramifications were indicated by *La Voz de México:* "the police are strongly hated among the lower classes."[24]

The police department had been reorganized in 1879 in order to professionalize the service and centralize control of agents. The police force that preceded the 1879 *Gendarmería Municipal* was based on the participation of the neighbors of the thirty-two *cuarteles menores* in which the city was divided. Inspectors and assistants were also residents; they walked around their neighborhood and helped in crime prevention while performing other duties, such as collecting taxes and fighting fires—corresponding with the comprehensive notion of *policía y buen gobierno* and the structure of colonial *alcaldes de barrio,* both inherited from colonial times.[25] The Porfirian reorganization, building on some of the reforms established by liberal governments and by the French intervention and Second Empire (1861–67), divided the city into eight *demarcaciones* or police districts and established a structure in which the inspector general of the police responded to the governor of the Federal District, himself appointed by the president of the Republic. The police force was to be composed of full-time members, clearly distinguished from the civilian population by their uniforms and accountable to their superiors rather than to their neighbors—whose relations with the force were to be kept within strict limits. The police, authorities hoped, were to become an instrument of the state, rather than an extension of barrio life. The apparent rationality of the model and the large percentage of the city's budget devoted to policing contributed to an image of order and increasing safety during the Porfirian period.[26]

As experienced in everyday life, however, the institution of policing did not radiate order and civility. The *comisarías* (police stations), since their establishment in the 1879 reform, were crowded, disorganized, unhealthy, and often dangerous.[27] Although the reforms mandated that each comisaría was to be staffed by a doctor and an intern and that gendarmes were instructed to take anyone wounded in the streets to the comisaría for emergency care, medical service at stations was so deficient that people avoided the police if they were in need of medical care.[28] Some victims and suspects were sent to public hospitals, further confusing emergency care and judicial functions. Emeterio Ortiz, suspected of battery, was transported to the White Cross hospital, where "someone told him that he could leave and come back tomorrow for treatment."[29] Emeterio was lucky, as he was declared fugitive but only suffered eight days of jail after he was reapprehended. Others, such as Jesús Torres, did not fare so well. Torres would spend a year, against his will, at the Juárez Hospital—more time than his attacker had been in prison.[30]

But the clearest conflict between modernization and everyday policing centered on the role of the police agent within urban communities. Gendarmes (as policemen were called since the reforms) were the most visible representatives of authority in city life. The force numbered around 3,000 men by the end of the Porfiriato. Their presence was obvious day and night at intersections, where their lanterns, placed on the corners, formed a long string of lights and marked the areas under vigilance. The breadth of policemen's duties suggests that they were expected indeed to be the keystone of order. Unlike their predecessors, gendarmes had to be literate and respond to a vertical structure of command. They saw that pulquerías closed on time and that neighbors cleaned their streets. They were also in charge of keeping private practices out of public spaces: among their duties was to prevent people from washing "clothes, dishes, buckets and other things at pipes and ditches, streets and public fountains," and to make sure that artisans did not perform their trade on the streets.[31] The police also had to arrest couples "having intercourse on the streets" and sleeping drunkards. These "civilizing" duties and the protection of the propertied were the priority in the use of police manpower. The greatest number of gendarmes was concentrated in the wealthy areas downtown, while barrios and colonias of the periphery were lightly staffed, if at all.[32]

Gendarmes' working conditions impeded these goals. Complete professionalization was still a distant goal by the end of the Porfiriato, as salaries were low and turnover rates high. Gendarmes themselves were subject to exacting disciplinary practices. Fines to maintain punctuality were often deducted from wages; a security deposit had to be paid for the gun and uniform; money was extorted by high-ranking officers. Yet, further attempts to improve discipline only prompted insubordination. In 1904, a leaflet incited gendarmes to call a strike in response to superiors' abuses. Their most common reaction, however, was desertion. Gendarmes moved in and out of the institution with ease, guided by the job market rather than any sense of professionalism. When providing their personal information in affidavits, they usually gave a trade other than "gendarme" or "employee." Some tersely stated that their occupation was "merchant currently gendarme."[33] Police duty was not a source of pride. Policemen often lacked the training and demeanor that would inspire respect from citizens, and they were frequently accused of excessive use of force, often in connection with the *leva* (impressment). Bribes were a feature of police activities at all levels, from extorting street vendors and pulquería owners to protecting gambling and prostitution to allowing the escape of prisoners.[34]

Yet, for the usual victims of crime, policemen were essential to preserve security and capture transgressors. Judicial evidence, rather than administrative reports, show gendarmes in a complex and close interaction with other actors. Probably drawing back to the policing traditions of the colonial period, gendarmes sought to establish a personal relationship with neighbors and thus gain their confidence rather than their fear. Key to achieving that trust was the gendarme's constant presence at or near his assigned intersection (the *punto*). Secundino Sánchez, for example, lived very close to his punto and received reports about ongoing fights from "a girl he knows." As with Secundino, victims and neighbors chased suspects and usually arrested them "with the help of the police."[35] The neighborhood's attitude must have been an important factor when gendarmes brought the detained to the comisaría, walking the suspect from his punto to that of the next gendarme, who then took the suspect to the next gendarme until they reached the comisaría.[36] Gendarmes who had a better relationship with their neighbors could count on their support. Salvador Luna, who lived near Estanco de Mujeres Street, tried to arrest Dionisio Cardiel because he was drunk and was using obscene language. Cardiel attacked Luna and, even though the agent made five shots into the air, Cardiel managed to wound him in the armpit. Then, according to the two men's testimonies, "the people" around subdued Cardiel and beat him for wounding Luna.[37]

Aware of negative reactions against police force abuses, and even when they were under attack, gendarmes such as Luna avoided using their guns. Most frequently, they shot their guns into the air to intimidate suspects and attract the help of other gendarmes. Excessive violence was not in their best interest: gendarmes were not immune to prosecution in the case of wounds or deaths resulting from their work. The common complaint in the press about gendarmes who abandoned their puntos in order to drink a glass of pulque with friends could be then understood not only as a sign of poor discipline, but perhaps as the agent's self-interested attempt to maintain relations with neighbors.[38]

Conversely, resistance to police intervention by neighbors sharply curtailed policemen's power. In one case in 1906, gendarme Luis Velis was slightly wounded when he tried to break up a fight between two domestic employees. The owner of the house denied Velis entrance to arrest the aggressors, and suspects and witnesses accused the agent of intervening after the fight had finished and of trying to plant a knife on one of the suspects. Later, during the trial, Velis did not appear for testimonies and crossexaminations because, the judge was notified, "he had resigned his job and cannot be found."[39]

City dwellers were not shy about expressing their disapproval of gendarmes who used excessive force. Gendarme Manuel Aguilar was accused and convicted of battery for using his gun against a former neighbor. Several witnesses testified to Aguilar's proclivity for drawing his gun in the middle of discussions. Aguilar declared that the victim and other neighbors called him *desgraciado tecolote*—damned owl, a common epithet against policemen—and threatened to stone him.[40] Individual defiance could reach epic proportions, as it did one day in 1906, when Elvira Peredo walked in front of a police station and called the second officer "viejo cabrón"—old goat. It took several hours to subdue her—and not before she broke the doors of two cells, bit and threw limestone on the employees, and insulted everyone up to President Díaz, who, she claimed, "sucks her dick, because she becomes a man when they do it." Her explanation, the next day, was that she had been drunk and that the chief of the comisaría had "ill will toward her, and always arrests her without justification."[41]

Were city authorities deceiving themselves when they entrusted the police with the reform of the lower classes' mores? Criminology, to be discussed in the following chapter, said repression did change culture. But the evidence suggests that gendarmes cannot be construed as mere executors of elite projects, nor as unbiased protectors of every citizen's life and property. Their role is that of unintended intermediaries between policies and traditions, between institutions and communities, and, as will be discussed later, between criminals and victims.

THE ISSUE OF NOMENCLATURE

One final episode in this brief history of the disputed capital shows the ambitions of urban reformers and the limits of official strategies to shape the way people used the city. The controversy over street nomenclature exhibited the reluctance of the majority of the inhabitants to accept passively progress when it threatened the way in which they knew and walked the city. In 1888, the city council decided to change all street names, establishing "a nomenclature in harmony with the advances of the population." It was argued that the existing style (which in most cases gave one name to each block) was "irrational . . . absurd" and provoked the hilarity of foreign visitors. Names such as Tumbaburros, el Tomepate, la Tecomaraña, were "ridiculous."[42] The proposed system divided the city along two axes that crossed one block east of the Alameda, identifying the streets by a number and a cardinal point. But the project soon provoked the opposition of various groups. The axes, argued critics at the city council, did not correspond with the middle of the city because of its asymmetrical growth and because "in the mind of all inhabitants" the center of the city was not a geometrical point but "a certain zone that now extends from the Alameda to the Plaza de la Constitución."[43]

When the changes were enacted they provoked confusion and protests. People used both old and new street names simultaneously. In 1893, city authorities returned the signs with the old names back to their original places but did not eliminate the new "official" names. The result was that most streets had two names: the old one used on a daily basis and the new one in official documents. In the recently established colonias San Rafael, Santa María, and Guerrero, however, the new names stuck, albeit temporarily, because people started using them. In even newer colonias, such as del Paseo, neighbors resisted the numeral system and preferred to use names of their own choosing. In colonias Condesa and Roma, the axis for the numbers was the Paseo de la Reforma, instead of the line established in 1888. According to Roberto Gayol, defender of the new system, the 1888 reform did not succeed because it lacked political support and because, in a number of new colonias, neighbors had been granted the de facto right to name the streets as they pleased, with no apparent intervention from city authorities.[44]

People continued to use the old names because they made more sense and corresponded with their way of viewing the city: as a group of *rumbos,* or "directions," associated with buildings or other urban markers rather than a grid. According to councilman Alberto Best, people knew the city well enough to make the numerical system unnecessary: "Each individual holds in his mind a number of street names that is enough for his business and occupations, and when he forgets or ignores one, it is easy to find it by only knowing the direction or proximity that it has with others that he still remembers." In 1904, the city council recommended that the old system be reestablished with only one reform—unifying the names where the traditional system had designated each block with its own name.[45]

Mexico City dwellers did not think of their town as a centralized space, but as a group of rumbos. Thus, the exchanges and movements that from the elite's perspective constituted an "invasion" of respectable areas, from the perspective of the urban poor were simply moves from one rumbo to another. Such movements responded to the immediate needs of social life and were not charged with the threat of disorder. Nevertheless, by naming and inhabiting the city in their own way, people undermined the model of rational order devised by Porfirian urbanists.

Judicial narratives attest to the meandering style of walking that preceded the committal of crimes. Leopoldo Villar gave the police a detailed description of his movements the day he was arrested for theft, beginning from his home in Málaga street to the Hotel Regis, then, with his friend Emilio Vera, to the Cine San Rafael, the Legislative Palace, San Rafael Avenue, Las Artes Street, and finally, at 11:00 P.M., to the sixth block of Miguel María Contreras Street, where he was arrested for stealing a wheel. Since Leopoldo lacked a stable job, he had to keep moving across the city, hanging around with friends and looking for an income.[46]

The lack of precision in the use of street names and addresses was also a way to evade authorities. When forced to give an address, people used vague references to locate their place in the city. Nineteen percent of those arrested in the 1917–18 campaign against petty thieves claimed to have no address, while others simply referred to a rumbo (e.g., "la Ladrillera," for a brick-making facility).[47] Josefina Ayala, arrested for begging in October 1930, gave two false addresses to the social workers who evaluated her ability to live by herself or be sustained by her family. Perhaps she feared that other members of her family might be further punished. She advised her son, Luis Barrios, not to use her name when visiting her in jail, but to ask instead for Isabel Gómez (who was a friend of Josefina, also in prison) so that he would not be detained for questioning too.[48] Josefina had probably undergone the same humiliating experience of Candelaria García, arrested in the same campaign: her clothes were burned, her head was shaved, she was sprayed with disinfectant, and was forced to wear an asylum uniform.[49] Social workers might have intended to help Josefina, but Josefina could only perceive this campaign (and other public policies toward the urban poor) as an ill-disguised aggression. Pressed by official harassment and by economic hardship similar to that which had forced Josefina to beg, the urban poor chose to use the city in their own way, crossing through the boundaries that were supposed to organize society and avoiding any contact with authorities.

CONCLUSIONS: CRIMINALIZATION AND THE ROLE OF URBAN COMMUNITIES

Although most of the problems and policies described in this chapter had antecedents in Mexico City's history, the peculiarity of the late Porfiriato and early postrevolutionary period resides in the clear confrontation between an authoritarian regime's projects to reshape urban geography and the opposing forces of subordinate groups' use of the city, demographic growth, and technological change. Besieged by unemployment, disease, and a lack of water and appropriate housing, the urban poor also lived in the respectable city, despite the fact that the police constantly reminded them of the capital's social boundaries.

Thus, the dispute about the use of the city became a matter of crime and punishment. Lower-class neighborhoods were identified as zones of danger and disease. City authorities placed the police in charge of punishing behaviors that challenged their idea of modernization—although policemen themselves had to cope with low wages and little prestige. Other efforts, such as the extension of sanitation and the control of alcohol consumption, were limited by the budget allotted to the marginal city and by the extent to which officials were willing to support the business of urbanization. The profits from real estate speculation and the pulque industry overrode the goals of social reform. It was easier and less costly to punish deviant behavior and to restrict the urban poor to the socially marginal areas of the capital.

Porfirian Mexico City's particular brand of modernization was characterized by an ongoing negotiation between the ideal city and the everyday city. The rules of behavior in public areas were not perceived (by their designers or by their subjects) as requiring strict obedience. Enforcement was determined by context. Certain transgressions could go unpunished if committed in the "dangerous" zone of the city or if the transgressor belonged to the upper classes. At the same time, practices such as public alcohol consumption, which the urban poor saw as harmless, became criminal. This generated broad skepticism about the fairness of the police and the criminal law. For the urban poor, justice could not be expected from above. They had to silently and constantly disregard regulations in order to survive in the city.

This chapter, finally, introduces one of the key actors in the story of Mexico City's crime and punishment, one that was not acknowledged by the Porfirian and early postrevolutionary state, and one only recently identified in the historiography: urban communities. Despite their diversity, colonias, barrios, and vecindades shared a willingness to respond to the vacuum left by city authorities concerning security and health. The prevention of crime was a source of cohesion for these communities, as will become clear when examining the reaction of victims, their neighbors, and relatives to violence and petty theft.

Although urban communities are more loosely defined than rural communities (due, perhaps, to the fact that the latter have been the subject of most scholarly research), they played a central role in the transformation of the city during this period of rapid growth. They were easy to identify. People associated their community with a rumbo, a geographical destination for their wanderings around the city. It combined work, nuclear and extended families, friends, and the public places of sociability where private life continued. The community contained the networks of support that were an essential element of survival in a world besieged by the drastic changes of capitalist modernization but lacking the material rewards of stable income and security.

3

The Construction of Mexican Criminology

Disconcerted by Mexico City's unruly population, the Porfirian intelligentsia focused on criminality to explain the government's lack of control over large sections of urban life. Criminals represented the reverse image of the progressive capital that the regime sought to build. Students of crime (called criminologists or criminal anthropologists) set out to classify social groups and give scientific legitimacy to the upper classes' sense of moral superiority. Perceptions and explanations of urban crime were a key element of the elite's views of society. Criminological discourse, however, was not simply an ideological construct to justify class rule.[1] Porfirian ideas about crime and punishment betrayed the ambivalence of educated observers toward their own society. The desire to discipline and regenerate society through scientific means was at the heart of criminology as an emerging science in Europe and the United States in the last decades of the nineteenth century. This inspired Mexican urban reformers' belief that repression could change the manner in which people used the city. Yet, despite the cosmopolitan goals, the specific ideas of Mexican criminologists could not be abstracted from Mexico City's reality. They were fascinated by the complex society that was the object of their research and failed to agree on a solution to urban problems. The explanations of society proposed by criminology, I will contend, emerged from an unstable combination of fear, eclecticism, and fascination that did not conform to the complexity of everyday life.

This attempt and its failure have been overlooked in contemporary accounts of the Porfiriato. Postrevolutionary interpretations of Porfirio Díaz's authoritarian regime dismiss his social policies as a simple instrument to maintain power and social control. Revolutionaries and later historians saw the social ideas produced by the *científico* group (influential officials and writers surrounding Díaz) as mere rationalizations of existing social and political hierarchies, proven inadequate by the same social rejection that overthrew the regime. Those ideas were all the more artificial, it is argued, since they were copies of French, English, or American intellectual constructs. Journalists denounced the police and penitentiary systems as the dictator's means to silence the press, obstruct electoral opposition, and repress collective disobedience. Under these premises, Porfirian ideas about criminality are little more than a subtheme of the intellectual history of the regime.[2]

Later approaches have reexamined Porfirian social reform on the premise that "social engineering" was more than an intellectual fashion, and that the científicos did in fact seriously try to discipline the lower classes to make them more obedient and fit for progress.[3] Regardless of the limited impact of social engineering on lower-class behaviors, I will add, its guiding ideas were not the product of a passive absorption of foreign knowledge: they involved the creative effort of writers and the curiosity of a broad Mexican audience. Images and analyses of crime in particular offered a key to explain a society that did not always measure up to the project of progress and order. Furthermore, by providing a critical perspective on social reality, criminologists sought to contribute to the redefinition of social policies. The discourse of criminality and punishment should not be interpreted, then, simply as means to an end but as a historical product, part of society's "mutually constructing configuration of elements."[4]

Writers, scholars, lawyers, and public officials produced these ideas. They identified themselves as the representatives of public opinion and as such claimed that their conclusions deserved to be applied in different areas of social life. Their views were informed by religious, journalistic, administrative, and even commercial interests, and their voices presented often contending opinions. All of them claimed the scientific validity of their assertions.

Yet science was only one component of these intersecting observations of crime. The process of importing criminological knowledge prompted resistance from sectors linked with the legal profession, while explanations of social diseases combined theory, ideology, and a morbid fascination with the world of crime. Born from social fears, but also from the desire to be modern, Mexican criminology built a scientific perception of urban society—if one that failed to provide a generally accepted formula for social reform.

PERCEPTIONS OF CRIME AND CRIMINOLOGICAL OBSERVATIONS

The Porfirian elite believed that turn-of-the-century Mexico had finally achieved peace, if not harmony, thanks to the patent moral superiority of its rulers. Urban society, however, offered a landscape much more complicated than they had wished. The persistence of areas of crime and the urban poor's "invasion" of respectable places suggested that the majority of Mexicans were not as virtuous and obedient as expected and that the line between good and evil was not so straight and "natural" as the one that divided the wealthy from the poor, or men from women. In order to achieve the necessary authority to inspect "the world of crime" and lower-class life that so fascinated them, educated observers appealed to science. Charles A. Hale has defined one important component of the elite's sense of superiority as "scientific politics": a strong government led by Díaz, guided by the methods of science and an interpretation of society that viewed it as an organism.[5] Criminology was thus a useful instrument to preserve old prejudices in the observation of new realities.

Statistics composed the first testimony of modernization, and public opinion found the figures that exhibited national growth very convincing. Starting in the last two decades of the nineteenth century, local, federal, and nongovernmental institutions gathered quantitative information about the economy and population. The Dirección General de Estadística, founded in 1882, the Sociedad Mexicana de Geografía y Estadística, and the Consejo Superior de Salubridad were among the main publishers of statistics. Authorities and observers believed crime statistics in particular to be an objective measurement of the behavior of society. This rationale had been present in the mind of public officials and social observers since the last third of the nineteenth century and reemerged after the 1910 Revolution. The compilation and publication of statistical series based on judiciary and police sources sought to demonstrate the state's adequate handling of the problem.[6] The international promotion of Mexico's image was also behind the publication of crime statistics. The Dirección General de Estadística compiled and published the 1871–1885 series with the express goal of showing at the International Exposition of Paris "the moral progress that has been achieved" in Mexico.[7]

Testimonies about the reception of these series, however, suggest that they often worked against their goals. They failed to impart an "objective," moderating counterpoint to contemporaries' alarmed perceptions of recurring "crime waves." When public discussions of crime mentioned statistics it was to attest to the "terrifying" growth of crime.[8] Because of the negative potential of quantitative information, the series chosen to be collected and published were subject to the changing concerns of different authorities and thus lacked continuity. Most series in the first half of the twentieth century resulted from efforts to have them published when they seemed useful, not from routine record-keeping. Authorities could change the criteria of quantification or stop publication altogether when the information revealed negative tendencies.[9] Critics denounced court- and police-based statistics of criminality in the capital, published since 1890, for their lack of consistency. Carlos Roumagnac considered them "useless" because of their inaccuracy.[10] In 1896, pulque traders defended their business against accusations that it caused crime, arguing that the official statistical information, although nicely printed in tables, did not account for the circumstances of arrests, the number of acquittals, and the growth of the population. They concluded that official figures failed to render the exact number of crimes committed and that only specialists could extract meaningful information from them.[11]

Statistical accounts of the city conveyed a growing crime rate. Earlier in the Porfiriato, the official report was that criminality was not increasing in Mexico City because jobs were abundant, the population was more educated, the police and the judiciary had improved, and political stability had curbed the demoralization caused by civil war.[12] This idea, however, did not last long. In 1890, Mexico City's correctional judges complained that arrests were exceeding the capacity of their courts. In 1896, police arrested 29,729 "scandalous drunkards," 94 beggars, and 910 prostitutes. The public attorney stated that whereas 8,108 individuals were convicted in 1897, in 1909 the number had more than doubled to reach 16,318. Figures showed the violent nature of most recorded crimes: between 1885 and 1895, 78 percent of offenses were crimes against persons. Homicide rose from 179 presumed murderers arrested in 1891, to 481 in 1895. Figures condemned the Mexican capital as one of the most dangerous cities in the world.[13]

Contemporary images of Mexico City also exhibited, perhaps with more accuracy than statistics, the embarrassing face of progress. Porfirian observers condensed the life of the lower classes in visual accounts of corporal degradation and wretched housing that contrasted with the "comfort" of progress. In 1897, Miguel Macedo described unhealthy dwellings, humid and without ventilation, where the *petate* (matting) was the table during the day and the bed at night, and where the same blanket that protected from rain or cold, covered sleep and sexual intercourse. In the streets, the dirty and emaciated bodies of the poor were as evident as the clouds in the clear skies of the city, yet they often became victims of trolleys.[14] *El Hijo del Ahuizote* denounced the "general embarrassment" caused by the gendarmes who arrested a drunken woman of the lower classes ("una mujer del pueblo"). When she forcibly resisted arrest, they grabbed her and in the struggle completely stripped her, transporting her with her feet tied "like a pig."[15] The nude and hungry bodies of alcoholics lying in the streets became an essential datum of arguments against alcoholism.[16] *Santa,* a widely read novel by Federico Gamboa published in 1903 and peppered with scientific meditations on deviance, epitomized the ambivalent attraction that Mexican readers felt for scenes of vice and crime. The novel, a great sales success, depicted morbid and prurient images of the life and body of its main character, a Mexico City prostitute.[17]

This imagery made a great impact on public opinion through newspapers. The daily press depicted crime graphically and voiced the elite's indignation at the contrast between their project to create an elegant city and the behavior of a population who did not share those concerns. The *Gaceta de Policía* was a magazine devoted entirely to local police news and supported by police inspector Félix Díaz. *El Imparcial,* a vehicle for the opinions of powerful científicos, and also subsidized by the government, devoted a considerable portion of its space to crimes, suicides, and assorted quarrels. Even the respectable *La Voz de México,* organ of the Catholic church, gave daily reports of criminal incidents. In their coverage of crime, newspapers used narratives as well as diagrams, photographs, engravings, summaries of trial debates and testimonies, and often editorials.[18]

Newspapers' treatment of police news was criticized from several perspectives. Authorities decried exaggeration in the press of the "quantitative and qualitative" increase of criminality. Liberal *El Hijo del Ahuizote* denounced *El Imparcial* for preferring to deal with "frivolities" like high society dances and gruesome killings over real problems. A sensationalist press, declared the mutualist magazine *El Bien Social,* encouraged wrongdoing by its "sick" and "greedy" coverage of some stories and inspired new crimes with reports of homicides among the upper classes.[19] *Don Cucufate* (a satirical weekly) mocked the "imparcialadas" in its doggerel: "twenty five crushed/and a lot of suicides/ . . . /That's how they enlighten the mob,/with gossip and dirty lies."[20]

Instead of the moralizing practiced by respectable newspapers, the popular press satirized the other side of the tension between civilization and barbarism in the streets of the capital: namely, judicial, administrative, and police repression. Weekly illustrated magazines denounced the duplicity of the institutions of order, which condemned the vices of the lower classes (particularly pulque consumption) while turning a blind eye toward upper-class alcoholism and failing to pursue real crime. In a drawing from the front page of *El Diablito Bromista* (subtitled "Semanario de la clase obrera, azote del mal burgués y coco del mal gobierno"), one pulquería patron asked another why a policeman arrested his friend (dressed in the traditionally Indian white cotton trousers, sandals, and a plain shirt) when another customer (with suit, hat, and shoes) was obviously the drunker of the two. The answer was an old Mexican saying: *el hilo siempre se revienta por lo más delgado* (literally "the thread always breaks at its thinnest part"), indicating that the crime of public drunkenness only happened when a poor person committed it.[21]

Regardless of the publication's ideology, press coverage of criminality in Mexico City was determined by the social background of suspects and victims. Journalists used demeaning terms to depict collective phenomena. To refer to petty thieves, they used words like "plague," "epidemic," and *rata* (rat) or *ratero* (petty thief). Names like "sons of Gestas" or "sons of Caco" referred to an ancient and obscure family of thieves. Reports of fights or traffic accidents seldom mentioned the names of offenders and victims, using instead generic expressions such as *una mujer del pueblo* (a lower-class woman) or, referring to ethnicity, *una indita* (a little Indian woman). Detailed reporting was reserved for the rich or the particularly gruesome. According to the editors of the *Gaceta de Policía,* if a man of the lower classes killed his lover and attempted suicide, the event would be buried in a small article. However, if the people involved happened to be Manuel Algara y Terreros and actress María Reig, the event caused "sensation" and reached the front page.[22] These famous cases set themselves apart against a background of anonymity.

Anonymity became an obsession for Mexican criminologists and police, due in part to the demographic growth of the city. Either criminals did not have names or they were all known by the same aliases: in 1889, the name Antonio Hernández is listed twenty-three times in the records of Belem jail, and that of José Hernández, seventeen. It was not clear to what extent this was the product of repeat offenders. According to a judge in the High Court of the Federal District, authorities punished recidivism perhaps only once in three hundred cases because of their inability to identify criminals and because of the latter's mendacity. Another judge explained that identification of criminals in Mexico was difficult because the majority of them belonged to the indigenous race who, like the Chinese, possessed "a uniform pattern" in their features.[23]

This perceived similarity nullified the identification methods used by Mexican police, based on the declarations of the prisoners and superficial observation of the suspect's appearance. Criminologist Ignacio Fernández Ortigoza promoted the use of the system of identification devised in France by Alphonse Bertillon, based on the measurement of criminals' bodies and a more accurate use of photography. Since Bertillon employed a classification of small, medium, and large sizes of various parts of the body, Fernández Ortigoza personally measured the heads, feet, ears, hands, and arms of eight hundred criminals in Mexico to calculate a "national" standard.[24] Bertillon's files supported the assumption that criminal acts, as with any other vice, always left their marks on the body. In criminal trials, judges used the suspect's identification card to establish his or her previous offenses. The scars on the body, precisely recorded on the card, demonstrated the suspect's disposition to fighting. If the accused denied the existence of the scars, he was compelled to show the part of his body that bore the marks. Amid the public and the jury's laughter, the exhibition proved two things: that the suspect sought to defy science with lies and that his guilt as a criminal was written on his body.[25]

As the methods for identifying criminals were largely ineffective, journalists, lawyers, and policemen preferred to understand crime as an activity confined to a particular segment of society and criminals as a professional group. Statistics might suggest that criminality was expanding continuously, but police officers and store owners assumed that there existed an identifiable core of professional, expert thieves, or rateros. The *Gaceta de Policía* published a "Black Page" with police archive portraits of criminals, listing their name, alias, and modus operandi. The information, the *Gaceta* claimed, was useful for police officers, travelers, store keepers, the general public in Mexico City, and the railroads.[26] As will be discussed in chapter 7, rateros became, in the perception of the law and the authorities, the nucleus of the Mexican criminal profession.

Yet, the line between the respectable and the criminal population was not as clear as desired. From the perspective of Porfirian observers, falsehood characterized criminals. Miguel Macedo correlated criminals to *léperos*—lower-class men whose contacts with the cultured classes had allowed them to "refine the Indian's astuteness."[27] Roumagnac compiled a dictionary of the unintelligible jargon used by prisoners to refer to criminal actions. The *Gaceta de Policía* listed and explained the favorite tricks used in the streets of the city. These tricks required an additional ability: criminals could dress well, have good manners, and pass as honest people. Sometimes defrauders went so far as to pretend to be (if they were not already) plainclothes policemen or health inspectors.[28] Therefore, despite the racial prejudices of urban elites, crime crossed the somatic divisions of the population. In the eyes of the Porfirian ruling classes, criminals included the two extremes of anonymity: the faceless and anonymous masses on one side; and shrewd, well-dressed individuals, hidden among respectable people, on the other.

Rather than the minutia of criminalistics, it was violent crimes that fascinated the general public. The crimes that provoked greatest attention from the press were the so-called crimes of passion, not the least because they were common to all classes, ages, and eras, and defied traditional conceptions of a male honor that "protected" women from violence.[29] Crime also fascinated because it frequently subverted traditional gender roles.[30] To the surprise of scientists and journalists, women could also be agents of transgression. The famous case of María Villa (a.k.a. "La Chiquita"), who killed

Esperanza Gutiérrez, received great attention because one woman used a gun against another in a case involving a man of higher status.[31]

Disrupting gender divisions and moral roles, crime incarnated the attraction underlying readers' scrutiny of lower-class life. Santa, the prostitute in Gamboa's novel, ran the gamut of possibilities of transgression and disease in Porfirian society. She came from the countryside to the metropolis, where she served wealthy individuals and anonymous léperos. She loved both handsome and ugly men, witnessed a crime and testified in Belem. Another woman sexually approached her and she finally fell from youthful health to alcoholism and cancer. The public devoured *Santa* with the same interest that it devoted to crimes of passion. But such attraction was almost sinful and posed for the Porfirian intelligentsia the duty of representing and explaining vice while preserving the moral and scientific distance of social hierarchy. The resulting tension was an important element in Porfirian studies of the darker spaces of the city.

The best way to limit the disturbing impact of deviance was to establish the scientific basis of social difference. Scientists and journalists constructed a discourse about social diseases that conceptually isolated them from the "good" or "high" parts of Mexican society, thus renewing the links between class and morality. According to Macedo, the sense of personal security of the Mexican ruling classes was sound, notwithstanding that the rate of homicides in Mexico was thirteen times higher than in Corsica. The reason was clear: crimes were committed by members of the lower classes against their peers. While their morality was "the lowest," the morality of the well-to-do was "elevated." Wealth, intelligence, and mores clearly divided the two classes. The only connections were "to command and to obey, to serve and to be served." This separation corresponded with a visible difference. Macedo divided society into three groups: individuals wearing plain shirts were the lowest class, followed by those who wore jackets and, at the top of the scale, the group that used frock-coats. The identification of the groups that participated in criminality also had important racial elements: "pure Indian" and "predominantly Indian" formed the "delinquent classes."[32]

To set themselves apart from their object of observation, these writers began by condemning, on moral and aesthetic grounds, the cultural context where drinking and transgressions took place. Pulquerías were "nauseating" places, and most Mexican prostitutes were "ugly."[33] The curative and heating effects attributed by the poor to alcohol belonged with other strange beliefs like traditional curing systems that "damaged the spirit," according to Gamboa, "without healing the flesh."[34] Thieves who used a religious medal for protection were only "imbeciles."[35]

But turning away from reprehensible cultures was not enough. In order to account for these realities, the educated groups tried to systematize their observations of the urban poor. The locus of these observations was the domestic environment. Descriptions of poor, unhealthy dwellings, such as that of Macedo in 1897, became a common theme of the literature about urban social ills. Luis Lara y Pardo asserted in 1908 that the origins of crime and prostitution were inside vecindad rooms: "Within those four walls there have been nights of drunkenness and lust involving parents, siblings, friends and lovers. The father, his mind clouded by alcohol, would often (perhaps intentionally) caress his daughter instead of his lover."[36] Years later, Alberto J. Pani repeated the central elements of these descriptions. In *La higiene en México,* he noted that vecindad rooms were "true foci of physical and moral disease . . . the theater of all miseries, vices and crimes."[37] These images repeated, and thus claimed the same scientific legitimacy of, mid-nineteenth-century French descriptions of life in working-class areas. French writers looked inside workers' homes for the roots of the social ills connected with industrialization and were struck by the lack of amenities, incest, and "degeneration" found in proletarian dwellings—even if those conditions already existed in earlier periods of industrialization. Fiction writers and socialist thinkers like Jean Joseph Blanc and Jean Léon Jaurés warned about the lack of separation in working-class life between work and home, the spheres of men and women.[38] The apparition of these scenes in Porfirian literature resembled those produced by Victorian "urban explorers" of London who, at least symbolically, also entered the poor's dwellings and denounced scenes of degeneration. Upper-class writers and readers in London, just as their Mexico City counterparts, sought to crystallize the social geography of the city, identifying, describing, and explaining the spaces of poverty and danger.[39]

The gaze that entered workers' homes also elucidated social diseases outside. In his ambitious 1901 study of crime, Julio Guerrero described the "filthy hovels of the barrios," and departed from previous descriptions by asserting that the worst cases of immorality in Mexico City did not take place inside those dwellings, but among the groups whose only home were the streets or public dormitories.[40] Among Mexican criminologists, Guerrero placed the greatest emphasis, not only methodological but also explanatory, on the visual; according to the logic of Guerrero and his contemporaries, the thin and pure atmosphere of the Mexican highlands made sight more acute, views of degradation and misery more precise, and people less restrained. His description of the landscape of the Valley of Mexico predated two themes of twentieth-century literature. One was the transparency of the air of the valley, later reiterated by writers such as Alfonso Reyes. The other was the contrast between the clearness of the city's skies and the darkness of its slums. Men in the barrios were "very ugly" and people in general were dirty. In his descriptions of the city, Guerrero, a poet himself, conveyed the importance of visual detail and uncovered the affinity of perspective and style between criminologists and writers.[41]

Fictional narratives on urban themes also focused on the darker areas of life in the city. Writers used greater detail in their descriptions than did the newspapers. They made a more explicit effort to establish their point of view and moral authority, the distance between observer and observed, in order to freely and closely explore the abominable world of urban crime and vice that fascinated them and their readers. An example of this play between distance and proximity is *La Rumba* by Angel de Campo. The novel, published in newspapers between 1890 and 1891, followed the steps of Remedios Vena, a poor but honest seamstress who killed her common-law husband. Frequent changes of perspective and narrative point of view betrayed de Campo's search for a compelling voice. In the first chapters, precise descriptions of the misery of lower-class life combine with colorful dialogues among the inhabitants of one neighborhood. Then, switching to the style of police news and including a diagram of the crime scene, de Campo analyzed the details of the murder. After the jury acquitted Remedios, the narrative returned to its sympathetic scrutiny of life in the neighborhood.[42]

As authors became more familiar with stories of urban vice and crime, narratives gained in authority and popularity. The central character of Gamboa's *Santa* learned about "people and events that many will ignore until their death even if they live for years in the city, read the newspapers, attend the jury trials, and cultivate the friendship of authorities and policemen."[43] Gamboa used two alternating points of view to deal with the same tension between fascination and moral authority as in de Campo. On the one hand, *Santa* told the story of a blind pianist's love for the prostitute. Hipólito's adoration of Santa could remain pure and noble because it was based on other people's descriptions of her. On the other hand, Gamboa narrated the degradation of Santa's body, from healthy youth to the worst vices and, finally, death from cancer. To establish his authority, Gamboa stressed the ignorance of the characters and his own scientific knowledge of internal physiological processes. Once Santa became a prostitute, she soon lost all sense of morality, probably because "she had in her blood the germs of an old lasciviousness from some great-great-grandfather, coming back to life in her with all its vices."[44]

Jails were another field on which to play with the tension between objective observation and the world of crime. In one of the narrative shifts of *La Rumba,* de Campo uses the first person to describe a visit to Belem jail. Allowed into the jail by a journalist and a warden, the narrator climbs to the roof of the old convent and "spies" the crowd in the patios of the prison.[45] Gamboa, too, visited the cells of infamous San Juan de Ulúa prison, in Veracruz. In his diary, he wrote "I needed to see them [the prisoners] with my own eyes, to be able to describe them in my book." The description resulting from that visit stressed the similarity between prisoners and animals ("their elbows and knees of trained felines . . . their feet open and close like those of birds") and referred to Italian criminologist Cesare Lombroso's theory that the crania of criminals revealed "the insanity that had pushed them to crime."[46]

Guided by literary and criminological descriptions, the public saw the heart of the criminal world in the overpopulated jail of Belem. In this building, convicts and suspects endured prison terms ranging from one night to twenty years, sharing the limited space with criminal courts. In 1895, Heriberto Frías painted a grim image of Belem: typhus was endemic, garbage was everywhere, wardens ignored sick prisoners, violence occurred between inmates, and children were abandoned.[47] In spite of this apparent disorganization, Porfirian commentators saw in Belem a certain coherence that further isolated the criminal world from their conception of order. Prisoners established an internal world of power and loyalties. In the minors' section, quasi-military hierarchies structured discipline. Food and commerce inside the jail were under prisoners' control, and conjugal relationships were formally established and respected—even when both spouses were of the same sex. It was this close knitting of personal relationships, sometimes sanctioned with religious links, that made the world of Belem seem more dangerous. After all, critics claimed, prisoners "enjoyed" the company of their peers even more than the society of civilized people outside the prison.[48] The world of crime quickly absorbed the few innocents in Belem. While they endured long months before the beginning of their trials, they learned all the secrets of the profession. Belem, everyone agreed, was an enclosed space for the re-creation of criminality rather than a place for punishment or regeneration.[49]

Jails were the setting for the first systematic criminological observations in Mexico. "The hospital is the doctor's laboratory," wrote Francisco Martínez Baca and Manuel Vergara in 1892, "the asylum is the alienist's; for those who study criminal law and forensic medicine, it will be the prison. There we find together all the elements of social fermentation and putrefaction. There is no better place than this for observation."[50] This belief lies behind the most important and extensive works about Porfirian jails and criminals: Carlos Roumagnac's *Los criminales de México* and *Crímenes sexuales y pasionales.* In the former, Roumagnac explained that Mexican jails were "endless mines" for researchers. His anthropological exploration tried to harmonize with the practical need to know the identity of criminals and the truth behind their language. His goal was twofold: to assist in prevention and punishment and to expose individual cases before they became "units of criminal statistics."[51]

Although Roumagnac was acquainted with the "realm of theory," he stressed the wealth of empirical information contained in Mexican jails. He based both books on interviews with inmates of Belem and the penitentiary, which he entered with the authorization of the Minister of Gobernación (Interior), Ramón Corral, to whom Roumagnac dedicated the first volume.[52] Through the reiteration of a basic structure of questions and explanations, plus file photographs and the measurements of each prisoner, interviews linked individual cases to the social dimension of criminality. Roumagnac also explored the practices of the prison world and the intricacies of criminals' language. He pointed out the lying and "endless verbosity" or just plain "obscene" expressions used by inmates. Roumagnac did not reproduce obscene words, but compiled a small dictionary of the criminal argot to help the development of "scientific policing."[53] The study of language reinforced Mexican criminologists' belief that deviance appeared within a particular set of cultural values and references that caused their persistence. In *La llaga,* Gamboa referred to a criminal vocabulary that "tortures . . . and steals" everyday language without becoming a language in itself. Truth could not be conveyed through this language: because of "prison decorum" inmates seldom referred to the crimes of their fellow prisoners.[54]

Despite their rich detail, criminological observations did not reduce the strength of the biological explanations and class prejudice inherent in the scientific discourse about criminality. Asserting the universality of crime, Roumagnac wrote: crime is common to "all species [*especie*] of men—I was going to write animals."[55] Roumagnac, as well as Gamboa, had to harmonize the imperative of direct observation with the scientific methods and theories brought from abroad, fitting their conclusions into the framework of prevalent ideas about social hierarchies. As Marie-Christine Leps notes for European criminology, early exponents of the discipline based their arguments on their ability to assemble the pieces of a variegated knowledge about urban social ills.[56]

CRIMINOLOGY AND SOCIAL ANOMALIES

As science offered the basic formula for social order, it was also expected to make sense of its anomalies. In the last decades of the nineteenth century, criminology systematized the main theoretical and methodological elements of the study of criminality and alcoholism, combining older ideas about anatomy with contemporary notions from positivist sociology. Italian criminologists such as Lombroso, Ferri, and Garofalo, often read in Mexico in French translations, and French authors such as Tarde and Lacassagne lent Mexican texts an international flavor and informed the very empirical foundation of Mexican criminology.[57] Criminology legitimated the literary fascination with the world of vice. Mexican authors, particularly those familiar with positivism, did not mind using multiple, even contradictory theoretical sources and transcribing long paragraphs from their sources. This suited criminology very well as the discipline itself had a polemic and eclectic character. Its founding fathers stressed the scientific quality of their observations while buttressing them with examples from variegated sources and periods, on the premise that criminals were a separate "variety" of the human race.[58]

Cesare Lombroso loomed as the discipline's greatest name. Although indebted to earlier studies of phrenology, he claimed to have discovered patterns among the anatomical features of "born criminals" and thus announced the possibility of distinguishing criminals from "healthy" people. In other words, and in a break with classical penology, Lombroso and his followers concluded that criminals could be therapeutically eradicated from society. His notion of atavism (individual retrogression to the features of primitive races) posited both a causal theory and a rationale for that eradication. He dismissed his critics as "philosophers" who pretended that theorizing was more valuable than empirical observation but who could not "descend from the nebulous regions of metaphysical speculation to the humble and arid earth of jails."[59] Lombroso attracted Porfirian readers because he defended a racial hierarchy based on the study of criminals' anatomy. As in Italy, criminal anthropologists saw themselves as destined to play an important role in the construction of a strong nation.[60]

Despite Lombroso's long shadow, the adoption of criminology in Mexico did not have a defining moment and a single emissary, as sociology did with Gabino Barreda. Criminologists lacked the academic structures that sanctioned the introduction of other scientific bodies of knowledge. This relative marginality derives from the fact that, during their early discussions about society and progress, Mexican positivists stressed colonization and education over the treatment of social diseases. This changed by the end of the century, when, in *México, su evolución social,* Miguel Macedo and Justo Sierra (the most influential científico writer) listed the treatment of crime and other social problems among the main areas of state action.[61] Discussion of such problems reached the new generations of lawyers and physicians educated under positivism during the last decade of the nineteenth century. Among the first public discussions of the "Italian Positivist School" was Macedo's criminal law class at the School of Jurisprudence. Although the teacher was aware of the new theories, he had been reluctant to include them earlier in his course because they did not harmonize with the "classic" tenets of the Mexican Penal Code of 1871. Questions from students Manuel Calero, Jorge Vera Estañol, and Jesús Urueta prompted Macedo to talk about criminology. In an informal fashion, the group continued with the study of the Italian masters.[62]

Macedo knew that criminology did not lack opponents. Lawyers had a mixed reaction to these novelties. The new editors of the legal journal *El Foro* promised in 1898 to spread the nascent ideas of Lombroso, Ferri, Tarde, and Lacassagne, because their theories were true "masterpieces of the modern spirit." One of those editors, Urueta, proclaimed the need to adapt the criminal law to the new scientific certainties about crime. On the other hand, no less influential groups within the legal profession stated their concerns about the exaggerated claims of Lombrosians. The *Revista de legislación y jurisprudencia* published several essays clearly adverse to Italian criminology, and even doubtful of its scientific status.[63] The reluctance among criminal lawyers to accept the penal consequences of criminology would prove to be a strong and long-lasting obstacle for thorough reforms to the 1871 Penal Code, achieved only in 1929 and then only to be undermined by lawyers and replaced by another code in 1931.

Although Mexican criminology was not organized by a single academic institution or scholar, it manifested certain coherence around the search for the particularities of crime in Mexico. According to a Spanish author, a number of works of criminology in Mexico made "important contributions" to the science: *Estudios de antropología criminal* (1892), by Martínez Baca and Vergara, Macedo's *La criminalidad en México* (1897), Guerrero's *La génesis del crimen en México* (1901), Roumagnac's *Los criminales de México* (1904) and *Crímenes sexuales y pasionales* (1906), and Luis Lara y Pardo's *La prostitución en México* (1908).[64] Mexican criminologists moved from physiological research toward approaches that underlined the social causes of crime. In 1885, Rafael de Zayas Enríquez published in Veracruz *Fisiología del crimen: Estudio jurídico-sociológico,* where he began by discussing crime from a perspective based on medicine and in connection with mental diseases. In 1892, Martínez Baca and Vergara published an analysis of the crania of criminals stored in the museum of Puebla's penitentiary. The authors' goal was to establish "the physiological knowledge of the soul" and thereby correct deviations. However, these attempts did not have a great impact. By 1904, Roumagnac considered Lombroso's ideas about atavism and the physiognomy of criminals to be exaggerated, since research on the connection between crime and anatomy had not produced precise results. After all, the data available in Mexican jails were still "very rich" and unexplored, and required a specifically national approach. Mexican specialists had to descend to the horrifying depths of crime and vice of the underworld and come up with national explanations and solutions.[65]

This sense of urgency and its own eclecticism weakened criminology's claim to cover the entire discourse about social diseases. The boundaries of the discipline themselves imploded under the pressure of the multiple voices that tried to address the central dilemma in Porfirian intellectuals' explorations of Mexican society. On the one hand, the statistics and images of crimes and vice in the capital were impressive, although their meaning was not yet precise and raised many questions; on the other hand, criminality had to remain alien to the upper classes' own world for fear it would defy the elite's moral superiority. Scientists, public officials, criminologists, and journalists identified and classified criminals. Their discourse combined moral condemnation with professedly systematic analyses of social phenomena. Because elites vacillated between scientific interest and social fear, however, empirical observations and analyses did not follow a logical sequence and at times were difficult to reconcile.[66]

The first task of the discourse about social diseases was to formulate a legitimate explanation for the internal, physiological, and psychological processes that turned an anonymous citizen into an anomalous individual. The premise was that human behavior had somatic origins—thus "the philosophical importance of anatomy," according to Roumagnac—and the mechanisms of transmission of these anomalies were biological rather than social.[67] At the same time, writers confined criminality to the world of the city's lower classes, thus adding a social qualification to the biological theory. This created a characteristic tension between everyday perceptions and scientific accounts of crime.

Crime itself was not clearly separated from other ills, such as alcoholism. Therefore, different groups answered these questions with explanations that varied according to their agendas and perceptions of society at large. In the liberal press aimed at the working class, alcoholism received greater attention than crime because it separated criminals from industrial workers and artisans. These publications emphasized hard work, steady effort, and discipline to build working-class identity, but also reflected the importance of alcohol as part of workers' recreation. *San Lunes,* for example, championed the moral correction of workers and even tried to infuse respect for gendarmes. On the opposite side, *La Guacamaya* announced without shame that its publication was interrupted one week because the director had had so stupendous a binge that he had "a loose bolt" in the head and was locked up in jail. Too severe a stance regarding this vice could alienate readers. *La Guacamaya,* which supported the prohibition of public drunkenness in 1907, had earlier run a column in which two pulque drinkers expressed editorial opinions with lower-class language. *El Hijo del Fandango* promised to fight against alcoholism, but also used alcohol for humorous purposes and advertised cantinas and pulquerías.[68] One thing was clear: workers might get drunk sometimes, but they were not criminals leading a "dissipated" life and working only sporadically. One of the main targets of the popular press was the official newspapers' depiction of workers as "debased" and the double standard among the press and gendarmes regarding workers and gente decente.[69]

Catholic writers shared with liberals the perception of alcoholism and criminality as essentially moral issues, framing their views in terms of the moral opposition between vice and family. Drunkard parents, they claimed, disrupted the harmonious coexistence of working-class households. Catholic newspapers reporting on crime portrayed it as sinful behavior requiring Christian expiation. This, more than race or physiology, was the cause of criminality and the degeneration of nations. Scientists' analyses of criminals' brains, asserted *La Voz de México,* were chimerical: the true virus of crime was free thinking, the ideas of Martin Luther and Voltaire. Lay Catholic writers contended that Mexico had advanced too quickly in material terms, outdistancing moral progress. Alcoholism and criminality were important elements in the Catholic criticism of the secular project of scientific politics: material progress without morality promoted vice.[70]

Scientific explanations eventually had the greatest impact on public opinion. It would be misleading, however, to oppose a scientific approach to that of Catholics and liberals. Writers from all backgrounds accepted science as truth and used ideas and instruments borrowed from science. Even *El Periquillo Sarniento,* a publication directed at a popular Mexico City audience, published an "odd-looking romance / like those of doctor Lombroso," about three pregnant young ladies.[71] The scientific quality of knowledge functioned more like a rhetorical device than a clear mechanism to exclude "nonscientific" writers. Criminologists themselves felt free to slip moral judgments into their research.

A closer look at their explanations will explain why Mexican criminology was so persuasive. Metaphors that implied the similarity between human behavior and other biological phenomena were readily incorporated into science. The notion of "contagion" was particularly useful because it encompassed culture but preserved the priority of biological mechanisms. Macedo proposed that the state rescue the orphans who roamed the streets from the "nursery" of crime. To guarantee their regeneration, authorities should not concentrate them in shelters, since that environment would allow further transmission of the knowledge of vice. Instead, Macedo suggested giving the children to families willing to adopt them.[72] Belem jail, mentioned previously, was considered to be another vehicle of contagion: the "criminal population" of the old convent shared its vices and then went out to spread "the disease of typhus and the disease of crime."[73] Writers also argued that newspapers could disseminate information about methods of crime, providing inspiration and valuable techniques to imitate. A variation on the theme of contagion was the notion of "imitation," formulated by French criminologist Gabriel Tarde. According to Tarde, crime was not merely the product of the "biological individual" but also of the influence of society. This theory, he alleged, combined Lombroso's ideas about the physiological, inherited causes of crime with those stressing the influence of the social environment.[74]

Imitation and heredity converged in the sphere of the family. As in Europe, children from overcrowded Mexican lower-class dwellings received there the genetic seeds of their weaknesses and saw the models for their future behavior. Lara y Pardo, cited above, described the images of claustrophobic rooms that generated prostitutes. Boys saw their parents drinking and fighting, and it was only natural that they would go out to the streets, try a glass of pulque—which cost only a centavo—and imitate acts of violence and sensuality. Everything was transmissible from parents to children: physiognomy, tastes, abilities, weaknesses, and customs. This enclosed environment rendered education, the científicos' favorite instrument of cultural modernization, an ineffective weapon to reform the "dangerous classes."[75]

To delineate this process, the notion of degeneration was used more frequently than that of heredity because of its double meaning: (a) degeneration alluded to the moral condition of criminals, prostitutes, and beggars, and (b) it described the effects of alcohol consumption and low morality on heredity. The discourse about social diseases placed degeneration at the center of its explanation because it linked the individual, family, and national levels of observation. Trinidad Sánchez Santos mentioned several "stigmata" of psychological and physiologic nature transmitted by alcoholics to their descendants.[76] Thus, degeneration was victimizing the whole society without being noticed, even by specialists. Crime and alcoholism spread insidiously outside the reach of prophylactic measures, impossible to isolate because "we carry [them] inside ourselves," declared Roumagnac.[77] Sánchez Santos calculated that an alcoholic could produce 640 "degenerated" descendants, populating the darker spaces of the city and making of each child a candidate for the penitentiary.[78]

Race was a useful instrument to deal with degeneration at a social level because racial categories worked as an extension of the organic conceptions of society and politics. Martínez Baca, in Puebla, made sweeping racial generalizations the basic elements of his anatomical comparisons. He contended that the brains of Indian criminals were smaller than their European equivalents because the indigenous race was "quite degenerated."[79] Sánchez Santos argued that Indians had lost "beauty and vigor" after the Conquest, because the colonial government lifted the strict pre-Hispanic punishments against alcoholism.[80] Continuing the historic process of racial decadence, civil wars in the independence era caused criminality because they relaxed the boundaries between patriotism and mere personal profit. The perspective for Mexico was grim: weak individuals formed weak races and nations, incapable of defending themselves and prone to crime. Nations could preserve their "virility" only through temperance and virtue; otherwise, their survival was not certain.[81]

For those such as Roumagnac, who stressed a social explanation of deviance, race provided a seamless way to assess its impact on Mexico—although the biological meaning of race itself was diluted in his writings and those of other authors concerned with Mexico's "national race." In his study of "criminal anthropology," he hesitated over whether to follow the theories of crime that espoused external or those that stressed internal causes—causes in the environment or within the individual's psyche. He chose to limit the "internal" causes of crime to the "influence of race," transmitted by heredity.[82] Guerrero declared that crime was a complex social phenomenon, "the individual manifestation of a general phenomenon of dissolution," that reached all members of society. Thus, he looked at the individual life of the criminal in the context of "coexisting phenomena of society."[83]

Porfirian educated groups became concerned that degeneration could seize the whole country and destroy the aspirations of progress. One of Roumagnac's original motives in beginning his study of Mexican crime was to reject the idea that the Mexican people were one of the most criminal in the world. The belief in the importance of race did not overcome nationalism, but blended with it in a formula that crystallized in postrevolutionary anthropology. Some foreign writers had founded an image of bloodthirsty Mexicans based on official statistics and the historical accounts of

Aztec human sacrifice. Despite Roumagnac's efforts, observers considered urban social diseases evidence that criminality and alcoholism were national particularities. If in 1882 Mexican criminality was considered mostly an outcome of sudden passions, by 1900 Guerrero had defined a Mexican "type" of alcoholic, and portrayed Mexican criminals returning to the barbarous ways of the Aztecs, who needed war to satisfy their lust for blood. He warned about the Indians "thinking of blood and extermination," which could cause a "great tragedy" if prompted by political events.[84]

In this grim scenario, criminology afforded an essential tool to reestablish conceptual order: a convincing rule by which to classify humans. Lombroso had proposed the existence of criminal "types" recognizable by their anatomical differences, and subsequent authors produced multiple, not always compatible, classifications of the different criminal types. Mexican criminologists, like the Chinese encyclopedia mentioned in a Jorge Luis Borges story, were not too concerned about the internal logic of their taxonomies, drawing with ease from variegated criteria.[85] Yet Mexican divisions stressed external signs of difference. Macedo's classification based on dress inspired the 1900 Regulation for Penitentiary Institutions in the Federal District, which established that authorities had to divide prisoners according to their "class." The first class was formed by "individuals of good standing who wear suits or frock-coats," the second by those wearing jackets, shirts, or trousers, and the third by those using the traditional combination of cotton blouse and trousers.[86]

Julio Guerrero shared Macedo's perception of a deep separation between classes but did not consider it so simple (e.g., "high and low," or "masses, middle class, and aristocracy") or obvious (e.g., "shirt, jacket, and frock-coats"). Instead, he based his classification on the features of private life. The basic rule for Guerrero's division was the character of conjugal relationships: at the bottom of society were the groups dominated by promiscuity and degeneration, followed by those where polygamy still survived, concluding with groups where unions were monogamous and definitive. Industrial workers were in the middle of the scale: they were almost monogamous and had just started to acquire discipline, but still needed close supervision of their behavior. At the top of his classification, almost as an ideal model, Guerrero placed the Creole middle- and upper-class woman, "*la señora decente,*" sum of all moral virtues. This "exquisite . . . psychical variety of the human kind" had inherited the virtues of the colonial period and strengthened them during the "bloody" age of civil wars. Although the model belonged to the urban, educated groups of central Mexico ("our directing classes"), Guerrero avoided establishing a causal relationship between virtue and class, basing his construction instead on a gendered moral division.[87]

When applied to the control of anomalies, criminology's classifications were not aimed at constructing a more homogeneous and egalitarian society, but at reinforcing the signs of social difference that constituted the foundation of the classifications themselves. For government officials, it was more important to identify and isolate the agents of transgression than to prevent social diseases. If criminals were cut off from the rest of the population, Macedo argued, criminality would no longer be a cause of public concern. At the inauguration of the San Lázaro penitentiary, in 1900, Macedo celebrated the beginning of "the reign of silence and solitude" for criminals.[88] A product of modern science and techniques, the discourse about criminality did not seek to extend the benefits of progress to the entire population. On the contrary, it provided an acceptable justification for the exclusion of large sectors of society from the fruits of modernization.

CONCLUSIONS

Criminologists were the privileged social observers of urban society during the Porfiriato, but their legacy did not end with the regime. They bequeathed many of their instruments and premises to the project of regeneration of the Mexican people appropriated by the revolutionary state. After the Revolution, criminologists' influence did not suffer the same violent attacks as did Comtean positivism. Even though Mexican criminology continued to develop and produce new studies in the twentieth century, it did not achieve an autonomous institutionalization, but remained part of juridical research at academic centers. Its influence was perhaps stronger in the realm of penal practice, where the ideas of the Italian masters are still cited. Its extreme biological tendencies, however, have been effectively countered by the development of other social sciences and their stronger explanations about social ills.[89]

The historicity of the discipline explains its failure and its continuity. Faced with the limitations of their moral superiority as an instrument of social hygiene, Porfirian intellectuals tried to create a space of scientific legitimacy with which they could organize the fight against social diseases. The results undermined the basic liberal tenet of equality, as it naturalized the difference between deviants and citizens. And, as Guerrero acknowledged with some despair at the end of his book, positivism failed to become a source of moral influence on the Mexican lower classes.[90] The majority of his contemporaries were more optimistic; however, as the next chapters will show, Guerrero seems to have been closer to the mark. In spite of its wide audience and its ability to provide a discursive support for state intervention, criminological knowledge had a limited impact on penal legislation and new penitentiary institutions, which failed to check crime or change the social biases of the police and judicial system.

Criminology provided classifications and explanations of urban lower-class life but failed to eliminate crime from the modern capital. The detailed observations undertaken by Mexican criminologists proved that, despite all their prejudices, educated men were fascinated with life in the darkest corners of the capital. This tension between fascination and ideology caused the Mexican discourse about criminality to lack the conceptual and institutional coherence that would translate into public policies. Yet, the categories developed by Mexican criminology formed a central component of elite's views of society. In order to understand the external causes for the failure of criminology as the basis of social reform, and the realities that escaped that view, the next chapters will depart from the elite perspective and begin an exploration of Mexico City's underworld.

II

THE PRACTICES

"Scientific" descriptions of urban crime have a limited value as sources of information about crime itself. The next three chapters (dealing with violent crimes and theft) will depict criminal behaviors as they emerge from judicial testimonies and, to a lesser extent, administrative records, newspapers, and the few criminological passages that avoided the generalizations discussed in the previous chapter.

The perspective shifts here to suspects and victims. Chapter 4 focuses on crimes committed in public places in which persons of the same sex, usually linked through work or place of residence, used violence to resolve disputes over reputation. I contend here that honor, although seldom mentioned by actors, was a central concern for the urban lower classes. Fights that echoed the rules of upper-class duels expressed this concern, but they generated little interest among authorities.

Chapter 5 examines violence by men against women. This includes cases of spousal abuse and rape. As these crimes usually involved victims and offenders linked by kin or friendship, the chapter examines the limits of the notions of honor discussed in chapter 4; it examines the privacy of marriage and contends that violence played a key role in the construction of gender roles. Beating or raping women was not simply conducive to male domination, but also served to modify household and labor relations, as women entered the labor market and began to autonomously use the city's public spaces. Young women who suffered sexual abuse did not become the cause of further retaliatory violence; instead, their parents negotiated the victims' marriage with the attackers, or their continued stay, in a subordinate role, in the paternal household. In contrast to views of violence as irrational behavior, these two chapters emphasize the expressive use of physical force and its role in the construction of social networks among the urban poor.

Chapter 6 looks at theft in the household and in the workplace, and underscores the function of monetary exchanges in the urban poor's economy of survival. The disruptive effect of wage relations and other cash transactions provides an alternative way to assess the cultural impact of capitalism in Mexican society. Yet, theft was not simply an expression of class tensions, since the urban poor were the most common victims of the offense. In contrast with well-off victims, and rather than involving the police, they negotiated with offenders for the recovery of stolen property. In so doing, they stressed the nature of theft as a monetary transaction. Simultaneously, employers made every worker a suspect, and distrust the keystone of labor relations.

Before tackling specific crimes, an amendment to criminological generalizations is in order. One of the dearest "facts" of positivist criminology was that deviance was ascribed to a "criminal population" that could be counted and individually identified. The best measure of the size of such a population was the number of arrests, convictions, or prisoners. The first problem with this criminal census, however, is that official statistics of criminality were patchy and only partially reliable.[1] And, even if those data are deemed accurate enough, as I contend they are, to establish a few general facts about criminality, the question remains: Can a set of common features be ascribed to most offenders, if not to a well-defined criminal class? What follows is a description drawn from those statistics and from a sample database of 209 cases, involving 282 accused, 197 victims, and 402 witnesses.

Although the personal information of suspects suggests a lower economic and educational level, they cannot be typified as a distinct cohort within the city population. They were 80 percent male, a fairly common proportion in modern societies, but other traits do not depart from the demographic data of censuses, suggesting a similarity between suspects and the majority of the population. Their median age was twenty-five, right in the middle of the largest age group of the population.[2] The literacy rate of suspects was very close to the average: 124 of the 282 accused (43 percent) were able to sign their statements, compared with a 40 percent literacy rate among the city's population. One difference is meaningful: those found guilty, out of all the accused, seem to have had a lower literacy level. Only 41 of the 132 found guilty signed (31 percent).[3]

Evidence is not conclusive about the ruthlessness of criminals. As in other societies, only 20 percent of suspects were married. This percentage is lower than that of the city, where 43 percent of those sixteen years or older were married in 1895. However, as discussed in chapter 5, several of those stating their marital status to be "single" were in fact united in stable relationships.[4] Fewer suspects were born in Mexico City than was the case for the city population overall: 34 percent in the database against somewhat less than half of city inhabitants in 1900—although the difference would probably decrease if census figures on place of birth also considered age. Fifteen percent of suspects came from the state of Mexico and 33 percent came from the states of Guanajuato, Hidalgo, Querétaro, Michoacán, Puebla, and other localities in the Federal District. The trades stated by suspects (see appendix, table 7) show them holding jobs common to the lower classes but by no means marginal to the city economy. Official statistics confirm that the majority of suspects were artisans. In 1900, they accounted for 33 percent of those who faced a jury trial, but they were listed in the census of that year as only 10 percent of the employed city population. One note of caution about trade information should be added. Many suspects, victims, and even witnesses declared to the police that they had a trade clearly different from the occupation that emerged from their testimonies. Many gendarmes declared that they were "employees" or had another trade besides police work. Some changed their statements: Miguel Delgado declared first that he was a *mecánico* (mechanic) but then added that "since he does not currently have occupation in mechanics, he makes his living with a device that gives electric discharges to those who desire it."[5]

One pattern does emerge: those whose trade placed them in the streets tended to be involved in crimes. Shoemakers and cobblers (both called *zapateros*) composed only 2 percent of the population, but they made up 6 percent of the database (accused, victims, and witnesses) and 14 percent of the sentenced in 1900. Construction workers were also overrepresented: they represented less than 2 percent of the population in 1900, but 6 percent in the database and among those sentenced in 1900.[6] Like Miguel Delgado, many cobblers, construction workers, and lesser artisans peddled their services in public places, becoming more exposed to conflict and more visible to the police's eyes.

4

Honor and Violent Crime

On February 27, 1924, an ambulance brought Luis Chávez to the Seventh District's police station. He had knife wounds to the right hand, nose, and right armpit, suggesting they came from a fight. Despite the agents' questioning, he refused to name his attacker and died minutes later. Altagracia Cerda identified the body. She declared herself his "illegitimate sister" and added that she did not know who might have killed her brother, who "was not a troublemaker, nor a drunkard, nor had he personal enemies, and he was devoted to his work." Later, at her first hearing with the judge, Cerda promised to "try to conduct the necessary investigations." Sure enough, on April 8, she returned and declared that María de Jesús Medina had informed her that, on the day of the event, she had seen near the place where Chávez was found a man named Rafael Trejo with blood on his hands, bragging that he had fought with Chávez. Medina later declared that Chávez and Trejo used to eat together at her taco stand and that they had quarreled because the latter had tried to collect two pesos that Trejo owed him. Medina also provided a detailed description of Trejo's appearance, the clothes he wore, and the pulquerías he frequented. Cerda provided a photograph of her brother standing with Trejo and another man (fig. 3). The picture, noted Cerda, proved that the two "were very good friends."

On May 15, Rafael Trejo was brought to the police station after Altagracia

3. Luis Chávez and Friends. "Friends the three of them." Rafael Trejo at center; Luis Chávez on the right, ca. 1924. Source: AJ, 19334, Homicide, 1924. Courtesy Tribunal Superior de Justicia del Distrito Federal and Archivo General de la Nación.

Cerda saw him near a pulquería and asked two policemen to arrest him. Trejo declared that Chávez was only an acquaintance and that on the day of the murder Chávez had asked him to pay for the pulque they were drinking. When Trejo refused, Chávez tried to take the money from him, hitting him in the face and pulling a knife. Therefore, Trejo had to defend himself and used his own knife, wounding Chávez. As proof, Trejo showed a scar left by the fight. After the fight, Trejo stayed at home for two weeks without bothering to find out what had happened to Chávez. But Altagracia brought María de Jesús Medina and her daughter, Altagracia Benítez, to declare against Trejo. Benítez had been "romantically involved" with Chávez some months before his death, and later Trejo confessed his crime to her. She declared that, on the day of the event, Trejo only had scratches in his hand, not the wound he claimed was made by Chávez. Nevertheless, one year after the arrest, a jury acquitted Trejo because he had acted in self-defense.[1]

The preceding summary of a trial record found in the Federal District's judicial archives contains all the typical elements of violent crime in Mexico City: the setting (a pulquería in colonia Guerrero), the motive (a disagreement over a debt), the weapons (knives), the actors (two male friends of the lower classes in their early twenties: the victim, a street fruit vendor, the accused, a cart driver), the response of authorities (leaving the investigation in the hands of the victim's family, dragging out the proceedings for months), and the jury (acquitting the suspect against compelling evidence).[2] This chapter will try to answer some questions posed by this story: Why did friends Rafael Trejo and Luis Chávez engage in a deadly fight over little more than a day's salary? Why did Chávez refuse to tell the police the name of his attacker? And finally, why did Trejo tell the victim's girlfriend and other people that he had fought Chávez? Did he know that he was going to be acquitted?

Violence was a feature of life in Mexico City. Official statistics, condensed in table 8 in the appendix, show that violent crime was a frequent occurrence. Battery constituted more than half of the felonies brought to trial. Homicide rates were very high compared to other contemporary urban areas and were on the rise. In 1900, for example, the Federal District had 13.30 people sentenced for homicide per 100,000 inhabitants; in 1909 the rate reached 31.53, and in 1930, 37.17. That same year, the relatively high homicide arrest rate in Buenos Aires was 21.00 per 100,000.[3] An unknown number of violent crimes did not enter criminal statistics either because minor cases were dealt with as fights (*riñas*) by administrative authorities or because victims did not report them to authorities out of fear that policemen and judges could punish them as well as the offender.

Criminologists and historians have regarded violence as a meaningless and self-destructive fact of urban lower-class life. A close look at the ways in which violence was used, however, reveals that most confrontations resulting in battery or homicide followed precise rules that resembled those governing elite duels. Fights usually involved contenders in equal conditions: man against man or woman against woman, with similar weapons and in a public place free from police interference. These conditions allowed the outcome of the fight to reaffirm the reputations that had been challenged. The urban poor, after all, had a great deal at stake in social perceptions of their individual value. Honor mattered as much to them as it did to the upper classes.

HONOR AND VIOLENCE

In the late nineteenth century, Mexican elites still thought of honor as social status; *honra* was clearly signified by external signs, such as clothes, mores, language and caste. Such a view was rooted in the structure of colonial society, which had not been completely erased by independence and the revolts of the first half of the century. Yet the defeat of monarchism in 1867 and triumph of the liberal 1857 Constitution established an egalitarian citizenry, where visible social differences had no legal embodiment. Honor, as in other modern societies, was associated with internal virtue and integrity, rather than with inherited status. Honor was not completely redefined during the República Restaurada and Porfiriato, but represented a compromise struck between the demands of tradition and modernity—best expressed as a code of honor containing precise rules governing duels and other disputes. This solution, of course, applied only to the gente decente. For them, the urban lower classes remained strangers to honor, although now as a result of their ignorance rather than demeanor or birth.[4]

Understanding common criminal violence as a product of honor demands a review of the meaning of honor. Contemporary historians often embrace the definition formulated by Julian A. Pitt-Rivers in his classic studies of Mediterranean culture: honor is "the value of a person in his own eyes, but also in the eyes of his society." The formulation is productive because it links the internal and external aspects of honor and allows for an interpretation of individual behavior under the light of collective judgment. Any analysis that is not based on the intertwining of both aspects is bound to be partial.[5] The following analysis is therefore based on the premise that observable behaviors recorded in criminal archives have a close relationship with an internalized sense of the actors' self-worth and their disposition to respond accordingly. Violence is a reflection of suspects' readiness to defend their honor and their knowledge of the rules governing the riposte to challenges. Yet the relationship between the two aspects of honor in Pitt-Rivers's definition is not automatic or unconscious, as violent episodes would suggest. The knowledge of the rules of confrontation signifies not only that contenders knew how to respond, but also that they possessed an honor worth defending. Honor, therefore, has to be considered as a right: the right to be respected and recognized as a member of a group of equals. A challenge conferred honor and a fight demonstrated the ability to defend it, regardless of the result. Poverty did not exclude anyone from the claim to that right: to the contrary, it made its defense, as in the Algerian societies observed by Pierre Bourdieu, all the more meritorious.[6]

Understanding honor in modern Mexico City demands some corrections to the Mediterranean model. Honor was not an exclusively male, upper-class concern. Everyone invoked honor when defending his or her reputation. Honor not only signified status, but also involved other aspects of individuals' relations with their communities: reliability, resourcefulness, loyalty. In lower-class neighborhoods, where life was marked by job instability and deprivation, one had to rely on the support of the same neighbors and co-workers who were the audience for confrontations. Violence created a sense of equality as it demonstrated that everyone deserved respect and was ready to defend it.[7] Honor was a right that had to be defended daily, against many threats, and at a very high cost. Paradoxically, therefore, liberal equality can be said to have increased the cost of the defense of honor: it eliminated the visible markings of group equality while, in the case of the urban poor, restricting access to the code of honor and the legitimate use of violence.

Penal legislation reinforced the connection between violence and honor. The 1871 Penal Code's definition of battery (*lesiones*) and blows (*golpes*) established the guidelines for classifying and punishing most cases of violent crime. Battery was defined by "wounds, excoriations, bruises, fractures, dislocations, burns, [and] any other injury leaving a trace on the human body."[8] Sentences or fines for battery varied according to the severity of the corporal damage. When the injury resulted in "an incurable disease . . . impotence, the loss of a member or organ" the sentence could be up to six years in prison. If the wound was on the face, the punishment could be increased according to the judge's discretion. The length of sentences could also be increased or decreased according to the life-threatening nature of the injuries or the circumstances surrounding the offense. "Treachery" (*alevosía* and *traición*) referred to the use of surprise, deceit, or the betrayal of confidence by the offender against the victim. The maximum prison term for battery with aggravating circumstances was twelve years.[9] The code granted legitimacy to the use of force by "honorable" men in defense of their reputation, particularly when taking place in public sites or when actors followed the code of honor. The code presumed that battery committed in a fight deserved a milder sanction.[10] Blows, defined as physical violence that did not cause injuries, were only punished if inflicted "publicly" or in a fashion "that public opinion would regard as dishonoring." Convicts could receive up to four months of prison, "according to the circumstances (*circunstancias*) of the offender and the victim."[11] Thus, blows were not a crime if exchanged between people of the same social standing and in circumstances that did not affect their reputation or lack thereof.

The code conceived the defense of honor as a male affair; therefore, it protected men and reduced the punishment for violence performed by those with positions of family authority. If a father, for example, committed battery after finding his daughter "in the moment of intercourse" with another man, he would receive one-fifth of the prescribed sentence. The spouse who found his or her mate committing adultery would receive one-sixth of the regular sentence for battery and a shorter sentence in case of homicide. Battery would go unpunished if "performed in the exercise of the right to punish the victim, even if the correction is excessive."[12] Conversely, the code gave men broader powers to seek legal remedy than women in cases of adultery and stressed the protection of paternal authority and male physical integrity. Battery committed by a descendant of the victim would be punished with two years added to the regular sentence. Castration was specifically punished by article 533 of the 1871 Code with ten years of prison and a fine of 3,000 pesos. Far from becoming obsolete, and despite the absence of any case of castration in published statistics, this provision was strengthened in the 1929 and 1931 codes.[13]

Honor, conceived as status, was explicitly acknowledged as a mitigating circumstance. The 1871 Code established that the accused was exempted from criminal responsibility if he or she acted "defending his or her person, honor or properties, or those of another," and judges could consider as mitigating circumstances the "good customs" of the suspect.[14] Honor was indeed mentioned in cases involving middle- and upper-class actors, such as the 1923 homicide of Carlos Susan. The suspect, Francisco Torres, had asked Susan to stop annoying his wife at the movie theater. Torres declared that he told Susan, whom he did not know, to behave "in a decent way, out of respect for the families" in the place. Susan threatened Torres, slapped him, and invited him to go outside. Torres asked a bystander to take care of his wife, followed Susan out, and shot him dead. He later declared that while they were outside Susan told him "to fuck his mother and that lousy whore, his wife." When a policeman approached Torres after the shooting, he surrendered, saying that "he was not a vulgar criminal, but an army colonel." During the trial, he presented several letters and witnesses attesting to his "good behavior" and "absolute honesty." He was unanimously acquitted by the jury because he had acted "in defense of his honor" defending his wife. Her role was instrumental in what was essentially a dispute about status and competence: Susan himself had threatened Torres saying that he was a worthy person with friends in the police.[15]

Colonel Antonio Tovar, author of the 1891 *Código nacional mexicano del duelo,* had foreseen the situation faced by Colonel Torres and framed it within the code of honor. "A gentleman," wrote Tovar as an example of the usefulness of the duel, "goes to the theater in the pleasant company of his young and beautiful wife, whom he loves." When they are leaving, someone says, "*¡me gusta!*" ("I like her" or "I like it"). The gentleman has three options. He could engage in a fight in situ, but this would lead to a judicial process, a "social scandal," and would expose the lady to the obligation of testifying in court. "Is this morality?" asked Tovar. He could file a civil suit, but it would only achieve a fine against the offender and, continued Tovar, "Is this the reparation?" To challenge a duel, instead, would be more discreet and legitimate enough to allow the gentleman to continue patronizing the theater and thus make his wife "proud to have as a husband a man who possesses the necessary dignity and courage to make her respectable and respected."[16]

In the latter decades of the nineteenth century, the duel provided socially accepted rules for the use of violence to solve disputes among the upper classes. Translation of European codes of honor, articles and pamphlets for and against dueling, and even Tovar's Mexican code were published during this period. These unofficial regulations established detailed procedures governing the ritual and weapons involved in combats.[17] Judicial authorities treated duelists with leniency. Antonio Martínez de Castro, the author of the 1871 Penal Code, acknowledged in 1870 that the duel was commonly used by the Mexican upper classes, had the support of public opinion, and could not be confused with the "common wounds and homicides . . . inflicted in a fight where contenders are drawn by the almost irresistible force of vulgar preoccupations"; thus, he explained, legislators had decided not to punish it as homicide or battery. A sign of modernization among the elite, the duel was particularly useful for congressmen, military officers, high-ranking bureaucrats, and journalists during Porfirio Díaz's rule. Strict punishment of duelists was not desirable, Martínez de Castro added, because "the nation would be deprived of the important services of some of its most respectable men."[18] The 1871 Code devoted a twenty-seven-article chapter to the duel and punished homicide in a duel with up to six years in prison and 3,000 pesos. But popular rebellion, the increasing use of firearms, and new political conditions contributed to the decadence of dueling after the Revolution.[19]

The impact of this legislation beyond the political elite was nil. The complex ritual sanctioned by the code of honor and the cost of swords and dueling pistols prevented the urban poor from employing them. When stressing the respectability of dueling, observers and legislators contrasted it with lower-class violence. In 1897, Miguel Macedo noted that duels were less frequent each day, because "the upper classes denounce crimes against reputation," referring their disputes to the courts instead of dueling, while for "the inferior classes," disputes were solved "through quarrels or revenge." Macedo, who in the same text denounced the "barbaric" character of Mexican criminality, inadvertently linked dueling with lower-class violence—in that both dealt with matters concerning "reputation."[20] According to liberal newspaper *El Popular,* the Mexican people did not resort to the law to settle their disputes because they believed doing so was a sign of "cowardice." Demonstrating an "atavism of medieval origins," poor people preferred to use force.[21]

From this perspective, the violent defense of poor men's reputations, according to an 1896 pamphlet, was a sign of the lower classes' "loss of any notion of dignity, duty and decorum." The same pamphlet, produced by the powerful association of pulque distributors, noted that the excessive concern for virility was a distinctive defect of the poor man, whose "pride is based on his virility, and only feels insulted when his courage and strength are in doubt."[22] Criminal violence was the product of the "irrational" nature of the Mexican lower classes: writers and legislators believed that fights and homicides were triggered by banal causes, or by macho whims that barely disguised greed, jealousy, or lust. Renowned novelist Federico Gamboa, for example, stated that "homicidal lunacy" characterized the majority of Mexicans. These perceptions have had a lasting impact on contemporary scholarship. Poor people do not fear death and they engage in senseless violence, it has been argued, because they entertain a fatalistic acceptance of the harshness and brevity of life, embodied in a typically Mexican "subculture" of poverty and crime.[23]

Despite the pulque distributors' argument, alcohol intoxication, rather than machismo, was the most common explanation of violence. Writers and authorities blamed alcohol for creating both the environmental and psychological causes of violence. This view derived from the obvious fact that fights often took place outside pulquerías and cantinas, and that many of the arrested presented signs of recent alcohol consumption.[24] Drunkards easily turned into violent criminals: one minute fraternally embracing each other over their glasses, the next confused in a bloody fight triggered by "trivial" motives. The lower classes' concern for reputation, therefore, amounted to "insignificant reasons" that only alcohol could escalate into life-or-death issues.[25]

Intoxication framed but did not cause violence. Beyond its physiological effects, which are not conclusively linked with aggression, "alcohol provides a culturally accepted excuse for violence."[26] In Mexico City court records, drinkers' disposition to fight generated standardized accounts of the behavior associated with intoxication. Suspects stressed the fact that they had been drinking together with their rivals before the fight broke out. They were thus able to avoid responsibility by declaring that violence had started "without any justified reason" or arguing that they could not account for their violent acts, as alcohol had erased their memory.[27] Conversely, victims and suspects could place the blame on their rivals by declaring, as Leandro Méndez did, that his nephew Luis Martínez attacked him without justification because "every time he gets drunk . . . he loses his mind completely and becomes like an insane man."[28]

Suspects had good reasons to exaggerate their drunkenness, since article 34 of the 1871 Penal Code stated that "complete inebriation that deprives the use of reason entirely" excused penal responsibility. At police stations, doctors classified suspects' degree of drunkenness in three levels: "alcoholic breath" but otherwise normal behavior; "incomplete drunkenness" characterized by faster heartbeat, red cheeks, and nervous behavior; and "complete drunkenness" defined by ataxia, "lack of will," and "loss of consciousness." The latter supported suspects' claims that they "did not remember" the deeds of which they were accused and helped them obtain leniency.[29] Their testimonies thus complemented, rather than contradicted, elite notions that denied honor to the poor and despised the environment of pulquerías.

Judges accepted a "threatening" stare and any degree of alcoholic intoxication as attenuating circumstances. The unspoken rationale for this leniency was the reverse of that applied to duelists: the lower classes were so utterly devoid of honor and rationality that trying to prevent further crimes by means of incarceration was futile. Critics of judicial practices noted that, by considering drunkenness an attenuating circumstance, the penal code tied authorities' hands in the fight against delinquency. Several proposals to make inebriation an aggravating circumstance were dismissed by a special committee set up to revise the 1871 Code. Citing Italian criminologist Rafaelle Garofalo, committee chairman Miguel Macedo argued instead that the penal code's provision should be maintained because alcohol only exaggerated the "criminal instincts" of offenders who were already born criminals.[30]

The result of these ideas was a general acceptance of violent crimes regardless of the actors' status. Battery was punished less severely than other offenses. Table 9 in the appendix shows that those convicted of battery received prison terms of no more than a month in 80 percent of the cases, while theft was punished with more than one month of arrest in three-quarters of the cases.[31] In most trials for battery, judges dismissed the cases for lack of evidence or released the suspects because they had spent a longer term in jail than the established sentence. Table 10 in the appendix compares official numbers for arrests and sentences in the years for which such information is available and shows that only one out of three battery suspects was sentenced—the largest proportion after sexual offenses. This leniency, which may have encouraged violence, was a manifestation of the historically specific ways in which violent crime was defined and punished. During the latter decades of the nineteenth century, certain offenses like highway robbery, rebellion, or even petty theft were severely prosecuted as serious threats to national progress and social order.[32] Prosecutors saw the common and bloody fights between lower-class men and women as a self-contained phenomenon, not deserving of the interest devoted to other offenses.

Tolerance toward violence, however, did not make police intervention welcome among suspects. Conditions in jails and police stations were so bad that both authorities and suspects regarded a night's stay enough of a punishment. And when trials started, they could drag on for months, while suspects languished in jail or Juárez hospital. Judges commonly delayed pressing formal charges against the arrested, thus obstructing families' attempts to post bail for suspects. More importantly, police intervention did not guarantee that responsibilities were sorted out in a fair manner. In practice, it often meant that victims and offenders were equally punished. Policemen broke up fights when they anticipated a tumult and then arrested whoever was at hand, including the victim. At the police station, many suspects complained about what they saw as an unjust detention and claimed to be mere bystanders. Policemen would also arrest any bleeding or otherwise wounded persons (despite their claims that the wound was the product of an accident) and take them to the police station. Only after examination by doctors and an initial declaration—taken, as in the case of Luis Chávez, on the brink of death—were victims sent to Juárez Hospital, where they had to stay until the judge issued a release order. Confined to a hospital bed, victims had to disprove the authorities' assumption that they had also been offenders.[33] The inadequacy of arrest practices responded to officials' presupposition that lower-class victims and suspects were hard to discern, since accounts from either were untrustworthy.

Discouraged from appealing to the penal code's regard for honor as a justification for violent behavior, suspects availed themselves of arguments that reinforced assumptions about the "moral depravity" of the urban poor. Many, as noted above, blamed their acts on alcohol and momentary fits of rage. Others, such as homicide suspect Jesús Rodríguez Soto, simply recognized their fault and vehemently asked the members of the jury for mercy. Against all evidence and the defense attorney's argument of self-defense, a majority of the jury concluded that Rodríguez Soto did not produce the wounds that induced his rival's death.[34]

Suspects of violent crime almost never used the word honor to justify their behavior. While colonel Francisco Torres, in the 1923 case described above, cited his own status, lower-class suspects emphasized specific signs of honor, such as masculinity or reliability, which defined honor as the right to be an equal member of their community. Those accused of battery, for example, could construe their violent acts as an expression of their virility. In 1917, Pedro Zamora fought Manuel Pinzón and Carlos Gutiérrez because they had suggested that Zamora was homosexual. He called them cowards and all ended up seriously wounded and in jail. In 1931, after wounding Alfonso Campos, Carlos Torres told a witness to call the police. He was not afraid of them, he declared, and announced "that he was very macho and that everyone 'can kiss my ass.'"[35] Others adduced their *honradez* (honesty) as workers or merchants. Regino Mena, accused of stealing from a store in 1915, denied the charges, arguing that he was a tailor and that "he is incapable of committing a crime such as the one committed today, and is ready to present honorable people to guarantee his conduct as an honest and hard-working man, always busy looking for food for his family."[36] Possession of currency demonstrated that one was "honest" (*honesto*) and not "one of those persons who as soon as they earn a peso spend it, without thinking about the future."[37] As in the case that began this chapter, a dispute about a two-peso debt was clearly worth engaging in a potentially fatal confrontation, since such a dispute implied a challenge to one's honesty.

RULES OF CONFRONTATIONS

Because the defense of honor was not clearly articulated, the examples cited above seem to support the notion that the urban poor countenanced a rather primitive and "excessive" *machismo.* In order to reconstruct the actual concerns about honor behind these cases, it is necessary to go beyond the first level of suspects' testimonies and look at the circumstances surrounding the crime. These can be examined through the ways in which violence was performed—the weapons employed, the actions of offender and victim. The importance of honor—like most such concepts—was better expressed through actions than words.[38] From a distance, fights might have seemed quick and confusing events, and their consequences upsetting and undignified, but in Mexico City they had clear patterns that participants acknowledged as rules.

Lower-class contenders had to observe proper behavior to obtain a valid outcome, one that the public would perceive as fair. Friends, neighbors, or relatives participated to ensure fair play regarding weapons and police intervention—much as in elite duels. One-on-one fights were acceptable, while numeric superiority was judged unfair. A neutral, public place had to be used to guarantee that no one had an advantage. Contenders interrupted disputes that started inside a cantina or pulquería and moved to the streets, where force could be openly used. "Let's go outside" amounted to a formal invitation to fight. In 1911, *Nueva Era* reported the case of two young men who quarreled after a billiards match. They left the poolroom, took a coach to the Calzada de la Verónica on the outskirts of the city, and fought each other with knives. One of them died.[39]

Going to all that trouble only to resolve a billiard match might seem strange if they could have fought just as easily on the sidewalk, but another precept in the use of violence was to avoid police intervention. Those apprehended by the police during a fight would usually deny that there was a quarrel at all and, as Luis Chávez, refuse to name their attacker. Aside from the unreliability of the police, it was not proper to seek outside help to solve a conflict. The right approach was to not complain about wounds and to wait for a better occasion to get even. Lorenzo Rivas and the brothers Manuel and Albino García had an increasingly dangerous conflict. According to Rivas's father, the two brothers first wounded Rivas in the face; Rivas refused to denounce them to the police, arguing that he was feeling better. Two weeks later, Albino and Manuel "challenged him," and the next day Rivas was found dead, wounded with a knife and holding another in his hand.[40] If they sought to avoid the fights, neighbors and friends of the contenders would intervene themselves, even at risk of being wounded, before the police were called.[41]

Friends were more reliable than the police. They intervened as "seconds," making sure that conditions were fair, or to fight in their friend's place. In 1920, *El Universal* reported that Manuel Belmont and Francisco Sánchez had "agreed on a duel" in the *plazuela* of Tepito. Belmont hesitated and recanted the words that had offended Sánchez. But Belmont's friend, Alberto Cornejo, insisted that Belmont should not lose that opportunity to behave "as a brave man," so he himself slapped Sánchez in the face. Sánchez pulled a knife and sank it into Cornejo's stomach, leaving him almost dead.[42] The rule, as in duels, excluded women. When Carlos Morales got into a knife-fight with another man, Morales's wife, Magdalena Guevara, placed herself between the contenders and was wounded. Back home, Morales was angry and asked her "why in the hell didn't she mind her own business"—prompting Guevara to accuse him of causing her wounds.[43]

Another key rule of confrontations was that contenders use equivalent weapons. Most fights involved only fists but, despite the penalties for blows established by the penal code, very few of them were ever reported to the police, much less brought to trial. The terms used in trial depositions to designate blows often implied their light nature: *moquetes* (taps), *cachetadas, bofetadas* (slaps). Stones, sticks, and other objects were also used in cases of battery, but the most common weapon, and the one that in itself implied the equality of contenders, was the knife. Knives were even used in suicides. They were both offensive and defensive weapons, and their widespread use determined the frequency of bloody wounds that prompted police intervention. Until the Revolution broke into the city, it was unusual to see guns used against knives. In 1903, Faustino García attacked Carlos Rivas, an off-duty policeman, with a knife. Even though Rivas sustained wounds in his face, he used his gun only to hit García, and fired into the air to attract the help of other policemen.[44]

Using and carrying a knife was part of a person's character. Some suspects would have two or more. Francisco Guerrero, the famous murderer and rapist known as "El Chalequero" was carrying a knife and a pair of scissors when he was arrested in 1888. He told one of his victims that "he never left his weapons behind."[45] Elpidia N. mocked her husband by declaring publicly that he was *poco hombre* (not much of a man) because "he does not even carry a weapon."[46] Knives were key objects in the representation of violence. Prostitute María Villa, a.k.a. "La Chiquita," convicted of murder herself, believed that if a knife fell to the floor, a fight was surely forthcoming.[47] Multiple words designated these weapons. According to Roumagnac's dictionary, the knife, or *cuchillo,* was called *danza, charrasca,* or *filero,* and *sutiar* meant wounding with a cutting weapon. Arnulfo Trejo's lexicon of criminals added other Mexican synonyms for knife: *alfiler, barilla, belduque, estoque, faja, fierro, filosa, gancho, horquilla, limpiadientes, peineta, punta, sacatripas, rofi.*[48] Such ample vocabulary was not exclusive to "the criminal class." Regardless of their name, size, or intended use, knives were both weapons and tools in everyday life, and thus readily available. María Villa acknowledged in her trial that she always carried a pocket knife, although she was not a skilled handler of the weapon.[49] Hence, fighting with a knife was not a sudden and treacherous act, nor something peculiar to the "world of criminals," but a legitimate way to defend personal reputation in front of the community.

Battery and homicide suspects used razor blades, carving knives, switchblades, and many other instruments, but the tools used by shoemakers to cut hides for sandals and shoes (*cuchillos de zapateros,* also called *chavetas*) were by far the most common, since they could easily be bought at scrap metal booths in the streets. They had a short and strong blade, the shape of a large nail, and a short handle that fit inside the hand. They were used to cut rather than to puncture. Since they were necessary for work, the accused could claim that they were working tools, not weapons—perhaps explaining shoemakers' overrepresentation among the accused. Inside Belem jail, where many inmates worked as shoemakers, this type of blade was always present in fights and suicides.[50]

Different kinds of wounds had different meanings—according to the causes of the confrontation or the victim's perceived fault. Sweeping strokes would be used in a fight where contenders faced each other in equal conditions and indicated that both had an opportunity to measure each other's courage. The cobbler's knife could be used *apuñada*—with the blade coming out between the fingers, as an extension of the fist. The contenders used a slashing motion to attack (*de rasgoncito*), rather than trying to puncture the victims' body. The stroke aimed at the gastric area, sought to *sacar el redaño* (take out the intestines) or *dar un vacío.*[51] The resulting wounds had a strong visual impact: *El Imparcial* described a mural painting at a pulquería in colonia de la Bolsa depicting a "thug . . . raising his knife, the hat covering his eyes and serving also as a shield, looking at his rival, who had just fallen down with his entrails open."[52] *Charrasquear* meant "to wound in the face," and street fights would often end with the disturbing sight of facial wounds. As in other societies, the head was the locus of personal honor, and facial scars were perceived as signs of a violent personality.[53] Visible scars were always registered in prison records: since they were presumed by authorities to be caused by knives, they became an undeniable record of the individuals' violent behavior. By contrast, wounding with stabbing motions (*picar*) was used against an unwary victim and implied that the attacker did not leave room for a reply. When Lino Calderón was mortally wounded outside of a pulquería, witnesses reported that he scolded his fleeing attacker: "You ingrate, you are not supposed to hit like that."[54]

All these rules varied but were not eliminated when women were involved in fights. The meaning of wounds on a woman's face, for example, represented not a mark of bravery but a demonstration of her man's power.

J. Carmen Ramírez waited for his common-law wife Consuelo Vázquez at home and wounded her in the face because his friends had told him that she was very good looking, and he had suffered the neighbors' mockery for his jealousy.[55] Prostitute Luisa M. was cut twice in the face by a pimp, leaving "the horrible scars" visible in her portrait. Later, another woman told Luisa, "You must be naughty to have your snout cut like that!" She replied that no prostitute had done that, but a man, and killed her.[56] In his defense of a homicide suspect, law student Palemón Serrano reasoned: "What is dearest to a mother more than her son? Therefore, what would be dearest for a prostitute, more than her face? Is not the face what the prostitute uses to attract the sympathy of men? Cut, stain, transform it—as the victim did—and you will see how the prostitute's feelings explode."[57]

Women were considered weak but "explosive" fighters, "an organism lost to unrestrained passions, a ferocious animal," rather than self-conscious actors in the practice of violence.[58] Serrano's argument seemed all the stronger, as it corresponded with the perceived feebleness of women. Mexican apologists of the duel were adamant against women's access to the practice. Female duels, as described in Mexican treatises, moved from the ridiculous to the sublime: women could fight with their umbrellas in the Alameda, or uncover their "rich and turgid breasts" during a combat in Vienna.[59] Thus, violence between women was never construed as the defense of honor, but as the product of female "weakness" vis-à-vis passions and vices.

Yet regulated violence could be as useful for women as it was for men. Women were as likely to commit violent crimes as they were to be involved in other offenses. In 1895 and 1900, women composed one-quarter of those arrested for battery in the Federal District, while they were 22 percent of those arrested for all crimes. When accused of battery, they were as likely as men to have fought someone of the same sex.[60] Poor women also had a reputation to defend, since many of them shared with men a concern for public perceptions of their courage and reliability. Their honor was not always attached to that of their spouses, nor were knives beyond their reach. Judicial testimonies suggest that a degree of autonomy was granted to female fighters: quarrels between a man and a woman would logically be continued by two men, while it was not proper for men to instigate women to fight. Although women also used knives and aimed at their enemies' face, a few cases suggest less concern among women about the kind of weapons used. Ana Villorín and Agustina Carrillo fought because the latter told Villorín that she was a "wretched woman." Villorín bit Carrillo on a breast, while Carrillo hit her in the head with a plate. Facial wounds and hair pulling were common elements in women's fights, as contenders sought to shame their rival.[61]

A well-documented case is that of María Villa, "La Chiquita," who killed fellow prostitute Esperanza Gutiérrez, "La Malagueña," in 1897. She and Esperanza had verbal confrontations over their relationship with a middle-class man, Salvador Ortigoza. At one point, they publicly traded blows and spat on one another. Since Ortigoza was not willing to decide which one he liked best, María and Esperanza agreed on a duel in a neutral place. They both would be armed because Villa was stronger with her hands. Other prostitutes intervened and they were dissuaded. But Esperanza continued mocking Villa in public places. On the night of the crime, Villa went to Esperanza's house, expecting to find her with Ortigoza. He was not there, but Villa killed Esperanza anyway, using his pistol. The case attracted great public attention, because a woman had used a gun in circumstances that resembled male confrontations. The exceptional nature of the event was portrayed in one of José Guadalupe Posada's prints about the crime of Tarasquillo Street, in which María fires at Esperanza's face using the typical stance of a pistol duelist.[62]

Insults, the intervention of friends, a level field: women's confrontations mirrored honorable masculine encounters. Duel-like confrontations between women were not restricted to high-price prostitutes. In January 1906, two women, forty and sixty years of age, engaged in a duel with knives to end a protracted dispute over some chickens. According to *El Imparcial,* they and their witnesses met at La Piedad Road and followed the dictates of the "code of honor." The newspaper mocked the honorable pretensions of the combatants and described the fight itself as a "quarrel." Yet, the report conveyed the tensions between the duelists' domestic roles, the legitimacy of the confrontation, and the views of the authorities:

> The victim, Saturnina Elizalde, brought her small son to the duel. Before they began the fight, she left the baby under a tree, blessed and kissed him, telling him that perhaps that was the last time she would see him. Her fears proved

> right, as she died minutes later next to her son. . . . The killer has confessed, but claims not to have committed any crime, because her rival could also have killed her. The case, however offers no difficulty for prosecutors.[63]

EXPLAINING HONOR

What kind of honor is this, that can lead people to kill over chickens or neighbors' gossip? In order to establish the attributes of lower-class honor, it is necessary to delve into the explanations offered by those involved. Reputation, or public opinion about one's honor, emerges from judicial testimonies as a very valuable asset—one worth fighting for. But actions and explanations also reveal that honor was not limited to its external manifestations and included an intimate sense of self-worth, expressed by the immediate reaction of the challenged party.

This reflexive aspect of honor explains why, in their statements, suspects stressed the immediate causes of the crime (e.g., the accidental shooting of the gun or the blind rage caused by alcohol) while, without any fear of contradiction, advancing explanations for the deeper causes of the conflict. Heliodoro Sandoval and Casimiro Zamora were old and "intimate friends," living in the same vecindad and working together as gardeners at the Alameda. One night in 1909 they were drinking at a pulquería. Suddenly and without any apparent reason, according to Heliodoro, Casimiro "hit him and pushed him to the ground . . . telling him that he was a son of a bitch." They continued fighting outside the pulquería, punching and kicking one another, until they decided to walk back home together. At the *callejón* (alley) de la Santa Veracruz, Heliodoro turned around and wounded Casimiro in the chest with his knife. Heliodoro explained that at that point he remembered the insults and blows he had received at the pulquería from Casimiro and "could not contain his repressed anger." Heliodoro's sentiments were an essential fact, and they explained the delay in his reaction. Casimiro had gotten his job because Heliodoro recommended him. The day of the events, a Saturday, they had been paid at the Alameda. Casimiro collected the money that other co-workers owed him for pulque he had paid for in previous days, but Heliodoro, who owed him sixty cents, only gave him fifty. They did not have an argument at that time, but later they met at the pulquería, where they drank and talked, and the fight began. The disagreement, after all, challenged work hierarchy, friendship, and reputation.[64] In disputes over a debt, the motivation was not to recover the money but to reestablish the name of debtors and creditors—a vital concern in the monetarized economy of the urban poor. "A glass of pulque," therefore, amounted to more than a triviality.[65]

In this and other cases, contenders' explanations always referred to their community as the audience for the defense of their reputation. Such communities could be the vecindad, the pulquería, or work, but more often than not a combination of the three. In a 1905 fight in which all of the accused, victims, and witnesses were porters (*mecapaleros*), between fourteen and thirty years old and illiterate, none of the participants referred to their obvious competition for patrons at a corner. Instead, they talked about issues of precedence and reputation, friendship and feelings of "envy," "resentment," "affection," and "confidence."[66] Worries about reliability were particularly important for merchants. Almost one-third of those involved as witnesses, suspects, or victims in the cases of violent crime in the database defined themselves as such.[67]

In the 1909 shooting of Manuel Sordo by Francisco Pérez, the primary audience for the reputation of both contenders were male Spaniards—six of the seven persons involved in the trial—who worked and lived in close proximity. The case contained all of the elements involved in an expanded definition of honor: violence, old and recent tensions, economic subordination, and sexual decorum. Both were Spaniards, Pérez twenty-two years old and Sordo thirty-eight, and they knew each other well. Sordo owned the store and cantina "La Sevillana," on the corner of Arcos de Belén and Revillagigedo. He had been Pérez's boss a couple of years ago and now Pérez delivered sodas to "La Sevillana." At noon, on May 5, Sordo was behind the counter of his store when Pérez came in. After they talked briefly, Pérez headed toward the door. But he suddenly turned around and shot Sordo twice. A policeman came in and disarmed Pérez. Striving to explain the disturbing event, two of Sordo's employees declared that the problem had started the day before, when one of Sordo's maids, Filomena Galicia, went out of the house to buy eggs. Pérez broke the eggs and gave her money to buy more, and then took her to his room. She returned half an hour later. Sordo reprimanded Pérez that night, at the cantina, and Pérez insulted him and ran away. The morning of May 5, Sordo told Pérez that he was going to fire Galicia and then he could have her. Pérez first denied his interest in her, but then from his car he told Sordo, "Yes, I fucked the maid and I am going to fuck you too," and left despite Sordo's demands that he step down to fight. Pérez added, "I'm your father, and I'll fix you when I finish delivering the sodas," to which Sordo replied "any time and any place you want."

With his open challenge, Pérez had made Galicia's seduction the key to the other issues between him and Sordo. Sordo, who survived the shooting, declared that when Pérez had been his employee, he had seduced another maid. The morning of the crime, Sordo told Pérez "not to distract [the] maids, because it would cause a bad impression among strangers to know that his family knew and accepted those disorders." Besides the reputation of the house, control over labor was at stake. Filomena Galicia confirmed that Pérez was trying to seduce her and that he had promised her to talk to her mother so she could leave the house where she was working.

According to witnesses, the two men had contrasting personalities. Pérez "is a cheerful person . . . he is weak and good-natured, so he does not respond when he is provoked." Sordo, on the other hand, "is very dominant . . . and always likes physical play, frequently with Pérez, sometimes abusing him without Pérez complaining." Sordo's physical play had become more than a game in recent times. Sordo declared that in the morning of the events he had shaken Pérez by the arm and told him that he was "a son of a bitch," adding, "Go away, I don't hit you because I don't want to abuse my force." Pérez replied, "Don Manuel, you might push me around abusing the fact that you are stronger, but man-to-man you would not dare." Pérez used a 32-caliber Browning pistol in order to even the field. But he knew that the use of the gun could cast a shadow over his victory. Thus, in a half-hearted effort to prove that the fight was honest, he left the gun on the counter after he had shot Sordo once, and told him: "Now, you can kill me." Sordo reached for the gun but Pérez changed his mind, grabbed the weapon, and shot Sordo again. Fallen behind the counter, Sordo told Pérez "you have killed me, coward." The gun solved the dispute, but undermined its public meaning.[68]

Pérez's deliberate movements (he came back after delivering the sodas, he did not resist arrest) suggest that he was moved by the power of certain people and places. Violence emerged and was resolved in the community to which actors belonged, yet it was not concentrated in specific areas of the city. According to the data from the cases examined, out of 218 accused and victims of battery, 108 lived a few blocks from the place where the crime was committed. In most cases, the victim and the offender knew each other well. According to table 11 in the appendix, the areas of greater frequency of violence were police districts I, II, III, V, and VI. These districts (encompassing the crescent moon outlined in chapter 1) surrounded the city's central area and included the majority of lower-class colonias and barrios. They also contained the greatest number of pulquerías in the city as well as areas of commerce and lower-class housing.[69] Although this association might seem the fault of alcohol consumption, it would be more accurate to say that violence occurred most commonly where vecindad, social life, and work converged.

The inhabitants of urban communities had a clear sense of the significance of their collective worth. Fights could pitch two vecindades against each other, as in a Boston Street battle started by a group of children and continued by adults.[70] In Tepito's Casa Grande vecindad, described in Oscar Lewis's *The Children of Sánchez,* the forceful defense of the community's reputation was expected from boys and girls. The community itself could demand proper behavior from its members—honesty, courage, and respect. Fights inside vecindades could start when residents asked neighbors "to go and speak their words somewhere else because there were ladies and girls in the vecindad, so that kind of language was not acceptable."[71] In that context, the use of knives and fists did not challenge, but rather supported the social concern over good reputation and conformity to gender and age roles.

The role of communities in fights should not be construed as evidence of disdain for violence and death, for if lower-class audiences accepted the fair rules of combat, they also feared and condemned violence. Despite the lack of interest among the police and judges, there were strong social reactions against these crimes. Relatives of the victims, for example, actively sought punishment for those perceived as culprits. In the homicide of Luis Chávez, described at the beginning of this chapter, his sister Altagracia Cerda played a central role in the investigation. In the homicide of Lorenzo Rivas, who refused to accuse his rivals and died in 1900 with a knife in his hand, the victim's father and sister accused brothers Albino and Manuel García. While Albino was arrested and later released because of lack of evidence, Rivas's relatives looked for Manuel for years. Every time they saw Albino they would insult him and accuse him of Lorenzo's death. Finally, in March 1908, Manuel was arrested by the police, yet he and Albino were dismissed again in July because the prosecutors lacked enough evidence to proceed any further. They did not try too hard to find it: although an order for his arrest for murder had existed since 1900, Manuel García had been twice arrested for other reasons after that date, and twice released without reopening Rivas's case. The fact that there were two attackers and one victim explains the tenacious search of the latter's family. Social reaction against homicides or fights perceived as unfair remained strong despite, rather than because of, the inaction of the judicial system and the police.[72]

Neighbors and relatives summoned the police when deemed necessary, testified in court, and even negotiated for an apology by offender to the victim, but their intervention was not circumscribed by the results of judicial action. Jesús Rodríguez knew this full well when, at his jury audience for battery charges, he asked his victim's relatives "to abstain from bothering his brothers."[73] Incarceration, in contrast, often failed to satisfy the communal need to reintegrate the offender—whether after an apology or the restitution of stolen property. Judicial and police intervention was accepted when it coincided with the preventive goals of the community, but such intervention, often guided by the criminological ideas about popular violence, failed to take into consideration the codes for the legitimate use of violence or the mediation of neighbors in disputes.

The formalization of Mexico City lower-class violence was not conveyed in any single literary, journalistic, or scientific text. Its coherence, nevertheless, emerged in the public acts and testimonies of offenders and victims. They were contenders in confrontations that were open to the inquiry of authorities and the judgment of the community's opinion. It did not matter so much who prevailed in a fight, nor who was accused by the police: what mattered was demonstrating one's bravery and loyalty—those virtues that educated people called "honor." While upper-class males could look to judicial institutions for recognition of their honor, the urban poor trusted the judgment of the collectivity. Each fight was, essentially, an appeal to that judgment. Therefore, if violence was performed according to the rules, it did not disintegrate social links, but strengthened the ties and exchanges necessary to survive in an adverse urban context.

The defense of honor, however, was costly. Violence was always more than an expression of the concern about reputation. Judged by its results, rather than its motives, violent crime was demeaning and, in the perspective of many victims, signified the uncontested use of force. Equality might have been the goal, but it was rarely the result. Several victims of homicide and battery (such as Luis Chávez) managed also to hurt their attackers and were thus (unlike Chávez, who died too soon) charged by the police. The data about victims who were not accused (a total of 96) suggests that many did not have that opportunity: 37 of them were women (38 percent, against 18 percent among homicide and battery suspects), and their median age (thirty years) was two years higher than that of the accused.

CONCLUSIONS: DISRUPTIVE GUNS AND DANGEROUS VIOLENCE

Violence became a more disruptive phenomenon during the latter years of the Porfiriato as the increasing use of guns in common crimes diluted the positive meaning of violence in public settings. Facial knife wounds, after all, rarely endangered the victim's life, but guns represented a lethal threat and limited contenders' ability to control the effect of their weapons—thus unwittingly subverting the rules of honorable confrontations.[74] Guns are probably one of the causes of the increase in the proportion of homicides among crimes after 1916, while battery was becoming less frequent (see table 8).[75]

Firearms became cheaper and more abundant by the late Porfiriato yet their use remained exceptional until the Revolution, when guns became readily available in the city. In numerous cases after 1913, violence came from strangers and tended to be more deadly. Soldiers of the different occupying armies used their weapons in personal disputes, and quarrels in cantinas and pulquerías usually ended in gunfights. The police, ill-prepared to use their own guns, often required the help of military officers to subdue suspects. From the men arrested for public drunkenness in 1917, the police seized dozens of firearms of different brands and calibers—large-caliber Colt and Smith and Wesson pistols being the most common. Many of the arrested were themselves policemen, guards, soldiers, or officers detained for disorderly behavior after firing their guns into the air.[76]

Firearm use among civilians continued to grow after the civil war was over. In 1921, acknowledging the trend, President Alvaro Obregón decreed that licenses to carry arms in the Federal District, "for safety and legitimate self-defense," would be issued to adults who could prove their "honor-ability" and pay a ten-peso fee.[77] During the 1920s, guns were customarily carried in Congress. Personal reputation remained a central element in parliamentary debates through the 1920s. Guns often emerged in the context of discussions about the "virility," "loyalty," or "honesty" of deputies. In December 1921, during a closed-doors session, a fight between two representatives almost led to gunfire. Deputy Luis Espinosa restored order by pulling his own gun, but another fight in 1924 resulted in a deputy's death, and Espinosa himself died in 1926 in a confrontation with a fellow senator.[78] Among the poor, on the other hand, the cost and regulation of guns still limited their use. Guns were not so easy to acquire in pawn shops and larger calibers were officially restricted to the police and the army.[79]

Few shootings followed honorable rules. *El Universal* paid particular attention to a 1916 case in which an apparently trivial dispute between two young friends resulted in the death of one of them, an army officer. Octavio García ("very well known in social circles") tried to recover a pawn ticket that he had given to his "intimate friend" lieutenant colonel Carlos Chico as a guarantee for a loan. Chico refused and García simply pulled his gun and killed him.[80] The reporter explained the tragedy as the result of "a moment of insanity" and the influence of alcohol on García. But the sudden appearance of guns was in itself disturbing, as in revolutionary general Juan Banderas's death, in 1918, at the hands of federal deputy Miguel A. Peralta. Banderas pushed Peralta at a cafe, because the latter had attacked Banderas in a speech at the Chamber. Peralta, aware of Banderas's fame as a violent fellow, shot him. According to witnesses, when Banderas was on the floor and before Peralta emptied his gun in him, he regretted not having used his weapon first. Now, he mumbled, "I'm screwed."[81] Fights, he should have known, were not the same as they used to be.

Although the frequency of battery decreased after the Revolution, violent crime also appeared more unpredictable and dangerous, the work of strangers. In many cases, the offenders were unknown to the victim. Authorities posted in public buildings photographs of anonymous bodies found in the streets, in the hope that relatives or friends would identify them. Automobiles caused many of these deaths. In 1924, there were 32,537 automobiles registered in the country; in 1930, the number rose to 63,073. Between 1930 and 1940, records show that 6,648 persons died in traffic accidents.[82] Yet, due to judicial corruption, drivers enjoyed a great margin of impunity if they happened to run over a pedestrian.[83] Among urban communities, as a consequence, violence lost some of its value as the legitimate way to solve disputes about honor. Danger was less often a face behind a knife, and more often a stray bullet or a speeding car.

This multiplication in the sources of danger may explain why violence has been accepted by twentieth-century observes as a permanent feature of the life of the urban poor—an "endemic" phenomenon not easily susceptible to a historical approach. This ignores, first, the rules of violence prevailing before the appearance of guns and the (modified) rules that survived it. More importantly, the thesis of a "subculture of violence" limits the danger of unrestricted and meaningless violence to certain quarters of the city, thus unduly narrowing the scope of research on urban violence. Paradoxically, anthropological studies of Mediterranean honor have not helped in breaching the gap, as one of their premises is that the community's size is inversely proportional to public sanction of reputation. Thus, the ethical aspects of honor would be harder to scrutinize in a large city.[84] The idea fits well with sociological views about the changes associated with urbanization (anonymity, mobility, anomie). In contrast, this chapter's argument challenges the belief that modernization diluted social links and weakened concern for other people's opinions. As judicial testimonies show, violence in early-twentieth-century Mexico City was not the effect of the weakening of individuals' ties to their communities but, on the contrary, signaled a heightened concern for personal reputation in the eyes of those communities—coeval, it should be noted, to an increase in dueling among the upper classes.

A look at honor that stresses the interconnection of its internal and external aspects is useful in order to link evidence that includes both actions and explanations. The sense of honor implied the belief that it was a person's right (regardless of class and gender) to be recognized as a trustworthy, reliable, and resourceful member of the community. In lower-class neighborhoods, where life was marked by job instability and deprivation, one had to rely on the support of the same neighbors and co-workers who were the audience for confrontations. Violence created a sense of equality by showing that everyone deserved respect and was ready to defend it; shame (the rejection by that audience) was to be avoided at all costs.[85] Masculinity was demonstrated by fighting, but the sex of violence was not male: women also engaged in fights. In so doing, they proved that they also had reputations to defend and that they were equal to any man or woman who faced the daily struggle for survival in Mexico City.

Honor dictated a code of behavior ultimately tested by the ability to deal with violence. While the rich saw honor as status and used violence according to a legalized code, for the lower classes the defense of honor was worth the risk of incarceration. Luis Chávez, who preferred to die as a brave man rather than accuse his friend Rafael Trejo, could have subscribed to Jorge Luis Borges's verses in memory of the bravery of turn-of-the-century Buenos Aires in the poem "Milonga de Jacinto Chiclana":

Entre las cosas hay una
De la que no se arrepiente
Nadie en la tierra. Esa cosa
Es haber sido valiente.[86]

5

Violence Against Women

The *Gaceta de Policía* reported in 1905 the "tragedy of Amargura [Bitterness] Street." On October 23, Arnulfo Villegas killed his fiancée Carlota Mauri because she had told him she wanted to break off their engagement. The article included portraits of the killer and his victim, and a drawing of the moment of the murder, when Villegas forced Mauri to sit on his lap and shot her in the face (see fig. 4). According to the *Gaceta,* this was just another example of the lower classes' ferocious jealousy. "For these people of low morality," added the report, female rejection "equals the greatest of insults." Women, editorialized the *Gaceta* some months later, "were born to be loved . . . from the cradle, to the nuptial bed, and to the grave. Men are strong, and they can punish all of their wives' mistakes with the force of affection or condemnation. They should not use the homicidal weapon because that does not cleanse the stained honor but turns these same men into criminals."[1]

Was Arnulfo Villegas trying to cleanse his honor? The previous chapter drew only the public face of violent crime. Violence also occurred in private contexts and was not always organized as fair confrontations. Perhaps as common as battery and homicide, violent and sexual offenses against women constitute their reverse side—for notions about honor that prompted many fights in defense of reputation also justified the abuse of the weakest members of the family. When husbands, relatives, or lovers com-

GACETA DE POLICIA 7

La tragedia de la Calle de la Amargura

CRIMEN HORRENDO UN ABRAZO DE MUERTE. LA DESPEDIDA A TIROS

Si hay delitos llamados á sacudir dolorosamente á la sociedad, seguramente el perpetrado en la calle de la Amargura por Arnulfo Villegas, es uno de ellos.

Éste hombre, cuya juventud no hacía presumir en él instintos de salvajismo y crueldad tan refinada, dió muerte a tiros á una infortunada joven, á quien su mala estrella había llevado á cultivar relacionesamorosas con el que á la postre debía ser su verdugo.

La historia de tales amorios es una sucesión de disgustos, de exigencias y de celos, que hacían presumir una desventura completa, para caso de llevarse ácabo la unión que Arnulfo proyectaba, fingiendo hipócrito rendimiento, simulando dulces afecciones y demostrando, como un consumado comediante, un carácter tranquilo, excento de arrebatos y de maldades.

¿Qué fue lo que motivó esta tragedia? Nada; un «no te quiero ya» que es para esa gente de bajo nivel moral, igual á la mayor de las injurias, pues que más que un cariño que no son capaces de sentir en todo el altruismo de la frase lo que sienten herido es el amor propio de valentones, que exije, como cosa natural, el que la mujer en quien ponen los ojos, debe ser siempre suya hasta la abnegación, hasta el sacrificio, hasta la abyección.

Señorita Carlota Mauri

Arnulfo Villegas

Entrémos en detalles

Joven, en la plenitud de la vida, hermosa, con esa hermosura que dice inocencia y bondad se veía día á día tras el modesto mostrador de un estanquillo de la calle de la Amargura, á una joven llamada Carlota Mauri, tentación de los parroquianos que penetraban en el pequeño esblecimiento y objeto de codicia para los galanes del rumbo que asediaban á Carlota con pretenciones amorosas siempre rechazadas y sin cesar renovadas.

Carlota que tenía actualmente diez y ocho años desdeñaba esos amorios de lance y muchas veces habia manifestado que el día que tuviera un

Villegas en el momento de hacer el segundo disparo sobre la Señorita Carlota Mauri

4. "The Tragedy of Amargura Street. Horrendous Crime. A fatal embrace. The shooting farewell." Source: *Gaceta de Policía* 1:2 (29 Oct. 1905), p. 7.

mitted violent crimes against women, they sought to reinforce proper male control of families and matrimonies. The outcome was not always positive. The exercise of unanswered violence may have buttressed men's sense of their rights and self-worth; if their reputation gained anything by it, however, those gains were upset by the victimization of women and their exclusion from the benefits of an honorable equality. This chapter will revise what the previous one proposed: instead of asserting the positive value of honor, the following pages will address the contradictions at the roots of violence and its high social cost.

Two paradoxes shall be addressed. The first relates to class. As with the man-against-man confrontations, public opinion judged domestic violence differently according to the socioeconomic background of those involved. While the press construed upper-class marital homicides as "crimes of passion" that resembled famous European cases, the same offenses among lower-class couples were interpreted as demonstrations of the machismo and irrationality of the poor.

The second paradox refers to social reactions to these crimes. Despite the outcry and curiosity caused by some causes célèbres, the public and authorities generally overlooked domestic and sexual violence that, although frequent, did not result in death or alarming bloodshed. The idea permeating this double standard was that many of these cases belonged in the family realm, where passion was a dangerous emotion: parents could punish their children, and women were not entitled to seek redress for the abuse they suffered. Life, however, did not easily adapt to the divisions between the public and the private spheres implied in the modern notion of the family as a nuclear, self-sufficient unit.[2]

The question that these paradoxes pose is not so much what caused private violence, but how it was culturally constructed. The intimate reasons that motivated some men to beat their wives easily avoid the historian's grasp. They can be approached, however, by asking instead about the reasons why public opinion could contemplate such violence as a natural part of domestic life, and how those men could avoid punishment. Patriarchal traditions are only part of the explanation. The answer also lies in the transformation of early-twentieth-century Mexico City, as urban communities adapted to the challenge of survival in an urban environment characterized by labor instability, migration, and an authoritarian regime. Marital instability and the need to control the family's labor were the factors which, in this context, made sense of private violence.

CRIMES OF PASSION, HIGH AND LOW

Published depictions of domestic violence stressed the differences between the "vulgar" violence among lower-class men and women, and romantic "crimes of passion" of the upper classes. Writers condemned the former, but did not give it nearly as much attention as the latter. Daily newspapers often depicted crimes of passion, some occurring in Europe, in which violence, sensuality, and glamour formed an appealing combination. These narratives often referred to the "insanity" and "blind passion" of those involved—thus the interest in a case where the female aggressor, a Russian woman, threw vitriol at a Polish man's face. He had refused to marry her and "insulted her by proposing that she be his lover, as he was already engaged to a beautiful American woman."[3] This account highlighted the sorry plight of women using force and the cosmopolitan undertones of the story. Stories about local crimes of passion also stressed the elegant lifestyle of those involved and probed the couples' past life to explain the "tragedy." In September 1913, *El Imparcial* devoted approximately one-fourth of its front page to the killing of Ana Ortiz Borbolla by her husband Rafael Pinedo. He had killed her because she did not want to give him "more money for his debauchery," and then committed suicide. The affair authorized some literary expansion:

> Every once in a while, from the palatial residences where the rich magnates dwell, amidst the luxury and comfort of European villas, there comes the black chronicle, mourning a tragedy, and blood flows in burning ochre over the polished stairs of Carrara marble and soft carpets, with the same clamorous cry of the plebeian Othello, the popular wife-killer, with the same insanity and obfuscation.[4]

The mention of the "popular wife-killer" hinted at the parallels of these crimes with lower-class cases. If committed by the urban poor, the same patterns became a parody of the prestigious European model, the product of brutality and the "pride based on virility" of poor males.[5]

For contemporaneous readers, this class-biased perception of passion crimes did not seem contradictory as crimes of passion evoked both scientific knowledge and the commonsensical defense of husbands' rights. Most criminological classifications did refer to "passion criminals" as the type defined by the exceptionality of the criminal act, a product of rage without premeditation. According to Lombroso, the passional criminal was different from common offenders because his jealousy responded to love and "urged [him] to violate the law by a pure spirit of altruism." Passion criminals, therefore, were not properly criminal: their facial traits were fair and they acted in response to legitimate causes.[6] In Mexico they were also exceptional, argued specialists. Carlos Roumagnac, who devoted a book to this "perfectly defined" kind of crime, maintained that Mexican cases never reached the "monstrosity" of those committed in "more civilized nations." Francisco Guerrero, "El Chalequero" (examined below) was not, according to Roumagnac, a passion criminal, as he "has never been moved by love."[7] The cases of homicide against women and other "horrible" kinds of violence inside the family were scarce in statistics, stated authorities, and journalists saw them as unusual.[8]

The rarity of these cases made them seem all the more straightforward. The triggering emotion was typically jealousy, but what else could be expected in defense of male honor? The *Gaceta de Policía* suggested that women took advantage of the protection of the law to insult men in public places. Nothing, the *Gaceta* claimed, could be worse for a man than to be publicly mocked by a woman. Being cheated on by a wife, popularly symbolized by horns growing from the man's forehead, was so humiliating that it attenuated responsibility in cases of homicide. Cleofas Nájera, a "peaceful man" from Coyoacán, had no legal resource to make his wife come back home, so he killed her. The prosecutors agreed with Nájera's defense that the crime was not a premeditated homicide and reduced the sentence from twelve years to eight.[9] Courts interpreted most cases of domestic violence in the same way that they viewed same-sex violence among the urban poor: a feature of the less "civilized" areas of urban life but nothing to be too concerned about. The press merely gave passing mention to such cases and was interested in stories such as the tragedy of Amargura Street only when a gun caused death—and then only as "one of our vulgar popular dramas."[10]

In the most notorious cases officials preferred to impose "the anathema of execution" on lower-class uxoricides. Unlike most of those sentenced to death, convicts in these cases did not benefit from presidential clemency. Arnulfo Villegas, the murderer of Amargura Street, was sentenced to death, denied clemency by President Díaz, and executed on February 12, 1908.[11]

Punishment had to be exemplary because although domestic violence was a male prerogative, a right, it was also a duty. The harshness of the punishment demonstrated, in harmony with criminological views, that the abuses of such power could only be exceptional.

Paradoxically, public opinion was reluctant to deal with more common practices in which men's rights translated into women's victimization. Judges and the police tended to excuse physical abuse if it did not lead to murder or bloodshed. As noted in the previous chapter, the law condoned husbands' use of violence to solve conjugal disputes. Few cases of wife beating reached the courts, and those that did usually involved lovers or witnesses who did not belong to the nuclear household. The courts and the press distinguished acceptable private violence from that which deserved punishment and based the distinction on the family's ability to avoid unnecessary publicity. Violence and the intervention of the police were cited as evidence of the lower classes' shamelessness and the weakness of their families. But the only perceptible class difference in these cases was the shroud of discretion afforded the well-off. Criminal legislation supported men's ability to deal privately with internal challenges to family hierarchy. The 1871 Penal Code punished adultery with two years when the woman was married and the man was not, but with only one year in the reverse situation.[12] Antonio Martínez de Castro explained the difference with anthropological sagacity:

> It cannot be denied that, morally speaking, the same transgression is committed by the adulterous husband and wife, but the consequences are certainly not the same; because the husband is dishonored . . . by the infidelity of his spouse, and the wife's reputation is not clouded by her husband's faults: the adulterous woman defrauds her legitimate offspring, by introducing foreign inheritors to the family, and that does not happen to the adulterous man who bears children outside his marriage.[13]

Thus implicitly linked with property, the husband's ability to use judicial channels was greater than that of the wife. Women's right to press charges against their adulterous husbands was restricted to cases in which the husband committed adultery in the couple's home, had a concubine, or caused scandal.[14] The official reluctance to intervene was clear in upper-class domestic conflicts. A "well-known" case mentioned by Luis Lara y Pardo in his study of prostitution depicts public attitudes toward elite marital problems. Health inspectors surprised the wife of an unnamed "honorable professional" at an expensive brothel, where she had gone with her lover. The officials, "thinking rightly that regulations should not be imposed at the cost of sacrificing a family," ordered policemen to protect the woman from arrest or any public humiliation.[15] Although punishment was probably forthcoming for her, authorities preferred to leave the matter to the husband.

Regardless of class, violence against women was legitimate, if not legal, because it maintained the man's honor without the intervention of third parties—including the judiciary. Divorce, legislated since 1915, rarely solved problems, especially when there was no legal union to begin with. The predicaments of outside intervention in marital disputes are exemplified by the crime of Libertad Street, in which Catalina Aranda was killed by Emilio Romero on June 26 of that year. Emilio had found Catalina at a girlfriend's house, in Libertad [Freedom] Street, and he wanted her and their two-year-old son to come back home, which Catalina had left after a fight. Catalina accepted but asked for some time to prepare her clothes. However, they continued to argue and he pulled a .44 caliber gun, shot her in the stomach, took the child and ran away. A policeman tried to stop him but he threatened to use his gun again. Fearing that he would hurt the boy, the policeman followed Emilio to a store, where Emilio telephoned his nephew and asked him to take care of his son, and then surrendered himself to the police.

Such was the conclusion of a ten-year relationship in which Catalina and Emilio had eight children. Six had died, two girls survived but lived in Spain, and the son's paternity was uncertain. Witnesses declared that fights were frequent between the two. According to Emilio's testimony, in the years they had been living together Catalina had left the house fourteen times, taking jewels, money, and clothes. She did not drink, but was irascible and would hit him. Each time she left home, he managed to bring her back "after being humiliated and giving her presents of clothes and jewels." The reason for her behavior was not alcohol, he explained, but the influence of Catalina's father and sister, who received money from Catalina. Things seemed to improve two years earlier, when Emilio was born and they married though not by civil law, at the Church of Regina. Disputes continued and, twenty days before the murder, Catalina left with her child. Emilio found her and they argued in the middle of the street. A policeman brought them to a civil court, where they signed an affidavit stating that Catalina did not want to live with Emilio anymore. The day of the homicide, Emilio informed the judge, he had asked her to come with him to Spain but she replied, "I hate you, the one I really love is Pedro Martínez," and insulted him further. That caused the struggle that led to the gun shot. But, concluded Emilio, he had not intended to cause her any harm. This part of his account, however, was contradicted by two direct witnesses of the murder.

Catalina Aranda's side of the story was recorded in the affidavit she signed at the civil court. She stated that she did not know the father of the child born to her in early February of 1913, but she was sure it was not Emilio's. The child had his last name "because he was born in the house in which she and Romero lived," on Cuauhtemotzín Street. Together they had traveled to Spain after the boy was born. A witness to the murder, Tirsa Torres de Alvarez, declared that Catalina had sought help at her home on Libertad Street because Emilio "beat and mistreated her." Catalina told Tirsa that she was going to get a job and would only stay for a couple of days. During her stay, added Torres, Catalina was "always serious and well behaved, very careful with her child, never going out to the street." The record stops at July 8, 1915. Emilio was probably released, as were many other prisoners during Zapatista incursions into Mexico City. Perhaps he took his son and fled to Spain.[16]

The crime of Libertad Street illustrates the complex and contradictory pressures weighing on unions that lacked the markings of legitimacy. It was a clear example of the limited reach of the judiciary and the police. For Catalina Aranda, they did too little, too late, and their tepid response fueled her husband's complaints. Emilio Romero may have loved Catalina and their son, and probably longed for the respectable privacy of other unions, but he saw her efforts to live and work on her own as a challenge. Despite the quarrels, their testimonies document a prolonged effort to maintain a stable relationship. Why then did it end in violence?

MARITAL VIOLENCE IN CONTEXT

From the perspective of legislators, policemen, and journalists, domestic violence was a legitimate consequence of male defense of family honor and punishable only when it resulted in murder or excessive publicity. This justification, however, begs two questions. First, why did women also commit violent crimes against their husbands or lovers, if they supposedly did not have to worry about the defense of honor? Several cases compiled by Carlos Roumagnac show that women also used violence in conjugal disputes, and in ways similar to men. Carmen V., for example, killed her common-law husband, who was seventeen years younger than she, because she felt "jealousy, anger, fury, and had drunk some pulque." Besides, "he did not give her money for expenses."[17] Isabel M., a prostitute, killed her pimp because he hit her. Isabel's justification resembles male explanations of violence: "When someone touches me it is natural that I defend myself, and that night I was not in the mood to take that."[18] In 23 of the 114 cases of battery and homicide in the sample database of crime in Mexico City from 1900 to 1930, women were the accused. In 13 of those 23 cases the victim or rival was a man. Examples reviewed in the previous chapter, however, show that women could also engage in public fights to defend their honor and, as did Carmen and Isabel, they would also invoke jealousy and alcohol. A strictly gendered explanation risks missing this point: violence did not always have the result of reinforcing male domination, even if it were intended to defend the family's reputation. It is more accurate to assess the role of private violence in the larger context of community networks, I argue, than inside the nuclear family.

The second question may provide the answer to the first, and it is an additional reason to discuss private violence in a larger context. What is the role of the household economy as a factor of violence? Considering these crimes merely as pathological cases of patriarchal authority gone awry, the jealousy or blinding passion of "vulgar popular dramas," fails to illuminate the complex stories recorded in judicial archives. Violence in lower-class households (which unsurprisingly constitute the majority of these cases) resists explanations based on the neat private-public divide that the elite embraced as the rule for "respectable" modern families. The case of Catalina Aranda, among others, shows that beatings and murder were one aspect—the most salient, but not the only one—within disputes in which both women and men had much to lose. In order to fully understand the implications of violence in the domestic life of Mexico City's lower-class suspects, we must look at the conditions that characterized their marriages.

It is here that Carlota Mauri's death on Amargura Street can elucidate the fate of Catalina Aranda. Criminologist Carlos Roumagnac devoted one chapter of his book *Matadores de mujeres* to Arnulfo Villegas. Roumagnac's account, based on court proceedings and interviews with the accused, depicts a complex relationship between Arnulfo, Carlota, and her mother. Twenty-six-year-old Arnulfo was the owner of a small but promising butcher shop. Sixteen-year-old Carlota had recently moved with her mother to Amargura Street, where they established a small store. Her mother sent Carlota to the butcher shop every day, for no apparent reason, but always nicely dressed. This continued, according to Arnulfos' testimony, until he understood the visits to be an implicit offer, so he wrote a very formal letter to Carlota, in which he declared his love. With her mother's authorization, Carlota and Arnulfo began to see each other every day. The relationship lasted for nine months, until Carlota told Arnulfo that she could not bear his excessive jealousy and asked him to stop seeing her, thus setting the scene for the murder.

Arnulfo Villegas's account suggests that the cause of Carlota's willingness to date him, and then her sudden break, was her mother's interest in a profitable marriage. Proof of this was the cursory way in which the engagement was arranged. Arnulfo had a church marriage and two children. His wife had not separated from him until he was already dating Carlota. He had also fathered another child when he was sixteen. Carlota's mother knew all of this, but still encouraged her daughter's religious and civil wedding plans. She allowed them to sleep together and, according to Arnulfo, knew that Carlota had become pregnant and had had an abortion. This permissiveness, Carlota's mother confessed to Arnulfo, derived from the fact that a few years ago Carlota had been "dishonored" by another man, who was released from jail only after he promised to marry her. Carlota had received the dowry, but the wedding did not take place. Arnulfo's account implied that Carlota's mother used her daughter for profit and, inadvertently, caused the tragedy. It was not uncommon for parents of raped women to negotiate a convenient marriage, and Carlota's mother had done it before. Nevertheless, Arnulfo promised Carlota that he would take her to the altar dressed in white—despite her mother's opposition, as "everyone knew that her daughter had been abducted." More than his lover, Arnulfo wanted to make Carlota "his wife in front of God and the law."

His wish would not be fulfilled. Another man, the owner of a neighboring store that sold *rebozos* (shawls), began to court Carlota at the same time that Arnulfo started to lose money in his business, largely, he claimed, because of his presents to Carlota and loans to her mother. Both lovers were aware of the difficulties in arranging an honorable marriage. In their letters, published by Roumagnac, Carlota complained about the fact that Arnulfo was already married and his wife had come to denounce him. Carlota asked him to prevent this scandal again "because it is not very proper that she knows that we have relations." Arnulfo was also concerned about respectability. In his first letter to Carlota, he proposed to her, stating that "the only thing I wish and hope to have found in you is someone to live with happily with God's blessing, someone I can proudly name a substitute for my mother." He referred again to his mother in another letter, where he asked Carlota "to understand that I love you as I loved my mother, with the only difference that that was a sacred love and ours is the love and sweetness between husband and wife."[19]

Arnulfo's longing for a respectable relationship revealed the tensions caused by marital instability. Conjugal relations among the urban lower classes usually existed outside the civil law and, even before the legalization of divorce, enjoyed a great degree of flexibility. Urban common-law couples lacked the social and legal legitimacy of their upper-class counterparts. Extended families, vecindades, colonias, or barrios, thus played a central role in legitimizing informal unions, and nuclear families were not isolated from these networks. Male violence tried to legitimize those relations by publicly reinforcing prevalent gender roles in the family: men exercised force and control, women sacrificed themselves, and relations were stable.[20]

Census data shows that in the Federal District a smaller percentage of adults married than in the rest of the country. Aware of this, observers of urban society linked violence, and crime in general, with the high frequency of common-law unions, separations, and sexual disorder. Criminologist Julio Guerrero saw these features as the defining moral trait of the lowest stratum of Mexican society, the one most reluctant to progress and prone to crime. Roumagnac suggested that the greater flexibility of sexual life was one of the factors that attracted criminal men and women to the capital. Journalists feared that divorce would further sap the decency of the population. In 1930, *El Universal* blamed it for the growing waywardness of women and the frequency of passion crimes: "Divorce . . . is one of the causes of women's immorality, even though today marriage is not the formal, solemn, and sacred act of other times, and family ties loosen and break."[21]

Elite perceptions overstated the fluidity of lower-class couples, since fewer marriages did not mean that fewer people formed unions. Marriage, in fact, was only one of the often overlapping terms used to name different types of relationships. Manuel Alcazar called Petra Rosas "the lady, that is, my wife," but, despite living together, both declared themselves "single"—as Emilio Romero and Catalina Aranda did.[22] The ambiguity stemmed in part from the different meanings of civil and religious marriages. As a consequence, bigamy was seldom prosecuted.[23] The cost of a religious ceremony or a banquet was beyond the reach of the lowest-income groups, and a church ceremony did not confer legal status to unions. Yet for many, civil marriage was only a legal duty, preliminary to the "real" marriage in the Church. Francisca Montaño declared herself single in front of the judge at a criminal trial. She later added that she was "married only by the Church" to Lorenzo Calderón, who also defined himself as single, but called Montaño his wife.[24] Given the limited ability of both legal and religious ceremonies to publicly declare their conjugal status, spouses could easily move between partners. Marital life (whether legalized or not) was only possible when housing was available for the new couple. Miguel Velázquez's address was in Regina Street, but only his sisters lived there. On a daily basis, however, he visited his "common-law-wife [*amasia*], Elisa Reyes, whom he has lodged with his godmother . . . on Zarco Street" (less than two miles northeast of Regina).[25]

Amasio or *amasia* was the most common word used to designate conjugal partners. Among the upper classes, *amasiato* had a clearly pejorative ring—as it has today in Mexico. The word *mancebía* also designated relationships that were not legally or religiously sanctioned. Yet amasiato had a more positive connotation among the rest of the population and it applied to long-term relationships in which partners were fully committed. Living in common-law marriage offered advantages to both parties, such as easily moving in or out of the spouse's house, yet appearing as a couple in front of the community. Lorenzo Rivas had been living with María del Refugio Rodríguez but they had frequent quarrels and finally separated. Nevertheless, they still met every night to walk in the streets of their neighborhood. María del Refugio's sister, Dolores, had a fourteen-year on-again-off-again relationship with Manuel García—whom María del Refugio suspected of killing Lorenzo. Gendarme González Escobedo and Rita León lived four years in common-law marriage until she left him and went back to the state of Michoacán. She returned to live with him and they split up again. González, however, took the relationship very seriously. After a failed attempt to bring her back, he killed her and then committed suicide.[26]

Wedlock (both legal and otherwise) was only as strong as spouses wanted it to be. The community's acknowledgment of marital ties required both men and women's forceful protection of their partners against rivals and, perhaps more importantly, against the gossipy intrusion of families, coworkers, and neighbors. In 1908, Alberta Rodríguez and Matilde Sánchez wounded each other with knives over their relationship with another Manuel García, who denied being the amasio of either woman. Both were prostitutes and had been friends. The fight was the conclusion of a protracted, public dispute in which both claimed to have a stable relationship with García and accused the other of being jealous. The crime resembled in many ways that of Tarasquillo Street, eleven years earlier, in which María Villa killed fellow prostitute Esperanza Gutiérrez over a lover. In both cases, suspects implicitly appealed to the rules of honor discussed in the previous chapter.[27] The unofficial nature of these unions and their openness to public scrutiny were precisely the reason for the constant negotiation of relations and the use of violence.

There was one difference between male and female justifications of violence. Alberta and Matilde accused each other of being jealous of García because, as it codified and legitimized male violence, jealousy was unbecoming for women. For men, jealousy (even if expressed by violence) was a valid demonstration of love. Antonio V., who killed his rebellious wife, regretted his deed in front of Roumagnac: "I loved her and I still love her!" he declared, "I would have liked to have her in a place where I could see her all the time, where she could not leave." This would have avoided the accusations and gossip of the people. But she wanted to be free and show her pride, in her words, "with the reboso halfway over her head."[28] Agustín C. killed Modesta H. because she humiliated him in front of his mother and neighbors but, he told Roumagnac, he still loved her in his dreams. Despite his claim that he did not premeditate the murder, Agustín H. was sentenced to death.[29]

Indifferent to the threat of the death penalty and moved by a sense of obligation, most offenders surrendered to the police after killing their wives or girlfriends. Others attempted or committed suicide. Almost all showed remorse and assumed the consequences of punishment. "God forgive me," Rosalío Millán said, "but she was too flirtatious [*coqueta*]."[30] When murder was not the result, however, trials did not offer a satisfactory expiation, because they involved the shameful intervention of the courts. Amador Santos declared, after being sentenced to one year for battery, that he only regretted not having killed Joaquina Prieto, "so he would be punished for something really serious."[31] The reaction to betrayal (or the suspicion of it) had to be prompt and strong, even if less tidy than honorable confrontations. Responding otherwise could mean public humiliation and a loss of self-esteem.

Behind the lack of social recognition for lower-class unions, at the roots of domestic violence, lies the inability of the urban poor to hide private disputes from public scrutiny. Jesús Viscaya was arrested after a man saw him beating his wife because she did not provide bread for dinner and had addressed him disrespectfully. The passerby (a stranger to Viscaya and his wife) hit him with a stone "and then, on top of all the evils, called a policeman."[32] The problem for Viscaya and other suspects was that domestic disputes took place in the semipublic space of vecindades, where many activities were conducted in the hallways and squabbles could be heard through walls, making vecindad concierges frequent witnesses in criminal trials. The limits between public and private life were further blurred because the inhabitants of vecindades and mesones had to conduct most of their everyday lives in the streets and other public places. Thus, despite criminologists' perceptions of popular immorality, lower-class couples did worry about the pressures of public opinion, and even victims could reject outside intervention and avoid police intervention.[33] Male violence was silently condoned because it was a legitimate instrument to secure, in front of public eyes, men's honor and women's submission.

Homicides such as the crimes of Amargura and Libertad streets attested to the high cost of this use of violence, but also to its inevitability. Witness the repeated invocations to death as the ultimate sanction of true love in the letters exchanged between Arnulfo Villegas and Carlota Mauri. Arnulfo signed his first letter as "The one who loves you and swears to love you beyond the grave." Later, Arnulfo warned Carlota that if she repeated what she had done the night before, "then we certainly will not see each other in this life of illusions and disappointments, but maybe we will see each other in the other life," and concluded: "Your love or death." Carlota signed one of her letters: "Carlota M., who will [not] forget you until death."[34]

After Arnulfo was executed, a leaflet reproduced by Roumagnac warned men on the danger of loving women too much:

Al pobre Arnulfo Villegas
Ya le llegó la malhora
Pues el miércoles temprano
Lo despacharon a La otra.

Carlota Mauri señores,
Fue la causa, claro está;
Por ser tan veleidosita
Arnulfo la fue a matar

Le hubiera dicho tan sólo
Aunque fuese de mentira
Que se casaba con él
Y no pasa la desdicha.

Villegas con loco brío
Dos balazos le tiró
Y muerta le hacía papachos
Como demente feroz.

El fallo de la justicia
Fue la "Pena Capital"
Que ya sufrió en Belemitas
Sin poderlo remediar.

Su esposa Doña L. B.
Lo mismo que su hijita
Lloran las pobres a mares
Por la desgracia inaudita.

Miren lo caro que cuesta
El amar a las mujeres
Los que casados ya son
Y usan esos procederes.

Tomen ejemplo hombres
De este tristísimo término,
Y contengan su locura
Para no morir tan presto.

No sean celosos terribles
Ni quieran con tanta furia;
Porque esto la causa ha sido
De desdicha tan segura.

No se entreguen tanto, tanto,
A mujer ninguna, no,
Porque ellas de cualquier modo
Son siempre la perdición.[35]

THE SEXUAL CONTENTS OF VIOLENCE AGAINST WOMEN

The eloquence inspired by crimes of passion was absent when violence against women included sex. In such cases, circumspection seemed the best option for all actors, even victims. This silence makes it harder to place sexual offenses in their social context. One case in point is that of Francisco Guerrero (a.k.a. "El Chalequero" or Antonio "El Chaleco"), who raped, robbed, and killed women in the northern outskirts of Mexico City between the early 1880s and 1908. Unlike most other sexual offenders, El Chalequero attracted the interest of the press and science.[36]

After his 1888 arrest for the murder of two women, he was compared with the London figure of Jack the Ripper: both targeted prostitutes of approximately forty years of age, both left gruesome wounds on their victims' bodies, both were blamed for previously unsolved crimes, and rumor had it that both were physicians or at least educated men.[37] The trial, in 1890, attracted such public interest that specialists, including Roumagnac, were called upon to decide if he was criminally responsible. Experts concluded that he was not mentally ill but a "born criminal." In applying criminological categories to his case, however, specialists and prosecutors avoided calling attention to the sexual nature of his attacks. Criminological classifications lacked a specific genus for sexual offenders. What defined El Chalequero was the cruelty of his murders, rather than his violent sexual practices—which included rape, attacks against minors, and biting his sexual victims. Neither was he a passional criminal, according to his examiners, for "he has never acted for love." In the end, Roumagnac accepted Guerrero's own explanation of his behavior: the victims had wounded "his self esteem as a man [*su amor propio del macho*]."[38]

A closer look at El Chalequero's interactions with his victims, however, reveals that his murders were only the extreme consequence of relations that included sexual abuse and exploitation. Antonio Mayorga, who first accused him, declared that Guerrero was the man who "took the prostitutes of Peralvillo . . . and after cheating them—by having forcible intercourse—robbed them and slit their throat."[39] Female witnesses at his trial were afraid of him because, rather than an anonymous threat, his was an open one; he often told prostitutes near the Río Consulado that he was El Chalequero in order to scare them and obtain their submission. Soledad González declared that Guerrero had wounded and robbed a friend of hers and later demanded to have intercourse with her for one peso; when González refused, he forced her to go to a lonely place near the river and told her that he was El Chalequero. He put four coins in her hand, a knife against her throat, and "abused" her. When he had finished, he took back the four coins, plus another she was hiding inside her mouth. Other victims declared that Guerrero had stolen the clothes they were about to wash in the river. He raped several women and then demanded money or pulque. Guerrero knew the fear he inspired in the rumbo of Peralvillo; no woman dared denounce him, and no man tried to settle any score with him until Mayorga testified against him.

The murder victim who finally led to Guerrero's arrest in 1888 was Mucia Gallardo, a woman who seemed to wield some influence over him. She was his amasia and ran some of the brothels of the area. Guerrero's relationship with Gallardo involved the exploitation of prostitutes, violence, and the stealing of other victims' meager properties. Together, for example, they robbed and wounded Josefa Rodríguez. His association with Gallardo probably forced prostitutes to accept her protection, working in one of her houses rather than by themselves in the streets. Even Guerrero's nickname, "El Chalequero" or "El Chaleco," came from "his habit of forcing woman to accept his will." In popular speech, *a chaleco* meant "by force." Nobody wished to accuse Guerrero because the violence he so openly exercised was part of the business of illegal prostitution in the northern margins of the city. El Chalequero was finally found guilty of the death of Mucia Gallardo, which he later acknowledged, and of that of Francisca N., "La Chíchara"—because of the similarity of her wounds to those of Gallardo.[40]

Murder distinguished El Chalequero's exploits from most recorded cases of sexual abuse, where violence was not the end but the beginning of a negotiation between suspects, policemen, judges, doctors, the victim, and her family. Thus, unlike the crimes of Peralvillo, most sexual offenses were surrounded by a decorous silence. Underlying silence and negotiations were public perceptions of sexual abuse which did not regard it as equivalent to the physical aggression found in battery and homicide. For offenders, the police, prosecutors, and juries (all of them male), most sexual crimes did not involve violence because, they thought, intercourse always took place with the consent of the victim. Ultimately, as El Chalequero's crimes suggested and victim's accounts will show in the following pages, young women's labor was at stake in the negotiations following sexual abuse.

From the victims' perspective, rape was in fact a painful and humiliating crime, and the use of physical force and moral pressure associated with sexual intercourse were never clearly differentiated. Their narratives stressed the treacheries (such as induced drunkenness or promises of marriage) used by offenders to lead them into situations in which sexual violence became possible. Fourteen-year-old Guadalupe Rodríguez, who accused Dolores Méndez of statutory rape, declared that Méndez took her from one cantina to another, making her drink until she was intoxicated. They knew that Rodríguez's parents would hit her if she arrived late and drunk, so Méndez offered to take her to an aunt's home in Santa Anita. They started walking, but he stopped in another cantina and made her drink even more. He told her that he had to take a room at a hotel to wait for a cousin. At the hotel, he promised "to set up a house for her, and buy her dresses and shoes" if she had intercourse with him. She stayed at the hotel for three days before returning home.[41] Other accounts exposed the pressure exercised by offenders who were related to them by kinship ties or work. Roumagnac reported the case of José D., who was convicted of committing incest with his daughter M. To obtain her consent, José threatened her and read her some articles of the penal code that proved, according to his interpretation, that "nothing could happen to them." At the trial, José called his daughter "a light-headed woman whom only I can judge, since I have lived with her in concubinage for more than a year."[42]

Placed against the authority of suspects and the skepticism of officials, victims' narratives often had considerable gaps. Physical violence was the central component of victims' experience of rape, yet few testimonies actually described it. One exception was the case of ten-year-old Juana Espinosa, who was raped by the uncle in whose house she lived as domestic help. The trial records also present the complex relationships that united victims and offenders in cases of sexual violence. On July 23, 1921, Teresa Corona, Juana's mother, brought her son-in-law Manuel Alvarado to the police station, accusing him of having raped Juana. Corona declared that Alvarado had married her daughter Nieves Carmona one year ago. At that time, Alvarado asked Corona that "the girl Juana go to her sister's house to serve as a little maid [*criadita*]." Corona agreed and "gave the girl to them." Later, Corona brought her daughter back home because of the disputes between Alvarado and Carmona. One week later, however, Corona sent Juana again to help at Alvarado's house. Days later, Juana called her mother and told her that she "felt ill" and that she had been raped by Alvarado. Corona accused Alvarado first of statutory rape and then simply of raping her daughter. At the trial, Juana Espinosa described the violence exercised against her body with straightforward language. She declared at the police station that she always brought breakfast to Alvarado at his work. The day of the crime, when he had finished eating, "he put her on the ground and without telling her anything pulled her skirt, opened her legs, and introduced something hard that made her feel pain and cry" and caused her to bleed. Alvarado offered to buy her shoes and a reboso if she did not tell anyone what had happened, and he told her that the blood was coming from her nose.

Manuel Alvarado, a thirty-two-year-old coach driver, did not deny the accusation but tried to portray the events in a different light. He said that after breakfast he was "a little bit drunk" from some pulque and that he and Juana started to play. He declared that Juana had kissed and enticed him saying that "she wanted to know what he did to her sister Nieves." Alvarado declared that he penetrated Espinosa only briefly and did not ejaculate in her. He added that Juana was not crying but "happy" afterwards. In front of the judge and later in the jury audience, Juana denied Alvarado's account and again detailed the physical violence involved. She declared that she did not cry for help because she was very scared, and that she did not voluntarily accept his advances. In a cross-examination with the accused, she maintained her story. Despite Juana's valor, the prosecution against Alvarado was centered on her age rather than on the violence of her attacker. The report of the medical examination at the police station and the Juárez hospital confirmed the recent deflowering and wounds in the victim's vagina, but stated that the body of the victim did not exhibit "signs of violence." Alvarado's attorney alleged that the victim "willingly offered herself, without the mediation of seduction, deceit, or violence." The judge indicted Alvarado for statutory rape, not rape, and the jury found Alvarado guilty of having had intercourse with "an honest and chaste woman," using seduction, but not violence, to obtain her consent. The judge sentenced him to five years in prison, half of what he would have received if convicted of the rape of a minor.[43]

This outcome was not unusual because forced penetration was not considered a form of violence. The detail provided by Juana in her accusation was missing from other rape cases, where the victims' language was usually indirect. They were afraid of challenging their attackers' versions and further shaming themselves by providing details of the attacks against their bodies. *Hacer uso* (to make use) of the female victim or *deshonrar* (to dishonor) were frequently employed as synonyms for intercourse. Others said that the accused *se burló* (deceived) them.[44] The careful selection of words had larger implications since victims had to choose between clearly acknowledging physical violence or stressing the damage to their honor. When victims chose to stress violence, their claims were not guaranteed to have an impact, for judges and juries gave precedence to the opinion of forensic doctors who examined the victim. Evidence of deflowering, even if accompanied by profuse bleeding as in the case of Juana, was not considered proof of violence.[45] Even relatives of the victim, such as those of thirteen-year-old Esther Zúñiga, preferred to press charges concerning the use of the victim's labor rather than to stress the sexual aspects of the offense. Esther's aunt, Teresa Zúñiga, declared that she had brought Esther to work at a home north of the city and that, she learned later, one Marcelina Ayala had taken her niece to the military barracks, where a soldier paid twenty-five cents to rape her. Teresa accused Ayala of corrupting a minor, and Ayala was found guilty and sentenced to four months detention, but the soldier who forced Esther was not accused of any crime, even though he appeared as a witness.[46]

Public perceptions of sexual abuse reinforced this neglect. Press accounts of sexual crimes were sparse and did not depict them as offenses deserving of serious public attention. In the case of El Chalequero, murder, rather than rape, dominated the interest of readers. Other times, sexual offenses seemed little more than a joke. In January 1897, *El Imparcial* reported in a brief note that a man had been accused of statutory rape and jailed because he spent a night in the company of two female minors. Should the accusation prove true, the reporter ironically commented, "there will be a difficult dilemma: which one of the two will he marry?"[47] Since elite observers saw promiscuity and incest as normal features of lower-class households, the victim's suffering was subordinated to her interests and those of her family—insofar as the offender was ready to marry her. The parents of the two victims in the *El Imparcial* report, like anyone in their situation, may have pressed for the wedding, but, as the report suggested, they would have a hard time convincing the judge that a crime had been committed.

The reluctance to recognize sexual abuse as a crime was based on flexible definitions of sexual offenses. Rape (*violación*), statutory rape (*estupro*), and abduction (*rapto*) were felonies sanctioned in the penal code. But they were loosely defined, making convictions difficult to obtain for the most serious crimes. The 1871 Code catalogued them as "Crimes against the order of families, public moral and good habits." Rape was defined as sexual intercourse with the use of violence, regardless of the age and sex of the victim. It was punished with six years of prison if the victim was more than fourteen years old and ten years if the victim was younger than fourteen. Statutory rape was "intercourse with a chaste and honest woman, whose consent is obtained through seduction or deceit." It was punishable by four years of prison if the victim was ten to fourteen years old, eight years if the victim was less than ten years old, and up to eleven months of detention if the victim was older than fourteen and the offender had falsely promised to marry her. Thus, statutory rape did not include intercourse with a woman older than fourteen to whom the offender had not promised marriage. Abduction was defined as seizing "control of a woman against her will, through physical or moral violence, deceit or seduction, in order to satisfy a lascivious desire or to marry her." The punishment was four years in prison but could extend to twelve years if the offender did not reveal the whereabouts of the victim. These crimes were punished more harshly when there was kinship between the offender and the victim or the former exercised some kind of authority over her. Neither statutory rape nor abduction, however, was punished if the offender married the victim.[48]

The legal definitions allowed for lax enforcement. Policemen, judges, and juries usually construed rape cases as abduction and statutory rape because they perceived deceit, rather than violence, as the defining trait of sexual misconduct. Judges and prosecutors categorized cases as statutory rape even when the accusers used the word "rape." Fourteen-year-old Asunción Gómez accused Margarito Villavicencio of "statutory rape, abduction, and rape," but the judge downgraded the accusation to statutory rape and then to abduction. She claimed that he had intercourse with her after promising marriage, so she had not returned home. Villavicencio claimed that he had "asked for a testimony of her love, and she did not resist until he tried to have intercourse with her, when she declined and he did not insist." The jury unanimously acquitted him.[49] The ambivalence could confuse victims. Juana Espinosa and her mother claimed that Manuel Alvarado had used force to have intercourse with the girl, but they hesitated to accuse Alvarado of rape or statutory rape. The judge, the jury, and the doctors who examined Espinosa did not see any violence involved in the case, and indicted Alvarado for statutory rape.[50]

The prospect of having to prove violence was as painful for the victim as the crime itself. The failed accusation of Asunción Gómez against Margarito Villavicencio, mentioned above, illustrates the physical and moral violence endured by victims during the judicial process. The practitioners who examined her at the station established that she had been recently deflowered. Two days later, however, doctors examined her again by request of the judge and determined that she had not been deflowered.[51] In these inspections, doctors had to answer some specific questions: Was the victim pubescent, had violence been used, was the victim recently deflowered, and what was her "probable" age? This involved an examination of the victim's whole body and descriptions of her genitalia and breasts.[52] Unlike in other violent crimes, physical evidence was essential to support the accusation, as the victim's testimony was not enough even to prove her age.

The search for physical evidence created a vicious circle. The mere fact that a victim had endured these procedures, with the consequent humiliation, reduced her credibility as accuser. Therefore, victims avoided examinations. They knew that doctors and medical students functioning as practitioners at police stations performed repeated and often unnecessary examinations of women, regardless of the reason that had taken them to the station. Teresa Mejía, victim of a rape, declared to the jury that when she was abandoned by her aggressor, "a policeman . . . brought her to the police station and advised her not to allow the practitioner to examine her, but to wait until the doctor had arrived."[53] Some victims resisted what they saw as abusive probes. Taken to the station as an alleged victim of statutory rape in 1927, María Venegas refused to undergo a medical examination, "confessing not to be a *señorita* (virgin) any more."[54] In 1929, the city government established that no woman had to be examined at police stations unless she had serious wounds. According to newspapers, this decision sought to avoid the "embarrassing inspections" because "many people who work at the stations find out about the results of these examinations, and this has prompted complaints from the victims of such improprieties."[55]

Judges' concern about physical evidence was coupled with the notion of "female weakness" and the perception that any woman who decided to turn her disgrace into a public issue lacked honor. The penal code's articles on abduction implied that women needed, in all cases, special protection against male deception. Article 811 established that "the use of seduction will be presumed in any case in which a woman under sixteen years old voluntarily follows her abductor." Martínez de Castro explained that a younger woman, "not being yet mature in her judgment, gives her consent due to her shyness and the weakness of her sex, or because of deceiving illusions."[56] Questioning by the police, judges, and defense attorneys tried further to undermine the victim's credibility by forcing her to describe the circumstances of her loss of honor.

It is not surprising, then, that victims and their families were reluctant to go to trial. An offer of marriage seemed preferable to pursuing punishment to its final resolution. The case of Guadalupe Rodríguez, discussed above, is again an example. When she accused Dolores Méndez of statutory rape, he denied having had intercourse with her at the hotel. He added that on the way to the police station, she had confessed to him that she "had had a relationship with a blacksmith" who deflowered her months ago after they had been drinking. She declared to the judge that the story of the blacksmith was not true, but she had told it to Méndez because he threatened that if she accused him, "she would have to spend two months in prison and he would only stay four days." Guadalupe insisted that she was a virgin until Méndez had intercourse with her. The medical examination confirmed that she had been recently deflowered. Nevertheless, she dropped her accusation against Méndez when he promised to marry her.[57]

That was the wise thing to do. Sixteen-year-old Teresa Mejía and her mother chose instead to pursue legal action against Teresa's paternal uncle, who had raped her in a hotel and abandoned her in the street afterward. The victim went so far as to request that the police examine her, so as to prove the effects of the rape and the blows she had received when she tried to resist. Authorities were not receptive to her accusations, however. With the jury present, the defense attorney and the judge claimed that the victim's mother,

Socorro Torres, was shamelessly working for her own interests because she was a widow with illegitimate children and because another daughter of hers had been "dishonored" but did not marry the offender. Torres denied those charges and complained that the hearing was taking place without the presence of the attorney who had conducted the accusation during the proceedings. Yet, the jury unanimously acquitted Mejía.[58] The shame of appearing in the courtroom during a jury audience, which usually attracted a crowd, and the attitudes of the judge and jury members further discouraged the use of judicial channels. Aware of this, relatives would obtain the arrest of the suspect and drop the charges as soon as an arrangement was made.[59] Many trials abruptly ended when the accusing party dropped the charges.

As table 13 in the appendix shows, the possibility of a conviction in rape cases was very small: one in five cases in 1897 and 1900, and one in three cases from 1937 to 1939. Compared to other types of crime, rape had a higher conviction ratio (accused/sentenced) (see appendix, table 10). For abduction and statutory rape, the chances of a guilty verdict were even slimmer: during the first period, convictions were obtained in one in seventy cases, and between 1937 and 1942 the ratio decreased to three.

The intervention of the victim's family partially filled the vacuum opened by the judicial system, but it rarely achieved punishment for the offender. Relatives, not only judges, changed the accusations of rape to statutory rape, even when violence had been present, because that increased the possibility of negotiating the marriage of offender and victim. The mother of Carlota Mauri, the victim of Amargura Street, had made a deal with the man who first dishonored her daughter before arranging her tragic liaison with Arnulfo Villegas. Carlota received a dowry and a promise of marriage in exchange for dropping the charges. In that case, as probably in most, the gamble did not pay off: the intended groom avoided the wedding and Carlota's only satisfaction was a few days in jail for the offender. Abduction cases followed a similar pattern. The mother of the victim, or sometimes the father, would denounce to the police the disappearance of the daughter and name the suspect. After the accused was arrested and a medical examination of the victim was performed, negotiations would follow and the offender would be released on bail, for lack of evidence, or after the accusing party dropped the charges.

An additional reason to avoid a trial was that parents sought redress usually through the action of the mother. Exempted from the obligation to use violence, she could be fearless in her pursuit of the suspect. Eligia Alvarez, for example, was aware of the "romantic relationship" between her daughter, Aurora Gutiérrez, and Juan Villarreal, a man of whom she did not approve. When her daughter failed to come back from work, Alvarez went out to look for her. Thus, she charged Villarreal with abduction and statutory rape. The next day Alvarez found the couple and had Villarreal arrested.[60] The father played a minor role because it was his reputation that suffered the most, as the loss of the daughter's virginity revealed his lack of control over the household, and public dealings with the issue only highlighted his inability to keep family problems private. The offender's relation of kinship or neighborhood with the victim further weakened the nuclear family's authority. María Guadalupe Bárcenas, for example, accused her stepbrother Manuel Rosete of having promised to marry her in order to have intercourse. When he reneged, it was her father who pressed charges, stating that he did so only to force Rosete to marry his daughter.[61]

Parental action also aimed at reinforcing authority within the household. For many victims, the dilemma was whether to go back home and face parental punishment or to accept their attackers' proposals and stay with them. This points to another key element of young women's victimization: even if it were voluntary, others would interpret her sexual initiation as a break with her role in the family. All female victims were suspected of consenting to intercourse. Thus, by pressing charges, parents also punished the victim, for she had to suffer the shame of the judicial inquiry. Many cases that began as sexual violence generated additional conflict within the family. Aurora Gutiérrez, for example, declared at the police station that she had left home because she did not like living with her sister and she and Juan Villarreal were arranging their wedding. Her mother, added Gutiérrez, "instead of acting in a prudent way, arrived with a policeman," to arrest them both.[62] Some victims, like Aurora, worked outside the home, thus limiting the reach of parental vigilance. Esther Zúñiga, the minor raped by a soldier in the case mentioned above, decided to stay with Marcelina Ayala, the woman who delivered her to the soldier, because she was afraid of her and because Ayala bought her a dress.[63]

Some cases of abduction or statutory rape were in fact the product of the daughter's decision to elope, in order to sever her links with the family. Young women knew that their "dishonoring" would radically alter their relationship with their parents. When her father asked the police to subject her to a medical examination, Raquel Osorno, who was fourteen years old, declared that "it is true that she is already a *mujer de mundo* [woman of the world]" because she had been deflowered one year ago by a boyfriend whom she did not see any more. Now, she declared, she was abandoning her house "because it was not favorable for her, because her parents kept her in complete slavery."[64] Judicial records of sexual violence are at times difficult to distinguish from other kinds of domestic conflict over honor and labor in which parents punished independent-minded daughters. Angela Rodríguez kept her twenty-six-year-old daughter María Mora locked up in her house for ten months in 1909, after she learned about Mora's brief relationship with a man seven years earlier. Rodríguez deprived Mora of food and clothes, and forced her to do all the household chores. Brought to the police, the victim refused to press charges, declaring that she wanted only to be free.[65] Guadalupe Rodríguez's father, she declared, "mistreated her because he did not want her to work" away from the house.[66] Work could be the beginning but also the resolution of these conflicts. Sixteen-year-old Concepción Cerón, who became pregnant after escaping with her boyfriend, preferred to start working as a prostitute in a house at Tabaqueros Street rather than to return to her parents, "because she was afraid of being scolded."[67]

Despite the silence that surrounded them, sexual crimes unmask the essential contradiction of honor, their meaning shifting when experienced by those at the bottom of family hierarchy. This would not appear a contradiction were it not for the initiative that those young women were unafraid to use. Judicial records witness to their courage when they detailed a rape in front of their attackers and the public or when they deliberately chose freedom over honor by making illicit sexual intercourse an indelible marker of their release from domestic work.

By contrast, from the perspective of parents, control of daughters' labor was indistinguishable from honor. This coincidence made possible the pragmatism demonstrated by their negotiations after rape, never mind that the bargaining and the publicity involved in court procedures further humiliated the victim, who suffered not only the violence of offenders but also the intrusive investigations of policemen and lawyers. The violence inflicted against the victim remained the basic fact of sexual crimes. Despite the ease with which husbands could abuse their wives to defend their reputation, the evidence suggests that they avoided violence to redress the dishonor of a daughter.

CONCLUSIONS

Silvia Arrom has noted an increasing respect for wives' rights in the first half of the nineteenth century conveyed by cases of ecclesiastical divorce. Although the evidence discussed in this chapter should be distinguished from that of civil courts, it is possible to agree with Arrom in that marital abuse survived in a "gray area," encouraged by lax legal definitions that justified the state's reluctance to intervene. Statistics suggest an improvement in the conviction ratio for sexual crimes after the Revolution. However, it is difficult to situate the evidence from the early twentieth century in the context of long-term progress or even the modernization of patriarchal structures studied, for later periods, by other authors.[68]

The Revolution, despite the armed participation of women, did not bring a transformation in the social attitudes that decried domestic violence while demanding greater male control of the family. *Excélsior* observed that the 1929 Penal Code was lenient with killers who claimed the defense of honor as their motive. This, noted the editorial, would only increase "conjugal criminality" in "a country like ours, where human life is despised."[69] Men's duty to protect women became even stronger. In 1930, *El Universal* stated the need to return to Porfirian severity against "wife killers." "Women's emancipation," warned the editorial, had created the illusion that they could defend themselves. Despite the claims of feminists, added the newspaper, "women are organically weaker, they need protection . . . as long as they do not become masculine, and men remain in charge of the public use of force."[70] Audiences at jury trials and the newspapers' police reports welcomed and developed the image of women as victims who had to take justice in their own hands. After 1916, and until the elimination of jury trials in 1929, several cases defended by famous lawyers obtained the acquittal of women who had killed men. The vocabulary used in these defenses highlighted the organic and psychological weakness of women, which prompted them to take fatal actions against strong and dangerous men.[71] By stressing the innocence of the accused, these dramatizations of women implied that their overall situation in society did not have to change. On the contrary,

Excélsior noted again, women should return to the behavior that made them the "honor and decorum of Mexican society" in a mythical prerevolutionary past.[72]

Between 1900 and 1931, and probably beyond, the perspectives and interests converging in sexual and matrimonial crimes pointed to the conclusion that violence itself is a cultural construct but one that is slow to change. "Crimes of passion" among the elite were "vulgar dramas" when performed by the urban poor. Most actors did not perceive as criminal the use of force in the everyday relations between parents and children, or husbands and wives. For the urban poor, the forceful control of wives and daughters helped to redress the lack of legitimacy in their marriages and to deal with the tensions created by their failure to keep a clear separation between private life and the public realm.

Sexual crimes often remained outside of the public eye because police and judicial officials disallowed the sexual nature of male violence against women and because victims' relatives downplayed the fact that, for the victim, sexual intercourse itself could be a form of violence—for rape wounded not only the victim's reputation, but also her body. Only victims, and usually at the cost of humiliating exposure, would state the criminal character of these cases. It was always convenient for most everyone involved to keep these matters, like other forms of domestic violence, confined to the private realm. Still, the examples discussed in this chapter did not unfold exclusively inside the private sphere, since they were open to the inquiry of judicial authorities and the interest of urban communities—not to mention the self-serving curiosity of the historian. Nevertheless, judges, witnesses, offenders, and victims defined many of these cases as private and in effect kept them beyond the reach of punishment.

This chapter stresses the perspective of urban households who received fewer benefits from patriarchal structures of power. Tight control of lower-class victims' sexuality was less consequential than the issue of who would benefit from their labor, since there was no inheritable property to be lost to illegitimate children or an unfavorable marriage. The crime of Amargura Street showed the results of a negotiation where the interests of Carlota Mauri's mother and Arnulfo Villegas reached the greatest tension. Violence resolved it because, in his view, that was the best way to cleanse his honor. In the cases in which parents and daughters decided to seek punishment of sexual offenders, the judicial system reminded them that the urban poor could not trust the state and the law to recognize their honor.[73]

Nevertheless, urban communities placed the urban poor's version of honor—one that stressed reliability and resourcefulness—at a central place in their social life. Violence, both public and private, was the consequence. Men and women had to defend their personal reputation when it was challenged by their equals, and thus claim their rightful place in their community. But young women, who were still under the control of their parents, could not make the same assertion. Yet, they emerged here as more than passive victims of shame. In doing so, they exposed the contradictions of honor as sanctioned by tradition. If the contenders of same-sex fights paid dearly to reconstruct a sense of and a claim to honor, those who used violence against their wives and daughters only proved the costly and unstable nature of that honor.

6

Money, Crime, and Social Reactions to Larceny

In 1901, traveler Ethel B. Tweedie recorded elite attitudes toward theft with a wealth of detail that Mexican writers preferred to avoid:

> The first thing to teach a Mexican Indian is to be honest; by nature he is a most awful thief. Warning:—Take nothing to Mexico of value, only what is absolutely necessary, and never leave anything unlocked. In the street the Mexicans will seize a purse or a brooch during broad daylight; or take a man's pin out of his scarf! Fraudulent notes and silver are in constant circulation; short change is invariably given to strangers. . . . Look at the door-mats; they are chained to the floor. Look at the seats in the chief shops of the City; they are secured to the counter. Look at the ink-bottles in the General Post Office; they are sunk down into the tables so that they cannot possibly be moved. Even the combs and tooth-brushes (yes, public tooth-brushes!) may be seen chained to the walls in hotels. Everything is done to try and prevent theft; yet innumerable pawn-shops groan beneath the weight of ill-gotten property, kodaks, opera glasses, and endless articles stolen from houses as well as travelers' trunks.[1]

The kind of petty larceny Tweedie described was not the most damaging or dangerous, and probably not even the most frequent type of theft. Pickpockets, shoplifters, and their kin rarely had access to large amounts of money, nor did they resort to physical violence against their victims. Nevertheless, they alarmed "decent people" because their crime seemed to touch any object or person, regardless of class, in the streets and other public places. Theft was threatening for the Mexico City elite because, in Miguel Macedo's words, it "built a bridge" between classes. It turned bosses into victims and workers, domestic servants, and the poor in the streets into suspects. Battery, homicide, and sexual violence, on the other hand, were an internal problem of the lower classes.[2] The "weight of ill-gotten property" was a measure of the losing battle that authorities were fighting against the crime that crossed the class divide.

Tweedie and Macedo ignored the evidence that most thieves' attention was not limited to "kodaks [and] opera glasses." In the majority of theft cases, victims did not belong to the elite, nor was larceny a systematic manifestation of social discontent with inequality. Although many people suffered deprivation, relatively few decided to break the law, and theft was condemned by all classes.

Historical literature has inherited this neglect toward the subject of urban theft. Scholars have stressed the role of Latin American bandits in expressing social tensions in the countryside and their repression as part of the process of state building. Urban larceny, however, has largely been ignored because its connections to social and political movements are less apparent.[3] From the perspective of those situated at the lowest end of the income scale, whether victims and offenders, theft expressed the drastic transformations of urban society caused by demographic growth and an economy dominated by monetary exchanges of goods and labor. In order to redress the lack of interest from studies concerned with larger political and economic processes, one must take a close look at the economic and cultural aspects of larceny.

Theft was one among many small-scale and nonwage economic activities that provided the urban poor with additional income and the ability to cope with economic instability. Thus, theft needs to be studied not merely as a predatory offense, but also with regard to the social reactions it triggered. Larceny was a marginal strategy because potential offenders balanced need and opportunity against the cost of punishment and public shaming. Nevertheless, the penal reaction against theft transformed this calculation. Petty theft was not new in Mexico City during the early decades of the twentieth century, but only then did it become the axis of the relationship between the urban lower classes and state social reform policies. Tweedie's prepossession and the intellectual construction of a social category of urban thieves (*rateros*), would justify harsh but largely ineffective penitentiary strategies. Both chapters 6 and 7 are based on a common thesis: crimes against property were as much a product of economic conditions as the result of cultural attitudes toward class difference and crime.

THE ECONOMICS OF THEFT

Mexico City had been at the center of a large market economy for centuries, but it was during the Porfiriato that money became a factor of instability in the lives of the urban poor. Rodney Anderson observes that many workers displaced from their lands since the 1890s became wage laborers on haciendas and in the cities, "whereas before they had not often been part of the national money economy."[4] The wage-earning population of the country tripled between 1861 and 1895. In the latter year, according to Stephen Haber, the number of consumers whose income was enough to buy manufactured goods neared five million, although the overwhelming majority of the country's population belonged to a lower class defined by its meager income.[5] Among artisans, according to Carlos Illades, the tendency during the nineteenth century was toward a greater "transparency of the relationship . . . established between artisanal masters, on the one side, and officials and apprentices, on the other."[6] The volume of circulating currency increased twelve times between 1880 and 1910. In Mexico City, monetary exchanges were particularly intense compared with the rest of the country. In 1910–11, retail sales per inhabitant in the Federal District were five times greater than in the rest of the country, and more cash was available in the capital.[7]

More money and more salaried jobs in the economy did not mean better conditions for everyone. During the last decade of the Porfiriato, economic downturns had quick and unsettling effects on the subsistence of the general population. The 1905 adoption of the gold standard caused price increases and made the Mexican economy, which had traditionally relied on silver exports, more vulnerable to global economic cycles, as was soon proved by the impact of the 1907 economic crisis on living conditions. The latter years of the Porfiriato saw a dramatic increase in the price of foodstuffs and in unemployment, caused by drought and reduced production. Thus, cash scarcities made economic slumps more difficult to endure.[8] After 1907, and particularly in 1913–16, when revolutionary turmoil hit with the greatest severity, currency and prices became a true obsession for the majority of Mexico City inhabitants. During those times, silver coins became scarce, military occupation and the campaigns around the Valley of Mexico caused further shortages, and authorities printed paper money with little concern for its immediate devaluation. A recovery began in the 1920s, but slowed down after 1926 and was interrupted by a new depression in 1929.[9] Hard times for the capital's population translated into a daily struggle to come up with cash.

Loans and pawning increased in times of crisis and often involved stolen objects as guarantee. Strongly rooted in a tradition of popular credit, pawn shops loaned customers amounts below the value of the objects pawned. Customers kept a ticket until they could pay the loan back plus interests and recover their possessions. The principal moneylender for the poor was the Monte de Piedad, a colonial charitable institution supervised by the city government, whose business soared during the late nineteenth century. Interest rates on loans guaranteed by property were at least 8 percent per month for amounts of less than one peso and 6 percent for larger amounts, plus a 5 percent fee. Attracted by the increasingly lucrative business during the Porfiriato, private pawn shops competed with the Monte de Piedad, although exacting higher interest rates. Authorities acknowledged the role of loans in the economy of the urban poor, and, from the times of famine in 1915 through the 1930s depression, tried to make loans more easily available. Credit between fifty cents and ten pesos, used to purchase food or lodging, was very common during this period.[10]

It is not surprising, then, that economic pressures had a clear impact on crime. The links between the economy and theft had been noticed by observers since the colonial period, and the inequalities and poverty that made theft possible in the first place had deep roots in Mexican society.[11] After battery, theft was the crime most frequently reported. Between 1895 and 1938, theft constituted 21 percent of all sentences and 18 percent of all arrests.[12] Tables 14 and 15 in the appendix provide the total number of those arrested, accused, and sentenced for theft between 1871 and 1938. The trend is one of growth during the last years of the Porfiriato and decline after the 1910–15 gap in the series. The average number of sentences per year and rates per 100,000 inhabitants (see appendix, table 16) fell sevenfold from 1895–1909 to 1927–38. Shorter-term variations in theft rates coincide with periods in which lower-class living standards were negatively affected by the economy, such as the increases after 1903, 1907, and 1928. Data for 1916–20 renders a lower average of sentences per year than the previous cycle, but evidence from qualitative sources suggests that in 1915 there was another peak in thefts, coinciding with hard times for the capital's population due to civil war. Theft trends declined afterwards. Although the national economy was still in shambles in the early 1920s, reconstruction was well under way in Mexico City. Depression hit again in the second half of the decade, contributing to an increase in committals after 1928.[13] The statistical data are reinforced by qualitative sources that point to periods of increase and stability in cases of theft.[14]

Caution is advisable: The correlations between economic indicators and theft (see appendix, table 17) render weak causal relationships. This is in part due to the scarce number of cases observed. Additionally, statistical series on theft are not fully reliable, for official attitudes and data collection methods varied throughout the period. The police, for example, arrested suspected "habitual thieves" during the sporadic campaigns undertaken by city authorities, although in many of those cases no offense had been committed to justify the arrest. According to police data, less than half of those arrested—in some years, just one-tenth—were formally indicted.[15]

The historically specific relationship between living conditions and crime in the late nineteenth and early twentieth centuries reveals its complexity in the statements of contemporary observers. Criminologists explained theft as the combination of misery and immorality among the poor. In 1900, Julio Guerrero suggested the reasons why petty thieves would stay in the cities, despite the periodic transportation of hundreds of them to the forced labor camps of Valle Nacional, Oaxaca. They lacked a steady job or enough income, wrote Guerrero, so they preferred to live from crime than to endure "the uncertainty of the great competition . . . and jobs that involve a great number of tasks and pay only what is necessary to satisfy their animal needs." Guerrero denounced the miserable living conditions of the lower classes, which, in his view, caused crime. Yet, he and other authors agreed that the urban poor lacked the morality needed to resist the temptations created by an urban environment where, thanks to progress, wealth was now publicly exhibited.[16] But rather than temptation, the category of *miseria* (extreme poverty) articulated the connection between theft, economic stress, and moral weakness. In 1882, the designers of the new penitentiary reasoned that miseria pushed "men of good nature to seek a means of subsistence through attempts against property" and drove women to prostitution. These impulses, added the report, were the same in the rest of the world, "the result of a general cause whose effects are sure and unavoidable."[17]

Aware of such explanations, theft suspects mentioned hunger to justify their crimes. In a letter to President Francisco I. Madero on January 19, 1913, Belem inmate Consuelo Hernández asked for a pardon on the grounds that need had forced her to steal. But rather than describing poverty as an "unavoidable" cause, her missive presented the multiple calculations linked with larceny:

> I, your servant, have been a widow for the last six years and have two children, and have always worked in different jobs, but for a year now I have had trouble finding work, and the day when I committed this shameful act I had no bread to give to my children, who had not eaten for the whole day. I was looking for a lady who had been recommended to me, but I had forgotten the street number, so I entered a house where I had been knocking at the door. I saw a reboso on the railing and I, who was only thinking about my children, had the thought of taking it. As soon as I had grabbed it, the maid came out and I was arrested.

The rest of the letter shows that, contrary to what elite writers thought, Consuelo did not think that miseria meant shamelessness:

> Believe me, sir, that I felt like dying, not for my sake but for my abandoned children. I have no family and they are orphaned. As you will understand, they took the whole thing as theft in an inhabited house and sentenced me to five years. I have been here for a year of bitterness, consumed in thinking about my little children, now living with strangers who helped me by taking them in but, as you know, the hanger-on soon grows tiresome.[18]

Consuelo was not granted a pardon, even though she was asking the president to redress a situation in which punishment had only worsened the problems that prompted her to break the law. After all, Consuelo made the deliberate choice of reaching for a shawl that she could easily pawn. She implied this when she acknowledged that, despite the confusion caused by hunger, she "had the *thought* of taking" the reboso while she was "*thinking* about my children" (my emphasis).

Like many other offenders, Consuelo conceived of theft as a form of economic exchange mediated by money—an aspect lost to the moralism of criminologists. Cashing in the stolen goods, even if they had small monetary value, made arrest less likely because it replaced the clothes, tools, and any small goods (which the legitimate owner could recognize and reclaim) with anonymous cash. Pawnshops were easily accessible in the city, and many businesses, including pulquerías, accepted goods as payment.[19]

Consuelo also knew that the possibility of prosecution was part of such exchanges. Judges could use the attempt to pawn objects as the only evidence of the crime. The police pressed suspects to explain the origin of the objects they were caught pawning, and a weak explanation was enough to justify a guilty verdict. Such was the case of Regino Valdéz, a minor, who in 1914 was arrested and sentenced to six months of imprisonment in a penal colony after he tried to pawn a gun. He confessed that he wanted to sell the gun but no pawnbroker or merchant would accept it because it was a type of gun used exclusively by the army. He sold it for two pesos to an old man who later denounced him.[20]

The cost of converting stolen property into cash increased according to the size of the booty. The story of two cows stolen in 1915 illustrates the great variation in the price of stolen properties. Daniel Ocaña, José Cruz, and Federico Rodríguez were accused of stealing the cows, valued at 1,800 pesos, from Ocaña's boss, José Díaz. According to Cruz, Rodríguez paid him and Ocaña 20 pesos to steal the cows. Rodríguez sold the cows to Rosario N. for 50 pesos. Rosario N. sold the cows to Enrique Sánchez, who insisted that he bought the cows, without knowing they had been stolen, for 275 pesos each.[21] Merchants knew the risks of buying goods of unknown origin, as a resourceful victim could always trace his or her property back and obtain a court order to have it returned or seized. Mechanic Adolfo Barrera told the judge in a theft case that he had not bought stolen tools from suspect José Mejía "because he has the precaution of never buying tools that are offered to him; when he needs tools he goes to the hardware store."[22] Any monetary transaction, in sum, could be linked to theft. Yet, as it became clear during the Revolution, access to cash was the key to everyday survival.

SCARCITY, DISORDER, AND COUNTERFEITING IN THE MID-1910S

Poverty, instability, and monetarization compounded and concentrated their effects on the urban lower classes during the years of the Revolution. The effects of the civil war began to be felt by the population of Mexico City in February 1913, during the ten days known as *Decena Trágica,* when an unknown number of civilians were killed amid a military rebellion against President Francisco I. Madero. After the 1914 defeat of Madero's successor, Victoriano Huerta, the city was handed over to Constitutionalist general Alvaro Obregón and was alternately controlled by Constitutionalists and the Revolutionary Convention's alliance of Zapatistas from Morelos and Villistas from the north. It was not until it was finally recovered by Venustiano Carranza's Constitutionalist armies in August 1915 that the municipal government began to return to its customary order.[23] Political labels soon lost their meaning for the urban poor, as they learned the high price of political instability. Hunger became a reality for anyone without savings or goods to pawn. Francisco Ramírez Plancarte vividly described how the upheaval

> caused great distress among the people, whose hunger became so extreme that, in the lower-class quarters, many people would faint, and many of the dispossessed would pick up fruit skins from the floor and eat them voraciously even though they were covered with dirt; others would dig with a stick in the piles of rubble around markets, looking for any leftovers from poultry, fruits, vegetables, or entrails, even rotten, to placate their hunger.[24]

The civil war was a threat coming from outside. Newspapers singled out the Zapatistas for creating communications problems south of the city by attacking trains and roads. When Obregón was approaching the capital from the north, in 1914, a letter signed by fifteen hundred residents asked that interim president Francisco Carvajal have the Federal army relinquish the city, because its presence would expose half a million people to "the horrors of a siege." The letter argued that the capital had suffered enough already without having to feed a fighting army or face popular revolt.[25] There was no siege, but the transitions between authorities forced city residents to sharpen their survival skills. When Carranza left for Veracruz in late 1914, abandoning the city to Zapata and Villa, people hurried to buy food and charcoal, even if they had to pawn their belongings to do so. They knew that new authorities meant more problems, particularly inflation. In late 1916, *El Universal* compared current prices of basic staples with 1912 prices: A load of corn had increased from 4 to 19 pesos; a kilo of sugar, from 8 to 40 cents; a kilo of beans, from 8 to 20 cents; salt, from 6 to 15 cents.[26] Prices, however, were only one aspect of the retail nightmare. According to *El Demócrata,* the weights were rigged, merchants demanded payment in advance or mistreated the clients, prices varied if you paid with bills or coins, and false currency was widespread.[27]

Monetary chaos was the greatest source of anxiety. Different authorities imposed different monetary units, creating confusion, inflation, and further scarcity. Despite each faction's decrees to force circulation of their currency and exclude the enemy's, city dwellers had to use whatever money was available. In June 1915, for example, José Rodríguez stole Pomposa González's purse, which contained the following items: "one Constitutionalist one-peso bill, three cartons of twenty cents, two of five cents, five silver pesos, fifty pesos in bills, one fifty-cent bill from Chihuahua, two quarters of a Michoacán lottery bill, and six five-cent copper coins."[28] Pomposa did not know which of these units would be accepted by merchants, as their relative value shifted daily according to political conditions. Currency itself became scarce because merchants and the better-off kept the "good" coins and bills that reached their hands, leaving the poor with money of questionable quality. Forced loans and seizures by the government further depleted the circulation of cash, particularly coins. As early as 1913, Huerta's government authorized banks to print fifty-cent bills, and encouraged stores and industries to use tokens.[29]

Another costly outcome of the civil war was the weakening of the city police. The Federal Army and the revolutionaries thought that control over the capital granted them the right to seize property and engage in a variety of excesses. This made it hard for the police, decimated by draft and desertion, to maintain order, especially as this often meant facing unruly soldiers. In 1914, the Carrancistas sacked the police armory and enrolled several gendarmes before abandoning the city to the Zapatistas, who in turn opened the doors of jails before leaving. Ramírez Plancarte attested that "the police were nonexistent; many gendarmes fell victim to robberies and revenges . . .

nobody tried to prosecute the crimes, and those who stayed in their job protecting order soon abandoned their posts."[30] While, for the Porfirian oligarchy, the irruption of revolutionaries in the capital meant the seizure of homes, cars, and much valuable property, for most inhabitants of the capital the new situation meant a generalized feeling of danger. The wrong look at a "Carranclán" or failure to buy him a drink or yield a tramway seat could easily provoke a shooting.[31]

The job of gendarmes became a dangerous one, mainly due to gratuitous attacks from the revolutionaries. Benjamín Pérez was at his punto in Arcos de Belem Avenue when a group of Constitutionalist soldiers (witnesses called them "yaquis," a feared indigenous group from northeastern Mexico) saw him and said "there's a *tecolote,* let's get rid of him." Shots were exchanged and Pérez was captured by the soldiers, who also caused damages and wounded witnesses at a restaurant. Pérez was summarily executed later by order of the military authority. In the few cases where a soldier was arrested for committing a common crime, even after the judicial system had been restored, the suspect could be released by military orders or the "Zapatista mob." Gendarmes were also attacked during the sacking of food stores.[32]

Weaker policing opened a space for the concerted action of workers and women, often through food riots. During the revolutionary years, street demonstrations were at first prompted by political events, but they soon became channels for protest or simply food distribution. Accounts of early gatherings suggest that the police never had full control over them. On May 24, 1911, for example, a crowd walked from the Chamber of Deputies to the National Palace, demanding Porfirio Díaz's resignation and shouting "Viva Madero!" When a member of the unpopular plainclothes Policía Reservada shot at the demonstrators, he was lynched on the spot. In the Zócalo, police fired again and things spun out of control. There were nine deaths and fifty-two wounded, and some stores were looted; Díaz resigned the following day. People took to the streets again in February 1913, when a military rebellion threatened President Madero, but the crowds were scattered by chaotic artillery barrages. Yet, under Huerta's regime, workers organized by the anarcho-syndicalist Casa del Obrero Mundial marched in Mexico's first May Day celebration. By 1915, authorities were powerless to prevent collective demands for food. Mobs ransacked stores and were brought to order only by military intervention.[33] Spontaneous food riots expressed popular hunger and resentment against merchants, but they were often difficult to distinguish from actions by revolutionary troops. In July 1915, for example, the Inspección General de Policía reported to the city council that a gang of "fifty armed men" broke into a cantina and stole 3,500 pesos worth of merchandise and jewels. A few days later, "a group of the lower classes" sacked 200 pesos worth of merchandise from another store, also on San Antonio Abad Avenue.[34] Although hunger might have been the cause of the latter attack, the impunity of the "armed men" of the former probably invited action. After all, nobody was free of blame. Despite the popular image (at least among historians) of humble Zapatistas asking for bread after their army entered the city, they were also accused of violent attacks against property.[35] A few cases triggered judicial action but, as judicial authorities and the police were reduced to powerlessness during those days, punishment was a matter of chance.

Things seemed to be upside down: those in power were committing crimes, judicial and political matters were not clearly separated, and women were commanding men. One 1915 theft file conveys the sense of disorder and danger brought about by the Revolution. On May 14, a group of soldiers led by a female officer whom they addressed as "coronel [*mi coronela*]" entered the apartment of Juana Ayala and her sons, in colonia Doctores, with a search order to look for weapons and ammunition in the house. The officer was not wearing a uniform but a blue skirt, a white blouse, and a white hat with three stars. She looked very young, her hair was cut short, and she had some scars on the left side of her neck. Someone at the vecindad had accused the Ayala family of being Carrancistas. Juana Ayala, the mother, replied "that neither her nor her sons are Carrancistas, that they are *carniceros* [butchers]." The soldiers found a box with 1,763 pesos in silver coins. When she found the silver coins, the coronela told Ayala "this is why money is not circulating, because you monopolize it." The soldiers also took a clock and other objects. Neighbors gathered around the door of the Ayalas, but they were dispersed by the coronela, who warned them that they would be shot if they did not go back to their homes. The officers forced Ayala to sign a receipt stating that 134 pesos in bills and coins had been seized, and then they took off in two cars.

Unlike most other similar operations, the search at the Ayala's home triggered a response by the police and judges. Several suspects were arrested and then released after they showed that the search had been ordered by military authorities. The judge then issued an arrest warrant against "a woman who claims to be coronela." When she was arrested, on July 9, she gave her name as Celia Hernández Salazar, seventeen years old and born in Cuernavaca. She declared that, even though she did not wear her insignia, she was in fact a colonel and a member of the staff (*estado mayor*) of General José Flores Alatorre. She denied all the charges, but several witnesses—some of whom said that she was a prostitute in a brothel of Cuauhtemotzín Street—recognized her and she was arraigned in Belem jail until a letter signed by Colonel Juan Flores ordered the judge to release her. Before the order could be obeyed, Zapatista troops leaving the city in late July freed her along with other prisoners.[36]

"Coronelas" such as Celia Hernández were not unheard of during the Revolution, particularly among the Zapatistas. Not all coronelas actually possessed a colonel's rank, but they did lead units of up to several hundred men.[37] Although some of them hid their sex, that was not the case with Celia. This, her youth, and the debatable "revolutionary" character to the search at Dr. Lavista Street explain the fact that she was arrested, albeit briefly. In the eyes of the Ayalas and their neighbors, Celia Hernández was a stranger in several senses: she represented the unassailable threat introduced by the Revolution into the smaller world of their community.

Encouraged by the ambiguity of the situation, civilian crowds targeted stores suspected of hiding food and owned by hated Spanish merchants. Such actions, defined by the law as crimes, were becoming quite acceptable. Some food riots dispersed without police intervention and even prompted the revolutionary government to allot five million pesos to buy grain. Other actions were defined as crimes, but even then judges were tolerant. On August 13, 1915, for example, Clementina Núñez, from Spain, told police that her store and cantina at the corner of Imprenta and Palomas streets had been robbed of four hundred pesos worth of bottles of cognac, sherry, and eggnog. The store had been robbed in recent days by the Zapatistas. This time, Núñez had caught fourteen-year-old Jesús García with some bottles in his hands. García explained that other neighbors were taking bottles from the store, and that he did it "to sell the bottles that he found because he is hungry and has to feed his mother." In November, citing a decree by Primer Jefe Venustiano Carranza, "which does away with the rituals that in the past obstructed the fair and prompt administration of justice," Judge Julio Montes de Oca declared García guilty but set him free at once. The judge set a low price to the bottles, which got lost in the police station, and mentioned the accused's need to feed his mother as a demonstration of "the difficult and anguishing situation in which, because of the recent political revolt, the poorest class of people live."[38]

Official reactions were less benign if, instead of simply asking for bread, crowds addressed the sensitive issue of currency. On July 1915, a group of women and children looted stores in La Merced, this time in reaction to general Pablo González's decree taking Villista bills out of circulation. Carrancista soldiers opened fire against the demonstrators, leaving several wounded.[39] In 1916, two general strikes demanded the payment of wages in a stable currency. They again met with prompt repression from Venustiano Carranza.[40]

Money, after all the anarchy, had become the most direct representation of political authority. Alfonso Taracena described an August 1915 play entitled "Su Majestad el Hambre" ("His Majesty Hunger"), where these beliefs were played out. Allegorical characters represented different aspects of economic trouble: a poorly dressed man portrayed a revolutionary bill, while an elegant lady was the National Bank note; they had to deal with *coyotes* (middlemen) who made exaggerated profits from exchange. Dialogues alternated with scenes in which "real" female domestic workers and male factory workers complained about the price and bad quality of food, and proceeded to plunder a market. "Vile monopolists," they claimed, were to blame for the situation. Another play in the Teatro Lírico made comedy out of monetary confusion: actors, ballerinas, and singers represented *revalidados altos y bajos* (high- and low-denomination validated bills), Villista and Carrancista bills, rubles, francs, and dollars.[41] A series of decrees published by Carranza in April 1916 vowed to put an end to anarchy by replacing the old notes with new "unfalsifiable" bills. The measure, which forced other currencies out of circulation, triggered further unrest and contributed to the unpopularity of Carranza and his minister of finance, Luis Cabrera.[42]

While bills danced, the poor had trouble finding bread. Who was to blame? Counterfeiters and looters proved that the line between criminal behavior and mere subsistence was a matter of perspective. While looting could be condoned, counterfeiting became the clearest criminal symptom of the impact of political instability. Due to the chronic shortage of money, forging coins and using tokens were common practices in Mexico City since the colonial period; but they became more noticeable during the last decade of the Porfiriato and proliferated during the days of revolutionary turmoil. Like food riots, counterfeiting expressed the diminished legitimacy of political authorities. Its specific ideological meaning, however, is less obvious. The practice was primarily an expedient for survival, and offenders never claimed the moral justification of demonstrators asking for bread. Nevertheless, merchants, the first victims of counterfeiting, denounced the crime and sought police action. They would bite the coins to test them and would reject those that failed the test.[43]

Their complaints at times prompted investigations by the Policía Reservada, but not always, since excessive scruples risked obstructing commerce altogether. In August 1915, for example, a woman selling tortillas in the streets refused to accept a twenty-cent *cartón*. The customer called a gendarme, who forced the *tortillera* to receive the token. Two agents of the Reservada intervened and decided that the token was indeed suspect. The gendarme fought the agents, declaring that he "was tired of working for this lousy [*pinche*] government"; a squabble ensued, and he was arrested.[44] The confrontation portrays two points of view about counterfeit money. In the streets, the concern of most people was to circulate the currency, whatever its source—thus the street policeman's decision to force the tortillera to take the token—for political authorities, represented by the plainclothes policemen, the kind of money circulating was a greater concern.

Counterfeiting carried harsh punishment. The 1871 Penal Code set prison terms from three to eight years and fines of up to 2,500 pesos for falsifying the national currency. The penalties applied if six or more coins were found in the suspect's possession. In December 1903, a reform that increased penalties for theft without violence also increased the penalties for counterfeiters. The sentence for falsifying paper bills issued by a bank was set at ten years, plus a fine of up to 3,000 pesos, and only three coins had to be found in the suspect's possession to punish him or her as a counterfeiter. Catholic newspaper *La Nación* noted in 1912, however, that continuing arrests only proved that "counterfeiters do not learn, despite the strong penalties which they receive."[45] During the Revolution, counterfeiters faced greater rigor from military authorities intent on forcing the circulation of their bills and ready to use capital punishment for exemplary purposes. In August 1915, Rafael Meza was executed for printing low-value bills. His son had unwittingly incriminated him, when he assured a store clerk that the bills he was using to pay for candy were good because his father had made them. *El Demócrata* justified the sentence, arguing that laws had to be harsher during wartime, and Meza was guilty of increasing the misery of the illiterate people.[46]

Supporters of strong punishment believed that the production of good-quality counterfeit money required criminal skills and organization. That seems to have been the case during the nineteenth century and most of the Porfiriato. In 1900, the Policía Reservada arrested several suspects who produced fake coins that, according to *El Imparcial,* circulated in great quantities around the city. The gang's workshop was located in Tepito, and it contained all the tools and materials required. Two women, also arrested, used the coins in provincial fairs and in the capital.[47] Skilled offenders did not let the Revolution interrupt their activities. Eduardo Carreón Suárez, sentenced in 1914 to five and one-half years for counterfeiting, had two previous convictions for the same offense. The police found a number of tools and materials in his house, although he claimed that he was only keeping them for a friend. In 1916, reported *El Universal,* plainclothes agents arrested gold currency counterfeiters of "true mastery."[48]

Economic crises and monetary anarchy, however, made counterfeiting more than an exclusively criminal trade. The ranks of skillful printers and coiners were joined by small-time forgers of coins and tokens, who used readily available tools and materials (see fig. 5).[49] According to the *Gaceta de Policía,* in 1906 counterfeiters were a heterogeneous crowd:

> Among the apprehended there are those who produce bad-quality coins in humble workshops, and those who use expensive machines to produce money of such perfection that it is difficult to distinguish it from the legal bills . . . there are those who dress badly and live in the dangerous barrios, and those who dress like dandies and mix with high society.[50]

Raids of lower-class neighborhoods to round up counterfeiters, sometimes called *cachuqueros,* became common news in the popular press. During the revolutionary years, monetary chaos placed counterfeiting within everyone's reach, as authorities issued tokens and bills that were poorly designed and easy to imitate.[51]

More than printing skills, counterfeiting required audacity. The risk lay in introducing coins or bills into circulation, particularly if the forged currency was of bad quality. Fake coins were thus used mostly in small transactions. Rosario Cerón and Maximino Salgado, sentenced to five years of prison in 1914, confessed that they produced twenty-cent coins. Every day,

5. Counterfeiters. Criminals with a bag of coins in a home, ca. 1925–30. Source: Fototeca Nacional, Fondo Casasola, 74987. © INAH.

they would spend four to five pesos worth of these coins. A common stratagem was to pay for a product with good currency, receive the change and substitute one of the coins with a forged one. The offender would then act as a victim and demand that the bad coin be exchanged for a valid one. In most cases, however, the accused simply tried to pay for basic products with forged coins. Catalina Ayala was arrested in 1913 for using a fake fifty-cent coin to pay for bread, coffee, and sugar from a small store in Nonoalco Avenue. The owner of the store called the police and a judge sentenced Ayala to two years and six months in prison. Ayala and other accused invoked their poverty and ignorance about money to explain their fault. Paula Iglesias declared that she had paid for clothes in La Merced with two fifty-cent false coins out "of her ignorance, because she does not know money perfectly."[52] Authorities rarely believed these claims. They are meaningful, however, as they refer to the havoc wreaked by monetarization on the urban poor's economy of survival.

The brief and intense events of 1915 left their mark on the historical experience of Mexico City. They gave theft an ideological significance that went beyond that historical moment. Public opinion during those days became more receptive toward theft as a product of inequality and ignorance. These explanations had an impact on judges' decisions, as in Jesús García's trial. In giving García a short sentence, the judge echoed the feelings expressed in food riots, placing some of the blame for crime on *abarroteros* (small store owners) who caused hunger.[53] But such political construal of theft risks overlooking the predatory nature of the offense. Statistics of criminality were not compiled between 1911 and 1916, but it is clear that thieves continued to be prosecuted. In October 1914, police stations handed over more than two thousand complaints to judicial authorities. Many cases were never brought to court, as administrative and judicial functions were weak vis-à-vis revolutionary commanders in control of the city. Nevertheless, officers made a policy of punishing petty thieves with exemplary rigor, just as they did counterfeiters.[54]

THEFT AND URBAN COMMUNITIES

A more balanced image of social reactions to theft emerges when we turn to burglary, a very common occurrence but one often ignored by political authorities. Rather than the law, it was the collective reaction of neighbors that protected lower-class victims from burglary. Although understandable as a product of "the difficult and anguishing situation" of the poor, larceny was not a welcome occurrence in the life of the urban population. Thieves took advantage of the ambivalent divisions between private and collective spaces in vecindades, and challenged the ties of trust that united families and communities. Approximately half of the cases of theft in the database involve victims and offenders who resided close to each other or were related by kin, friendship, or work.[55]

A 1909 case reveals the complex links that often united victims and offenders. In January 13, eight-year-old Ricardo García was caught by neighbors and arrested when trying to break into the house of a Chinese resident of Delicias Street. Questioned by authorities, Ricardo produced a number of contradictory statements about himself: that his name was not García but Vázquez and that, contrary to what he first told the police, "he has no address, because he sleeps wherever he finds an opportunity . . . that he has no trade nor father, only his mother, but she does not have an address either, because she sleeps in the restaurant where she works as a maid." The ensuing testimonies showed that Ricardo was not so isolated from his community.

He lived with some relatives in a vecindad on the same Delicias Street. The previous year Ricardo and other boys had stolen thirty pesos and a clock from neighbor Rafaela Romero's house. Ricardo returned the money, and Romero decided not to call the police because the boys' families asked her not to and promised to give Ricardo "a good whipping." Ricardo and other children formed a gang that used to meet every day to engage in burglaries, steal money, or pawn the products of their thefts and divide the profit. The victims were usually their neighbors and relatives. This time all the suspects were discharged except for Ricardo, who was ordered by the governor of the Federal District to be interned for six years in a correctional school.[56]

The harsh treatment met by Ricardo was the consequence of the Delicias Street vecindad's inability to support household hierarchies. Young offenders in this and other cases of theft withheld the respect owed to their elders. They also linked play and other social activities with a remarkable ability to acquire and spend money. Cash obtained from pawning stolen goods bought tramway tickets, pulque, or nice clothes.[57] Thieves tended to be younger than other offenders. The average age of the accused in the cases of theft examined was 25, while the average age for those accused of battery and homicide was 28 and 31 respectively. In contrast, the victims of theft were generally older, with an average age of 32.[58] The average age of theft suspects would probably decrease even further if cases never brought to court were considered. Juvenile delinquency worried government officials, and it became one of the foci of social policies after the Revolution. While Ricardo faced the usual harshness of Porfirian policies against thieves, post-revolutionary juvenile offenders benefited from well-meaning but largely ineffective welfare and educational institutions.[59]

Thieves like Ricardo also betrayed the confidence of their neighbors by waiting for victims to leave their property unsecured. Many thefts took place in vecindades where neighbors shared a common space in the building's patio and spent many hours together. Since relations at the vecindad level were less hierarchical than those between family members, thefts prompted public disputes in which each party's reputation was at stake. *El Universal* reported that María Guadalupe Rivera found her best clothes missing from the clothesline where they had been drying. She went to the room of her neighbor Antonia Aguilar and asked about the clothes, thinking it was a prank. But Aguilar was angered by her suggestion and insulted Aguilar. The victim declared that she saw the clothes in a corner of Aguilar's room and picked them up; she then went to the police and accused Aguilar.[60] Given the fact that thieves took advantage of trust to gain access to the homes of neighbors and relatives, the moral of the tale seemed clear for victims and witnesses: trust no one.

But they had to. Communities did not prevent thefts by severing ties with the suspects or by locking up their property. When victims, their neighbors, and relatives caught the offenders, they tried to deal with the problem without calling the police, because official intervention could only increase the distance between them and suspects. Ricardo and his friends had committed a number of offenses that were punished simply with "a good whipping." In order to avoid thefts and the ensuing confrontations, people made a common cause in the protection of their neighbors' property.

At the first line of defense, vecindad concierges played an important role in the prevention of theft. *Porteras* (usually women) lived at the place and witnessed the comings and goings of neighbors, since their rooms were usually placed at the entrance of the building.[61] Whenever the victim was not present, the concierge would call the police and even detain the suspect. When María Guadalupe Hernández returned to her house in May 1915, she found that the lock of her room had been broken, "but that the concierge had already sent the ratero to the police station, where Hernández found her belongings." Inés Camacho, the portera in this case, was watering the street in front of the tenement when she saw suspect Antonio Pérez, a stranger to her, enter and shortly afterward leave with a suspicious bundle. Camacho went into the vecindad, where she found a door open. She followed Pérez and asked for help from the police. Protecting the vecindad was not only a matter of solidarity. Since proximity created suspicion, the concierge had to take action against theft at her building, lest she became the first suspect. Carlos M. Tello accused his concierge of theft, even though he did not really know who had broken into his house and stolen his jewels. The accused, Policarpo Lozada, declared that he saw two suspects entering the building and noticed that Tello's door had been forced, but he did not notify the police.[62] His failure to act was interpreted as evidence of complicity.

Everyone knew that quick reaction was necessary when a theft had been committed. By questioning witnesses and cornering suspects, lower-class victims established face-to-face negotiations with the goal of recovering the stolen property before anyone had to go to jail. Victim Sara Prado, for example, declared that she only wanted suspect María Vargas to return the purse she had taken and that she was not interested in having her punished. No one benefited from the incarceration of offenders, since experience indicated that the stolen property would be more difficult to recover once the police and courts became involved. Manuel Martínez saw Manuel Torres in a pulquería wearing the sarape that had just been stolen from Martínez's house along with a sewing machine. Before bringing the suspect to the police station, Martínez "begged him to confess where he had put the sewing machine, but the suspect refused."[63] Negotiations could even take place even after the police were summoned. Teodora Rodríguez offered to give some money to her accusers at the police station. A police officer escorted her to her house, but she could not find her husband nor produce the money, so she was officially arrested and later found guilty. Violence was not a common part of these negotiations, although it was always a latent possibility. As mentioned in chapter 4, battery could be the result of an unresolved dispute about property.[64] Since violence could attract police attention, however, it was a counterproductive way to deal with theft. By contrast, if the gendarme on the nearest corner agreed to intervene, as in the case of Teodora Rodríguez, he could make a credible threat of incarceration, prompting the suspect to confess and, more importantly, to surrender the stolen objects.

Negotiations gave considerable latitude for victims to decide between punishment or restitution. When Dimas Barba accused portera Eulalia Pérez of stealing a bundle of his wife's clothes, she offered to lead the police to another suspect, José Vázquez. Pérez told the judge that Vázquez was guilty because he had signed a paper promising to pay the victim for the cost of the stolen clothes. The file indeed contains a paper signed by one Raymundo Vázquez in which he promises to pay the victim fifty pesos if the charges against José Vázquez were dropped. The suspect's proposal had to satisfy the victim; otherwise, it could be used as evidence of the accused's guilt. María de la Luz Ruiz did not accept money from José Ramos in exchange for the clothes that had been stolen from her house. Ramos, who lived in the same building, blamed another man he had invited to his room that night; fearing jail, he begged Ruiz to drop the charges, which she did not. She doubted that he would keep his word, since she had known him for only three days and, she added, he was "effeminate."[65] For Ramos and many other suspects, the threat of incarceration was a good reason to negotiate with their accusers. The difference between the suspects' fate in these two cases illustrates the role of communities in defining the possibility of negotiation. Dimas Barba knew José Vázquez, so he accepted the promise to pay. On the other hand, María de la Luz Ruiz did not trust José Ramos and did not lose much by having him arrested.[66]

Theft emerged in a city of suspects, where privacy, property, and the hierarchies of families and communities were flexible and open to negotiation. Porteras and neighbors sought to protect the people they knew from strangers; they suspected everyone, but they also wanted to preserve trust within the vecindad. Their reactions explain why petty larceny was reported relatively less frequently than other crimes, such as battery and homicide. In the latter offenses, the police did not wait for the victim to press charges, whereas in cases of theft police usually acted only at the victim's request.[67] Assuming, as the evidence strongly suggests, that the urban poor dealt with most occurrences of larceny without official intervention, it is possible to argue that the participation of victims and their communities played a larger role than official punishment and the police in the prevention and resolution of the problem of theft.

THEFT AT THE WORKPLACE

A similar readiness to deal directly with suspects occurred in another significant setting for larceny. Theft at the workplace, and often just the fear of it, played a key role in the cultural construction of class relations in modern Mexico City. It was in stores, workshops, restaurants, and domestic service where embezzlement "built a bridge," to use Macedo's phrase, between classes. Employers and supervisors took investigation and punishment into their own hands, because they doubted all workers. Always the object of suspicion, workers risked little by supplementing their income with borrowings from work.

Taking tools or raw materials home had been traditional practices at the workplace since the colonial period, and both workers and bosses avoided dealing with them as crimes. In some industries, these "loans" were informally accepted as a way to complement workers' wages. By the twentieth century, however, bosses' attitudes had begun to shift toward a strict criminalization of these practices, even if they occurred in small shops. Article 384 of the 1871 Penal Code specifically addressed theft at the workplace, setting a sentence of two years, regardless of the value of the stolen object, when "the theft is committed by an employee or a domestic worker against the master [*el amo*] or his family," and "when it is committed by operators, artisans, apprentices, or students, in the home, workshop or school in which they normally work or study."[68] The code's description suggests that these fears did not express the distance that elites tried to build between classes, but the close relationships between owners, managers, and laborers in places where work often mixed with private life.

The reference to "the master or his family" in article 384 suggests that the most common source of mistrust was not found in factories or workshops, but at the home of "the master," where privacy and work mixed in the absence of explicit contractual relations. Many workers slept at their workplace, thus creating suspicious circumstances. María Torres was a tortilla maker for María Trinidad Franco. After fifteen days of work, Torres asked Franco to allow her to sleep at the store "because she did not have a place to sleep." Two weeks later, a scale and some clothes were stolen from the place, and Franco accused Torres.[69] The convergence of housing and work was the defining feature of the relationships between employers and domestic workers—most of them female. Although a salary was usually agreed upon between the *amo* or *ama* and the maid, the relationship was also an extension of household hierarchies, and wages included housing, food, and clothing for the worker and sometimes for her children too. According to Julio Guerrero, servants were "incorporated into the house where they serve, being subject to the unconditional orders of their masters at any time they are needed."[70] Closeness did not prevent mistrust. If employers believed that their "unconditional orders" had been disregarded, they did not hesitate to call the police. When a one-hundred-peso bill left on a table by Rosa Vázquez's boss was missing, all workers in the house were searched and taken to the police station. The police interrogated and threatened the suspects, including ten-year-old Mariana Espinosa, Vázquez's daughter, and her nine-year-old brother, Felipe, until Mariana confessed and she and her mother were arrested.[71]

The intervention of the police in master-servant relations became official in the 1879 Reglamento de Criados Domésticos (Regulation for Domestic Employees) issued by the Governor of the Federal District. Like prostitutes in their 1873 regulation, domestic servants (including waiters, coach and cart drivers, launderers, and the employees of billiards, inns, ice cream parlors, public baths, and pulquerías) had to register with the Inspección

General de Policía where they received a booklet. At the conclusion of his or her work with a "master," the employer was to return the booklet to the worker, with the annotations that the latter "deemed fair." Such annotations had to be registered with the police and checked by future employers. The 1879 regulation presumed that domestic workers were suspects: lack of annotations after a job "will justify the presumption that the servant has not maintained good behavior"; the registered servant who remained jobless for a month "will be considered and treated as a vagrant." The connection between domestic work and embezzlement was tersely expressed in article 12, which established that "all domestic thefts" had to be reported to the Inspección General de Policía, which would investigate and record the event in the registry—although these records were not mentioned in the trials examined.[72]

Domestic workers lived under permanent suspicion, individually and as a group. Newspapers warned their readers that maids would wait until their bosses left the house to steal clothes or money, or to inform burglars about such an opportunity. In his treatise on prostitution in México, Luis Lara y Pardo wrote that domestic workers were always sought after in Mexico, even if they were lazy, sick, or thievish. He portrayed theft as an implicit part of the working arrangements for a maid, as she "always . . . enjoys lodging and a salary of approximately eight pesos a month, without considering the small amounts that she fraudulently appropriates." Lara y Pardo concluded that maids were prone to prostitution, since "domestic work is one kind, albeit less clear, of degeneration."[73] Guerrero characterized female domestic workers by the somatic signs of their degeneracy ("prognathism . . . deformed ears, or any other stigma") and their "very relaxed morality," both sexually and in their labor relations with employers. Domestic workers not only stole from the homes where they worked, wrote Guerrero, but they also revealed to their friends the intimate lives of their bosses. The descriptions of Lara y Pardo and Guerrero were less explicit, however, regarding male bosses' expectations about their female servants' sexual favors.[74]

Concerns about the integrity of domestic workers justified precautions such as asking candidates for a letter of recommendation. Newspaper adds seeking domestic workers usually required these references, but workers could also be hired without such letters if they could produce another maid's verbal recommendation. These precautions did not, of course, prevent cases such as that of Luz Ramírez, who managed to earn the complete trust of her employers and then ran away with most of the family's clothes.[75] But theft by domestic workers was rarely the clearly defined crime conceived of by the law. A host of relationships and arrangements were part of the transactions between bosses and domestic workers. According to Margarita Tinoco, her employer, Carlota Alpuchi, had accused her of theft because Alpuchi did not want to pay for the nine days Tinoco had worked at her house. Alpuchi responded that she suspected Tinoco because she did not complain when Alpuchi discounted from her wages some money that was missing from the house. Tinoco explained that she had accepted her employer's decision to deduct 2.70 pesos from the 2.90 pesos owed to her for nine days of work "to avoid trouble," and she was indeed released for lack of evidence.[76] Suspects explained their acts as responses to employers' violation of their agreements—although their claims were not always accepted by judges. Judicial intervention derived also from challenges to the authority of the alleged victim, as in Uriel González's case against María Rueda. González accused Rueda of stealing money from his bedroom at the house of General Manuel Arenas, where he lived and she worked. But Rueda claimed that she was innocent and accused González of mistreating her and trying to get her fired by her real boss, General Arenas. González responded that Rueda was his employee, too, because he gave money for the house's expenses. In other words, Rueda argued that she was under the protection of General Arenas, while González sought the intervention of the police and the judge not only to recover the money, but also his authority.[77]

Suspicion and embezzlement were not limited to "the master's" household. Theft, along with alcoholism and laziness, was a recurring theme in elite descriptions of Mexican workers in general. Even the liberal *Diario del Hogar* admonished the Mexican worker that if he wanted "to improve his class status . . . he needs to be honest, formal, deserving of respect."[78] Store clerks or factory workers were usually accused of taking merchandise or materials home. Employees at restaurants could be accused of simply keeping the money made during the day. Mistrust was, according to observers, the dominant note of work relations. Julio Guerrero described the class of salaried industrial workers as increasingly disciplined, thanks to the time they spent in workshops. Nevertheless, he noted, they were still prone to abandon the virtues of honesty and tidiness so painstakingly taught to them:

"A great deal of vigilance is needed from supervisors to prevent *raterismo* among them; there are special employees that search their clothes at the end of the work day."[79]

Employers saw the aggressive prosecution of suspected thieves as part of their job. Supported by the rigor of article 384 of the penal code, bosses extended their authority into the jurisdiction of the police and the courts by interrogating, threatening, and punishing suspects. When the police were called, it was always to give additional muscle to boss rule. This biased intervention of officials in labor disputes prompted criticisms from jurists. In July 1919, a correctional judge wrote to the governor of the Federal District about the "excessive penalties" imposed on workers because of their misguided use of raw materials. "The factories of the Federal District, particularly the textile mills," wrote the judge, "complain every day about thefts committed by their workers, consisting of pieces of cloth or threads whose value seldom exceeds one peso. . . . These small *raterías* are prompted by ignorance rather than criminal intent . . . as offenders ignore the severity of the penalties they face."[80]

The judge proposed that signs be posted informing workers about the provisions of the penal code. His opinion, however, did not challenge the traditional extrajudicial authority of labor supervisors.

The paradoxes of this use of the criminal law as part of labor relations did not escape the perception of workers. Organized workers resented being defined as a vice-ridden class. On the contrary, their claims for respect as a class stressed their differences from criminals.[81] In addition, it was clear to many accused workers that other illegalities were overlooked if they benefited employers. The difference (which made workers criminals) was that supervisors were able to act on the basis of suspicion, while judicial action against other illegal practices, such as fraud or violation of agreements by employers, was comparatively rare.

This paradox was particularly clear in workplaces like the municipal slaughterhouse (*rastro*), where the aggressive vigilance of employers coexisted with multiple irregularities in the retail sale and distribution of meat. Public complaints about official corruption, traders' speculation, and the stealing of by products—such as the blood traditionally sold to the poor at low prices—were common. In 1911, cart drivers bringing stock to the rastro created a near-riot, arguing that corrupt inspectors overlooked official regulations to benefit large companies and made no effort to prevent increasing violence and an "invasion of a plague of rateros."[82] In contrast, a 1915 case of theft at the slaughterhouse reveals how supervisors used the police to harass suspect workers. On June 10, Antonio Montiel, in charge of security at the slaughterhouse, brought night watchman Vicente Nieto to the police station, accusing him of stealing a belt used by the rastro's machinery. Two days later, Montiel told the judge that he had accused Nieto because, at the time of the theft, he was drunk and had abandoned his place of work to shoot dice. Montiel acknowledged, however, that he had no indication that Nieto had actually committed the crime, and the charges were dropped. On July 5, Montiel now presented Joaquín Mireles, accusing him of the same theft. Montiel claimed to have found Mireles selling the stolen belt at a used hardware booth in the Tepito market. Mireles explained that he had worked at the rastro for four years, but because of the decrease in the number of animals slaughtered he had to look for another job. Even though he did not confess to the theft, Mireles offered to pay Montiel for the cost of the belt, in order to avoid arrest. The fact that Montiel did not pursue his accusation against Mireles may suggest that the proposal was accepted.[83] When suspects offered to pay for the stolen property, they implied that theft was part of a negotiation aimed at improving their share of the wages exchanged for labor.

From the point of view of workers, the "loans" interpreted by the boss as theft were not a crime, but a way to redress an unfair relation or simply to complement wage income. Eduardo Tamayo, a painter, accused his employee Marciano Chávez of stealing 4.5 pesos worth of brushes and paint. Tamayo declared that Chávez committed the theft because he had been fired for being drunk at work. The accused countered that Tamayo refused to pay the wages he had earned. Chávez was acquitted, but not until four months after his arrest.[84] His claims of innocence might have convinced the judge, but Chávez's imprisonment only reinforced Tamayo's authority, who successfully defined as theft what, in the eyes of his employee, was merely a wage dispute. From the workers' perspective, unpaid or underpaid work could also be construed as a violation of reciprocal trust. In such context, taking raw materials or tools home was not really a crime. Since suspicion was always against them and instability characterized work in Mexico City, workers had little incentive to desist.[85]

CONCLUSIONS

Theft resembled other economic exchanges, but it faced the adverse reactions of members of all classes. Despite elite notions about the intrinsic criminality of the Mexican lower classes, portrayed by Ethel Tweedie, the fact remains that theft was contained by social disapproval, largely stemming from the same groups accused by elites of being criminal. This explains why only a relative minority of the urban poor resorted to theft during periods of scarcity and unemployment. Collective reactions against practices such as devaluation and price fixing also expressed city dwellers' interpretation of the causes of their penury and were not universally defined as crimes. Yet, theft articulated the conflictive nature of capitalist expansion. Like violent crime and the crowd actions studied by E. P. Thompson, larceny was not a meaningless, "spasmodic" behavior, but reflected the complexities of modern urban societies.[86]

Was capitalist modernization the cause of theft in modern Mexico City? The rise in theft—or at least increased anxiety about it—was encouraged by the growing importance of money in labor relations and the everyday survival of poor households and by increased mobility between residences, jobs, and social networks. For many people, modernization meant the disruption of allegiances and the loss of traditional structures of patriarchal control, but it also meant more opportunities to exchange goods and labor for money. Yet, theft was not new in Mexico, and neither were employers' aggressive reactions against suspects at the workplace, or communities' attempts to establish negotiations between victims and offenders.

Contemporary interpretations of punishment in capitalist societies argue that the development of the modern penitentiary was the result of elites' desire for a disciplined working class.[87] The case of Mexico City, however, suggests the need to examine punishment of specific crimes. Counterfeiting, increasingly practiced and punished during the civil war, demonstrated how the state's authority to define practices against property could be widely contested. In a larger context, increasing punishment of counterfeiting also reveals a broader project by the state to undermine customary, if illegal, practices. Theft at the workplace had two meanings in this context: it gave employers a rationale to maintain their extrajudicial authority and to articulate labor disputes as crimes, and it gave workers an informal way to redress labor relations they perceived as unfair. From an elite perspective, the goal of control at the workplace was not the creation of a new, clean, reliable, and obedient class of workers so much as the preemptive vigilance and exemplary punishment of an otherwise unredeemable working class.[88] What was unique in the early twentieth century was the criminalization of petty theft at the workplace, and the consequent elite construction of the urban poor as a class of potential thieves, a subject to which we now turn.

III

THE CONSEQUENCES

Punishment is supposed to follow crime. Yet, the literature on both topics in Mexico has stressed a juridical perspective, and even historical accounts tend to focus on policing and penitentiary institutions. The previous chapters have shown how criminal practices and public policies shaped one another. In order to restore the proper conceptual sequence between crime and punishment, the following pages will continue to underline the interactions between discourses (criminological, legal, and political) and practices (criminal, police, and penitentiary), but will trace changes back to the latter years of the nineteenth century and up to the period of legal reforms concluded by the elimination of jury trials in 1929 and the abrogation of the 1871 Penal Code.

The focus on punishment, however, introduces a problem that had been absent from the preceding discussion, namely, the construction of collective and individual identities through the actions of penal institutions. *Rateros,* examined in chapter 7, were the product of criminological explanations of and police strategies against urban theft. Although elite descriptions and arrest campaigns were in fact directed at the urban poor in general, an identifiable group did emerge from the lower classes: professional, "modern" criminals. Chapter 8 examines how penitentiary practices shaped the identity of prisoners as a group, and how they acquired a political voice when conditions made it possible.

While the introduction to part 2 described the profile of suspects based on statistical data, such a method is not possible here. The commission of crime provides a reasonably clear criterion with which to identify a group, but the impact of imprisonment on identity went beyond the economic and cultural factors that made transgression possible in the first place. The identity of rateros was constructed out of committal, true, but also out of institutional interventions. The meaning of punishment in early-twentieth-century Mexico City is, to put it simply, the creation, through violence and isolation, of the social differences between "criminals" and "normal" citizens—differences which criminologists considered natural.

7

The Invention of *Rateros*

In his book *Las colonias de rateros,* published in 1895, Antonio Medina y Ormaechea argued that thieves disrupted "modern society" by "introducing fear inside homes, disturbing peace in the streets, planting mistrust among social classes, and undermining the authority of the government." Medina y Ormaechea proposed that thieves, whom he called *rateros,* be banished from the cities and sent to forced labor colonies.[1] Other opinions were even stronger. In 1897, both Miguel Macedo and the editors of *El Imparcial* recommended the flogging of thieves.[2] Their advice did not fall on deaf ears. In early-twentieth-century Mexico City, the state supported by the dominant classes took a radical stance toward the problem of theft: they adopted Medina y Ormaechea's method and preserved the time-honored prejudices upheld by Macedo and *El Imparcial.*

The ideas of these influential writers formed the basis for one of the largest experiments in social reform undertaken in the first decades of the century. Policemen and the press defined rateros as a social group of thieves. Positivist criminology lent scientific authority to these ideas by arguing that criminals were a particular kind of human being. Finally, legislators reformed the criminal code and established transportation to penal colonies as an instrument to rid the city of rateros—as if they were foreign invaders, or an exotic type of epidemic disease. In the perspective of all of these groups, punishment became the weapon to fulfill the goals of progress and civilization in Mexico City.

The war against rateros was not free of tensions, however. In the first place, the crackdown against thieves imposed on many innocents the consequences of police suspicion. Some political authorities and lawyers criticized these strategies as neglecting due judicial process. More importantly, policies against thieves contradicted the ways in which city dwellers dealt with theft in their homes or at the workplace. Those policies increased the role of the police and the judiciary in mediating disputes that had traditionally remained in the realm of households or neighborhoods. The result was a self-fulfilling prophecy in which the stigmatizing punishment of petty thieves combined with the increasing use of guns to create a modern kind of professional urban criminal. Although few in number, these criminals became the focus of public fears about crime and police corruption.

DEFINING THE TRADE OF THIEVES

In order to systematically eradicate rateros, turn-of-the-century Mexican criminologists had to construct them as a collectivity—even though, as the previous chapter shows, theft was the result of individual decisions. The Porfirian discourse about crime provided a general explanation beyond the economic context of theft. Criminologists, officials, and journalists equated petty thieves with rateros: a clearly defined social group, identifiable by its criminal skills and its presence in certain spaces of the city. This was all the more convincing as it reconciled scientific knowledge, public policies, and class prejudice. Unlike other notions from criminology, the category of ratero evoked the experience and vocabulary of city dwellers. The term had long been part of the common Spanish language to reference petty thieves. *Ratero* connoted moral lowliness and was often related to the nouns *rata* or *ratón* (rat, mouse) and the adjective *rastrero* (crawling, but also vile, despicable).[3] People used the word *ratero* to point at strangers in the immediate context of theft, as a synonym of *ladrón*. The word simply stated a fact based on immediate evidence: "He is a ratero because he is fleeing with my belongings."[4]

Criminological definitions of rateros oscillated between biological explanations and empirical observations. Scientists and journalists sought to demonstrate the collective identity of rateros by referring to the genetic origins of their "decadence." Trinidad Sánchez Santos listed rateros among the kinds of degenerated offspring of alcoholic parents. The press referred to them as "rats" who arrived in "plagues," "waves," or "invasions."[5] Julio Guerrero called *raterismo* an "endemic" phenomenon in the capital.[6] Most frequently, however, writers identified and discussed them based on direct observations of life in the streets of the capital. In *Las colonias de rateros,* Medina y Ormaechea defined *rateros* as those thieves who stole less than one thousand pesos and did not use violence. He stressed the poverty and lack of social ties that prompted their crimes:

> Those little tricksters, those untidy women, those shirtless men [*descamisados*] who wander the city streets until they find the most favorable opportunity to dispossess pedestrians of any objects they might be carrying, those burglars . . . are almost all minors, have no family ties, education, or work.[7]

Medina y Ormaechea's description was precise in contrast with others that liberally applied the label to any lower-class suspect in the streets. *El Universal* wrote in 1916 that, using the "pretext" of economic difficulties, "the lazy one becomes a ratero."[8] That winter, the newspaper printed on its front page pictures of alleged rateros, including several beggars and a destitute mother with her children. The text warned that many beggars and peddlers were in reality rateros and swindlers, and should be removed from the streets.[9]

These descriptions established a relationship between the lack of social attachments and the proliferation of rateros, thus implying that the "plague" was a consequence of recent migration to the capital. Rateros were thus an urban phenomenon, a group that naturally thrived in the cities but was not born there. They were intruders, "the rubbish from other cities," who came to the capital to profit from anonymity.[10] According to *El Imparcial,* while the "non-ratero men" were willing to emigrate to places with a hot climate to get jobs and feed their families, rateros tried to stay in places with nice weather and avoid work.[11]

Observers located rateros in certain parts of the city traditionally regarded as areas of danger and intense commerce. The barrio of Tepito and the nearby Lagunilla market were the most notorious among these places. The Baratillo market was known as the "thieves' market," where stolen and second-hand goods were commonly bought and sold. An 1895 guide of the city warned visitors about La Merced market, which "is famous for the number of rateros who work there."[12] The experience of city dwellers supported these impressions. In October 1925, several individuals robbed José Sorribas, taking his hat and money. The following day, Sorribas told the police, he went to Tepito to buy a new hat, and he saw one of his attackers, Rafael Téllez, in the gardens where "many vagrants lie in the morning to take the sun." For Sorribas, as for many other victims, rateros belonged to the world of vagrants and criminals of certain areas of the capital.[13] These perceptions of rateros as a collectivity had an echo in the Mexican derivations of the word *ratero,* which included *raterismo* or the adjective *rateril* to refer to the group or trade of thieves.[14]

Criminological and popular notions concurred in the notion that raterismo was the trade that specialized in stealing. Rateros were the men skilled at picking pockets or breaking into homes, and then evading the action of the law. The daily press talked about rateros in terms that stressed their coordination and unified techniques. In 1897, liberal *El Hijo del Ahuizote* announced that "rateros not only pick pockets, but they also attack their victims with knifes, and can even slap policemen."[15] In 1923, according to *El Universal,* police repression had momentarily interrupted the activities of thieves, but now they "have started again their despicable activities," after the truce gave them an opportunity to "recover their strength."[16] According to these descriptions, evasiveness characterized the trade. Rateros could pass as "decent" citizens and fool the unaware, and they could also avoid punishment by fabricating lies and hiding their identity. Education was thought to be part of the trade: in 1918, Francisco Bárcenas was sent to the Islas Marías because, according to prosecutors, he was a "teacher of minor rateros in La Merced."[17] In 1929, *Excélsior* reported that the police had discovered "a true thieves' school" and arrested students and professors. The report described the school as having classrooms, complete regulations, and even a graduation ceremony. Graduates entered a gang of rateros working in coordination with the school, although applicants could be admitted to the gang simply by proving that they were *rateros conocidos* (well-known thieves).[18] *Excélsior*'s report is not supported by additional evidence about such a school, but the belief in the existence of a close-knit community of thieves did reach a wider sector of public opinion than, for example, the ideas about criminals as a primitive kind of human being. Even if upper-class readers could identify rateros with the poor in general, the ideas about raterismo as a trade were widely shared. As noted previously, neighbors and concierges saw among their duties the protection of their neighbors' property from intruders. In a city marked by clear, if unstable, social divisions, the category of *ratero* offered people a useful way to talk about those strangers.

Unlike popular reactions against thieves, that of jurists and scientists relied solely on punishment. For influential writers and officials of the Porfiriato, the existing laws were not satisfactory because they punished crimes, not criminals. The 1871 Penal Code defined theft according to the classical tenets of criminal law, by centering on the action to be punished rather than on the person who committed the crime. Theft (*robo*) was "the appropriation of a movable object without right or without the consent of its legitimate owner."[19] Theft was divided into "theft without violence" and "theft with violence against persons." The former received sentences ranging from three days to five years, according to the value of the stolen property and the circumstances of the crime. Punishment for the latter could result in up to twelve years' imprisonment or capital punishment in the case of the accused's participation in a highway robbery involving rape or homicide. Yet, experts blamed the repeated "crime waves" on the leniency and loopholes of the criminal code, and even the Ministry of Justice concluded that longer sentences were not enough to deter thieves. Implicit in these criticisms was the idea that dealing with rateros required special forms of punishment, even if such punishments violated the code's premise that only individual actions could be punished, and that all citizens were equal before the law.[20]

Observers of the penal system knew that the establishment of the San Lázaro penitentiary did not solve the problem of rateros, because the building housed less than seven hundred male inmates who had received sentences of more than three years or been deemed by authorities as "incorrigibles of bad behavior." Inspired by modern penal ideas, the new prison was not intended to inflict the humiliating and cruel punishment rateros deserved.[21] Raterismo demanded a large-scale solution without the enormous expense and delays involved in the construction of a new penitentiary.

Several reforms during the Porfirian period adapted the legal framework to the concern about the collective threat of thieves. These reforms established specific penalties and facilities for convicted thieves and gave political authorities greater influence in the penitentiary process. In 1894, an addition to the penal code authorized the president to designate the "places of work" where convicted thieves were to serve their sentences. According to the Ministry of Justice, the amendment's goal was to "repress theft and cease the alarm caused by the frequency and daring with which it is committed." Lawyers called it "the law against rateros," as it explicitly targeted "rateros" and others guilty of theft.[22] Another decree of the same month simplified the procedures for sentencing of theft. In December 1903, a new reform to the code increased the maximum sentence for theft committed without violence from four to nine years.[23]

The 1894 reform sought to facilitate the banishment of rateros to forced labor colonies and thus to formalize time-honored methods for removing criminals from Mexican cities. During colonial times, sentences for crimes such as vagrancy, disorderly conduct, gambling, and desertion often involved the assignment of convicts to the chain gang in Havana, or to hard labor building fortifications at Perote or the port of Veracruz. The Acordada tribunal commonly punished criminals with service abroad in the military or public works. But the system did not work smoothly. The tribunal had jurisdictional conflicts with the Sala del Crimen in Mexico City; prisoners waited for long periods before being sent abroad and frequently escaped. After Independence, convicts were commonly forced to join the army and, since 1867, the capital's political authorities had sent prisoners to forced labor camps.[24] After the 1894 law, the police arrested thousands of rateros and sent them to work camps in the Valle Nacional, Oaxaca, or Yucatán. Prisoners, but also *enganchado* (literally, "hooked" to pay off cash advances) workers, were sent to toil in plantations under such harsh conditions that many died there. Police officers in the capital were rewarded by plantation contractors according to the number of workers sent. American journalist John Kenneth Turner and the relatives of prisoners awaiting transportation equated the traffic with slavery.[25]

The most explicit formulation of the ideas about raterismo came in June 20, 1908, when a new law established the penalty of transportation to penal colonies (*relegación*) against rateros, counterfeiters, vagrants, and other "habitual criminals." Convicts would serve double the time of their sentence in the new penal colony of Islas Marías, in the Pacific Ocean.[26] The legislation targeted "habitual criminals, who constitute the veteran section of the army of crime, who commit the largest number of crimes . . . keep police constantly busy, and form the nucleus of the prison population." The reform derived from a proposal by Miguel Macedo's Comisión Revisora del Código Penal, which Congress passed with slight amendments. The idea of sending criminals to an island had been proposed to the committee in 1903, to forestall the poor conditions in existing prisons. The reform and the inauguration of the Islas Marías colony received the support of the press but, like the 1894 law, it did not attract the public attention drawn by the penitentiary in 1900.[27]

Based on the premise that rateros were an extraneous group among the city population, legislators expected to reverse the "invasion" by sending them to distant places of detention. Advocates of relegación depicted it as a progressive urban social policy, rather than simple retaliation. In *Las colonias de rateros,* Medina y Ormaechea presented to Mexican readers the new ideas about transportation discussed among international penologists. Transportation, noted Medina y Ormaechea, was more rational than flogging, which was a "barbaric" method tainted by its use among foreign invaders against Mexicans and expressly preempted by article 22 of the Constitution. Both practices stigmatized rateros and offered public examples of the state's strong hand against theft, but the former fit modern notions of punishment.[28]

Transportation affected an economic logic. Medina y Ormaechea described it as a profitable extension of colonization policies, in which lands and islands belonging to the nation would be put to use to regenerate criminals through labor. Prisoners' work, he suggested, could also be productively used in the construction and maintenance of highways and railroads.[29] Since rateros were an urban phenomenon, reasoned the *Gaceta de Policía,* penal colonies could transplant them to an environment where they would be rendered harmless and thus be forced to learn a useful trade. According to Julio Guerrero, the deportation of rateros from the Federal District in the late 1890s had already increased wage levels in the city. Transportation and industrialization would prepare the "people for democracy."[30] Transportation was thus envisioned as having a beneficial impact on the progress of urban society as a whole.

As a consequence of these ideas, authorities implemented transportation without much regard for the individual rights of suspects. Even after the 1908 law was passed, city officials often overlooked judicial procedures before sending rateros to penal colonies, as they had been doing since 1894. In 1910, officials apprehended 2,238 people and sent them to the islands, most of them for theft, although a large number were sent after official police "campaigns" against rateros, which involved collective and often indiscrimi-

s.[31] Despite the irregularities committed, the press and city au- fended these campaigns on the premise that, thanks to their daily of street life, the police could easily distinguish rateros from the rest of the population. According to *El Imparcial:* "A new war has been declared against this social plague, authorizing intelligent agents to round up subjects. . . . The activities of these agents have been very fruitful . . . because they know all rateros, the places where they can be found, and even their addresses."[32]

In 1906, the *Gaceta de Policía* declared triumphantly that these actions had prompted many rateros to leave for other cities, because they encountered more troubles in escaping the police and because they feared the penitentiary.[33] Although the statement might be biased (the police department, headed by Félix Díaz, helped publish the *Gaceta*), it reveals the connection between the police and the creation of rateros as a collectivity.

Officials and newspapers maintained that police action need not be encumbered with an excessive respect for the law. Although never publicly admitted, the police department had considerable leeway in using violence against rateros and other offenders. Beatings to obtain confessions were commonplace during the Porfiriato. Revolutionary forces in the capital captured a former policeman known as "El Matarratas," who had been accused of killing several rateros (hence his nickname) during Félix Díaz's tenure as police chief. El Matarratas was also accused of murdering political opponents of Huerta after 1913.[34] During campaigns against rateros, the police could arrest "suspects" without accusing them of any specific crime, arguing simply that they were "well-known rateros." Thus, in February 1914, Policía Reservada agent José Acosta detected Guadalupe Vega, a "well-known ratero," on Alhóndiga Street and decided to watch him. When Vega seemed to be about to steal bottles of liquor from a cart, Acosta arrested him. It took the judge only three days and no additional evidence to sentence Acosta to nine months of relegación.[35] Policemen often explained that the accused had been surprised in unspecified "suspicious activities" or found with objects whose origin he or she was not able to explain satisfactorily—regardless of their low value. Manuel González was arrested in March 1918 "because he was found with clothes whose ownership he cannot demonstrate, although nobody has claimed them as stolen." He was placed under the city council's authority, probably to be later transported to the

Islas Marías. The clothes he was carrying, however, were so dirty that the authority ordered them thrown away.[36]

These practices survived the Revolution, despite the new authorities' criticisms of the previous government's "laxity in the administration of justice and as a consequence the lack of personal guarantees."[37] During the Constitutionalist occupation of the capital, according to Ramírez Plancarte, police abuses, including the leva, increased "three hundred times" because police officials were appointed by military commanders from Pablo González's Ejército del Oriente.[38] In 1916, *El Universal* approvingly reported that the police chief was rounding up "an infinite number of rateros" and sending them to Yucatán and other distant places.[39]

The banishment of thieves remained a centerpiece of urban social policies under President Carranza. In his message to Congress in April 1917, Carranza announced that the government had taken steps to "repress with great severity the plague of raterismo afflicting the city."[40] This meant reestablishing the policy of transportation and a systematic campaign of arrests. Suspects were captured by the hundreds. They were warned to abandon the streets. If arrested again, they were summarily sent to the Islas Marías. The campaign was based on a seldom-used section of the 1871 Penal Code, which dealt with "Vagrancy and Begging" in the chapter on "Crimes against public order." Article 854 established that *vagos* (vagrants) were those who, "lacking property and rents, do not exercise an honest industry, art, or trade for a living, without having a legitimate impediment." Rateros were included in this definition, as they lacked an "honest" trade. City council records contain hundreds of records of arrests for reasons ranging from being a "sleeping drunkard" to urinating in the street, and to insulting the governor of the Federal District. Most of those arrested were defined as "well-known rateros" or "pernicious rateros."[41] Since the status of "well-known ratero" was established by political authorities without a trial, the decision to send suspects to the islands was largely discretionary. In December 1916, for example, governor of the Federal District César López de Lara personally selected one hundred rateros at the penitentiary to be sent to the islands. Another one hundred suspects were released.[42] The 1917 campaign only formalized this practice.

As in Porfirian times, the 1917 campaign relied primarily on policemen's eyes to detect rateros, but it also began to compile systematic information about criminals. After the arrest, city council employees gathered personal data about the suspect, including such information as birthplace, trade, age, address, and a brief physical description. In order to establish the status and connections of the suspect, personal files also included letters about their character signed by acquaintances, employers, or relatives of the arrested.[43] This information was then used to send rateros to the penal colonies the next time they were arrested, but it also served officials as the empirical foundation for their discussion of rateros as a clearly defined and numerous social group. In 1920, for example, the police chief painted an alarming image of the confrontation between policemen and rateros. Ten years earlier, he declared, the police had "seven thousand men, well equipped and armed"; but now that force had been reduced to "two thousand men without weapons." Of these, only seven hundred were in the streets at any given time. Yet, they had to face ten thousand rateros.[44]

Who were these rateros? The information compiled by the city council records for the 1917 campaign shows that rateros arrested in this campaign were a different lot from the suspects in judicial archives analyzed in the introduction to part 2. The police seem to have defined rateros as those suspects who were particularly visible in public spaces. Rateros were men. While women made up one-fifth of suspects in all criminal trials, only 7 percent of those arrested in the campaign were female. Merchants, artisans, construction workers, and cart drivers, many of whom peddled their services in the streets, supplied a higher percentage of rateros relative to suspects in judicial records. Journeymen and domestic workers were, in contrast, relatively fewer (see appendix, tables 7 and 18). More "respectable" trades were largely absent from the ranks of rateros: policemen and military men, 6 percent in the judicial database, were less than half a percent of those arrested in the 1917 campaign. Rateros were young. Their median age was twenty, five years less than that of judicial suspects, and only 12 percent of them were married—against 21 percent of the judicial suspects. Otherwise, ratero suspects resembled most of the city's population in that half of them were born there. In sum, those arrested in campaigns against rateros fit a profile that resembled more the criminological and police image of criminals than those who were suspects of actual crimes.

After the fall of Carranza in 1920, the Federal District's government carried out an "administrative exercise" against rateros that built on the foundations of the 1917 campaign. The rationale for the program, described by Teófilo Olea y Leyva in the 1923 First Criminological and Penitentiary Congress, was that the police were unable to act against certain rateros because the law was not flexible enough. During the exercise, administrative authorities (i.e., the police, without the participation of the courts) detained suspected rateros for fifteen days. A committee from the Supervising Board of Prisons (Junta de Vigilancia de Cárceles) interviewed each ratero. Based on the information thus collected, one of the members of the committee investigated the suspect's record in the archives of the Belem jail and the Department of Mental Hygiene, and interviewed other witnesses. The goal of the inquiry was to establish "a moral judgement about the arrested." Based on such findings, the administrative authorities could decide to banish the suspect to the Islas Marías (through the Ministry of the Interior), or simply to open a file, thus forcing the suspect to report periodically to the committee. If the accused was arrested again, he or she was immediately sent to the islands. According to Olea y Leyva, the 1923 experiment had been successful: 75 percent of the rateros arrested were not detained again, and those who were arrested by the police without proper justification were protected by the file that recorded their good behavior. There is no evidence that this "experiment" continued during the 1920s but, applying a similar mix of individual reporting and collective harassment, a 1931 campaign against beggars compiled personal data and monitored the individual behavior of offenders. Although this time social workers were in charge of the interviews, the campaign shows how criminological notions about raterismo had a lasting impact on social policies.[45]

Police campaigns and "administrative experiments" against rateros began to lose their uncontested force in public opinion in the 1920s. The impact of political changes on these strategies is clearly exemplified in the 1920 confrontation between the recently appointed governor of the Federal District, Celestino Gasca, and the city's chief of police, Jesús Almada. The dispute revolved around the authority of the police chief to deal with rateros independently from the governor and the judiciary. Gasca had personally intervened to reverse the illegal detention of many rateros kept in jail or in the islands from the times of Carranza's government. Almada then accused Gasca "of being the direct cause of the increase of criminality in the Federal District, because not only did he authorize the release of all the rateros in the penitentiary, but he also shielded the rats [*los ratas*] from persecution." Although Gasca claimed that he was only following the law, and accusations of police corruption were published, Almada and the newspapers succeeded in framing the debate in terms of the defense of society's interests (furthered by the police) against the legalistic and "puritanical" protection of criminals (by fastidious judges and the governor). *El Universal* published reports warning that the rateros released from the Islas Marías were coming back to the capital to take revenge against their foes and to increase the city's criminality.[46] The chief of police seemed to score a victory in the last days of Adolfo de la Huerta's presidency, when de la Huerta authorized Almada to round up rateros and send them to the Islas Marías. The dispute lingered, however, during Alvaro Obregón's presidency, when Almada asked for more autonomy and Gasca accused him of corruption.[47] Campaigns against rateros continued afterward, although they became less contentious than in the early 1920s and the press did not report them as news anymore. The departure of *cuerdas* (as the chain-gangs to the islands were called) became in the late 1920s a routine event that included suspects, convicts, and political prisoners. In 1934, President Cárdenas appointed a commission to examine the cases of prisoners at Islas Marías who had not been duly convicted.[48]

Despite their scientific undertones, campaigns against rateros generated strong opposition from the legal profession, whose intervention in the judicial and penal process was curtailed by the extrajudicial acts of political authorities. Harshness and distance from the city, lawyers claimed, did not translate into regeneration. In 1911, Antonio Ramos Pedrueza asserted that the 1894 law against rateros and the 1908 establishment of penal colonies had not reduced the number of thefts, which was still increasing. He directed at penal colonies the same criticism usually addressed at jails, namely, that they created more career criminals by placing "first time offenders" together with recidivists.[49] Banishment regulations and the increasing penalties against theft forced judges to hand out long sentences. Table 9 reflects this severity and the relative lack of concern of authorities about violent crime: while a quarter of those sentenced for theft received sentences of more than eleven months, only 3 percent of those convicted of battery received the same penalties. Prisoners, who indeed feared transportation to the Islas Marías, contributed to lawyers' dissent by using all available legal resources to avoid the execution of their penalty, and courts granted suspects' appeals against transportation. They and their families protested against the cuerda because it meant cutting short their trials. In June 1930, several suspects and their relatives alleged that city authorities were overruling a judge's ruling suspending the cuerda. Despite their appeal, the police forcefully took several prisoners from their hospital beds to the train station.[50]

Campaigns against rateros aroused protests and criticisms. Yet, they left several lasting legacies in Mexico City dwellers' understanding of crime and punishment. The first was to demonstrate in practice that rateros were a collectivity. The cuerdas, taking numerous suspects away from their city and their families, reinforced that idea. A second and more insidious legacy of these campaigns survives to this date in the belief that the police can identify and act against criminals without the burden of respect for individual rights.

MODERN RATEROS AND THE IDENTITY OF CRIMINALS

Criminological discourse and official campaigns against thieves fed the widespread belief that rateros were a distinct profession. But was there any reality behind this notion? While most arrests for *ratero conocido* were the product of police whims, there was indeed a relatively small group of offenders who embodied the ideas about rateros as a skillful and evasive trade. A product of the repressive policies outlined above, these modern professional rateros, who nevertheless avoided using the label, had greater knowledge about law-enforcement authorities and were more likely to use violence and a complex organization than typical theft offenders. Modern rateros, as I will call these professionals, caused a shift in public perceptions of crime: from the "invasion" of petty thieves feared by Porfirian elites to contemporary concerns about violence, corruption, and the indiscernibility of criminals and cops. This section will pay attention to the stories of several accused rateros, such as Higinio Granda, Rafael Mercadante, and Antonio Martínez. Evidence about their lives is scarce, but their identities, as perceived by the public and the historical record, were constructed around their criminal offenses.[51]

The new perceptions about crime were an offspring of the Revolution. Despite the unprecedented pressure imposed by the civil war on the economy of survival of the urban poor, petty crime did not experience a radical departure from Porfirian practices. Something similar could be said about punishment. Yet, the characters publicly associated with crime changed after

1913. The famous case of the Gray Automobile Gang portrays this shift. The gang became the focus of public attention and a symbol of modernization and danger in the capital; in the eyes of the population, it was clear evidence of the connivance between government officials and criminals that would distinguish the postrevolutionary era.

Since mid-1915, when the capital was under Zapatista rule, a gang of men dressed in uniforms and riding in a gray car (said to have been the one used to drive Madero to his assassination), entered the homes of several wealthy families and robbed them. Although these actions are in themselves difficult to distinguish from the expropriations executed by revolutionary leaders, the gang went on to become a legend in the annals of theft. Its members targeted upper-class victims, rode in elegant cars, and liked to spend their share of the take in fancy restaurants and cantinas. They used sophisticated methods to enter houses and avoided physical violence. Information from official sources allowed them to escape police intervention and target their prey. Their operations continued during the Constitutionalist occupation of the city.[52] The structure of the gang was complex: several groups, unknown one to another, performed special duties, while the "brain" of the system, Higinio Granda, coordinated them and received information and support from revolutionary officials. Writers characterized Granda by his intellectual virtues, which they contrasted with other members of the gang who were perhaps braver but too prone to alcohol. Granda's sophistication contributed to the cosmopolitan style associated with the gang. While Granda was Spanish, the driver of the car was said to be Japanese. One member of the Gray Automobile Gang bragged—just before being executed—that the gang's robberies would be the envy of thieves throughout the world.[53]

The gang was surrounded by an aura of technical prowess that resembled images imported in the form of movies and literature from Europe and the United States. In 1897, an article in *El Imparcial* entitled "The Evolution of Theft," signed by one Cestas el Roto, described the increasing refinement of theft. Old raterías seemed dull and backward when compared to the practices of contemporary swindlers.[54] Criminals seemed to take modernization very seriously. In 1914, members of a gang that specialized in opening safes were arrested. They confessed to having imitated the Black Glove Gang portrayed in Nick Carter movies.[55] In 1920, Interior Minister Manuel Aguirre Berlanga defended film censorship, arguing that the movie "Los misterios de Nueva York" had taught Mexican thieves to perform "high class robberies."[56] Foreign-born suspects such as Granda posed an additional threat because of their ability to pass as "decent" people—which thwarted the criminological perceptions of Mexican criminals as Indian or mestizo. Foreigners were blamed, particularly after the Revolution, of transgressions ranging from prostitution to theft to stealing Mexican women. The noticeable change regarding the methods and skills of thieves was portrayed in a 1925 editorial in *El Universal* entitled "Triumphant criminality." Recent robberies, noted the newspaper, could be classified, after Thomas de Quincey, as "works of art," and as demonstrations of "the technical advance of criminals." *El Universal* explained that "in the same ways that Mexico City is no longer a provincial city, pleasant and welcoming, and has become a cosmopolitan center, criminality, which used to wear diapers, has now grown and matured."[57]

The Gray Automobile Gang embodied another feature of modern crime: the use of automobiles. Cars gave criminals a "modern" and "dangerous" appearance. In the gang's operation, automobiles provided an advantage over pedestrian policemen and revealed the large investment involved in modern crime. As more cars appeared on the streets, stealing and selling them became a new and productive business. In 1912, the press reported the arrest of Luis Tapia (a.k.a. *La Muerte,* Death), who had been "devoted to stealing cars, the new fashion in the annals of theft." Tapia acted alone and without violence, relying on a device that, he claimed, could start up any car.[58] Seizing cars had become a common tactic among revolutionaries. Forced by political events, even revolutionary intellectual Martín Luis Guzmán had to take one at gun point, in broad daylight on Juárez Avenue.[59] Violence and larger crime organizations soon became an element of car theft. In October 1929, *Excélsior* reported a car theft performed "in the customary way": several individuals stopped a taxi, directed the driver to a deserted suburb and then assaulted him with their guns, took the car and left him by the road. This gang was probably the same one that the police captured in 1930. They had accomplices in Pachuca, state of Hidalgo, who obtained new license plates and sold the stolen cars as new. The extensive records of this trial, examined below, reveal the complex structure of organized gangs of thieves and their tendency to diversify their illegal activities. Stolen cars were in other cases disassembled and sold as parts, to avoid the possibility of detection.[60]

The defining trait in the perceptions of modern crime embodied by the

Gray Automobile Gang was its association with politicians. The gang had enjoyed the support of revolutionary officers since its beginnings in 1914. When entering their victims' houses, gang members wore uniforms and showed warrants signed by high military commanders, first Zapatista general Amador Salazar and then Carrancista general Francisco de P. Mariel. Warrants signed by general Pablo González, Mariel's chief, were also used. These warrants were apparently obtained through a network that involved a secret policeman, major José Palomar, who worked for González. This information, recorded by chronicler Alfonso Taracena and later by Juan Mérigo (an alleged accomplice), circulated in the capital by word of mouth, but no newspaper reported it.[61] The manner in which Constitutionalist officers dismantled the gang further supported suspicions about the involvement of some commanders. Higinio Granda and other gang members had been arrested by the Zapatistas but released in the transition between the Zapatista and Constitutionalist occupations. In September 1915, the Constitutionalists apprehended Granda, Rafael Mercadante, and others and placed them under the authority of a military judge. General Pablo González, who had promised to punish the users of "false warrants," obstructed the investigations of a civilian judge by ordering the immediate execution of two suspects. Sixteen alleged members of the gang were arrested in December, diffusing responsibilities even more; six of them were condemned by a military court and executed days after their arrest. Mercadante and Granda were spared, because they claimed to know the whereabouts of portions of the booty and the names of other accomplices. Mercadante died in his cell in December 1918; days later Oviedo, another member of the gang, declared at the penitentiary that he was going to make "sensational" revelations, but died shortly afterward in suspicious circumstances. Granda, in contrast, was released from prison in 1920 with the support of González, and worked as a clerk in criminal courts and as a land speculator.[62]

Accusations against Pablo González regarding his involvement with the Gray Automobile Gang became part of presidential politics and reflected public opinion about corruption among the new ruling groups.[63] González was known to intervene in "common" police business. In June 1915, for example, he unsuccessfully asked Veracruz governor Cándido Aguilar to use his influence in favor of a suspect being tried by the military judges of that state. In an effort to clean up his image before a frustrated bid for the presidential candidacy, González supported the production of the 1919 movie

El automóvil gris, in which the truth about the case would be exposed. Although the movie was a success, it did not improve González's image.[64] The "dirt" in the higher ranks of government had been a frequent criticism against the Porfirian regime, and Huerta was associated with alcohol and dishonesty, but the Carrancistas were, by far, the favorite target of popular scorn. The term *carrancear* meant "to steal."[65] Writer and official Luis Cabrera denounced corruption among other Constitutionalist politicians as early as June 1917, describing the use for personal profit of private property seized during military operations. The suspicions about high-ranking revolutionary officials were rarely substantiated in court. Cabrera refused to name names after his 1917 accusations, and even though González faced a court martial in 1920, his prosecutors did not bring up the allegations of corruption.[66]

The Gray Automobile Gang expressed the tenuous separation, in the perspective of the general public, between authorities and criminals. Since the mid 1910s, thieves used uniforms or badges to ease their way into the victims' homes. This was initially possible due to the confusion of uniforms and insignia brought about by the multiple armies that entered the capital. The ploy was also used in small frauds. In 1914, for example, a bread seller was forced to give his money to a uniformed man who claimed to be a Constitutionalist captain. One ratero, warned *El Universal* in 1917, had been committing burglaries and robberies at night wearing a Constitutionalist army uniform. Others would pass themselves off as inspectors of the Public Health Council.[67]

As these examples suggest, few were so glamorous as Granda and his associates. Eduardo Vázquez is a good example of the set of skills that characterized most modern rateros. On April, 1915, he was arrested after witnesses surprised him breaking into a house. Vázquez first claimed that it was his house, but his accusers were all neighbors of the victim and knew he was lying. Then Vázquez dropped a bundle containing clothes, jewels, and watches, and began running away. The victim asked officer Manuel L. Argüelles "to follow that individual dressed as a mechanic because he is a ratero." Argüelles caught up with Vázquez at his house, where he was changing his clothes. Once arrested, the suspect gave different names (first Guillermo Pacheco, then Eduardo Vázquez) to the police and the judge, arguing that he was embarrassed, but this ploy also failed. According to the archive of the municipal jail, Vázquez had been arrested for theft in 1913 and sentenced to five years in prison, but in July of that year he had been released to Huertista military authorities. He was probably discharged after the defeat of the Federal Army in 1914. On June 24, 1915, after his second arrest, Vázquez was summoned for a hearing, but the prison warden revealed that he was no longer there, because "he has been released to complete freedom by explicit order of the Ministry of Justice."[68] His change of clothes and name, his reluctance to confess, and his later release by order of the Secretary of Justice suggests that Vázquez had knowledge about the court system and the ability to obtain favors from political authorities. He was called ratero by witnesses, and proved in fact to be elusive and able to avoid long prison sentences.

Professional rateros had a common experience of frequent, if not prolonged, incarcerations. Higinio Granda's trajectory after his release from prison in 1920 (as law clerk and businessman) parallels those of other "well-known" rateros. He knew police and prison authorities because he had been in a Mexican prison before. In 1910, a letter signed by him and twelve other foreign prisoners in Belem asked Foreign Minister Enrique Creel for a pardon in commemoration of the centennial of Independence.[69] Like Vázquez, many of those accused of theft were persistent offenders, although this was difficult for authorities to prove.

Judges established the previous incarcerations of a suspect based on a report produced by the archivist of Belem jail, but the procedure was unreliable because suspects like Vázquez often changed their names. According to Roumagnac and other observers, published statistics underestimated recidivism by a great margin, particularly in the case of thieves. Some offenders, like Victoriano Jaramillo and Mariana Hernández, who were arrested in 1912 for fighting in their vecindad, could be very active and yet avoid long-term punishment. Since 1910, Jaramillo had been arrested nine times for theft and once for battery, and had been released each time for lack of evidence. Since 1901, Hernández had four arrests for battery (from which she was released once for lack of evidence) and eight for theft (released for lack of evidence in three instances). Critics of the penal code proposed reforms that eliminated short prison sentences, because they exposed first-time offenders to the teachings of seasoned criminals without reforming the prisoners' behavior.[70]

The ability of inmates to learn more about crime from one another inside prisons was a well-known fact, reported in 1871 by Antonio Martínez de Castro. He described prisons as true schools of crime, where "the ratero thief and the bandit; those guilty of fighting and the murderer . . . the guilty and those still on trial" live together in idleness, sharing stories and projects about past and future crimes.[71] Several of Carlos Roumagnac's interviewees told of learning criminal techniques in jail. Miguel N., for example, entered the Correctional School for the first time when he was nine years old. Small thefts caused him to be incarcerated five or six times, for periods of less than fifteen days, according to Roumagnac. Miguel took advantage of those incarcerations, he declared, by learning to pick locks, "for they have told him that you could make three hundred or a thousand pesos this way."[72] Mostly, incarceration reinforced favorable attitudes toward law breaking among inmates. The "three hundred or a thousand pesos" that attracted Miguel N. implied access to coveted goods and prestige. Would-be thieves associated with other inmates in jail and organized for future actions. Such was the case, for example, of Carlos Pineda and David Rojas, founders of the late-1920s car-stealing ring mentioned above. They admitted to the judge that the origin of their association was the penitentiary, where they devised a scheme to attack taxi drivers. The original members of the Gray Automobile Gang met in Belem jail and escaped together during the 1913 Decena Trágica.[73]

Better perhaps than technical knowledge, prisoners shared an accurate understanding of the weaknesses of police and judicial systems. On their way out of Belem, the February 1913 escapees burned the prison's archives, in order to clear their records and avoid re-apprehension.[74] A defining trait of successful professional criminals was the ability to avoid long incarcerations and even, as Eduardo Vázquez seems to have done, to use their connections to leave jail before the end of their trials. This ability was a double-edged sword, however. The thieves who had close contact with authorities could be labeled "well-known rateros" and become the target of unmotivated arrests.[75]

Antonio Martínez (a.k.a. "El Enterrador," the grave-digger) offers the best example of the connections and abilities that could be acquired during incarceration. In 1923, Martínez and Luz González were convicted for murdering their wealthy friend Ignacio Oliver, in a famous case that came to be known as "The crime of the Desierto de los Leones"—for the forest outside Mexico City where the body was buried. Martínez was released in 1929, thanks to a presidential pardon. He then approached the judge who

6. The Crime of the Desierto de los Leones. Luz González, "The Black Widow," and Antonio Martínez, "El Enterrador," during their trial. 1923. Source: Fototeca Nacional, Fondo Casasola, 69130. © INAH.

had sentenced him, asking for a job (see fig. 6). The judge assisted Martínez and he "worked during several months arranging pardons for several inmates of the penitentiary"—as Higinio Granda did in the early 1920s after his own release. In 1930 Martínez entered the car-stealing gang organized by Carlos Pineda and David Rojas. After his second arrest, he refused to confess and accused the police of torturing him and forcing other suspects to testify against him. Back in jail, his active involvement in prison life did not cease. In 1931, he and other inmates of the penitentiary signed a letter to President Pascual Ortiz Rubio asking him to fire a police officer who, they said, was corrupt and "had been a member of the well-known ratero gang called *Los de la Gorra Prieta* [The Black Cap gang]." The letter referred to Belem jail criminal files for proof of their accusations.[76]

Knowledge of police and judicial procedures gave rateros the means to cope with police persecution. Martínez, like other suspects, knew the police relied on confessions to obtain guilty verdicts, so he refused to make a statement and even, according to the police, forced other suspects to withdraw testimonies that incriminated him. He realized that there was no advantage in yielding to investigators' pressure to admit guilt because, despite the mandates of the law, judges never considered confessions as a mitigating circumstance. Confession was all the more important for prosecutors because the impact of witnesses' testimonies was often diluted in cross-examination or after witnesses failed to appear in later hearings. Eduardo Vázquez changed his clothes after committing the theft because he knew that victims' descriptions usually centered on the kind of clothes worn by suspects, and were rather vague regarding physical appearance. To counter accusations, suspects like Rafael Téllez appealed to the belief that criminals were clearly different from "decent people." Téllez claimed that he was an "honest" person whose relation to the rateros who were with him at the time of his arrest was only incidental. He was released after the victim failed to reappear in court.[77]

The strategies employed by suspects to avoid conviction were often nothing more than the use of rights granted by the law. *El Imparcial* reported the case of Refugio Rodríguez, "El Chaval," a "fine pickpocket ratero" captured in an 1897 raid. He had been sentenced twice to banishment in Valle Nacional, but had managed to stay in Mexico City by appealing his sentences. Legal resources to challenge judicial decisions were available to any citizen, but in fact seldom used. This made it possible to argue that only learned criminals could resort to appeals, or use several defense lawyers, in a subversion of the law intended to delay trial, the testimony of witnesses, and relegación. Even if only a few convicts were successful in their appeals, their cases reinforced police and newspapers' arguments for restricting their rights.[78]

Organized gangs of criminals—defined by the use of guns, a higher degree of planning, and some form of official complicity—shaped public perceptions about the existence of a criminal trade. They became a visible symptom of the modernization of criminality in the capital, particularly in the wake of the Gray Automobile Gang's exploits. The use of force had not been a common feature of urban criminality in the early years of the century, but robbery became the central element of public fears of crime after the Revolution. Thus, the category of ratero came to be associated with the use of violence—an element lacking in early Porfirian definitions of raterismo. According to judge David Fernández Jáuregui, criminality in 1920 was increasing, particularly in the form of robberies and assaults: "We no longer have to worry about the pickpocket who is satisfied with stealing a watch; now we are dealing with rateros who use their knife or gun to rob their victims."[79] Alarmed, the press reported that rateros were using violence not only against wealthy victims but against any person in the streets who carried items of the least value.[80]

The case against a car theft ring disbanded in 1930 documents the new modalities of organized crime. Its members included Antonio Martínez, whose experience in prison was mentioned above, as well as Carlos Pineda and David Rojas, who put together the gang from prison while serving three-year sentences for theft. Their testimonies and those of other suspects illustrate the complex system of hierarchies, loyalties, and rivalries that informed their work. According to Pineda's initial confession, he and David Rojas had stolen more than twelve cars. Pineda declared that in 1929 he met Leonor Jiménez, "seduced her," and invited her to join the gang, where she helped by tying up the driver's hands. This caused a fight, and Pineda and Jiménez committed some robberies without Rojas's participation. On his own, Rojas invited in Antonio Martínez and Manuel Castillo, and they stole other cars. Pineda and Rojas returned to work together later. In their robberies, they threatened the drivers with a gun or a knife and dropped them in a remote place. The cars were sold to Pino González, who had a garage in Pachuca, Hidalgo. González ordered the cars from Rojas and Pineda, or sometimes only asked for parts, such as tires. They agreed on the pay (between 400 and 500 pesos for each car) before the theft. González sold the cars as new for 700 pesos, changing the serial numbers on the engines and bodies, with the collaboration of the traffic chief of Pachuca, who provided false license plates.

Things did not always run smoothly. González declared that he had had disputes with Rojas and Pineda, particularly after González was unable to pay in full for a car brought by them in January 1930. Days later, Leonor Jiménez asked him for 400 pesos, to get Pineda and Rojas out of jail. González gave her 200 pesos, and one month later Pineda and Rojas brought him another car, a Ford. González declared that when he found out about Antonio Martínez's involvement in the robberies, he told Pineda and Rojas that he did not want to have anything to do with Martínez and expressed doubts about the other members of the gang as well. Pineda and Rojas told González that their accomplices were all "machos" and were not going to denounce them. After the former two were apprehended, the rest of the gang was arrested in Tulancingo, state of Hidalgo, where Martínez had planned to steal between 7,000 and 8,000 pesos from the chief of the railroad station and kidnap an hacendado. With the profits, "they were planning to leave the country, to South America."[81]

Official collaboration (be it in Pachuca, to obtain new license plates, or in Mexico City, to escape incarceration through bribes) was essential for the gang's enterprise. Police complicity encouraged rather than inhibited the use of violence, reflecting the increasing autonomy of police activities during the 1920s. As noted in chapter 2, Porfirio Díaz's reorganization of the city's police sought to turn the body into the government's instrument to impose progress on street life. Yet, the reality of police stations and gendarmes remained distant from modernizing regulations. Rumors of police corruption and violence at higher levels characterized the last years of the regime.[82] The prestige of the police suffered a severe blow during the Revolution. When rebel armies occupied the city, gendarmes were often no more than witnesses or victims of the disorders created by troops. Police offices continued to be the least desirable source of medical help for those in need, and the personal prestige of gendarmes continued to diminish. In 1920, Eufemia Rocha told her neighbor Lorenzo Baleriano, who was trying to quiet her down, that he might be the gendarme in his punto, but that in the vecindad they shared, "he was worth nothing [*una pura chingada*]."[83] In 1922, two gendarmes were arrested for three months because they beat some bystanders who protested their use of force during an arrest.[84]

After 1920, the police department became the target of public accusations of corruption, and presidents Adolfo de la Huerta and Alvaro Obregón got personally involved in redesigning the institution. At the beginning of his term, President Obregón fired the whole staff of the Policía Reservada—well known for its close involvement in political affairs. Beyond the need to have loyal officers, Obregón seems to have been interested in reforming the police along military lines, with decorations, uniforms, and guns similar to those used by the army. On May 3, 1922, without previous warning, army officials disarmed all gendarmes and removed them from their puntos. They were replaced by soldiers patrolling the city. Obregón replied to an alarmed telegram from the governor of the Federal District that the movement was part of a reorganization of the city police that he hoped to conclude in the next days.[85]

The measures responded to evidence of police corruption, now a visible phenomenon even at the lowest levels of police work. Witness the case of

Antonio Torres, who went to a police station to report a fraud (a customer who refused to pay for a cart). At the comisaría, he was informed that the cost of bringing the suspects to the authorities was 40 pesos, plus 10 percent of the value of the debt. Frustrated, the victim appealed to the judicial police, but no result was recorded in the file.[86] Everything had a price: a suspect could be released after the payment of 10 pesos to the officer in charge of the station; lovers caught in fraganti at public parks had to pay 5 pesos to the gendarmes who had turned the lights off to provoke the offense; police were bought and used by civilians "to commit robberies that stain the prestige of the corps"; gendarmes paid their superiors to be assigned to lucrative puntos.[87]

Antonio Torres' frustration, and the petty corruption that provoked it, were the result of the new autonomy of the police vis-à-vis local authorities and urban communities. The 1917 Constitution established that the prosecution of crimes was to be the exclusive responsibility of the government. What this meant in practice was that the policía judicial acquired greater responsibilities and received greater funding directly from the presidency. The judicial police emphasized investigation, rather than prevention, and became the only point of access to police protection for victims such as Torres. The Ministerio Público began to replace judges as the main prosecutors in trials. Simultaneously, gendarmes gradually lost the closeness to neighbors that they had tried to establish, against the official project, during the Porfiriato. Rather than a sign of greater security, the enhanced role of the judicial police often meant that police actions escaped public scrutiny.[88]

Accusations of corruption, however, reached higher in the 1920s, involving the press and even the presidency. Inspector general Pedro Almada was accused of exploiting brothels, gambling permits, and having subordinates who belonged to "terrible" criminal gangs and who dealt with stolen cars.[89] During the protracted public dispute between Almada and his superior, governor of the Federal District Celestino Gasca, over the policies to be followed against rateros, Obregón redefined the responsibilities of each functionary. Almada, however, seems to have won the president's support—despite Gasca's requests for his resignation, the inspector general received a performance bonus from Obregón and remained in office until 1925, into Plutarco Elías Calles's presidency. The city police had become a functional element in the political machinery of the Sonorenses. In 1924, opposition activists denounced the involvement of the gendarmes against candidates opposing Elías Calles.[90] In dealing with accusations against the police, the concern about loyalty seems to have prevailed over that about corruption.

These changes fostered the privatization of certain police services. The same entrepreneurial spirit that moved policemen to ask for money in order to look for suspects prompted the emergence of private investigation agencies and other less formal ways to aid in the search for suspects. Against regulations, police officers issued identification cards to private citizens who "collaborated" with their inquiries. Detective agencies peddled their services, arguing that the modernization of and increase in crime demanded new methods. "Oflodor Policía Privada Metropolitana," for example, guaranteed that no fees would be charged unless their agents achieved "complete success." Applications for licenses included letters of support from mercantile organizations. In its approval of one such request in 1933, a Ministry of the Interior memorandum cited the growing insecurity derived from the current economic crisis, the weakness of state institutions to respond to crime, and the existence of already numerous private agencies and individuals who sold their services. By 1934, however, private police agencies still lacked specific regulations.[91]

CONCLUSIONS

The "modernization" of criminals and policemen had upsetting effects on the ways in which the Mexico City population perceived and dealt with crime. As police and thieves seemed to live in their own world of money and violence, urban communities were left to prevent petty theft by their own means. Although this had been a function of vecindades and barrios from long ago, an increasing distance grew between them and the police. No longer was the gendarme on a corner the only thing a neighbor needed to deal with a problem: a heavy structure of corruption, guns, and long sentences now hung over the simple operation of seeking help from the representatives of the law.

The "modern" aspects of theft embodied by organized criminals were a result of the conjuncture of urban change, the criminological discourse of the late Porfiriato, and the political and cultural transformations brought to the city by the Revolution. Public perceptions of theft during the early twentieth century were marked by the construction of the category of ratero. Petty pickpockets and burglars became, in the eyes of the city dwellers, a dangerous and skilled criminal cadre, whose most advanced members formed the organized gangs that emerged during the revolutionary upheaval. The invention of rateros had been the empirical foundation for penitentiary reform and new policing strategies. These strategies were indeed the first and most systematic attempt to translate positivist criminology (and its inherited prejudices) into social reform. In practice, however, they buttressed the increasing specialization of law-enforcement institutions, the segregation of offenders who learned the crooked workings of the system, and the emergence of groups of robbers who became professional criminals.

The postrevolutionary practices of organized robbery never became as frequent as petty larceny, but they acquired a great resonance with the public. Professional criminals, such as the members of the Gray Automobile Gang, saw themselves as part of a cosmopolitan world of cars, guns, movies, and night clubs. Public opinion, on the other hand, suspected them of acting in cahoots with politicians and the police. Thus, urban robbers never became a variety of rural bandits. The homes of the wealthy were not necessarily their targets: car thieves attacked taxi drivers and made streets at night more dangerous for working women. Nor is there any evidence of redistributive intentions behind their conspicuous consumption. Rather than a critique of social order, their activities proved to the urban poor that innate criminal tendencies were not really part of class differences. Instead, such thieves confirmed the official double standard toward suspects: excessive penalties against petty rateros, but corrupt collaboration with big thieves.

8

Penal Experience in Mexico City

The prisoners of Belem jail had frequent nightmares. Some dreamt that they were flying, but not in a pleasant, carefree way. Maximino O. often felt as if he were falling, or that bulls were chasing him. Amada B. saw fearful objects in her flight. Other prisoners like María Villa or Carlos A. dreamt that their victims visited them and tried to take them away. Spending long months and years in prison, they had to get used to living with the uncertain sensations of their nightmares. The night before a jury decided his fate, Esteban M. dreamt that he was climbing the stairs to his trial, when a man told him: "If you stand on the left side, they will give you ten years; if you stand on the right, they will give you twenty." In his dream, he stood on the right side, because he did not know which side was the left. The next day, he received a sentence of twenty years (fig. 7).[1]

In order to analyze the uncertainty that prisoners experienced—of not knowing left from right—criminal law and prison life in Mexico City must be examined. Judicial and penal practices, like other aspects of civic life, were the object of political reexamination during the early twentieth century. The previous chapters show that punishment was a basic element of the urban poor's relation to state institutions. This relationship was not fixed, however. Despite the continuity of elite attitudes toward the urban poor,

7. Suspect during his trial, ca. 1912. Source: Fototeca Nacional, Fondo Casasola, 69013. © INAH.

the Revolution marked a clear departure from the way that the Porfirian regime addressed social ills. The periodization of political history is valid here because, according to Sergio García Ramírez, "Criminal law, in the broad sense . . . offers the most vivid testimony . . . about the authoritarian or democratic tendencies of a political regime." Political fluctuations had a more immediate impact on punishment than demographic and economic changes had on crime. During the Porfiriato, Mexico City prisoners suffered abuse and exploitation and feared the new Penitentiary and exile to the penal colonies. Their letters to President Porfirio Díaz beg for mercy and profess unconditional subordination to authority. The Revolution transformed their attitude. Prisoners in the 1920s organized to seek better treatment and to gain political support, which they received through material help and amnesty laws signed by President Alvaro Obregón. Their letters after the Revolution demonstrate a desire to make their voices heard. After the 1920s, the state adopted reforms to penal legislation and followed the advice of penalists who advocated more humane conditions for prisoners and greater intervention of social workers and lawyers in the execution of penalties, to protect due process and the general goal of "social prevention."[2]

This tale of improvement through revolution is basically correct, though too simple. Conditions in Mexican jails may have improved compared to Porfirian standards, yet they continued to be characterized by overcrowding, violence, and corruption, fostered by drug trafficking inside and outside.[3] Furthermore, this account suggests that politicians, helped by specialists, could mold at will the institutions and practices of punishment —thus neglecting the actions of those affected by the law. The Revolution meant not only a change of tone in state policies and elite attitudes regarding punishment, but also the participation of a greater number of actors in the public discussion of penal reform than had been the case during the Porfiriato. While lawyers challenged the power of criminology over punishment, prisoners became increasingly articulate against abuses.

Laws and institutions are not merely the straightforward expressions of a state project. In their everyday use, and despite disparities of power among actors, there is a permanent tension that gives shape to and transforms a political regime. As the previous chapter demonstrates, policies against rateros survived after the Revolution but were increasingly contested by prisoners and some members of the judiciary. In the realm of the elite project of order and in that of the everyday survival of prisoners, this tension explains the reciprocal ways in which discourse and "reality," science, public policies, and popular practices, modified one another. Both prisoners and lawyers can tell us much about the shifting rules of participation in the public sphere.[4]

LAWYERS AND PENAL REFORM

After almost sixty years of regulating crime and punishment in Mexico City, the 1871 Penal Code was replaced by an entirely new one in 1929, which was in turn replaced by a third code in 1931. In the process, penal reform became the focus of a public debate that was not restricted to ministry corridors. Criminologists claimed the support of science in favor of a radical transformation of the rules of punishment. Lawyers, on the other hand, successfully defended their control over the discussion and legislation of these issues.

Lawyers were not a homogeneous group, however. Influential penologists like Miguel Macedo and José Angel Ceniceros received good wages and senior jobs and participated in the drafting of the criminal law. At the same time, those working in penal courts suffered the material restrictions that would limit the impact of reforms. The budget allocated to the judiciary and the penitentiary system had been chronically low since the Porfiriato, and got smaller after the Revolution, prompting frequent complaints by public attorneys, court clerks, and other judicial workers. In 1931, Alfonso Teja Zabre argued that, as long as material conditions in jails and courts remained precarious, penal codes would be only a literary genre: "The heroic task of penal reform in Mexico . . . should start on the material and administrative side." These conditions fostered corruption in courts and police stations. Newspapers, politicians, and even judges denounced the routine use of bribes and extortion, beginning at the lowest administrative levels. Revolutionary leaders condemned venality in Porfirian courts, but the problem was never a central consideration in the discussions and legislative reforms that took place from the late 1890s up to 1931.[5]

Material problems in the practice of law contrast with the apparent progress of penal legislation. Penitentiary reform started under favorable auspices when, in 1896, Congress approved modifications to the penal code in order to prepare the way for inauguration of the new penitentiary in San Lázaro. The 1857 Constitution and the 1871 Penal Code had set the goal of establishing a "penitentiary regime"—meaning the adaptation of sentences to the prisoners' behavior and the abrogation (with a few exceptions) of the death penalty. The 1896–1900 reforms and decrees reorganized jails in the Federal District and gave administrative authorities greater power to decide the execution of sentences and prisoner labor. Porfirian elites perceived the new legislation as a break with the past, when empiricism and improvisation had characterized punishment. They thought scientific principles would now rule over incarceration by reforming those criminals who were receptive and by isolating for good those who could not be redeemed. Legal reform, however, was subordinated to the regime's penitentiary projects. The costly and highly publicized Penitenciaría de México received more official attention than the Palacio de Justicia Penal, which housed the criminal courts. President Díaz attended the inauguration of both buildings in 1900, although it was clear which one was his favorite. At the opening of the Palacio de Justicia, the President scornfully called it a "nice tenement." The Palacio, in fact, was but an addition to Belem jail, erected with fewer resources than the penitentiary.[6]

The penitentiary, on the other hand, was one of the great public works of the regime. Its modern panoptic layout was designed by architect Antonio Torres Torija, who drew inspiration from an 1848 interpretation of Jeremy Bentham's ideas by Mexican architect Lorenzo de la Hidalga. Construction began in 1885, but the building was not ready to accommodate prisoners until 1897. At the 1900 official inauguration, Federal District governor Rafael Rebollar praised the new prison as the beginning of "a new era in the evolution of repressive systems in Mexico."[7] Besides the architectural novelties, the penitentiary marked the start of a period of centralization of penitentiary institutions under the executive power.

The legislative changes enacted in 1896 began a discussion of criminal law that was closely supervised by the regime. In 1903, President Díaz appointed the ubiquitous Miguel Macedo as head of the Comisión Revisora del Código Penal. For a period of nine years, the Comisión Revisora compiled opinions about the penal code by lawyers and judges and drafted reforms to the 1871 Code. Even though it did not produce a comprehensive project of reform, the comisión did have the significant effect of keeping the discussion about penal reform within the boundaries of presidential power and channeling diverse opinions through the established hierarchies of the legal profession: Macedo had tight control over the commission sessions; his brother Pablo, a close collaborator of Díaz, was also a member of the científico group.[8] The Comisión Revisora provided a context to absorb and neutralize the fashionable positivist proposals of many writers who claimed to represent the modernization of penal legislation. Macedo, a jurist more than a criminologist, refused to tear down the 1871 Penal Code and write a new one from scratch; he limited the task of the Comisión Revisora to clarifying obscure passages of the old code, updating articles superseded by practice, and introducing a few novelties. Reforms could not be deeper, Macedo pointed out, because the new trends in criminology did not yet offer a comprehensive penitentiary alternative to the classic school.[9]

The Comisión Revisora garnered continued presidential support until it concluded its work in 1912, under President Madero, and published the four volumes of its proceedings, under Huerta, in 1914. Political instability prevented the commission from proposing extensive reforms to the penal code. However, the commission was able to draft the reforms that established the penalty of relegación examined previously.

The Revolution brought about a new range of attitudes toward judicial and penitentiary reform. Although positivist notions about raterismo remained strong among politicians, the social movement involved a critique of the corrupt and unfair practices of the police and judiciary, and even of the support lent by science to authoritarian policies. Revolutionary troops expressed this challenge with summary judgments against suspects or by breaking open prison doors; but ideologues also fashioned the impulse for legislative reform. The Zapatista faction proposed the most radical departure from the old status quo through a 1915 penal law whose basic idea was to make justice easily accessible to people without economic resources. The Zapatista proposal would have ended delays and the "monopoly of justice" by lawyers, and would have allowed judges and juries to sentence criminals without complicated proceedings. To deal with convicts, Zapatista lawmakers dismissed isolation. Specialists in "the science of Psychology" would supervise the inmates in the new "institutions for regeneration." The law asserted that jurisprudence was not a technical ability but a political function, derived from the premise that social inequality was the true cause of crime.[10]

Although many revolutionaries shared the ideas of the Zapatistas, institutional continuity prevailed over radicalism. Since late 1914, Carranza had signed several decrees that reestablished the administration of justice, limited the possibilities of appeals, and appointed new judges in the towns under Constitutionalist control. The 1915 "Programa de la revolución social encabezada por el ciudadano Venustiano Carranza" criticized the "immorality of courts" and the long delays in judicial proceedings caused by corrupt employees. The "Programa" included "reforms of judicial procedures with the purpose of making the administration of justice more effective and expeditious."[11] Once his faction defeated the Zapatistas and Villistas, however, Carranza showed that his main concern was for the reestablishment of judicial routine, Porfirian-style repression of "social plagues," and the continued centralization of the penitentiary system under the executive power as outlined in 1896 and 1897.[12] But not all groups in the heterogeneous winning coalition agreed with Carranza's approach. At the 1916–17 Constitutional Congress, deputies defeated Carranza's proposal to establish a centralized penitentiary system through article 18 of the new Constitution, dismissing the Carrancistas' reliance on scientific arguments and their emphasis on punishment as an instrument of social reform. In their speeches, the majority of representatives stressed a preference for tackling social inequality and their distrust toward the reestablishment of a Porfirian-style executive power.[13]

After Carranza's overthrow in 1920, attempts at penitentiary reform gained energy. According to the organizers of the First Criminological and Penitentiary Congress, in October 1923, crime and punishment were central aspects of social reconstruction. The summons to the Congress stated that the revolutionary regime had achieved "resolution of the most important political problems" and that the next step was to continue "the effort toward the radical and rational improvement of our society" with the help of scientific and technical knowledge. This time, however, technical reform would coincide with political changes and support a progressive social order. The congress included specialists from diverse disciplines (sociology, criminal law, anthropology, medicine, and education), and public officials from all over the country. They met under the sponsorship of labor leader Vicente Lombardo Toledano and Federal District governor Celestino Gasca—still struggling with police chief Almada over the treatment of rateros. The debates conveyed the new viewpoints of postrevolutionary penal reformers, particularly their concern about juvenile delinquency. Presenters stressed the explanation and prevention of crime as a social phenomenon, and even Miguel Macedo voiced his concern about the inequalities of the law toward the different classes.[14]

Legislative action did not come until the second half of the 1920s. Moreover, it was not the product of a clear consensus among penologists. President Plutarco Elías Calles appointed a committee in 1925 to propose "deep reforms, not a mere correction of classic ideas."[15] The committee's work led to a new penal code, which President Emilio Portes Gil decreed in 1929 through special legislative powers granted by Congress. The Almaraz Code (after its main author, Juan Antonio Almaraz) embraced positivist criminology and ideas about centralizing punishment under the executive power. The influence of Macedo's Comisión Revisora was clear in some sections, which borrowed verbatim from the 1912 project. At the same time, some passages of the Almaraz Code advocated the rehabilitation of criminals rather than their isolation, echoing the vocabulary of the 1923 congress.[16]

Despite or perhaps because of its innovations, the 1929 Code triggered the reaction of legal professionals, who protested the interference of political authorities in the adjudication and execution of sentences. The code had created a powerful Supreme Council of Social Defense and Prevention, which, as the depository of specialized knowledge about penal techniques, had the power to supersede judges' decisions. The authors of the new code justified the power afforded the council on the grounds that the new body could establish the suspect's "social responsibility"—as opposed to the classic, "metaphysical" idea of moral responsibility and individual free will. The premise of punishment was going to be the more flexible principle of "social defense," which allowed for the incarceration of those individuals deemed dangerous—regardless of their responsibility for a specific offense. According to the code, recidivists could be incarcerated for an indefinite time, until authorities decided that their "dangerous state" had disappeared. Citing the "exaggerated respect for individual rights" of the current regime, Almaraz even argued that constitutional reforms were in order to allow authorities to act effectively against crime before it took place.[17]

Criminal lawyers resented the way in which the code was introduced—without a broad discussion preceding it, literally by decree. Critics charged that the new code was difficult to put into practice, contained several conceptual and formal flaws, and introduced unnecessary novelties into the penal vocabulary, such as the substitution of *sanciones* for *penas.* Furthermore, critics argued, the Almaraz Code contradicted the Constitution in giving the Supreme Council (appointed by the executive) faculties to invade the jurisdiction of the judicial branch of government.[18] The responses undercut the code. One penologist accused the Ministry of the Interior, the government of the Federal District, and the High Court of the Federal District of "killing [the Supreme Council] by starvation" because they were not willing to relinquish any of their powers. New president Pascual Ortiz Rubio was not interested in affording the council the powers that his predecessor, Portes Gil, had promised to Almaraz.[19]

Resistance to the code threatened to go beyond cabinet politics. One of the new provisions of the 1929 Code was to punish negligence with stronger sentences. This provision was perceived by truck and taxi drivers to mean the elimination of bail for those who ran over pedestrians or caused accidents. The drivers' unions threatened to strike if those provisions of the code were not revoked. There were rumors that its enforcement would be postponed. The *Excélsior* stated that the mere publication of the 1929 Code had already increased violent crime in the capital. Congressmen and other newspapers denounced the code as an increased threat to public safety and suggested that Congress should repeal it; but members of the official majority came forward to stop further debate.[20]

The reaction against the 1929 Code resulted not in a return to the 1871 Code but in the prompt drafting and approval of yet another code, which proved to be a better synthesis of old practices and contemporary ideas about punishment. President Ortiz Rubio appointed a fresh committee to write a code that would "have reality in mind," seeking reforms that were "pragmatic and feasible." The committee declared from the outset that it "does not follow a certain school or penal system, but maintains a pragmatic and eclectic attitude."[21] The new penal code was passed in 1931 following a wider process of discussion than its predecessor. After the committee's initial works, the First Juridical Congress approved the project. Lawyers and judges celebrated the fact that the new code maintained the primacy of the legal profession in the administration of justice.[22] The result, still in force today despite multiple reforms, disposed of the stylistic extremes of the 1929 Code.

The codes of 1929 and 1931 had much in common: both reflected post-revolutionary changes in attitudes toward punishment and the social causes of criminality. With different terminology, both established the goal of rehabilitation and placed punishment under the responsibility of the executive power. The 1929 Code stated that the goal of sanctions would be "to prevent crime, to re-utilize delinquents and to eliminate the incorrigible, by applying to each type of criminal the procedures of education, adaptation and cure required for their conditions and for social defense" (article 69). The 1931 Code did not make such a doctrinaire statement, but it established that "the Executive power will apply the procedures deemed necessary for the correction, education and social adaptation of the criminal" (article 78). Thus, the crude language of the 1929 Code ("re-utilize delinquents") appeared in the 1931 Code as "social adaptation" of criminals, but maintained political authorities' control over the execution of sentences.

Both codes were more receptive to explanations of theft based on economic factors than were Porfirian ideas about rateros. The codes introduced the notion of *robo famélico* (starving theft), to define larceny committed without violence and caused by an urgent need of the accused and his or her family. Such offenses would no longer be punished. The notion demonstrated a common trait of revolutionary perceptions of the causes of crime.

In 1923, Lombardo Toledano had criticized those who supported the use of banishment against petty thieves, saying that it was unjust to impose such a hard punishment on someone who probably stole bread out of hunger. Alfonso Teja Zabre, coauthor of the 1931 Code, defined criminal law specifically as an "instrument for class justice" that would strengthen the state through "revolutionary legislation . . . to attract to its side the unorganized power of the dispossessed classes."[23] Henceforth, the failure of success of punishment would be judged as a function of the postrevolutionary regime's social policies. That reasoning prompted the Partido Nacional Revolucionario to include preventive policies and penitentiary reform in Lázaro Cárdenas's 1934 presidential program.[24]

THE IDENTITY OF PRISONERS

Thus associated with social policies, postrevolutionary penal reform went beyond a mere academic debate. Even if the mechanisms to legislate and impart justice were not radically transformed after the Revolution, new and old actors now felt entitled to participate in the public discussion of the law. The most numerous group to participate in the mediation between law and punitive practices were not lawyers, but prisoners. They were intimately concerned with the functioning of institutions and thus greatly interested in reform. There were limits, however, to their ability to participate in the public discussions mentioned above. Clearly, one of them was literacy: as noted in the introduction to part 2, the sentenced had a lower literacy level than did the indicted in general. Another obstacle was the "criminal" label that the judicial process and criminological discourse placed on them. If there was one idea from the intellectual constructions of criminologists that took root in public opinion it was the notion that a criminal was a type of person characterized by his or her constant drive to break the law and epitomized by the category of ratero. Therefore, people could interpret a criminal conviction or simply an arrest as a permanent mark on the suspect's identity: once a criminal, always a criminal. As noted previously, judges and the press construed the use of legal resources by prisoners in their own defense as further proof of their criminal nature.

One way for prisoners to struggle against these perceptions and deal with prison life was to build a public voice in defense of their interests. Departing from interpretations of prison life that posit the prisoners' loss of identity as an inevitable byproduct of penitentiary techniques, the following pages trace the reconstruction of political agency in the context of prisons.[25] In the 1920s, prisoners began to think of themselves as a community of interests and thus addressed authorities through the legal rhetoric that until then had excluded the uneducated and poor. In this way, they offered a radical challenge to the strategies of punishment based on isolation.

Prison life itself was the central theme of those claims. The idea that criminals belonged to a lower level of society had justified inhumane jail conditions, even if those conditions made a mockery of penitentiary reform. Descriptions of prison life in Mexico City painted a grim picture, but they also stressed the apparent happiness of inmates. In 1863, inspector Joaquín García Icazbalceta found that gambling, drinking, and violence were rife in Belem jail. García Icazbalceta, like many later observers, considered the place a "focus of corruption" and a "school of immorality."[26] In 1897, Miguel Macedo noted that even the construction of the new prison would not solve penitentiary problems, because prisoners were still corrupted and still enjoyed the company of their peers. Public prosecutor Emilio Rovirosa Andrade confirmed in 1903 that criminals liked the new penitentiary as well. After personally visiting several prisons, novelist Federico Gamboa wrote in 1913 that most of the inmates were happy with their life of idleness and their consumption of marijuana.[27] This evidence bewildered elite observers. They concluded that imprisonment, even in such degrading conditions, did not correct transgressive behavior, but fostered it.

Despite the alleged contentment of prisoners, jails were characterized by disease and danger. It was not uncommon to hear of cases such as the clerk who, after spending five months in Belem for battery, died two weeks following his release, from a disease "caused by the prison."[28] According to Heriberto Frías, typhus, neglect, and sometimes even starvation killed prisoners. Trials dragged on for months, even years, as defendants waited in prison. Fights were deadly and frequent, often related to alcohol or drug consumption. In 1900, the Supervising Board of Prisons discovered that there were not enough toilets in Belem. Dangerous filth floated about in the building during the frequent floodings. Additions and reforms to the building did not improve its hygienic conditions. In 1907, the *Diario del Hogar* described Belem with strong words: "It stands at the center of the city, like a cloister, infectious, revolting, spilling its harmful vapors over its walls, like a glass filled with poison."[29] Even officialist *Gaceta de Policía* recognized that the institution was a potential embarrassment "when a foreign visitor wished to visit it."[30]

Authorities had difficulties in establishing control over Belem jail. Increasing overcrowding was a problem throughout the prison's history. In 1863, the prison held 780 men and 336 women. In 1887, there were 1,299 men and 313 women. In 1906, up to 5,000 prisoners inhabited Belem. Because of the slow pace of the courts, suspects were a large factor of Belem's overpopulation. Criminal courts communicated with the prison through a window, called *el boquete* (the hole), where prisoners made their statements. The building contained multiple passages between sections and many subdivisions; there were seven patios and 116 "big and small" rooms. Prisoners gathered on the patios, making the work of guards more difficult. The inauguration of the San Lázaro penitentiary was an important propaganda event, but its impact on the city's prison system was slight. Overcrowding and violence in the penitentiary soon resembled the conditions of the old Belem jail. The power structure of both prisons proved more complex and resilient to change than reformers had expected.[31]

The hardship of incarceration encouraged informal practices aimed at improving life in small ways. Imprisoned since 1897, María Villa, "La Chiquita," finally found distraction in 1900, when she was allowed to acquire a guitar and a mandolin. María wrote in her diary, "It seems that God has sent me contentment." Prisoner Manuel T. kept a dog for company. Others played dice (presumably for money), stole things from one another, and killed time any way they could: organizing a lottery, buying and selling tequila.[32] The food prepared in prison was so bad that anyone who possessed a small amount of money from their work or from outside sources had their meals delivered daily through a window. Employees and inmates in charge of vigilance collected fees for their cooperation in allowing the entrance of food and drinks. They also profited from a vigorous commerce in bread, coffee, sugar, and cigarettes.[33]

Prison officials and penitentiary legislation sought to counteract the perceived contentment of prisoners with harassment, isolation, and internal divisions. In Belem, officials imposed arbitrary decisions, such as the sudden prohibition of all visits in 1890. Female prisoners were sexually harassed by the male staff. Catalina S. saw little use in complaining, she told Roumagnac, because nobody paid attention, and she could be punished for it. The internal hierarchies that separated prisoners were as strong as those dividing authorities and inmates. When a newcomer entered the prison for the first time, he faced the aggression of more experienced "sharks," who soon stripped him of his clothes. Separations within buildings reinforced hierarchies based on each prisoner's length of incarceration and social status. Regulations issued in 1900 officially established a *departamento de distinción* (preferential section)—to house prisoners "chosen by the authority" or, in other words, those whose social status was higher than the rest of prisoners—in addition to the sections for the arrested and the sentenced.[34] Following Miguel Macedo's classification of social strata, the reform established that employees had to register the "personal qualities of entered individuals," including trade, education, and "social class." The three classes were distinguished by prisoners' use of *levita, chaqueta,* or only *camisa* (frock coats, jackets, and shirts).[35] The isolation cells (*separos,* or *bartolinas*) housed prisoners of bad behavior and those sentenced to death. A separate section for former policemen prevented them from contact with other prisoners. Journalists incarcerated by the Díaz regime were also confined in a special area.[36]

Hierarchies among prisoners, partly based on regulations or previous status, developed further inside. Upon entrance, all inmates received two plates, a spoon and cup, soap, and a straw mat to sleep on. But they could also use their own clothes and furniture—which for the fortunate consisted of a bed and a table. Equality was not desirable for the better-off. María Villa enjoyed some benefits and, in her diary, highlighted the differences that separated her from the rest of the female prisoners. "They do not understand me and I do not understand them," she wrote. Rafael Tagle, who had attended high school, told Roumagnac that another prisoner who attacked him was a *pelado,* a pejorative term referring to the urban poor. Regulations prohibited prisoners from possessing money, newspapers, musical instruments, pornographic pictures, or alcohol. Yet the existence of material possessions, commerce, and work accentuated economic disparities and gave prisoners access to cash. By the end of the century, Belem had three shoemakers' shops, two for carpentry, and one each for cigar making, tailoring, production of matches, weaving, and hat making. There was also a bakery. Women did laundry and embroidering and were in charge of cooking for inmates in Belem and other city jails. Some inmates even became bosses.

Victoriano A., serving a twenty-year sentence, was the owner of a textile loom at which other prisoners worked.[37]

Differences of rank between prisoners involved the use of violence and influence. A select group of inmates in Belem and the penitentiary became members of the structure of vigilance that maintained control over the rest of the population. Each section of the prison had a "major" and several "presidents" appointed by the warden. These were prisoners armed with clubs, whose loyalty to prison authorities was stronger than any solidarity they might have felt with fellow inmates. In a failed attempt at escape led by inmate Alberto Tagle, in 1887, one president and an employee died. The intervention of other inmates, later rewarded by authorities, prevented Tagle and others from reaching a wall and escaping. The regulation of 1900 called these officer-inmates "corporals" and "adjutants," and established a salary of ten and four pesos per month, respectively. Although the appointments were to be based on records of good behavior, this was not necessarily the case. Rafael Tagle, brother of Alberto Tagle and accomplice in the escape attempt of 1887, later became a major. His rank seems to have derived from his social status and close relationship with prison authorities. He finally managed to escape prison in 1904. Francisco R. did not fear the ill will or ambition of other inmates while he was a major in Belem. He secured power by keeping a list of male homosexuals and by having a brother who was a police agent. As one of the first occupants of the penitentiary, however, he bitterly complained about losing his close relationships with authorities at Belem prison.[38] The higher strata among male prisoners were able to use violence, earn money, and manage the structures of power to get closer to authorities and to the possibility of escape. They commanded enough resources to cope with and, to an extent, benefit from prison life.

All these internal hierarchies and accommodations helped inmates to manage their limited resources, but were not enough to improve living conditions for most of them. The most common response of inmates to poor conditions, regardless of their rank, was to address authorities for help and to capitalize on their knowledge of judicial practices. Disease (against which holding a prison rank meant little) provided frequent reasons to appeal to authorities. In 1931, several Belem prisoners sent an unsigned letter to the city's chief of public health, complaining about an outbreak of flu inside the prison and about the lack of medical facilities. Poor food quality also prompted complaints to the press and authorities. A few prisoners denounced wardens' exploitation of their work, or employees' embezzlement of inmates' food.[39]

The slow progress of their trials concerned inmates more than any other circumstance of their incarceration. Delays and irregularities in the administration of justice were the rule, and prisoners often did not know the state of their cases or the date of their future release. Miguel Delgado, for example, was arrested on July 13, 1920, after a fight; on September 7, he was sentenced to eight days of arrest and released. Court clerks often had a larger role than judges in conducting judicial proceedings. They profited from the delays, demanding money to expedite the cases.[40]

The Constitution guaranteed that the poor would benefit from the services of public defenders, although there were never enough of them to staff city courts, and they played only a minor role in trials. In one case, a public defender asked the jury to find his defendants guilty. Such ineptitude explains why Guadalupe Ruiseñor could decline her right to appoint an attorney, as many other suspects did, arguing that she needed to do so because she had not committed any crime. Suspect Florencio Sánchez appointed his wife as his attorney, seeking perhaps to be able to see her, and correctly assuming that the decision would not hurt his defense. A few public attorneys, however, in particular Agustín Arroyo de Anda, were models of skill and tenacity. In the cases where he was involved, the accused party used its right to question accusers and demand corroborating evidence, sometimes with successful results. He uncovered the neglected clemency requests of prisoners and obtained overdue releases. But public defenders were often denied access to the prisoners, while private counsels were allowed inside to sell their services. Inmates and their families placed money on these hopes, often to be disappointed.[41]

Conditions in Mexico City jails, combining brutality, corruption, and internal hierarchies, could not be less favorable for the emergence of prisoners' agency. Yet, prisoners reacted, individually and as a group. A number of different strategies addressed judicial shortcomings. As we have seen, suspects used a number of methods to avoid legal intervention altogether, such as negotiating with victims, changing their names, and refusing to confess. Suspects also used the ambiguities of language and memory to deflect judicial interrogation, since prosecutors relied almost entirely on the testimonies of victims and the accused, and seldom on more than one witness or on crime-scene evidence. While some suspects cited their youth as an excuse, older defendants claimed that alcohol had clouded their recollections. If witnesses' accounts had gaps, the accused could even deny the existence of a crime. A common defense among those accused of theft was to say that they had found the stolen object on the street, and that they took it in the belief that it had been lost.[42]

Prisoners used procedural rules to avoid an unfavorable sentence. Some suspects delayed the proceedings in the hope that witnesses against them would disappear in the meanwhile. To achieve this, they would appoint and dismiss their counsel several times and for no apparent reason. Julián Lara and Andrés Tapia, accused of battery against each other, appointed and discharged as many as seven defenders during their case. The judge took six months to find them both guilty. Most commonly, however, the accused declined their right to appoint a defender, because they knew that it would only delay the trial. Theft suspects used other devices to avoid banishment to the Islas Marías and other penal colonies. Many convicts appealed their sentences, regardless of the probable outcome, because they knew that the appeal would take several months, thus entitling them to remain in Mexico City for the rest of their sentences. To avoid being sent to penal colonies, prisoners would attack and wound their victims, policemen, or fellow inmates, in order to have new charges brought against them for offenses punished with imprisonment in Mexico City.[43]

Cognizant of the politics of the judiciary system, prisoners often appealed to higher authorities. Letters requesting presidential pardon were common before the Revolution, and they continued under Madero and Huerta. These letters usually had a submissive tone, appealing to the president's or his wife's mercy. A letter by Agustín Ulibarri and others on the occasion of one of Porfirio Díaz's reelections, exemplifies their style:

> We suffer with submission the consequences of our disgrace, but we are also repentant and desire to alleviate our sad and miserable situation. Thus, we have decided to raise our humble voice to you, Mr. President, in these solemn moments in which the spontaneous unanimity of the Mexican People has reelected you for the high office that you occupy, causing the joy of the people.[44]

Such missives were not idle exercises. A letter often involved the cost of paper, stamps, and the fees of scribes who provided the good handwriting and formalities of style that promised greater impact.[45]

A closer look at these letters reveals that prisoners in Porfirian jails saw the advantages of accepting stigmatizing ideas about criminals as a class. An innocent verdict, after all, did not cleanse the stigma of spending days or months in prison. Francisco P. Díaz appealed to President Díaz's mercy, wisdom, and "noble heart," asking that the rest of his sentence be served in the army. Francisco did not claim to be innocent, and acknowledged his membership to that special group of society: "I am twenty two years old," he said, "and I have spent sixteen of these in the career of crime."[46] Others used criminological categories to argue for leniency, claiming to be criminals out of need rather than by "instinct."[47] Letters also asked for the president's intervention over judicial decisions because their trials were not fair. "We have faith in justice," inmates of Belem jail wrote to Díaz in 1900, "but, sir, we have more faith in you."[48] Perhaps concerned about these appeals, the 1900 prison regulation authorized officials to open letters to and from inmates, erase words from them, or forward them to other addresses.[49]

The Revolution linked prisoners' individual problems with larger political issues and changed the tone of their letters. During a military uprising against Madero in February 1913, artillery fire opened a hole in the walls of Belem jail, and hundreds of inmates fled in the middle of the battle. Most of them were later pardoned by the new president, Victoriano Huerta, even though they had not been re-apprehended. Other escapees joined the federal army. Many still in jail were released later by the Zapatista armies when they took control of the city. As a result, prisoners' letters soon incorporated revolutionary rhetoric, and the political or military situation of the country became their central argument. Eva Rojo and twenty-three other inmates of Belem requested Madero's pardon in order to fight for the Revolution in a feminine brigade they had already organized in prison. According to death-row inmate J. Guadalupe Cuéllar, authorities granted "several hundred" pardons in 1914 so that prisoners could enter the army.[50] Descriptions of suffering gave way to promises of happy sacrifice for the nation. Pioquinto Gómez and other prisoners in Galley 3 of Belem addressed President Obregón on October 1922: "We, your humble sympathizers since your candidacy until this precise moment, are ready to enlist among the true Revolutionaries of strong ideas and beliefs, to punish with a heavy hand all those traitors who only want to benefit by obtaining the best public offices. . . . We want to fight in the battlefields, rather than being slaves of the old Dictatorship."[51] By means of their patriotism, they intended to convert themselves from the punished into the punishers of those who had committed crimes against the nation.

Postrevolutionary letters from prisoners no longer simply begged. They demonstrated the increased willingness of prisoners to denounce corruption and intervene in the appointment or removal of prison authorities. In 1911, Emiliano Helguera accused Belem warden Wulfrano Vázquez of participating in a conspiracy against President Madero. In 1924, invoking "the ideals of the Revolution," prisoners requested a wider amnesty. In 1931, Antonio Martínez ("El Enterrador") and other prisoners of Belem thanked President Ortiz Rubio for the removal of certain prison officers and offered information about the illegal deals of one still in office. Offers of spying on political opposition came from the penitentiary in 1925. Although scribes were still hired to write some of these letters, the literacy rate among prisoners was rising after the Revolution, placing letter writing within reach of more of them.[52]

Several unprecedented attempts to formalize their collective actions are further proof of prisoners' willingness to enter the public sphere. Prisoners organized in order to pursue broad presidential amnesties. In 1921, the Pro-Freedom Association of Islas Marías inmates, supported by the Federation of Trade Unions of the Federal District, addressed the nation through a manifesto seeking amnesty from President Obregón. The Pro-Amnesty Penitentiary Union formulated a similar request to President Elías Calles in 1924 with Obregón's support. Prison organizers adopted the style of labor unions. In late 1922, prisoners in the same Galley 3 who had expressed their desire to be "among the true Revolutionaries of strong ideals and beliefs" informed President Obregón that they had organized the Prisoners' Union in order to fight corruption and fraud by lawyers, guards, and court employees. They also set forth to achieve alliances with "all organizations and trade unions," by defining themselves as an "autonomous union." The Prisoners' Union fully embraced the language of political mobilization fashionable in the 1920s. They adopted the same motto, "Health and Social Revolution," as the dominant Regional Confederation of Mexican Workers (CROM). Their goals, however, addressed institutional reform rather than class relations or government social policies. One of the objectives of the Union was to request the immediate removal "of any Employee who conspires against

8. Jazz band started by Belem Jail inmates, ca. 1930. Source: Fototeca Nacional, Fondo Casasola, 86628. © INAH.

or mistreats physically or verbally those under his custody." Obregón welcomed the union as an instrument to help resolve inmates' cases. There is no documentary evidence of further activities in the following years; in 1937, however, a union of penitentiary workers obtained control of the penitentiary's workshops.[53]

Hardly a political clientele, inmates nevertheless managed to use the new rules of public discourse for their own benefit. Presidents Obregón and Elías Calles granted several amnesties, and the former intervened in favor of inmates' welfare, using the resources of the powerful Department of General Provisions, controlled by Luis N. Morones, leader of the CROM. Although difficult to evaluate, particularly under the light of contemporary conditions, improvements in prison life resulted from this activism. From the "Belem Jazz Band," (see fig. 8) to the establishment of matrimonial visits and the right to choose transportation to the Islas Marías along with the family—evidence shows that conditions for Mexico City prisoners never sank again to the situation of the turn of the century.[54] Official attitudes concerning criminals had changed, but these measures also acknowledged prisoners' greater organization and ability to address authorities.

CONCLUSIONS

Postrevolutionary presidents were more receptive toward inmates and more considerate regarding the social causes of crime, but their popular generosity did not mean the defeat of the traditional and scientific uses of punishment. Positivist notions about the "innate" nature of criminals survived well into the 1920s and later. Legal professionals resisted the advances of scientists, not only in order to defend the Constitution, but also to protect their power within the judiciary. The Revolution was not a sudden opening into freedom, as many inmates of Belem thought that day in February 1913 when artillery fire breached the wall of their prison. Nor was it a radical challenge to prevalent ideas about crime, criminals, and the internal structure of prison life. The prison walls were repaired, and the institutions of punishment and justice survived political turmoil.

The real change belonged at the level of political participation. Punishment became the battlefield where lawyers, police, and suspects disputed the meaning of criminal law and its place in the larger context of postrevolutionary politics. The impact of this dispute over punishment can be appreciated in two areas. First, prisoners and their communities came to believe that crime responded to social and economic factors, and not merely to moral failures or the degeneration stressed by criminologists and authorities who wanted to isolate offenders. Second, the new participation of prisoners and lawyers in public debates about crime and punishment became part of the construction of revolutionary legitimacy. The inhabitants of Mexico City challenged the technocratic discourse constructed by Porfirian specialists on "social pathologies"; in return, prisoners expected concrete benefits from a more transparent relationship with penal institutions.

Becoming prisoners forced the urban poor to rethink their relationship with the law and political power. Activism inside penal institutions seldom became a matter of public discussion, unlike crime itself. Judicial sources, however, document the continuity of prisoners' and suspects' opposition to judges' and administrators' decisions. Resistance, in this context, meant survival through accommodation rather than open defiance of authority; it did not imply prisoners' outright rejection of the validity of the law, but rather its use and manipulation.[55] The active participation of Mexico City inmates in their own subsistence and organization demonstrates that penitentiary institutions, both before and after the 1896–1908 reforms, were less effective in isolating and reforming criminals than penologists had hoped. Prisoners' adoption of a public voice in the 1920s was an extension of the autonomy they had exercised inside Belem since Porfirian times. In adopting the language of political participation, however, prisoners contributed to changing the conditions of the dialogue between common citizens and a penal system that often victimized them instead of protecting their rights.

Conclusions:
Crime Contested

Crime in Mexico City between 1900 and 1931 developed in two distinct rhythms. One was swift: from the proud capital of Porfirian progress, through the besieged and hungry center of the civil war, to the optimistic heart of postrevolutionary reconstruction in the 1920s, the city experienced great changes in thirty years. The institutions and ideas around crime also changed at a fast pace compared to the periods of slower reform that preceded and followed those years. Never in the past had the Mexican state been so aggressive and resourceful against suspects: arrest campaigns, large prisons, leva, and transportation to penal colonies were brought to bear in rapid succession. Images of crime reinforced the impression of dizzying transformation, from the ragged, rural, knife-wielding pulquería fighters of the turn of the century, through the fearful revolutionary soldiers, to the sophisticated car-driving professionals of the postrevolutionary era.

Although these transformations left an imprint on public opinion, they masked changes taking place at a different pace. There were consistent rules governing violence, theft, the perceptions of and reactions to crime, and the negotiations established by all actors before and during the intervention of police and judges. The results of these interactions were not always positive; violence combined with male domination to silence young victims, and corruption, delays, and neglect defined the judicial process. Yet everyday patterns of crime were resistant to change and the chronological boundaries of this study could probably be extended in both directions without replacing the central elements of the preceding description. One fact, however, is a clear indicator that things were changing in the long term: crime grew in frequency up to (and probably during) the Revolution and it declined afterwards. This book has explored the multiple factors that explain such a shift. In a few words, it is at the intersection of politics and everyday practices that the history of crime in the city must be explained.

The first part of this book reconstructed the tension that emerged between the elite's project of urban modernization and the everyday uses of the city by its inhabitants. Since the second half of the nineteenth century, Mexico City's upper classes had understood urban design as part of the progress toward "civilization." Thus, the construction of wide avenues and impressive buildings went hand in hand with the division between safe neighborhoods and the dangerous zones where migrants settled. But Porfirian city planners could not change workers' need to come out of their homes and neighborhoods and make a living in the streets, the markets, and the residences of the wealthy. Lack of water in their houses and cash in their pockets prompted many to spend their days (and often their nights) in public places, where they came into contact with all classes of people. Bolstered by the development of tramway and railroad lines, the urban poor crossed and diluted the social borders designed by urban planners.

Mexican criminology was born of this contradiction. Science and a professional police came to the regime's aid to criminalize the everyday practices of the urban poor. Specialists set out to explain the complexity of urban life by defining criminals as a social group. They eclectically borrowed explanations and even descriptions from European books. Their observations of Mexico City's underworld amounted to somber assessments of the threat to progress posed by "social pathologies." Beyond this pessimism, however, Mexican criminology did not propose a unified set of social policies. Some authors thought it enough to use traditional racial and cultural prejudices in order to isolate the criminal population from "civilized" groups, while other writers were fascinated by the lives of prisoners and lower-class families. The intellectual legacy of Mexican criminology was ambivalent. On the one hand, it lent a scientific ring to authoritarian policies of social control in the cities, on the other, it stimulated empirical research into the life of the urban population among social scientists and writers.

The tension between modernization and everyday uses was clearly played out in specific areas of the city. The crescent moon surrounding downtown to the north, east, and south produced the images of crime that the elites feared, but it was mostly in the inner boundaries of that moon that conflict took place: the railroad station, the pulquerías north of the Alameda, the markets of Tepito, the tramway hub at the Zócalo, trade around La Merced, justice and punishment in Belem jail. Here, not in the wide avenues and grand buildings of the ideal city, is where urban life and elite discourses suddenly intersected and articulated conflicts.

The second part of this book looked at specific practices of crime that changed at a slower rhythm. In the perspective of urban communities, crime meant something more than conflicting ideas about the city. Violent offenses, to begin with, reflected the importance of honor. Although jurists dismissed most fights as caused by trivial disputes and alcohol, the unspoken rules that governed combat demonstrated that reputation and a sense of self-worth mattered as much to the lower classes as they did to upper-class duelists. Conversely, domestic violence exhibited the desire of lower-class spouses to consolidate strong nuclear families, despite the multiple economic and cultural factors that made matrimony unstable, namely, the lack of civil or religious legitimacy of their unions or the pressures on the household to maximize the use of its labor. Elite observers saw criminal violence as spontaneous and disorganized. Judicial records, in contrast, show that violence was justified, although not welcomed, as an assertion of particular rights, and that its adverse results could be contained through unspoken rules. Guns came with the Revolution to undermine the positive meanings of violence; like cars, they seemed random and lethal in their effects, but they were not as accessible as something like knives.

Sexual violence was the result of the same factors and contexts, though it casts a shadow over the interpretation outlined above. The historical approach demonstrated its limits when it tried to pair the public uses of violence with the intimate, yet eventually shaming, power of rape. No amount of evidence or interpretive effort can escape the conclusion that sexual violence had a negative impact on Mexican society. At the same time, it is not easy to dispel the intuition that, as in El Chalequero's deeds, all violence was sexual violence.

The role of neighbors in preventing crimes against property was less ambiguous. Albeit these offenses resulted from joblessness and lack of stable income among the urban poor (as clearly expressed by embezzlement and counterfeiting), most people saw larceny as nothing more than a crime. Potential offenders knew that victims, neighbors, and gendarmes would act promptly and force them to negotiate an acceptable solution. Criminologists and legislators, however, failed to notice these responses. This was partly due to the urban poor's understandable reluctance to involve authorities—the intervention of judges and police often meant the punishment of offenders and victims equally and the irretrievable loss of stolen property. Beyond these pragmatic motivations, however, theft lays open socially contested views on punishment. Official policies against lawlessness implied that crime was endemic in certain neighborhoods and isolation was the only solution. Urban communities condemned crime but preferred reintegrative punishment—that is, sanctions and negotiations that left a door open for the return of the transgressor into the community rather than stigmatization.[1]

A history of crime shows how these communities were steadily building themselves in spite of the state: authorities did not protect their security but punished their attempts to deal with trouble through negotiation and shaming. Law denied honor to their fights, legality to their dealings with thieves, virtue to the victims of sexual abuse. Mistrust was cast over both guilty and innocent, creating from above a true city of suspects. Yet, just as upper-class homes could not function without workers crossing the boundaries between the modern and the marginal city, urban governance was always implicitly based on the active response of urban communities to the problems of urbanization, from security to health and food supply. The city's impressive population growth cannot be explained otherwise, as the state consistently proved that its resources were spent according to narrow class and political demands. As argued by Oscar Lewis, neighborhoods, extended families, and vecindades contradict sociological views that associated urban life with anomie and anonymity.[2]

Invisible to the ambivalent attraction that guided the criminologists' gaze, these communities built themselves in several overlapping layers. They included the barrios that claimed a multisecular identity, such as Tepito and La Merced, or the more recent colonias whose internal cohesion came from the fight, against the state and developers, for the infrastructure that had been promised to them, as Guerrero, La Bolsa, and Obrera. But vecindades also formed communities, spatially tighter than barrios and colonias, and more intense in their interactions among inhabitants. Extended families accepted the modern gift of mobility and stretched their ties through the geographical divides of a city and between work and privacy. They were permanently challenged by the state and upper classes' derisive perception of amasiato and were often characterized by violence against women. Other communities—often precarious—were built around pulquerías and the hustle of corners. These appeared and disbanded every day, but integrated nevertheless strong horizontal groups of fellow workers, lovers, and friends, ready to fight one another to demonstrate their right to demand public respect. There were also the coerced but powerful communities of prisons, where inmates challenged the technologies of punishment to build their own networks of survival. Figure 3, the cracked photograph presented as evidence against Rafael Trejo, best portrays the multilayered nature of urban communities. Trejo and his victim, Luis Chávez, were friends before they fought, lived close to each other, ate and drank together, and their fatal fight involved the sister of the victim, Altagracia Cerda, who pressed on with the case, despite police apathy and an unsympathetic jury that acquitted the suspect.

Crime forged urban communities. This book has not put forward a stable definition of these communities because evidence reveals them as fluid, searching to negotiate their rights and boundaries with the state and among their own members. I can suggest a retroactive definition that, rather than attempting to enclose them, opens an avenue for further research: urban communities were the public opinion that judged crime, justice, and the value of their own members and, therefore, constantly redefined themselves in the face of conflict and the neglect and intervention of the state. Constituting an audience for conflict the size of which varied according to its ability to disseminate words and gestures, urban communities were mediators (of honorable fights, arrests, and negotiations between victims and suspects) and therefore actors in the prevention of crime.

The last part of this volume, back to a quicker tempo, shows that national legislators responded to the uncomfortable evidence of these communities with the invention of a hypothetical community of rateros—a trade, elite writers argued, but also a product of heredity. The punitive policies derived from such constructs had the unintended consequence of creating two groups that, although not deserving the name of communities, became important actors in the twentieth-century history of crime in Mexico City: professional criminals and specialized police—perennial suspects in city dwellers' views of crime. The stigmatization and isolation of convicts fostered the emergence of offenders expert in navigating the penal system and who soon became the focus of generalized fears about "modern" crime in Mexico City. While the frequency of crimes decreased after the Revolution, people learned to fear well-armed robbers because they understood that such criminals relied on the complicity of the police and judiciary, and that serious crimes often went unpunished. Herein the double meaning of a city of suspects: if criminology rationalized fears toward the majority of the population, people turned suspicion around and focused it on the representatives of the state.

The state created new kinds of suspects by stressing the use of policing and punishment as instruments of social reform. Judges and policemen had traditionally supported employers and protected the "respectable" victims of pickpockets and shoplifters. But the late Porfiriato and revolutionary period witnessed the unprecedented reliance of authorities on criminal law and the institutions of punishment to deal with the social groups that they saw as responsible for "social pathologies." The most comprehensive attempt to adapt social policies to criminological ideas came in the form of repressive policies against rateros. Based mostly on police suspicion and the neglect of due process, those policies resulted in the incarceration or banishment to penal colonies of thousands of suspects.

The outcomes of these policies are difficult to assess. On the one hand, the establishment of the federal penitentiary did not reduce crime and soon became the scene of complex power relations similar to those prevailing in older Mexico City jails. Prisons established the framework for the social construction of criminals, but also for challenges to collective stigmatization. Incarceration isolated suspects from their communities and, in the view of elites, created a strange world of criminals. After the Revolution, however, increased political participation allowed prisoners to adopt a more public stance regarding the administration of jails and courts and even to unionize. In so doing, they challenged the notion that criminals were not citizens and engaged the state in a dispute about the meaning of crime as a social problem. Labor discipline, on the other hand, underwent little change as a result of the new penal system; bosses and workers continued to deal with theft in the realm of the workplace. Meanwhile, penitentiary reform legalized the continuity of quasi-slave labor in regions far from the capital. Nevertheless crime rates soared. Political mobilization and institutional instability during the Revolution debilitated Porfirian control over the police and judiciary. While corruption became widespread, the state relaxed its stance toward petty theft. The results seemed benign. Crime rates show a persuasive decrease after 1920, as part of a long-term trend that lasted until the latter years of the century (undoubtedly related to the sustained growth in education and living standards achieved between World War II and the late 1960s).

Yet the narrative related above contains many elements of the problems of crime and punishment affecting contemporary Mexico. It has been a permanent temptation during the writing of this book to introduce evidence from life in contemporary Mexico City. Today, crime and punishment again occupy a central place in the intersection between state policies and everyday life. Criminality and violence have risen, particularly since the December 1994 economic crisis.[3] Popular ideas about raterismo remain strong, as do community reactions against larceny. A banner at the entrance of a busy commercial district in colonia Morelos greets customers: "Welcome. If a ratero tries to steal from you, let us know. The merchants of this market will gladly beat the crap out of him." Street commerce continues to be the source of income for a good part of the population and, as in the early decades of the century, their relationship to authorities is usually mediated by police intervention. Vendors and customers do not associate the presence of the police with greater security, but with bribery and further violence. Today, as in the early decades of the century, people prefer to avoid involving judges in their disputes, as the judiciary seems to retain the class and gender prejudices of old times.[4]

Criminal practices have adopted new forms in recent years, due to the growth of the drug business and, as a consequence, the multiplication of corruption. The use of guns, complex organization, and official connivance that defined the Gray Automobile Gang in the 1910s is now present in vastly larger and more profitable transnational organizations. Like their predecessors, modern criminals have an entrepreneurial spirit and are ready to use violence; but the rumors against Pablo González are laughable when compared with the accusations presented in court against Raúl Salinas de Gortari and other members of the political and financial elite during the administration of Raúl's brother, Carlos (1988–94). From the perspective of the public, this makes crime more threatening and anonymous. Violence is not restricted to formalized confrontations, but has become more deadly and widespread. As in the 1920s, new penal laws and police reorganization fail to redress spreading, blatant institutional corruption and impunity. Historical experience appears to be lost on the Mexican and U.S. governments as they turn the fight against drug trafficking into a national security priority. The use of violence in the "war" against the drug business (which has proven its high cost and meager results in countries like Peru, Colombia, and the United States) threatens to repeat past mistakes. Today's actions against the drug business only increase costs to traffickers, forcing them to spread their profits. It might be argued that the more people benefit from the drug business, the less likely it will be condemned by society. In contemporary Mexico, that war diverts resources from the population's real concerns about crime and further alienates the police and judiciary from the public.

As in the early decades of this century, in today's Mexico crime and punishment constitute the focus of tensions between state policies and civil society. The government relies on new jails, equipment, and weapons for the police. In 1996, for example, the Mexican Congress passed legislation designed to fight organized crime. Soldiers temporarily replaced police officers in the capital in early 1997, while the latter were sent to complete a retraining program. Politicians catering to the middle-class vote stress a discourse of law and order and the stigmatization of criminals.[5] But these policies weaken the ability of city residents to deal with transgression and preclude the reintegration of offenders. The convergence of state and public goals regarding crime and punishment may be one of the benefits of the long-awaited arrival of democracy. The election of the Federal District governor in July 1997 was a decisive step toward the accountability of city officials, but little of real value will be achieved until the judiciary gains citizens' trust.

The portrait of crime and punishment drawn above has sought to provide a sound perspective on contemporary questions by stressing the diverse but intertwined rhythms of historical change. Social scientists normally address criminality with policy-making urgency. This book seeks to revise those simplistic, conventional problematizations of criminality as a disease or imbalance of society. The history of crime in early-twentieth-century Mexico City shows that the frequency and character of offenses does not respond favorably to increased policing and punishment. On the contrary, crime becomes a more disrupting phenomenon for the majority of the urban population when the state applies stigmatizing policies against collective and individual suspects. A comprehensive approach suggests how crime itself prompted challenges to these policies and the identities thus created.

The parallels between past and present became clear to me one summer night in 1995, while I was walking my dog after a day of research in Mexico City's archives. Three teenagers on roller skates, in punk clothes and with spiked hair, held on to the back of a tramway, which pulled them on Lázaro Cárdenas Avenue. Several policemen on motorcycles, armed with machine guns, members of one of the special "elite" forces recently created by the Federal District's government, stopped them. The officers did not seem to have a clear reason for stopping the teenagers, who kept a defiant attitude, looking the agents in the eye despite being threatened and pushed. A small group of passers-by began to surround the scene, and one woman told an officer, "Let them go. Don't hit them." The officer turned toward her and asked, "Do you want us to let them go, so they can rob you? That's what you want?" The woman did not flinch, and the witnesses did not disperse. Finally, the policemen let the teenagers skate away.[6] The main elements of the story related in the previous chapters were present at that scene: city dwellers apprehended because of certain cultural traits, a dispute between authorities and citizens over the proper use of public space, and policemen guided by suspicion rather than knowledge of an actual crime. Despite the fear invoked by the officers, people in the streets made it clear that they were not so frightened by crime as to excuse police abuses, even in this city of suspects.

Appendix: Statistics of Crime

A Note on the General and Particular Biases of Criminal Statistics

Mexican statistics of criminality present conceptual and methodological problems. In 1907, Carlos Roumagnac declared that Mexican crime statistics were flawed and were only useful as an index of judicial activity. Other criminologists agreed with him.[1] Historians generally have criticized crime statistics for several reasons, the most important being: (1) victims of crime do not always approach the authorities, because the authorities do not always apprehend suspects and because suspects are not always guilty; (2) statistics usually reflect the interest of the authorities and the public for certain types of crimes; (3) statistics offer diverse results according to the institution that compiled them.[2]

In the case of Mexico, institutional instability must be added to all of these problems. The executive power, the judiciary, and the police forces of Mexico City often conflicted in their views and strategies concerning crime. Thus, the count of crimes from judiciary sources is much lower than the one produced by the police, which detained many drunkards and prostitutes in the streets and kept them in jail overnight. "Administrative" procedures of this kind were also used against minor thefts.[3] All the statistical series available until the 1930s come from sporadic efforts to have them published, instead of routine record keeping. Authorities did not hesitate to change the criteria for quantification or to stop publication altogether. For example, the public prosecutor of the Federal District appointed in 1902, Luis López Masse, left his mark in the judicial statistics by dropping the series that tracked arrests.[4] The Revolution suspended the continuity of all spheres of public administration, and there were recurrent changes in trial procedures, public order policies, and the penal system.[5] Changes in the jurisdiction of courts and police, furthermore, make the comparison between the rate of crime before and after the Revolution imprecise.[6]

Despite these problems, statistics of criminality can be considered as the account of the crimes "purchased" by the state, through its funding of police, prosecutors, judges, and juries.[7] The Pearson correlation between judiciary budgets and the rates of criminality gives a coefficient of 0.91 during the thirteen years before the Revolution: when the state spent more money on judges and prosecutors, the number of arrested and sentenced increased. It is more difficult to establish the relationship after 1916, because political decisions and changes in the organization of the penal system upset the budget for the judiciary.[8] Authorities might have found more criminals when they spent more money chasing them, but it is doubtful that they succeeded in deciding over the long-term trends of criminality.[9]

The first systematic publication of crime statistics for Mexico City and the Federal District is the Dirección General de Estadística's *Estadística del ramo criminal en la República Mexicana que comprende un periodo de quince años, de 1871 a 1885* (Mexico City: Secretaría de Fomento, 1890). The data after 1895 were published in the *Anuario Estadístico de la República Mexicana* (Mexico City: Secretaría de Fomento, 1894–99). Subsequent publications within the period of this book were: Ministerio Público del Distrito y Territorios Federales, *Cuadros estadísticos e informe del Procurador de Justicia concernientes a la criminalidad en el Distrito Federal y territorios* (Mexico City: Ministerio Público del Distrito y Territorios Federales, 1900–1909); Procuraduría General de Justicia del Distrito y Territorios Federales, Sección de Estadística, *Estadística de la penalidad habida en los juzgados del fuero común del Distrito y territorios federales durante los años de 1916 a 1920* (Mexico City: Talleres Gráficos de la Nación, 1923); *Anuario Estadístico de la República Mexicana* 1938 and 1940 (Mexico City: Talleres Gráficos de la Nación, 1939 and 1942); and Alfonso Quiroz Cuarón et al., *Tendencia y ritmo de la criminalidad en México* (Mexico City: Instituto de Investigaciones Estadísticas, 1939), 82–83.

The following tables attempt to establish extended series based on homogeneous counting procedures and sources. I use "Accused" to name those whose cases were considered by judicial authorities as indicted of a crime, usually corresponding with *consignados* in the sources. "Arrested" refers to those detained by the police, and sometimes counted as *arrestados* or simply *arrestos.*

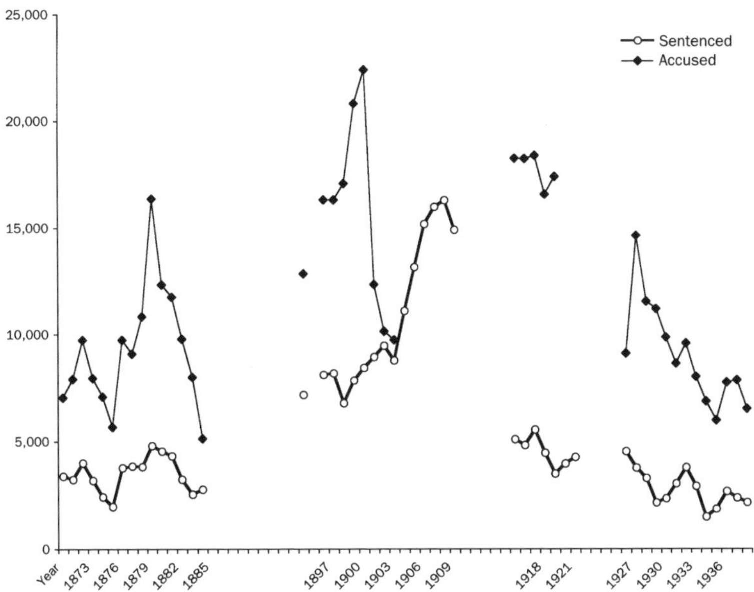

Table 1. Accused and Sentenced, Federal District, 1871–1939.
Compiled from statistics in Table 2.

Table 2. Sentenced and Accused. Federal District, 1871–1939

Year	Sentenced	Accused	Year	Sentenced	Accused
1871	3,403	7,038	1906	13,164	—
1872	3,249	7,923	1907	15,192	—
1873	4,018	9,745	1908	16,010	—
1874	3,207	7,965	1909	16,318	—
1875	2,440	7,078	1910	14,929	—
1876	1,991	5,672			
1877	3,782	9,750	1916	5,106	18,279
1878	3,865	9,100	1917	4,841	18,265
1879	3,836	10,843	1918	5,560	18,419
1880	4,803	16,374	1919	4,483	16,601
1881	4,554	12,332	1920	3,514	17,428
1882	4,322	11,754	1921	3,980	—
1883	3,252	9,796	1922	4,282	—
1884	2,558	8,004			
1885	2,780	5,135	1927	4,546	9,136
			1928	3,791	14,658
1895	7,165	12,838	1929	3,310	11,563
			1930	2,175	11,208
1897	8,108	16,333	1931	2,368	9,874
1898	8,194	16,330	1932	3,061	8,651
1899	6,783	17,094	1933	3,796	9,590
1900	7,848	20,837	1934	2,928	8,023
1901	8,441	22,427	1935	1,498	6,868
1902	8,956	12,344	1936	1,871	5,985
1903	9,470	10,155	1937	2,696	7,757
1904	8,782	9,740	1938	2,398	7,866
1905	11,114	—	1939	2,186	6,521

Sources: *Estadística del ramo criminal; Cuadros estadísticos,* 1900–1909; *Estadística de la penalidad;* Quiroz Cuarón et al., *Tendencia;* AE 1938; AE 1940.

Table 3. Accused. Mexico City, 1922–1926

Year	Accused
1922	27,689
1923	28,608
1924	29,809
1925	31,917
1926	21,971

Source: *Estadística Nacional* 3:47 (15 Jan. 1927).

Table 4. Arrested. Mexico City, 1885–1938

Year	Arrests	Arrests to judicial authorities	Year	Arrests	Arrests to judicial authorities
1885	32,893	10,114	1929	76,854	—
1886	35,421	10,107	1930	90,564	—
1887	34,972	10,335	1931	102,383	—
1888	39,542	12,064	1932	141,477	—
1889	44,377	14,813	1933	120,621	—
1890	44,074	14,064	1934	102,674	—
1891	47,408	14,358	1935	89,784	—
1892	49,577	14,776	1936	90,129	—
1893	43,684	14,352	1937	89,213	—
1894	37,798	16,110	1938	83,050	—
1895	38,577	16,795			

Note: The column "Arrests to judicial authorities" excludes those sent by the police to the authority of the governor of the Federal District for administrative infractions: prostitutes, drunkards, and beggars. Because the series is based on police sources and not all of those of the second column were formally indicted, the term "Accused" was not used.

Source: AE 1895; Quiroz Cuarón et al., *Tendencia;* AE, 1893–1899.

Table 5. Population of Mexico City, Federal District, State Capitals *, and Estados Unidos Mexicanos

Year	Mexico City	Federal District	State capitals *	National population	Mexico City as % of national population
1895	329,774	474,860	732,047	12,632,427	2.61
1900	344,721	541,516	774,233	13,607,272	2.53
1910	471,066	720,753	923,755	15,160,369	3.11
1921	615,327	906,063	926,475	14,334,780	4.29
1930	1,029,068	1,229,576	1,159,224	16,552,722	6.22
1940	1,802,679	1,757,530	1,431,007	19,652,552	9.17

* Includes cities of Aguascalientes, Ciudad Victoria, Colima, Cuernavaca, Culiacán, Chihuahua, Chilpancingo, Durango, Guadalajara, Guanajuato, Hermosillo, La Paz, Mérida, Monterrey, Morelia, Oaxaca, Pachuca, Puebla, Querétaro, San Luis Potosí, Tlaxcala, Toluca, Tuxtla Gutiérrez, Veracruz, Villahermosa.

Source: *Estadísticas históricas de México* (Mexico City: INEGI, 1994), based on figures of national censuses.

Table 6. Indices of Accused per 100,000, by District. Mexico City

		Judicial archives database		*Rateros* database
	Accused 1900	Accused's address	Place of committal	Suspect's address
Total Mexico City	1.00	1.00	1.00	1.00
I District	0.85	0.68	0.59	0.58
II District	1.02	0.83	0.70	1.07
III District	0.69	0.93	0.94	1.14
IV District	0.91	1.34	1.55	1.20
V District	0.91	0.67	1.03	0.53
VI District	1.28	0.92	0.84	0.46
VII District	0.62	0.94	0.73	0.52
VIII District	0.79	0.28	1.16	0.28

Note: Rates established by dividing arrests by the population of each district. The data from 1900 were normalized to that year's population. The other series were normalized to the 1921 population.

Sources: Databases; *Cuadros estadísticos* 1900; *Censo general de la República Mexicana verificado el 28 de octubre de 1900* (Mexico City: Secretaría de Fomento, 1901–1907); Departamento de la Estadística Nacional, *Censo general de habitantes: 30 de noviembre de 1921* (Mexico City: Departamento de la Estadística Nacional, 1928).

Table 7. Judicial Archives Database. Trades Stated by Suspects

Trade	No.	Percentage
Artisan	44	15.60
Merchant	24	8.51
Journeyman	23	8.16
Construction worker	16	5.67
Shoemaker, Cobbler	16	5.67
Domestic worker	15	5.32
Employee	12	4.26
Military	9	3.19
Police	9	3.19
Cart driver	8	2.84
Coach driver	6	2.13
Car driver	5	1.77
Railroad worker	5	1.77
Assistant	4	1.42
Apprentice	3	1.06
Gardener	3	1.06
Mechanic	3	1.06
Porter	3	1.06
Student	3	1.06
Butcher	2	0.71
Electrician	2	0.71
Homemaker	2	0.71
Launderer	2	0.71
Prostitute	2	0.71
Waiter	2	0.71
Other	20	7.09
Unemployed	2	0.71
No data	37	13.12
Total	282	100.00

Note: "Artisan" includes alfarero, peletero, sastre, sombrerero, tapicero, bizcochero, panadero, repostero, carpintero, herrero, peluquero, pintor, plomero, curtidor, talabartero, hojalatero, tejedor. "Other" includes nonartisans with only one representative in the sample.

Table 8. Accused and Sentenced for Violent Crimes. Federal District, 1895–1939

Year	Battery		Homicide	
	Accused	Sentenced	Accused	Sentenced
1895	8,054	—	481	—
1900	9,238	5,586	141	72
1901	10,582	6,169	131	163
1902	8,560	—	184	—
1903	6,707	—	191	—
1904	6,164	—	117	—
1905	—	7,388	—	90
1906	—	8,550	—	130
1908	—	9,526	—	121
1909	—	10,303	—	227
1916	—	1,292	—	46
1917	—	2,474	—	57
1918	—	2,851	—	101
1919	—	2,685	—	70
1920	—	2,363	—	55
1927	6,669	—	305	—
1928	10,801	—	492	—
1929	7,569	—	547	—
1930	6,277	—	457	—
1931	4,762	—	267	—
1932	3,758	—	369	—
1933	4,097	—	325	—
1934	3,630	—	460	—
1935	3,098	—	492	—
1936	2,671	—	438	—
1937	2,814	830	377	222
1938	2,852	752	486	228
1939	2,664	771	411	226

Sources: *Cuadros estadísticos* 1900–1909; *Estadística de la penalidad;* Quiroz Cuarón et al., *Tendencia;* AE 1938; AE 1940.

Table 9. Length of Sentence by Crime (percentages). Federal District, 1900

	Theft	Battery	Murder	Rape
Reprimand	0.28	1.82	0	0
Fine	0	0.86	0	0
Up to 30 days arrest	25.44	81.54	0	0
Up to 11 months arrest	50.42	12.42	0	25
Prison, more than 11 months	23.86	3.36	42.86	75
Capital punishment	0	0	57.14	0
Total	100.00	100.00	100.00	100.00

Source: *Cuadros estadísticos* 1900.

Table 10. Conviction Ratio (Accused/Sentenced) by Selected Crimes. Federal District, 1895–1942

Crime	Rate
Theft	2.68
Battery	3.23
Homicide	1.77
Rape	3.60
Abduction and statutory rape	24.40
All crimes	2.78

Sources: *Cuadros estadísticos,* 1900; AE 1940.

Table 11. Battery and Homicide Accused by District of Committal (per 100,000 population). Mexico City, 1900

District	Battery	Homicide
I District	2,533.15	30.56
II District	2,846.63	35.37
III District	2,108.23	30.55
IV District	1,902.14	28.42
V District	2,785.51	25.50
VI District	2,867.21	27.28
VII District	1,387.87	15.42
VIII District	1,621.11	33.20

Source: *Cuadros estadísticos,* 1900; *Censo general . . . 1900.*

Table 12. Arrested by the Police for Sexual Crimes. Mexico City, 1885–1926

Year	Statutory Rape and Abduction	Statutory Rape	Abduction	Rape
1885	41	–	84	59
1886	22	–	72	49
1887	113	–	14	43
1888	124	–	35	22
1889	132	–	2	47
1890	221	–	0	18
1891	139	–	2	30
1892	105	–	6	47
1893	150	–	4	57
1894	131	–	16	36
1895	177	–	30	72
1922	41	58	185	91
1923	30	112	197	80
1924	8	65	180	140
1925	66	79	253	109
1926	23	89	244	146

Source: AE 1896; *Estadística Nacional* 3:47 (15 Jan. 1927).

Table 13. Accused and Sentenced for Sexual Crimes. Federal District, 1897–1942

	Abduction and Statutory Rape		Abduction		Statutory Rape		Rape	
Year	Accused	Sentenced	Accused	Sentenced	Accused	Sentenced	Accused	Sentenced
1897	43	0	136	3	26	1	23	7
1900	43	0	126	0	50	2	30	4
1901	—	—	—	—	—	—	—	6
1905	—	—	—	—	—	—	—	8
1906	—	—	—	—	—	—	—	3
1908	—	—	—	—	—	—	—	16
1909	—	—	—	—	—	—	—	10
1916	—	—	—	—	—	—	—	1
1917	—	—	—	—	—	—	—	2
1918	—	—	—	—	—	—	—	33
1919	—	—	—	—	—	—	—	2
1937	229	49	—	—	—	—	53	24
1938	305	54	—	—	—	—	104	28
1939	217	65	—	—	—	—	98	37
1940	535	54	—	—	—	—	59	28
1941	474	56	—	—	—	—	118	37
1942	438	74	—	—	—	—	128	31

Source: AE 1898; AE 1940, 1942; *Cuadros estadísticos*, 1900–1909; *Estadística de la penalidad.*

Table 14. Accused and Sentenced for Theft. Federal District, 1871–1939

Year	Accused	Sentenced	Year	Accused	Sentenced
1871	–	1006	1905	–	2222
1872	–	1032	1906	–	2675
1873	–	1223			
1874	–	1197	1908	–	4055
1875	–	804	1909	–	3229
1876	–	753			
1877	–	1584	1916	–	1395
1878	–	1566	1917	–	1330
1879	–	1789	1918	–	1578
1880	–	2202	1919	–	813
1881	–	1312	1920	–	422
1882	–	923			
1883	–	646	1927	941	–
1884	–	386	1928	1777	–
1885	–	463	1929	1687	–
1895	2636	–	1930	2241	–
			1931	2567	–
1897	2343	1230	1932	2078	–
			1933	2480	–
1900	3404	1083	1934	1562	–
1901	4420	1178	1935	1382	–
1902	2025	–	1936	1347	–
1903	1893	–	1937	1324	586
1904	2164	2145	1938	1615	581
			1939	1347	536

Sources: *Estadística del ramo criminal; Cuadros estadísticos,* 1900–1909; *Estadística de la penalidad;* Quiroz Cuarón et al., *Tendencia;* AE 1938; AE 1940.

Table 15. Arrested for Theft. Mexico City, 1885–1826

Year	Arrested	Year	Arrested
1885	459	1894	1935
1886	484	1895	2123
1887	592		
1888	778	1922	6391
1889	977	1923	6421
1890	1046	1924	6346
1891	1493	1925	6481
1892	1758	1926	3954
1893	1773		

Source: AE 1895; *Estadística Nacional* 3:47 (15 Jan. 1927).

Table 16. Sentenced and Accused for Theft. Federal District, Yearly Average per Period

			Per 100,000	
Period	Accused	Sentenced	Accused	Sentenced
1871–1885	—	1,032.00	—	355.60
1885–1895[a]	1,219.82	—	369.90	—
1895–1909	2,343.00	2,183.50	325.08	302.95
1916–1920	—	1,330.00	—	146.79
1922–1926[a]	5,918.60	—	575.14	—
1927–1938	1,651.00	581.00	93.94	33.06

Sources: Tables 14, 15; Ariel Rodríguez Kuri, *La experiencia olvidada. El ayuntamiento de México: política y administración, 1876–1912* (Mexico City: El Colegio de México, 1996); *Estadísticas históricas.*

[a] Data for arrested in Mexico City.

Table 17. Correlations Arrested, Accused, Sentenced per 100,000 and Food Prices. Federal District (r=)

	Sentenced total	Accused total	Accused theft
Corn, 1885–1895			0.80
Corn, 1895–1910	0.75	0.75	
Corn, 1900–1901,1904–1906, 1908–1909			0.05
Pulque, 1900–01,1904–1906, 1908–1909			0.71
General index of food prices, 1927–1939	−0.07	−0.06	−0.31
Bread, 1927–1939	−0.21	−0.22	0.04
Corn, 1927–1939	0.12	0.31	−0.35

Sources: *Estadísticas históricas; Estadísticas económicas del porfiriato: Fuerza de trabajo y actividad por sectores* (Mexico City: El Colegio de México, n.d.), 68; Tables 1, 8, 9, 10, 12.

Table 18. Campaign Against *Rateros.* Trades Stated by Suspects

Trade	No.	Percentage
Artisan	220	25.46
Merchant	164	18.98
Assistant	38	4.40
Cart driver	38	4.40
Shoemaker	36	4.17
Construction worker	25	2.89
Delivery	20	2.31
Journeyman	19	2.20
Apprentice	17	1.97
Industrial worker	16	1.85
Coach driver	15	1.74
Shoe shiner	15	1.74
Car driver	13	1.50
Domestic worker	13	1.50
Unemployed	2	0.23
Other	72	8.33
No data	141	16.32
Total	864	100.00

Source: AHA, Vagos y rateros, 4157–60.

Notes

ARCHIVAL ABBREVIATIONS

AE [year] *Anuario Estadístico de la República Mexicana.* (See bibliography for publication data.)

AGN, DGG Archivo General de la Nación, Fondo Dirección General de Gobierno.

AGN, FIM Archivo General de la Nación, Fondo Presidente Francisco I. Madero.

AGN, GPR Archivo General de la Nación, Fondo Gobernación: Período Revolucionario.

AGN, PG Archivo General de la Nación, Fondo Presidente Emilio Portes Gil.

AGN, POC Archivo General de la Nación, Fondo Presidentes Obregón–Calles.

AGN, SJ Archivo General de la Nación, Fondo Secretaría de Justicia.

AHA Archivo Histórico del Antiguo Ayuntamiento.

AHA, BE Archivo Histórico del Antiguo Ayuntamiento, Fondo Bebidas Embriagantes.

AHA, PG Archivo Histórico del Antiguo Ayuntamiento, Fondo Policía en General.

AHA, PPP Archivo Histórico del Antiguo Ayuntamiento, Fondo Policía Presos Penitenciaría.

AJ Archivo del Tribunal Superior de Justicia del Distrito Federal, Reclusorio Sur.

APD Archivo Porfirio Díaz, Universidad Iberoamericana.

ASSA, BP Archivo Histórico de la Secretaría de Salud, Fondo Beneficencia Pública.

ASSA, EA Archivo Histórico de la Secretaría de Salud, Fondo Establecimientos Asistenciales.

ASSA, SP Archivo Histórico de la Secretaría de Salud, Fondo Salubridad Pública.

CP 1871 Antonio Martínez de Castro, *Código penal para el Distrito Federal y Territorio de la Baja-California sobre delitos del fuero común y para toda la República Mexicana sobre delitos contra la Federación. Edición correcta, sacada de la oficial, precedida de la Exposición de motivos dirigida al Supremo Gobierno por el C. Lic. . . . Presidente de la comisión encargada de formar el Código* (Veracruz y Puebla: La Ilustración, 1891).

CP 1929 *Código penal para el Distrito y territorios federales* [1929]. Mexico City: Talleres Gráficos de la Nación, 1929.

CP 1931 *Código penal para el Distrito y territorios federales y para toda la república en materia de fuero federal* [1931]. Mexico City: Botas, 1938.

MPP Mexican Political Parties Propaganda, Benson Latin American Collection, University of Texas at Austin.

INTRODUCTION

1 Tables 1 to 4 synthesize the evidence from available statistics. On rates through the twentieth century, see Rafael Ruiz Harrell, *Criminalidad y mal gobierno* (Mexico City: Sansores y Aljure, 1998), 13, and Ira Beltrán and Pablo Piccato, "Crimen en el siglo XX: Fragmentos de análisis sobre la evidencia cuantitativa," in Ariel Rodriguez Kuri and Sergio Tamayo, eds., *Ciudad de México: Los ultimos cien años, los próximos cien años* (Mexico City: UAM, 2001).

2 I will not address, therefore, behaviors that are not predatory and do not face an adverse consensus, such as drunkenness and prostitution. For the role of public opinion in defining crime, see Leslie T. Wilkins, "Offense patterns," in *International Encyclopedia of the Social Sciences,* ed. David L. Sills(N.p.: Macmillan Company and Free Press, 1968), 3: 479.

3 See Alf Lüdtke, "Introduction: What Is the History of Everyday Life and Who Are Its Practitioners?" in Alf Lüdtke, ed., *The History of Everyday Life: Reconstructing Historical Experiences and Ways of Life,* trans. William Templer (Princeton, NJ: Princeton University Press, 1995); Geoff Eley, "Foreword," in *The History of Everyday Life,* viii.

4 See Michael Charles Scardaville, "Crime and the Urban Poor: Mexico City

in the Late Colonial Period" (Ph.D. diss., University of Florida, 1977); Gabriel J. Haslip, *Crime and Punishment in Late Colonial Mexico City, 1692–1810* (Albuquerque: University of New Mexico Press, 1999).

5 "Any generalizations about the nature of social life in the city must be based upon careful studies of these smaller universes rather than upon *a priori* statements about the city as a whole." Oscar Lewis, *Anthropological Essays* (New York: Random House, 1970), 60. See also Larissa A. Lomnitz, *Cómo sobreviven los marginados* (Mexico City: Siglo Veintiuno, 1975), 27; Mercedes González de la Rocha, *The Resources of Poverty: Women and Survival in a Mexican City* (Cambridge, MA: Blackwell, 1994); Susan Eckstein, *The Poverty of Revolution: The State and the Urban Poor in Mexico* (Princeton, NJ: Princeton University Press, 1977); Guadalupe Reyes Domínguez and Ana Rosas Mantecón, *Los usos de la identidad barrial: una mirada antropológica a la lucha por la vivienda: Tepito 1970–1984* (Mexico City: Universidad Autónoma Metropolitana, Unidad Iztapalapa, 1993).

6 Practice (defined as "habitual or customary performance") will refer in the next pages to those "places where what is said and what is done, rules imposed and reasons given, the planned and the taken for granted meet and interconnect." Michel Foucault, "Politics and the Study of Discourse," in Graham Burchell, Colin Gordon, and Peter Miller, eds., *The Foucault Effect: Studies in Governmentality with Two Lectures and Interview with Michel Foucault* (Chicago: University of Chicago Press, 1991), 75. For the need to associate the study of everyday practices with that of narratives (such as judicial statements), see Michel de Certeau, *The Practice of Everyday Life,* trans. Steven Rendall (Berkeley: University of California Press, 1984), 78.

7 Pierre Bourdieu, *Outline of a Theory of Practice,* trans. Richard Nice (Cambridge, UK: Cambridge University Press, 1998), chap. 1. For the possibilities of judicial sources, see Edward Muir and Guido Ruggiero, "Introduction: The Crime of History," in Muir and Ruggiero, eds., *History from Crime* (Baltimore, MD: John Hopkins University Press, 1994); Lynn Hunt, "Introduction," in Lynn Hunt, ed., *The New Cultural History* (Berkeley: University of California Press, 1989), 14, 22; Robert Darnton, *The Great Cat Massacre and Other Episodes in French Cultural History* (New York: Vintage Books, 1984), 5.

8 See Michel Foucault, *Discipline and Punish: The Birth of the Prison* (New York: Vintage, 1979); Dario Melossi and Massimo Pavarini, *Cárcel y fábrica: Los orígenes del sistema penitenciario (siglos XVI–XIX)* (Mexico City: Siglo Veintiuno, 1980); David Garland, *Punishment and Welfare: A History of Penal Strategies* (Aldershot, Hants, UK: Gower Publishing Company, 1985); Douglas Hay, "Property, Authority and the Criminal Law," in Douglas Hay

et al., eds., *Albion's Fatal Tree: Crime and Society in Eighteenth-Century England* (New York: Pantheon Books, 1975); Michael Ignatieff, *A Just Measure of Pain: The Penitentiary in the Industrial Revolution* (London: Penguin, 1978); Robert A. Nye, *Crime, Madness, and Politics in Modern France: The Medical Concept of National Decline* (Princeton, NJ: Princeton University Press, 1984); Peter Linebaugh, *The London Hanged: Crime and Civil Society in the Eighteenth Century* (Cambridge, UK: Cambridge University Press, 1992); David J. Rothman, *The Discovery of the Asylum: Social Order and Disorder in the New Republic* (Boston: Little, Brown, and Company, 1971).

9 See Howard Zehr, *Crime and the Development of Modern Society: Patterns of Criminality in Nineteenth Century Germany and France* (London: Croom Helm, 1976); Eric A. Johnson and Eric H. Monkkonen, eds., *The Civilization of Crime: Violence in Town and Country since the Middle Ages* (Urbana: University of Illinois Press, 1996); J. M. Beattie, *Crime and the Courts in England, 1660–1800* (Princeton, NJ: Princeton University Press, 1986); Eric H. Monkkonnen, *The Dangerous Class: Crime and Poverty in Columbus, Ohio, 1860–1885* (Cambridge, MA: Harvard University Press, 1975); Eric A. Johnson, *Urbanization and Crime: Germany 1871–1914* (New York: Cambridge University Press, 1995).

10 Robert Buffington, *Criminal and Citizen in Modern Mexico* (Lincoln: University of Nebraska Press, 1999), 4. See also Paul J. Vanderwood, *Disorder and Progress: Bandits, Police and Mexican Development,* 2d. ed. (Wilmington, DE: Scholarly Resources, 1992); Lyman. L. Johnson, ed., *The Problem of Order in Changing Societies. Essays in Crime and Policing in Argentina and Uruguay, 1750–1919* (Albuquerque: University of New Mexico Press, 1990); Eduardo A. Zimmermann, "Racial Ideas and Social Reform: Argentina, 1890–1916," *Hispanic American Historical Review* 72:1 (1992): 23–46; Donna Guy, *Sex and Danger in Buenos Aires: Prostitution, Family, and Nation in Argentina* (Lincoln: University of Nebraska Press, 1991); Dain Borges, "'Puffy, Ugly, Slothful and Inert': Degeneration in Brazilian Social Thought, 1880–1940," *Journal of Latin American Studies* 23 (1993): 235–56; Thomas Holloway, *Policing Rio de Janeiro* (Stanford, CA: Stanford University Press, 1993); Ricardo Salvatore and Carlos Aguirre, eds., *The Birth of the Penitentiary in Latin America* (Austin: Texas University Press, 1996); Nancy Leys Stepan, *"The Hour of Eugenics": Race, Gender and Nation in Latin America* (Ithaca, NY: Cornell University Press, 1991).

11 David Garland, *Punishment and Modern Society: A Study in Social Theory* (Chicago: University of Chicago Press, 1990), 229. See also David Blackbourn and Geoff Eley, *The Peculiarities of German History: Bourgeois Society and Politics in Nineteenth-Century Germany* (Oxford: Oxford University

Press, 1984); James C. Scott, *Domination and the Arts of Resistance: Hidden Transcripts* (New Haven, CT: Yale University Press, 1990); Joan Wallach Scott, *Gender and the Politics of History* (New York: Columbia University Press, 1988); Judith Walkowitz, *City of Dreadful Delight: Narratives of Sexual Danger in Late-Victorian London* (Chicago: University of Chicago Press, 1992); Gareth Stedman Jones, "The Determinist Fix: Some Obstacles to the Further Development of the Linguistic Approach to History in the 1990s," *History Workshop Journal* 46 (1996): 30.

12 For resistance and peasant communities see Eric R. Wolf, *Peasant Wars of the Twentieth Century* (New York: Harper and Row, 1969); William B. Taylor, *Drinking, Homicide, and Rebellion in Colonial Mexican Villages* (Stanford, CA: Stanford University Press, 1989); Florencia Mallon, *The Defense of Community in Peru's Central Highlands: Peasant Struggle and Capitalist Transition, 1860–1940* (Princeton, NJ: Princeton University Press, 1983); the essays in Steve Stern, ed., *Resistance, Rebellion and Consciousness in the Andean Peasant World. 18th to 20th Centuries* (Madison: University of Wisconsin Press, 1987); Nancy Farriss, *Maya Society under Colonial Rule: The Collective Enterprise of Survival* (Princeton, NJ: Princeton University Press, 1992); and a path-breaking study of survival in Charles Gibson, *The Aztecs under Spanish Rule: A History of the Indians of the Valley of Mexico, 1519–1810* (Stanford, CA: Stanford University Press, 1964).

13 See for example Torcuato Di Tella, "The Dangerous Classes in Early Nineteenth Century Mexico," *Journal of Latin American Studies* 5 (1973): 79–105; Eric Van Young, "Islands in the Storm: Quiet Cities and Violent Countrysides in the Mexican Independence Era," *Past and Present* 118 (1988): 130–55; on slavery, Rebecca Scott, *Slave Emancipation in Cuba: The Transition to Free Labor, 1860–1899* (Princeton, NJ: Princeton University Press, 1985). For a revision of recent interpretative approaches on gender and modernization, see Margareth Rago, *Os Prazeres da Noite: Prostituição e Codigos da Sexualidade Feminina em São Paulo, 1890–1930* (Rio de Janeiro: Paz e Terra, 1991).

14 Gilbert M. Joseph, "On the Trail of Latin American Bandits: A Reexamination of Peasant Resistance," in Jaime E. Rodríguez, ed., *Patterns of Contention in Mexican History* (Irvine: University of California Press, 1992), 293–336; William B. Taylor, "Between Global Process and Local Knowledge: An Inquiry into Early Latin American Social History, 1500–1900," in Olivier Zunz, ed., *Reliving the Past: The Worlds of Social History* (Chapel Hill: University of North Carolina Press, 1985), 142. See also Nicholas B. Dirks, Geoff Eley, and Sherry B. Ortner, "Introduction," in Dirks, Eley, and Ortner, eds., *Culture/Power/History: A Reader in Contemporary Social Theory* (Princeton, NJ: Princeton University Press, 1994), 5; Steve J. Stern, "New

Approaches to the Study of Peasant Rebellion and Consciousness: Implications of the Andean Experience," in *Resistance, Rebellion and Consciousness,* 10–11; William H. Beezley, Cheryl English Martin, and William E. French, eds., *Rituals of Rule, Rituals of Resistance* (Wilmington, DE: Scholarly Resources, 1994).

15 See Ricardo Salvatore and Carlos Aguirre, "The Birth of the Penitentiary in Latin America: Towards an Interpretive Social History of Prisons," in Salvatore and Aguirre, eds., *The Birth of the Penitentiary;* Laurence John Rohlfes, "Police and Penal Correction in Mexico City, 1876–1911: A Study of Order and Progress in Porfirian Mexico" (Ph.D. diss., Tulane University, 1983) for a similar conclusion; and Lyman L. Johnson, "Preface" to *The Problem of Order in Changing Societies,* xiv; Nydia E. Cruz Barrera, "El despliege del castigo: Las penitenciarías porfirianas en México" (manuscript), 4 and 16.

16 Alan Knight, "Revolutionary Project, Recalcitrant People: Mexico, 1910–40," in Jaime O. Rodríguez, ed., *The Revolutionary Process in Mexico: Essays on Political and Social Change, 1880–1940* (Irvine: University of California Press, 1990). On social reform and immigration in Latin America, see Diego Armus, "La ciudad higiénica entre Europa y Latinoamerica," in Antonio Lafuente, ed., *Mundialización de la ciencia y cultura nacional* (Madrid: Doce Calles, 1993), 587–96.

17 Miguel Macedo, "El Municipio. Los establecimientos penales. La asistencia pública," in Justo Sierra, ed., *México, su evolución social: síntesis de la historia política, de la organización administrativa y militar y del estado económico de la federación mexicana; de sus adelantamientos en el orden intelectual; de su estructura territorial y del desarrollo de su población y de los medios de comunicación nacionales y internacionales; de sus conquistas en el campo industrial, agrícola, minero, mercantil, etc., etc. Inventario monumental que resume en trabajos magistrales los grandes progresos de la nación en el siglo XIX* (Mexico City: Ballescá, 1900) v. 1, pt. 2, 706. Miguel Macedo (1856–1929) was an influential lawyer, politician, and member of the *científico* group. Daniel Cosío Villegas, *El porfiriato: Vida política interior,* vol. 8 of *Historia moderna de México* (Mexico City: Hermes, 1972), 851.

18 José Enrique Ampudia M., "La penitenciaría de México (1882–1911)," *Boletín del Archivo General de La Nación: La Penitenciaría de México* 5:4 (1981–82): 5–8; Rohlfes, "Police and Penal Correction"; Tony Morgan, "Proletarians, Politicos, and Patriarchs: The Use and Abuse of Cultural Customs in Early Industrialization of Mexico City, 1880–1910," in Beezley et al., eds., *Rituals of Rule,* 151–72; William E. French, "*Progreso Forzado:* Workers and the Inculcation of the Capitalist Work Ethic in the Parral Mining District," in Beezley et al., eds., *Rituals of Rule,* 191–212; William H. Beezley, *Judas at*

the Jockey Club and Other Episodes of Porfirian Mexico (Lincoln: University of Nebraska Press, 1987); Antonio Padilla Arroyo, "Criminalidad, cárceles y sistema penitenciario en México, 1876–1910" (Ph.D. diss, El Colegio de México, 1995), 86–87. A closer look at the contradictions of judiciary practices and theory in Elisa Speckman, "Crimen y castigo: Legislación penal, interpretaciones de la criminalidad y administración de justicia: Ciudad de México 1872–1910" (Ph.D. diss., El Colegio de México, Mexico City, 1999).

19 The argument about political instability and social reform was formulated by Julio Guerrero, *La génesis del crimen en México: estudio de psiquiatría social* (Paris: Viuda de Charles Bouret, 1901), chap. 4. See also Alfonso Quiroz Cuarón et al., *Tendencia y ritmo de la criminalidad en México* (Mexico City: Instituto de Investigaciones Estadísticas, 1939), 100. For a critique of modernization as an explanation of crime, see John D. Roger, "Theories of Crime and Development: An Historical Perspective," *The Journal of Development Studies* 25:3 (April 1989): 312–28, esp. 314–15. For colonial rule and urban growth, besides the works by Scardaville and Haslip, see Louisa Schell Hoberman and Susan Migden, eds., *Cities and Society in Colonial Latin America* (Albuquerque: University of New Mexico Press, 1986); James R. Scobie, *Buenos Aires: From Plaza to Suburb, 1870–1910* (New York: Oxford University Press, 1974).

20 John Braithwaite, *Crime, Shame, and Reintegration* (New York: Cambridge University Press, 1989), 21; Alessandro Baratta, *Criminología crítica y crítica del derecho penal*, trans. Alvaro Búnster (Mexico City: Siglo Veintiuno, 1986), 71, 81, 87; Marvin E. Wolfgang and Francis Ferracuti, *The Subculture of Violence* (London: Tavistock Publishers, 1967); Albert K. Cohen, *Delinquent Boys: The Culture of the Gang* (New York: Free Press, 1955); David Garland, "Of Crimes and Criminals: The Development of Criminology in Britain," in Mike Maguire, Rod Morgan, and Robert Reiner, eds., *The Oxford Handbook of Criminology* (New York: Clarendon Press, 1994): 7–8; Albert K. Cohen and James F. Short Jr., "Research in Delinquent Subcultures," *Journal of Social Issues* 14:3 (1958): 20–37, esp. 22.

21 See Kai T. Erikson, "Notes on the Sociology of Deviance," *Social Problems* 9:4 (Spring 1962): 307–14; idem, *Wayward Puritans: A Study in the Sociology of Deviance* (New York: John Wiley, 1966); Howard S. Becker, *Outsiders: Studies in the Sociology of Deviance* (New York: Free Press, 1963).

1 THE MODERN CITY

1 Andrés Lira, *Comunidades indígenas frente a la ciudad de México: Tenochtitlan y Tlatelolco, sus pueblos y barrios, 1812–1919* (Mexico City: El Colegio de

México, 1995), 236, 238, 262. A pioneering and still unmatched study of expansion is María Dolores Morales, "La expansión de la ciudad de México en el siglo XIX: el caso de los fraccionamientos," in Alejandra Moreno Toscano et al., eds., *Investigaciones sobre la historia de la ciudad de México* (Mexico City: INAH, 1974), 189–200. On the modernization project see Mauricio Tenorio, "1910 Mexico City: Space and Nation in the City of the *Centenario,*" *Journal of Latin American Studies* 28 (1996): 75–104; Barbara A. Tenenbaum, "Streetwise History: The Paseo de la Reforma and the Porfirian State, 1876–1910," in William H. Beezley et al., eds., *Rituals of Rule, Rituals of Resistance: Public Celebrations and Popular Culture in Mexico* (Wilmington, DE: Scholarly Resources, 1994), 127–50; Paolo Riguzzi, "México próspero: las dimensiones de la imagen nacional en el porfiriato," *Historias* 20 (Apr.–Sept. 1988): 137–57; Estela Eguiarte Sakar, "Los jardines en México y la idea de la ciudad decimonónica," *Historias* 27 (Oct.–Mar. 1992): 129–38; Michael Johns, *The City of Mexico in the Age of Díaz* (Austin: University of Texas Press, 1997).

2 For example, report by city council member Luis E. Ruiz about the Eighth District, 19 Jan. 1904, AHA, PG, 3644, 1691. The name *colonia* derives from the nineteenth-century colonization legislation. Jorge H. Jiménez Muñoz, *La traza del poder: Historia de la política y los negocios urbanos en el Distrito Federal desde sus orígenes a la desaparición del Ayuntamiento (1824–1928)* (Mexico City: Codex, 1993), 9.

3 Governor of the Federal District to City Council, 2 Feb. 1897, AHA, PG, 3640, 1156.

4 *Boletín del Archivo General de La Nación: La Penitenciaría de México* 5:4 (1981–82). The eastern end of the city was a "zone . . . crossed by infected canals dragging all types of impurities" and bad smells, see Morales, "La expansión," 191; see also "El crecimiento urbano de la ciudad de México y la desecación del lago de Texcoco," *Relaciones* 19:76 (Fall 1998): 133–50.

5 Lira, *Comunidades indígenas,* 264; John Robert Lear, "Mexico City: Space and Class in the Porfirian Capital, 1884–1910," *Journal of Urban History* 22:4 (May 1996): 481–82. On the lack of sanitation at the colonia Obrera, see "Informe general" by the Medical Inspector of the Fourth District, 31 Dec. 1924, ASSA, SP, Sección Salubridad del Distrito Federal, 2, 28.

6 By the early twentieth century, according to John Lear, elite families living in the center would be seen "as conspicuous exceptions." The process of specialization in the use of urban space was concomitant to the "segregation of wealth." John Robert Lear, "Workers, *Vecinos* and Citizens: The Revolution in Mexico City, 1909–1917" (Ph.D. diss., University of California at Berkeley, 1993), 48, 467, 486. I contend, as it will be clear later, that this segregation was not fully accomplished. The move could take place several decades later,

as with the Gómez family. Larissa A. Lomnitz and Marisol Pérez Lizaur, *Una familia de la élite mexicana: Parentesco, clase y cultura 1820–1980* (Mexico City: Alianza, 1993), 91, 105. For the importance of water-sellers and fountains, see Antonio García Cubas, *El libro de mis recuerdos. Narraciones históricas, anecdóticas y de costumbres mexicanas anteriores al actual estado social, ilustradas con más de trescientos fotograbados* (Mexico City: Editorial Porrúa, 1986 [1904]), 207–14. As in Rio de Janeiro, running water shielded upper-class families from contact with the street. Sandra Lauderdale-Graham, *House and Street: The Domestic World of Servants and Masters in Nineteenth-Century Rio de Janeiro* (Austin: University of Texas Press, 1992).

7 *La Tribuna,* 16 Oct. 1912. For a similar campaign in 1893, see Lear, "Workers, *Vecinos* and Citizens," 51, 55. On sidewalks, see 1 May 1896, AHA, PG, 3640, 1143. For actions against *kioskos,* see AHA, PG, 3640, 1147. For colonial and early national concerns regarding control of behaviors in public spaces, Juan Pedro Viqueira Albán, *¿Relajados o reprimidos?: Diversiones públicas y vida social en la ciudad de México durante el siglo de las luces* (Mexico City: Fondo de Cultura Económica, 1987); Pamela Voekel, "Peeing on the Palace: Bodily Resistance to Bourbon Reforms," University of Texas at Austin, manuscript; Jorge Nacif Mina, "Policía y seguridad pública en la ciudad de México, 1770–1848," in Regina Hernández Franyuti, ed., *La ciudad de México en la primera mitad del siglo XIX* (Mexico City: Instituto Mora, 1994), 9–50; Anne Staples, "Policía y Buen Gobierno: Municipal Efforts to Regulate Public Behavior, 1821–1910," in Beezley et al., eds., *Rituals of Rule,* 115–26.

8 AJ, 453723, Abuse of authority, 1905; Lomnitz and Pérez Lizaur, *Una familia de la élite mexicana,* 82.

9 AHA, PG, 3644, 1691.

10 "Sobre el número y clase de presos que debe alojar la Penitenciaría de México," *Boletín del Archivo General de La Nación: La Penitenciaría de México* 5:4 (1981–82): 33, 36; Ministry of the Interior to Ministry of Justice, 20 Nov. 1907, AGN, SJ, 645, 634. On conditions in the orphanage in 1913, see AGN, GPR, 38, 60, fol. 21–22. On the asylum see ibid., 38, 19, fol. 1.

11 François-Xavier Guerra, *México: Del Antiguo Régimen a la Revolución* (Mexico City: Fondo de Cultura Económica, 1988), 1:338; *Estadísticas sociales del porfiriato, 1877–1910* (Mexico City: Dirección General de Estadística, 1956), 73; Keith A. Davies, "Tendencias demográficas urbanas durante el siglo XIX en México," *Historia Mexicana* 21:3 (Jan.–Mar. 1972): 505; Francisco Alba, "Evolución de la Población: Realizaciones y Retos" in José Joaquín Blanco and José Woldenberg, eds., *México a fines de siglo* (Mexico City: Fondo de Cultura Económica, 1993), 1:133.

12 *Estadísticas históricas de México* (Mexico City: INEGI, 1994).

13 Ibid.; Dirección General de Estadística, *Censo General de la República Mexicana verificado el 20 de octubre de 1895* (Mexico City: Secretaría de Fomento, 1898).

14 *Censo General . . . 1895;* Departamento de la Estadística Nacional, *Censo de población, 15 de mayo de 1930* (Mexico City: Talleres Gráficos de la Nación, 1934). In 1790, women made up 57 percent of the population of Mexico City and a majority of the immigrants arriving in the city. Silvia Marina Arrom, *The Women of Mexico City, 1790–1857* (Stanford: Stanford University Press, 1985), 105–7.

15 Guerra, *México, del Antiguo Régimen,* 1:339, 342. Guerra identifies women with "traditional Mexico" (the influence of the Church, the sexual connotations of caciques' rule). Alan Knight holds a similar view in *The Mexican Revolution* (Lincoln: University of Nebraska Press, 1990), 1:19, 2:207.

16 Heriberto Frías, "El Pueblo Revolucionario armado: Inercia de la clase media," *La Convención,* 18 Dec. 1914, p. 2.

17 Lear, "Workers, *Vecinos* and Citizens," 164; Ana Lau and Carmen Ramos, "Estudio preliminar," in Lau and Ramos, eds., *Mujeres y Revolución, 1900–1917* (Mexico City: Instituto Nacional de Estudios Históricos de la Revolución Mexicana, 1993), 13, 50; Jean Franco, *Plotting Women: Gender and Representation in Mexico* (New York: Columbia University Press, 1988), chap. 5.

18 *Estadísticas históricas; Censo General . . . 1895.*

19 *Censo General . . . 1895.*

20 Salvador Diego-Fernández, *La ciudad de Méjico a fines del siglo XIX* (Mexico City: n.p., 1937), 31 and, on railroads replacing canoes, 5; José Guadalupe Posada, *José Guadalupe Posada: Ilustrador de la vida mexicana* (Mexico City: Fondo Editorial de la Plástica Mexicana, 1963), 217; John H. Coatsworth, "El Impacto económico de los ferrocarriles en una economía atrasada," in *Los orígenes del atraso. Nueve ensayos de historia económica de México en los siglos XVIII y XIX* (Mexico City: Alianza Editorial, 1990), 196–97. For example of a short trip outside the city and a burglary committed in the meanwhile, see AJ, 705331, Theft, 1911.

21 *El Universal,* 1 Oct. 1920, p. 9. Quote from Diego-Fernández, *La ciudad de Méjico,* 12–13. Evidence on the relative price of fares is inconclusive. In 1902, the usual expense in tramway fares for a worker was 24 cents although it probably included several trips. AHA, PG, 3643, 1600; *El Imparcial,* 11 Aug. 1902, p. 1. Prices increased during the late Porfiriato and the 1910s. In 1920, according to the Compañía de Tranvías de México, the average fare was 9.5 cents. *El Universal,* 1 Oct. 1920, p. 9; Celadores Municipales del Ramo de Policía to City Council, 23 Apr. 1901, AHA, PG, 3642, 1353. According

to Spanish writer Julio Sesto, daily wages in the late 1900s for journeymen, seamstresses, or cigar factory workers was one peso. Julio Sesto, *El México de Porfirio Díaz (hombres y cosas). Estudios sobre el desenvolvimiento general de la República Mexicana. Observaciones hechas en el terreno oficial y en el particular,* 2d ed. (Valencia: Sempere y Compañía, 1910), 134–36. For the role of tramways and trains in the expansion and centralization of urban space in Mexico City, see Manuel Vidrio, "El transporte en la Ciudad de México en el siglo XIX," in *Atlas de la ciudad de México* (Mexico City: Departamento del Distrito Federal–Colegio de México, 1987), 68–71; Mario Camarena, "El tranvía en época de cambio," *Historias* 27 (Oct.–Mar. 1992): 141–46; Miguel Rodríguez, *Los tranviarios y el anarquismo en México (1920–1925)* (Puebla: Universidad Autónoma de Puebla, 1980), 66. The number of passengers in the Federal District increased from 11,000,000 in 1887 to 102,321,628 in 1923. Ariel Rodríguez Kuri, *La experiencia olvidada. El ayuntamiento de México: política y administración, 1876–1912* (Mexico City: El Colegio de México, 1996), 161. For the role of tramways in other Latin American cities, see Anton Rosenthal, "The Arrival of the Electric Streetcar and the Conflict over Progress in Early Twentieth-Century Montevideo," *Journal of Latin American Studies* 27 (1995): 319–41; Allen Wells and Gilbert M. Joseph, "Modernizing Visions, *Chilango* Blueprints, and Provincial Growing Pains: Mérida at the Turn of the Century," *Mexican Studies/Estudios Mexicanos* 8:2 (Summer 1992): 167–216.

22 Angel de Campo, *Ocios y apuntes y La rumba* (Mexico City: Porrúa, 1976), 199; Eaton Smith, *Flying Visits to the City of Mexico and the Pacific Coast* (Liverpool: Henry Young and Sons, 1903), 30–34; AHA, PG, 3644, 1689.

23 See Moisés González Navarro, *La pobreza en México* (Mexico City: El Colegio de México, 1995), 123; *Gaceta de Policía* 1:2 (19 Oct. 1905): 3; ibid., 1:10 (24 Dec. 1905): 2. For responses to automobile accidents, see AJ, 1051487, Battery, 1921; Antonio Gavito to Pablo Meneses, Jefe del Departamento Confidencial, Secretaría de Gobernación, 10 Jan. 1931, AGN, DGG, 2.014(29)12, c.2, exp. 25. For a driver who ran over a two-year-old boy and was released by court employees after two hours, see H. J. Teufer to Porfirio Díaz, 8 Feb. 1911, APD, 36, 2216–17.

24 AHA, PG, 3639, 1092; Carlos Roumagnac, *Los criminales en México: Ensayo de psicología criminal. Seguido de dos casos de hermafrodismo observado por los señores doctores Ricardo Egea . . . Ignacio Ocampo* (Mexico City: Tipografía El Fénix, 1912 [1904]), 11, 14; *Gaceta de Policía* 1:9 (17 Dec. 1905): 9; AJ, 705337, Fraud, 1911.

25 *Memoria del Ayuntamiento 1901,* 2 vols. (Mexico City: La Europea, 1902), 1:505. Governor of the Federal District to City Council, 22 Dec. 1898, AHA,

PG, 3639, 1222; Enrique Ignacio Castelló to City Council, 2 Aug. 1904, AHA, PG, 3644, 1689.

26 Manuel Gutiérrez Nájera, "La novela del tranvía," in *La novela del tranvía y otros cuentos* (Mexico City: Secretaría de Educación Pública, 1984), 159. On "the suburbs riddled with brothels, inns, bullrings, cockfights and gambling houses," see José Juan Tablada, *La feria de la vida* (Mexico City: Consejo Nacional para la Cultura y las Artes, 1991 [1937]).

27 AHA, PPP, 3664, 3. For a powerful first-hand account of these years, see Francisco Ramírez Plancarte, *La ciudad de México durante la revolución constitucionalista* (Mexico City: Botas, 1941). See also Alberto J. Pani, *La higiene en México* (Mexico City: Ballescá, 1916); Claude Bataillon, "México, ciudad mestiza," *Ciencias Políticas* 35:1 (1964): 161–84, esp. 167–68. A closer look at the economic impact of the Revolution on the capital's population is presented in chapter 6.

28 *El Universal,* 9 Oct. 1920, p. 9.

29 Jean Meyer, "La ciudad de México, ex de los palacios," in Enrique Krauze, ed., *La reconstrucción económica,* vol. 10 of *Historia de la Revolución Mexicana* (Mexico City: El Colegio de México, 1977), 273–79; *El Universal,* 2 Oct. 1920, p. 3; Jiménez, *La traza;* Ayuntamiento Constitucional de México, *Argumentos contra la iniciativa presidencial por eliminar el ayuntamiento de la ciudad de México. Envían presidente municipal L. L. Hernández y regidor encargado de la secretaría general J. Prieto Laurens* (Mexico City: Imprenta Francesa, 1919), 34.

30 Clipping from *El Imparcial,* 11 Aug. 1902, p. 1, AHA, PG, 3643, 1600.

31 *El Imparcial,* 6 July 1908, p. 4; Sesto, *El México de Porfirio Díaz,* 245; Ramírez Plancarte, *La ciudad,* 426–27. Near the downtown area, vecindades were the result of subdividing large upper-class homes and during the nineteenth century housed tenants from different economic backgrounds. The construction of tenements for the express purpose of renting apartments took place in newly developed areas or in demolished downtown lots. See Lear, "Mexico City: Space and Class," 476; Jaime Rodríguez Piña, "Las vecindades en 1811: Tipología," in Alejandra Moreno Toscano et al., *Investigaciones sobre la historia de la ciudad de México (II)* (Mexico City: INAH, 1976): 68–82.

32 Clipping from *El Imparcial,* 11 Aug. 1902, p. 1, AHA, PG, 3643, 1600. According to the Comisión Monetaria, in 1891 there were 8,883 houses in the city and by 1902 the number had increased to 11,024. José Lorenzo Cossío, "Algunas noticias sobre las colonias de esta capital," *Boletín de la Sociedad Mexicana de Geografía y Estadística* 47:1 (Sept. 1937): 11. On vecindades' interior, see *Nueva Era,* 9 July 1912, p. 4. An 1872 police regulation established

that vecindad patios were to be considered as "public streets" for police action. *Colección de leyes y disposiciones gubernativas municipales y de policía vigentes en el Distrito Federal formada por acuerdo del C. gobernador Lic. Carlos Rivas* (Mexico City: Imprenta y Litografía de Ireneo Paz, 1884), 2:120.

33 AJ, 518303, Battery, 1907. For conditions in mesones, see Morales Martínez, "La expansión," 68; ASSA, BP, Sección Asistencial, Serie Asilados y Mendigos, 8, 8, fol. 2; ibid., 9, 21. In the mid-nineteenth century mesones sheltered cart drivers coming from outside of the city and staying a couple of days, AGN, Fondo Secretaría de Gobernación, 1847, 227, 1. In 1907, city inspectors fined a mesón owner because of the lack of running water, exposed and clogged sewers, common bathrooms, overcrowding of the twelve rooms, garbage that was not disposed of daily, holes in the roof and floors. ASSA, SP, Sección Salubridad del Distrito Federal, 1, 24. Many of the beggars arrested in a 1930 campaign lived in mesones. ASSA, BP, Sección Asistencial, Serie Asilados y Mendigos.

34 *Memoria del ayuntamiento,* 2:275–76; Blanca Ugarte to City Council, 31 Aug. 1920, ASSA, EA, Dormitorios Públicos, 1, 5.

35 Miguel Macedo, *La criminalidad en México: Medios de combatirla* (Mexico City: Secretaría de Fomento, 1897), 14–15; Luis Lara y Pardo, *La prostitución en México* (Mexico City: Viuda de Bouret, 1908), 120–21; Pani, *La higiene,* 111, 221. For their foreign inspirations of these descriptions, see chapter 3.

36 Since the late colonial period, the absence of running water at home had thwarted the construction of nuclear families. Marcela Dávalos, "La salud, el agua y los habitantes de la ciudad de México. Fines del siglo XVIII y principios del XIX," in Hernández Franyuti, ed., *La ciudad de México en la primera mitad del siglo XIX,* 300, 281. See also Ilán Semo, "La ciudad tentacular: notas sobre el centralismo en el siglo XX," in Isabel Tovar de Arechederra and Magdalena Mas, eds., *Macrópolis mexicana* (Mexico City: Universidad Iberoamericana–Consejo Nacional para la Cultura y las Artes–DDF, 1994), 48. For drainage systems, see ASSA, SP, Sección Salubridad del Distrito Federal, 1, 33.

37 Diego-Fernández, *La ciudad de Méjico,* 4. For a description of baños públicos in Lagunilla and Juárez, see vice president of the Junta Inspectora de la Beneficencia Pública to Ministry of the Interior, 16 Aug. 1913, AGN, GPR, 115, 77, 1. See also ASSA, EA, Baños y Lavaderos Públicos, 1, 15; for the regulations of the public baths of La Lagunilla, see ibid., 2, 11.

38 In October 1917, AHA, PPP, 3664, 1. For Bourbon official concern about these issues, see Voekel, "Peeing on the Palace." The problem remained in 1930 in the colonia Doctores. Pablo Peña Borregó to Minister of Justice, 6 June 1930, AGN, DGG, 2.014(29)8, c.2, exp. 29.

39 M. Río de la Loza to City Council, 27 Dec. 1892, AHA, PG, 3639, 1020.

40 Report of the housing committees to the city council, 15 May 1901, AHA, PG, 3642, 1354.

41 On urinals for men, see Vicente Moyano and José Genaro Alonso to City Council, 11 Oct. 1892, AHA, PG, 3639, 1019; contract between the City Council and Francisco J. Báez, 29 Aug. 1895, ibid., 3639, 1056; Public Health Council to City Council, 8 Apr. 1892, ibid., 3639, 1016.

42 Roumagnac, *Los criminales,* 282; Serge Gruzinski, *La colonización de lo imaginario: Sociedades indígenas y occidentalización en el México español, siglos XVI–XVIII* (Mexico City: Fondo de Cultura Económica, 1991), 272–75; Viqueira Albán, *¿Relajados o reprimidos?,* 191. On availability of water, see report of health inspector A. Romero to Public Health Council, 10 Jan. 1902, ASSA, SP, Sección Salubridad del Distrito Federal, 1, 22; council member Luis E. Ruiz on the Eighth District, 19 Apr. 1904, AHA, PG, 3644, 1691.

43 AJ, 553759, Abduction, 1908. On pulquerías, see Raúl Guerrero Guerrero, *El pulque* (Mexico City: Joaquín Mortiz, 1986), 158.

44 City Council to José González Parres, 7 Dec. 1907, AHA, BE, 1337, 397. The 1902 Reglamento de Bebidas Embriagantes established an area of "first category" alcohol outlets around the center of the city, where cantinas had to follow stricter hygienic norms and were allowed to remain open longer than those in the rest of the city, the "second category" area. AHA, BE, 1332, 115. García Cubas, *El libro de mis recuerdos,* 221–22; José María Marroqui, *La ciudad de México. Contiene: El origen de los nombres de muchas de sus calles y plazas, del de varios establecimientos públicos y privados, y no pocas noticias curiosas y entretenidas* (Mexico City: La Europea, 1900), 3:189–211. For early attempts to control pulque consumption, see Virginia Guedea, "México en 1812: Control político y bebidas prohibidas," *Estudios de historia moderna y contemporánea de México* 8 (1980): 23–64.

45 Andrea Coquis to City Council, 1 Apr. 1916, AHA, PG, 3645, 1777; for seizures and arrests related to unauthorized selling of pulque, see AHA, Gobernación, 1112, 120–21; AHA, Gobernación, 1118, 4. After the Revolution, this concern was still alive. *El Universal,* 14 Dec. 1916, p. 3. For restrictions see AHA, BE, 1332, 115; Pablo Piccato, "'El Paso de Venus por el disco del Sol': Criminality and Alcoholism in the Late Porfiriato," *Mexican Studies/Estudios Mexicanos* 11:2 (Summer 1995): 203–41.

46 Letter signed by "comerciantes de abarrotes y cantina," 16 June 1909, AHA, BE, 1338, 511; also Gervasio Suárez to City Council, 24 July 1911, AHA, BE, 1341, 699; Ministry of the Interior to Governor of the Federal District, 7 June 1913, AHA, BE, 1781, 1130. On the pulque industry, see Juan Felipe Leal and Mario Huacuja Rountree, *Economía y sistema de haciendas en*

México: La hacienda pulquera en el cambio: Siglos XVIII, XIX y XX (Mexico City: Ediciones Era, 1982).

47 *El Universal,* 16 Feb. 1917, p. 1; ibid., 13 Jan. 1917, p. 6. See also AHA, BE, Antonio Aura to City Council, 4 Apr. 1899, AHA, PG, 3641, 1240; for a license to operate a phonograph, see ibid., 3639, 1060; for one to sell food, ibid., 3640, 1145.

48 ASSA, BP, Sección Asistencial, Serie Asilados y Mendigos, fol. 7.

49 Governor of the Federal District to City Council, 11 May 1903, AHA, PG, 3644, 1643. Merchants of Empedradillo Street to city council, 23 Aug. 1894, ibid., 3640, 1179; Dirección General de Estadística, *Censo general de la República Mexicana verificado el 28 de octubre de 1900* (Mexico City: Secretaría de Fomento, 1901–1907). For the images of vendors see Diego-Fernández, *La ciudad de Méjico,* 4; Dávalos, "La salud, el agua," 280.

50 Tomasa Pérez and seven other women to City Council, 3 July 1915, AHA, PG, 3645, 1768; Isabel Reza and twelve others to the president of the city council, 25 Jan. 1901, ibid., 3642, 1342; ibid., 3642, 1371.

51 For merchants' resistance to inspectors in the San Lucas market, see Comisión de Mercados to City Council, 24 Feb. 1899, AHA, PG, 3641, 1266; José Carpinteiro, who paid 13 cents daily, claimed that the value of the candy he sold every day did not exceed 10 pesos. AGN, SJ, 891, 3937.

52 Neighbors and landlords of Santo Domingo to City Council, 26 July 1901, AHA, PG, 3642, 1360; Santos Cisneros and thirty-three others to City Council, 11 Nov. 1897, ibid., 3640, 1180. The conflict continued after the Revolution. In 1917, *El Universal* triumphantly announced that the authorities would cease to extend any more licenses for peddlers on avenues between the Plaza de la Constitución and the Alameda. *El Universal,* 10 Jan. 1917, p. 1.

53 *Memoria del ayuntamiento,* 2:39–41. See chapter 6 for a discussion of pawning.

54 *El Imparcial,* 2 Jan. 1900, p. 3; *La Voz de México,* 29 Jan. 1890, p. 2.

55 *El Imparcial,* 1 Apr. 1897, p. 2.

56 *El Universal,* 24 Dec. 1916, p. 3; Carlos M. Patiño, 4 June 1912, AHA, PG, 3645, 1704; and reply by Comisión de Policía, ibid. A highly publicized campaign against beggars took place in 1930. See Beneficencia Pública del Distrito Federal, *La mendicidad en México* (Mexico City: Departamento de Acción Educativa, Eficiencia y Catastros Sociales, 1931).

57 AHA, PPP, 3664, 2. See *Nueva Era,* 3 July 1912, p. 4.

58 Proposal of city council member Algara to City Council, 25 Feb. 1895, and reply from police inspectors, AHA, PG, 3639, 1092; Fifth District police chief to City Council, 7 Apr. 1895, ibid. See also the descriptions by social workers

in 1930 in ASSA, BP, Sección Asistencial, Serie Asilados y Mendigos; *El Imparcial,* 18 July 1912, p. 7.

59 *El Universal,* 3 July 1930, p. 3a.

2 THE POLICED CITY

1 For a full discussion of "campaigns" against petty thieves, see chapter 7. See *El Imparcial,* 12 Oct. 1897, p. 3; ibid., 3 Jan. 1917, p. 5; *Gaceta de Policía* 1:10 (24 Dec. 1905): 2; AGN, POC, 121-G-I-4.

2 Andrés Lira, *Comunidades indígenas frente a la ciudad de México: Tenochtitlan y Tlatelolco, sus pueblos y barrios, 1812–1919* (Mexico City: El Colegio de México, 1995), 26–28.

3 Clipping of *El Imparcial,* 11 Aug. 1902, p. 1, AHA, PG, 3643, 1600. José Lorenzo Cossío, "Algunas noticias sobre las colonias de esta capital," *Boletín de la Sociedad Mexicana de Geografía y Estadística,* 47:1 (Sept. 1937): 5–9; Agustín Avila Méndez, "Mapa serie barrios de la ciudad de México 1811 y 1882," in Alejandra Moreno Toscano et al, *Investigaciones sobre la historia de la ciudad de México (I)* (Mexico City: INAH, 1974): 155–81; Lira, *Comunidades indígenas,* 66.

4 Eaton Smith, *Flying Visits to the City of Mexico and the Pacific Coast* (Liverpool: Henry Young and Sons, 1903), 28–29.

5 ASSA, SP, Epidemias, 32, 12.

6 Comisión de Obras Públicas to City Council, 18 May 1900, AHA, PG, 3641, 1289.

7 *El Imparcial,* 6 Jan. 1900, p. 2.

8 Smith, *Flying Visits,* 41–42, 26; Mixcoac neighbors to Public Health Council, 31 Jan. 1907, ASSA, SP, Sección Salubridad del Distrito Federal, 1, 36.

9 María Dolores Morales, "La expansión de la ciudad de México en el siglo XIX: el caso de los fraccionamientos," in Alejandra Moreno Toscano et al., *Investigaciones sobre la historia de la ciudad de México* (Mexico City: INAH, 1974), 190–91, cited by Lira, *Comunidades indígenas,* 240.

10 Antonio García Cubas, *El libro de mis recuerdos. Narraciones históricas, anecdóticas y de costumbres mexicanas anteriores al actual estado social, ilustradas con más de trescientos fotograbados* (Mexico City: Editorial Porrúa, 1986 [1904]), 231. On the pulque *garitas,* see Raúl Guerrero Guerrero, *El pulque* (Mexico City: Joaquín Mortiz, 1986), 118; Jorge Nacif Mina, "Policía y seguridad pública en la ciudad de México, 1770–1848," in Regina Hernández Franyuti, ed., *La ciudad de México en la primera mitad del siglo XIX* (Mexico City: Instituto Mora, 1994), 33. For the control of travelers coming into the city, see AGN, Fondo Secretaría de Gobernación, 1847. The wider area and the less

precise limits of the city are clearly expressed by a comparison of maps of 1886 and 1906: Antonio García Cubas, *Plano topográfico de la ciudad de México formado por el ingeniero Antonio García Cubas con las nuevas calles abiertas hasta la fecha y los ferrocarriles* (Mexico City: Antigua librería de M. Murguía, 1886) and *Plano oficial de la Ciudad de México. Edición especial para el Consejo Superior de Gobierno del Distrito Federal, con motivo de la reunión del X Congreso Geológico Internacional* (N.p.: 1906).

11 *El Imparcial,* 16 July 1912, p. 1; *La Nación,* 2 Sept. 1912, p. 1–2; *El Universal,* 21 Oct. 1916, p. 3.

12 Salvador Diego-Fernández, *La ciudad de Méjico a fines del siglo XIX* (Mexico City: N.p., 1937), 5; *Gaceta de Policía* 1:10 (24 Dec. 1905): 2; Miguel Macedo, *La criminalidad en México: Medios de combatirla* (Mexico City: Secretaría de Fomento, 1897), 14–16, 4–7.

13 *El Imparcial,* 3 July 1908, p. 1. See also AGN, SJ, 893, 4337.

14 Smith, *Flying Visits,* 72–73; *El Imparcial,* 3 July 1908, p. 1.

15 *El Universal,* 16 Feb. 1917, p. 1. *México y sus alrededores. Guía para los viajeros escrita por un Mexicano. Cuidado con los rateros* (Mexico City: Tip. Luis B. Casa, 1895), 15.

16 AHA, BE, 1331, 41, fol. 1.

17 Cossío, "Algunas noticias sobre las colonias," 23, 26–29, 31; Diego-Fernández, *La ciudad de Méjico,* 4; Lira, *Comunidades indígenas,* 253; Jorge H. Jiménez Muñoz, *La traza del poder: Historia de la política y los negocios urbanos en el Distrito Federal desde sus orígenes a la desaparición del Ayuntamiento (1824–1928)* (Mexico City: Codex, 1993), 191–92; John Robert Lear, "Workers, *Vecinos* and Citizens: The Revolution in Mexico City, 1909–1917" (Ph.D. diss., University of California at Berkeley, 1993), 56–58.

18 The city council's authority was greatly reduced by legal reforms in 1903 and disappeared in 1929. The institution had to negotiate many important decisions with the governor of the Federal District, appointed by the president. García Cubas, *El libro de mis recuerdos,* 146. For the 1903 reform and its consequences, see AHA, PG, 3645, 1701; Ariel Rodríguez Kuri, *La experiencia olvidada. El ayuntamiento de México: política y administración, 1876–1912* (Mexico City: El Colegio de México, 1996), chap. 2; Jiménez, *La traza,* 19, n. 88.

19 *El Universal,* 4 Jan. 1917, p. 4. AHA, PG, 3642, 1427; ibid., 3643, 1600. See also Miguel Vega y Vera to City Council, 24 Feb. 1892, AHA, PG, 3639, 1014. Several frustrated contracts up to 1889 show the reluctance of the city council to take street cleaning under its direct responsibility, AHA, PG, 3639, 1028; ibid., 3639, 1071; ibid, 3640, 1193. In 1898, prisoners swept the streets of the city, AHA, PG, 3639, 1231. Ayuntamiento Constitucional de México, *Argu-*

mentos contra la iniciativa presidencial por eliminar el ayuntamiento de la ciudad de México. Envían presidente municipal L. L. Hernández y regidor encargado de la secretaría general J. Prieto Laurens (Mexico City: Imprenta Francesa, 1919), 19, 32–33.

20 Public Health Council to City Council, 27 Sept. 1901, AHA, PG, 3642, 1368.

21 Twenty-seven signatures to Public Health Council, 13 Apr. 1901, AHA, PG, 3642, 1420.

22 Julio Sesto, *El México de Porfirio Díaz (hombres y cosas). Estudios sobre el desenvolvimiento general de la República Mexicana. Observaciones hechas en el terreno oficial y en el particular,* 2d ed. (Valencia: Sempere y Compañía, 1910), 231–34. Public Health Council to City Council, 5 June 1902, AHA, PG, 3643, 1534; ASSA, SP, Sección Salubridad del Distrito Federal, 1, 23, 35.

23 AHA, PG, 3644, 1689.

24 *La Voz de México,* 20 Oct. 1897, p. 3.

25 *Colección de leyes y disposiciones gubernativas municipales y de policía vigentes en el Distrito Federal formada por acuerdo del C. gobernador Lic. Carlos Rivas* (Mexico City: Imprenta y Litografía de Ireneo Paz, 1884), 1:284; 2:117.

26 Mexico City was, in the assessment of Laurence Rohlfes, at the forefront of modern police reform, as it "increased the role of the professional police at the expense of outmoded institutions which were legacies of the colonial period." His remains the best study on the topic. Laurence John Rohlfes, "Police and Penal Correction in Mexico City, 1876–1911: A Study of Order and Progress in Porfirian Mexico" (Ph.D. diss., Tulane University, 1983), 42, 9–12. For police budget, see Manuel González de Cosío, *Memoria que presenta al Congreso de la Unión el General . . . Secretario de Estado y del Despacho de Gobernación* (Mexico City: Imprenta del Gobierno Federal, 1900), 804–11.

27 Rohlfes, "Police and Penal Correction," 94.

28 The city government claimed to have changed policies in 1906, allowing for the wounded to receive medical attention before the police arrived, but the practice continued. *Gaceta de Policía* 1:26 (6 May 1906): 6; Rohlfes, "Police and Penal Correction," 94, 97–98, 41–42; Report to City Council, 19 July 1919, AHA, Justicia comisarías, 2717, 1.

29 AJ, 1027226, Battery, 1920.

30 Agustín Arroyo de Anda to Minister of Justice, 8 Apr. 1904, AGN, SJ, 481, 793.

31 "Reglamento de las obligaciones del gendarme" [1897], in González de Cosío, *Memoria,* 767. The use of policemen for similar purposes dates back to the *celadores* and *vigilantes* of the late colonial era. Nacif, "Policía y seguridad pública," 14; Rohlfes, "Police and Penal Correction," 45–46, 77, 81.

32 AHA, PPP, 3664, 3–4.

33 AJ, 1027244, Battery, 1920; AJ, 781332, Theft, 1902; AJ, 430159, Attacks to authority, 1904. Of eighty-two acting gendarmes participating as suspects, victims, or witnesses in the examined cases, forty-six reported another trade. According to Rohlfes, gendarmes had salaries competitive with those of skilled workers: set in 1879 at one peso per day; by 1903 they had increased to 1.50 pesos. Rohlfes does not take fines and other deductions into consideration, nor seven-day weeks. Rohlfes, "Police and Penal Correction," 104, 30, 40, 88. In 1898, 2.3 percent of the policemen were dismissed, and in general there were "incredibly high turnover rates." Most gendarmes, Rohlfes himself notes, "did not view police work as a lifelong calling," lasting an average two years and four months. Rohlfes, "Police and Penal Correction," 120, 109, 119, 127. On the strike, Moisés González Navarro, *El Porfiriato: La vida social,* vol. 4 of *Historia moderna de México* (Mexico City: Hermes, 1957), 315. Professionalization was also a problem for the rural police corps. Paul J. Vanderwood, *Disorder and Progress: Bandits, Police and Mexican Development,* 2d. ed. (Wilmington, DE: Scholarly Resources, 1992).

34 See AJ, 781364, Aiding escape, 1914. Rohlfes, "Police and Penal Correction," 31–32, 129–30.

35 AJ, 430159, Attacks to authority, 1904. See also AJ, 1067902, Battery and Theft, 1921.

36 For example, AJ, 430164, Attacks to authority, 1904.

37 AJ, 781323, Attacks to authority, 1913.

38 See engraving "La seguridad en México. Eficacia de la policía," *El Hijo del Ahuizote* 16:1746 (17 Feb. 1901): 76; for a drunken gendarme caught in a pulquería fight, see *El Imparcial,* 1 Apr. 1897, p. 2; Carlos Roumagnac, *Los criminales en México: Ensayo de psicología criminal. Seguido de dos casos de hermafrodismo observado por los señores doctores Ricardo Egea . . . Ignacio Ocampo* (Mexico City: Tipografía El Fénix, 1912 [1904]), 118; AJ, 434206, Battery, 1903; AJ, 19331, Battery, homicide, 1924; AJ, 430159, Attacks to authority, 1904; José González to President Francisco I. Madero, n.d. AGN, FIM, 70; Archivo Venustiano Carranza, Condumex, Mexico City, 70, 7653.

39 The two suspects were sentenced to fifteen days and one month of arrest, respectively. AJ, 518295, Battery, 1906.

40 AJ, 781369, Battery, 1913; others called a policeman "mule" and doubted his masculinity, AJ, 430159, Attacks to authority, 1904; another suspect called a gendarme "abject, son-of-a-bitch owl." AJ, 518295, Battery, 1906. Words for gendarme included "tecolote, dorais, cuico, garfin, tequis, choco." Roumagnac, *Los criminales,* 126.

41 AJ, 518271, Attacks to authority, 1906. She was sentenced to three months of arrest.

42 *México y sus alrededores,* 5, 13–14.

43 *Documentos relativos a la nomenclatura de calles y numeración de casas de la ciudad de México* (Mexico City: La Europea, 1904), 35–36.

44 Ibid., 28, 32, 38, 48–49.

45 Ibid., 102–3, 25, 80–82.

46 AJ, 1067901, Theft, 1922; on walking the streets as a "speech act" that challenges panoptic power, see Michel de Certeau, *The Practice of Everyday Life,* trans. Steven Rendall (Berkeley: University of California Press, 1984), 98.

47 AHA, Vagos y rateros, 4157–60.

48 Josefina was finally released after four months in prison, ASSA, BP, Sección Asistencia, 6, 3. See also, ibid., 6, 29.

49 Candelaria García to Josefa Castro, 14 Oct. 1930, ASSA, BP, Sección Asistencia, 7, 7.

3 THE CONSTRUCTION OF MEXICAN CRIMINOLOGY

1 "Discourse" is used here to encompass the statements produced, from different perspectives and through various media, around the theme of crime. See a similar use of the term in Marie-Christine Leps, *Apprehending the Criminal: The Production of Deviance in Nineteenth-Century Discourse* (Durham, NC: Duke University Press, 1992). See also Michel Foucault, *La arqueología del saber* (Mexico City: Siglo Veintiuno, 1979), and Robert Wuthnow, *Communities of Discourse: Ideology and Social Structure in the Reformation, the Enlightenment and European Socialism* (Cambridge, MA: Harvard University Press, 1989).

2 This interpretation was maintained during the Porfiriato by newspapers such as *El Hijo del Ahuizote* and later adopted by revolutionary speakers and writers. See "Energía gendarmeril," *El Hijo del Ahuizote* (13 Apr. 1902): 1279, in which policemen attack newspaper vendors but let thieves, murderers, and counterfeiters act freely. For a denunciation of the political uses of prisons during the Porfiriato, see the speech by Rafael Martínez in *Diario de los Debates del Congreso Constituyente* (Mexico City: INEHRM, 1960), 2:813. The *científicos* used "a philosophy brought from abroad and masterfully adapted here: European positivism," Arnaldo Cordova, *La ideología de la Revolución Mexicana. La formación del nuevo régimen* (Mexico City: ERA, 1973), 45, 63–79. See also Charles A. Hale, *The Transformation of Liberalism in Late Nineteenth-Century Mexico* (Princeton, NJ: Princeton University Press, 1989), and Leopoldo Zea, *El positivismo y la circunstancia mexicana* (Mexico City, FCE-SEP, 1985).

3 Allen Wells and Gilbert M. Joseph, "Modernizing Visions, *Chilango* Blue-

prints, and Provincial Growing Pains: Mérida at the Turn of the Century," *Mexican Studies/Estudios Mexicanos* 8:2 (Summer 1992): 171–80; William E. French, *A Peaceful and Working People: Manners, Morals and Class Formation in Northern Mexico* (Albuquerque: University of New Mexico Press, 1996); the essays of William H. Beezley et al., in *Rituals of Rule, Rituals of Resistance* (Wilmington, DE: Scholarly Resources, 1994). For the continuity of these themes after the Revolution, see Alan Knight, "Revolutionary Project, Recalcitrant People: Mexico, 1910–40," in Jaime O. Rodríguez, ed., *The Revolutionary Process in Mexico: Essays on Political and Social Change, 1880–1940* (Irvine: University of California Press, 1990).

4 David Garland, *Punishment and Modern Society* (Chicago: University of Chicago Press, 1990), 22. For recent studies that emphasize the political and racial motivations behind criminology and begin to establish the discipline's connections with other social sciences and popular culture, see Julia Rodríguez, "Encoding the Criminal: Criminology and the Science of 'Social Defense' in Modernizing Argentina (1880–1921)" (Ph.D. diss., Columbia University, 1999); Lila Caimari, "Psychiatrists, Criminals, and Bureaucrats: The Production of Scientific Biographies in the Argentine Penitentiary System (1907–1945)," in Mariano Plotkin, ed., *Argentina on the Couch* (Albuquerque: University of New Mexico Press, forthcoming); Cristina Rivera Garza, "The Masters of the Streets: Bodies, Power and Modernity in Mexico, 1867–1930" (Ph.D. diss., University of Houston, 1995); Elisa Speckman, "Crimen y castigo: Legislación penal, interpretaciones de la criminalidad y administración de justicia: Ciudad de México 1872–1910" (Ph.D. diss., El Colegio de México, Mexico City, 1999); and the works of Carlos Aguirre on Peru and Ricardo Salvatore on Argentina and Brazil. Robert Buffington, *Criminal and Citizen in Modern Mexico* (Lincoln: University of Nebraska Press, 1999) is the most comprehensive study to place criminological and penal discourse in the broader framework of nation building.

5 Hale, *Transformation of Liberalism,* 27.

6 On the need for and the advantages of compiling statistics of criminality, see Trinidad de la Garza y Melo, *Apuntes para la estadística criminal del Estado de Nuevo-León* (Monterrey: Imprenta del Gobierno, 1870); "Sobre el número y clase de presos que debe alojar la Penitenciaría de México, Proyecto de Penitenciaría del Distrito Federal, Junta formada por el gob. Ramón Fernández" [1882], *Boletín del Archivo General de La Nación: La Penitenciaría de México* 5:4 (Oct. 1981–Mar. 1982); Antonio A. de Medina y Ormaechea, *México ante los congresos internacionales penitenciarios* (Mexico City: Secretaría de Fomento, 1892), 294–95. For the authority of statistics in general, see Moisés González Navarro, *El Porfiriato: La vida social,* vol. 3 of *Historia*

Moderna de México (Mexico City: Hermes, 1957), 3–13; "La estadística en 1853 y 1924," *Boletín del Departamento de la Estadística Nacional* 2:1, no. 11 (May 1924): 23; Francisco Barrera Lavalle, "Apuntes para la historia de la estadística en México," *Boletín de la Sociedad Mexicana de Geografía y Estadística de la República Mexicana* 5:4 (1910); *Estadística Gráfica: Progreso de los Estados Unidos Mexicanos* (Mexico City: Empresa de Ilustraciones, 1896); Jorge Adame Goddard, *El pensamiento político y social de los católicos mexicanos, 1867–1914* (Mexico City: Universidad Nacional Autónoma de México, 1980), 204. After the Revolution, the use of statistics with propagandistic ends continued, see Alberto J. Pani, *La higiene en México* (Mexico City: Ballescá, 1916), 145; "Circular no. 54 del Gobierno Constitucionalista de México, 3 de enero de 1917," *Boletín del Archivo General de La Nación* 1:3 (Oct.–Dec. 1977): 44; *El progreso de México: Estudio económico estadístico del Departamento de la Estadística Nacional* (Mexico City: Diario Oficial, 1924), 7; see also "Ley por la cual fue creado el Departamento de la Estadística Nacional," *Boletín del Departamento de la Estadística Nacional* 1:1–2 (1923): 68. For a critique of the ideological presumptions that support the prestige of statistics, see Joan Wallach Scott, "A Statistical Representation of Work: *La Statistique de L'Industrie a Paris, 1847–1848,*" in J.W. Scott, *Gender and the Politics of History* (New York: Columbia University Press, 1988), 111–38; for the use of statistics in the construction of nationalism, see Benedict Anderson, *Imagined Communities* (New York–London: Verso, 1983), chap. 10; Mauricio Tenorio, *Mexico at the World's Fairs: Crafting a Modern Nation* (Los Angeles: University of California Press, 1996), chap. 8.

7 Dirección General de Estadística, *Estadística del ramo criminal en la República Mexicana que comprende un periodo de quince años, de 1871 a 1885* (Mexico City: Secretaría de Fomento, 1890), iii–vii.

8 Miguel Macedo, *La criminalidad en México: Medios de combatirla* (Mexico City: Secretaría de Fomento, 1897), 23, 4; Ramón Prida, *La criminalidad en México* (Mexico City: Soc. Mexicana de Geografía y Estadística, 1933), 707; Xavier Sorondo, "La necesidad de la pena de muerte," *Excélsior,* 21 July 1933, p. 5; Alfonso Quiroz Cuarón et al., *Tendencia y ritmo de la criminalidad en México* (Mexico City: Instituto de Investigaciones Estadísticas, 1939), 124–25, 111, 14–15.

9 For example, see Ministerio Público del Distrito y Territorios Federales, *Cuadros estadísticos e informe del Procurador de Justicia concernientes a la criminalidad en el Distrito Federal y territorios* (Mexico City: Ministerio Público del Distrito y Territorios Federales, 1900–1909). See note preceding the tables for the specific biases of published series.

10 Carlos Roumagnac, *La estadística criminal en México* (Mexico City: García

Cubas, 1907), 5. Carlos Roumagnac (1869–1937) was born in Madrid; in Mexico he worked as a journalist and with the Mexico City police. He was the most prolific criminologist during the period. In 1939, Quiroz Cuarón mentioned Roumagnac as one of the first "technical policemen," who died "in poverty," and whose contributions to science were still neglected, Quiroz Cuarón et al., *Tendencia y ritmo,* 129; *La Voz de México,* 6 Oct. 1897, p. 3. For an assessment of Roumagnac's influence, see Javier Mac Gregor Campuzano, "Historiografía sobre criminalidad y sistema penitenciario," *Secuencia: Revista de Historia y ciencias sociales* 22 (1992): 221–57.

11 Junta General del Ramo de Pulques, *Dictámen que presenta la comisión nombrada por la . . . al señor Gobernador del Distrito* (Mexico City: Tipografía Artística, 1896), 3, 8.

12 "Sobre el número y clase de presos," 32–34.

13 *La Voz de México,* 18 Jan. 1890, p. 2; Macedo, *La criminalidad,* 17, n. 5, 43; Ministerio Público, *Cuadros estadísticos e informe del Procurador,* 1900, p. 122–23; ibid., 1909, p. 5.

14 Macedo, *La criminalidad,* 14–15; Julio Guerrero, *La génesis del crimen en México: estudio de psiquiatría social* (París: Viuda de Bouret, 1901), 53; *Gaceta de Policía* 1:9 (17 Dec. 1905): 6.

15 *El Hijo del Ahuizote,* 10 Oct. 1897, p. 2.

16 Fernando Ponce was a physician, director of the Hospital of Tulancingo; Fernando Ponce, *El Alcoholismo en México* (Mexico City: Antigua Imprenta de Murguía, 1911), 4. See Pablo Piccato, " 'El Paso de Venus por el disco del Sol': Criminality and Alcoholism in the Late Porfiriato," *Mexican Studies/Estudios Mexicanos* 11:2 (Summer 1995): 203–41.

17 Federico Gamboa, *Santa* (Mexico City: Eusebio Gómez de la Puente, 1922 [1903]). On Gamboa's success, see José Emilio Pacheco, "Nota preliminar," in *Diario de Federico Gamboa, 1892–1939* (Mexico City: Siglo Veintiuno, 1977), 12.

18 *La Voz de México,* 28 Jan. 1890, p. 3. For an example of a narrative, see *La Voz de México,* 29 Jan. 1890, p. 3; and "Tragedia de la Calle de la Amargura," in *Gaceta de Policía* 1:2 (19 Oct. 1905): 7–10. For a graphic narration of a fight, see *El Imparcial,* 1 Jan. 1906, p. 3. For the use of diagrams, *El Imparcial,* 9 Sept. 1897, p. 1. An example of illustrations appears in *Diario del Hogar,* 16 Apr. 1901, p. 2. See Alberto del Castillo, "Entre la moralización y el sensacionalismo: Prensa, poder y criminalidad a finales del siglo XIX en la Ciudad de México," in Ricardo Pérez Montfort, ed., *Hábitos, Normas y Escándalo: Prensa, criminalidad y drogas durante el porfiriato tardío* (Mexico City: Ciesas-Plaza y Valdés, 1997). The *Gaceta* claimed to sell 11,000 copies, *Gaceta de Policía* 1:9 (17 Dec. 1905): 9. Several local police chiefs, mayors,

and *jefes políticos,* from places like Veracruz, Chalco, and Campeche, appeared as overdue subscribers of the *Gaceta, Gaceta de Policía* 1:26 (6 May 1906): 8; ibid., 1:43 (9 Sept. 1906): 3. The part devoted to police news in *El Imparcial* seems to have increased during the 1900s; by 1906, approximately 20 percent of the space, including part of the first page, was devoted to police news, and there were regular sections on Belem and the various police stations, *El Imparcial,* 23 Jan. 1906, p. 1.

19 Public attorney Emilio Alvarez, 1897, quoted in Quiroz Cuarón et al., *Tendencia y ritmo,* 81; *El Hijo del Ahuizote,* 15 Aug. 1897; Luis G. Rubin, "Los crimenes y la prensa," *El Bien Social,* 1 Aug. 1904, pp. 53–54.

20 *Don Cucufate,* 1 Oct. 1906, p. 1. See a similar mocking criticism in *El Diablito Bromista,* 18 Aug. 1907, p. 1.

21 *El Diablito Bromista,* 16 July 1907, p. 1. See also "Lamentos de Juan Tlachique," *El Hijo del Ahuizote,* 19 Jan. 1902, pp. 1046–47; ibid., 17 Feb. 1901, p. 76.

22 *La Voz de México,* 10 Oct. 1897, p. 3; ibid., 12 Jan. 1890, p. 3; *Gaceta de Policía* 1:14 (28 Jan. 1906): 7.

23 Letter to Ignacio Fernández Ortigoza from Judge Manuel F. de la Hoz, in Ignacio Fernández Ortigoza, *Identificación científica de los reos: Memoria escrita por . . .* (Mexico City: Sagrado Corazón de Jesús, 1892), 20, 8, 11; Roumagnac, *Los criminales,* 235, 360; *El Imparcial,* 1 July 1897, p. 1.

24 Fernández Ortigoza, *Identificación científica de los reos,* 38–39, 3. The digital system replaced Bertillon's method beginning in 1908, Carlos Roumagnac, *Elementos de policía científica: Obra de texto para la Escuela Científica de Policía de México* (Mexico City: Botas, 1923), 85. By the 1930s, criminal records still combined the two systems.

25 Demetrio Sodi, *El jurado en México: Estudios sobre el jurado popular* (Mexico City: Secretaría de Fomento, 1909), 149–50. Files also reported on tattoos. See Francisco Martínez Baca, *Los tatuajes: estudio psicológico y médico-legal en delincuentes y militares* (Puebla: Oficina Impresora del Timbre, 1899).

26 *Gaceta de Policía* 1:9 (17 Dec. 1905): 9; ibid., 1:10 (24 Dec. 1905): 2. The *Gaceta* emphasized the use of photography for identification purposes.

27 Macedo, *La criminalidad,* 12.

28 *Gaceta de Policía* 1:10 (24 Dec. 1905): 12; ibid., 1:11 (7 Jan. 1906): 12; ibid., 1:10 (24 Dec. 1905): 2; ibid., 1:31 (10 June 1906): 14. For a description of criminal skills, see Carlos Roumagnac, *Los criminales en México: Ensayo de psicología criminal. Seguido de dos casos de hermafrodismo observado por los señores doctores Ricardo Egea . . . Ignacio Ocampo* (Mexico City: Tipografía El Fénix, 1912 [1904]), 376–82. On thieves as policemen, *El Imparcial,* 7 Jan. 1897, p. 2; *Gaceta de Policía* 1:31 (6 Jan. 1906): 14.

29 *Gaceta de Policía* 1:14 (28 Jan. 1906): 2; Carlos Roumagnac, *Crimenes sexuales,* vol. 1 of *Crimenes sexuales y pasionales: Estudios de psicología morbosa* (Mexico City: Librería de Bouret, 1906), 5–6.

30 Roumagnac, *Los criminales.* Roumagnac's first volume of *Los criminales* concluded with an illustrated appendix about two Mexican cases of hermaphroditism.

31 Ibid., 117; see also Posada's leaflet about the crime, *José Guadalupe Posada: Ilustrador de la vida mexicana* (Mexico City: Fondo Editorial de la Plástica Mexicana, 1963), 237. See chapter 4 and Robert Buffington and Pablo Piccato, "Tales of Two Women: The Narrative Construal of Porfirian Reality," *The Americas* 55:3 (Jan. 1999): 391–424.

32 Macedo, *La criminalidad,* 19, 7–8, 16, 13, quoting Justo Sierra, "México político y social," *Revista Nacional* 1:14; ibid., "Discurso pronunciado en la ceremonia inaugural de la Penitenciaría de México" [1900], in Archivo General de la Nación, *Boletín del Archivo General de La Nación: La Penitenciaría de México* 18 (1981–82): 12.

33 *El Imparcial,* 27 Jan. 1906, p. 1; *Gaceta de Policía* 1:14 (28 Jan. 1906): 3–4; *La Guacamaya,* 30 Aug. 1906, p. 1; Luis Lara y Pardo, *La prostitución en México* (Mexico City: Bouret, 1908), 32–33; William H. Beezley, "The Porfirian Smart Set Anticipates Thorstein Veblen in Guadalajara," in Beezley et al., eds., *Rituals of Rule, Rituals of Resistance,*173–90.

34 Gamboa, *Santa,* 291; also see Eduardo Menéndez, *Morir de alcohol: saber y hegemonía médica* (Mexico City: Alianza-CNCA, 1990), 83–84; *El Imparcial,* 29 Jan. 1906, p. 1.

35 *La Voz de México,* 9 Jan. 1897, p. 2.

36 Lara y Pardo, *La prostitución en México,* 120–21.

37 Pani, *La higiene en México,* 111 and descriptions in Appendix 3.

38 William M. Reddy, *The Rise of Market Culture: The Textile Trade and French Society, 1750–1900* (Cambridge, UK: Cambridge University Press, 1984), chap. 6; Joan Wallach Scott, "'L'ouvrière! Mot impie, sordide . . .' Women workers in the discourse of French political economy, 1840–1860," in J. W. Scott, *Gender and the Politics of History* (New York: Columbia University Press, 1988), 149–51.

39 Judith Walkowitz, *City of Dreadful Delight: Narratives of Sexual Danger in Late-Victorian London* (Chicago: University of Chicago Press, 1992), 26–28. For descriptions of urban laboring-class life as "the necessary condition" for the emergence of criminology, see Leps, *Apprehending the Criminal,* 5.

40 Guerrero, *La génesis del crimen,* 137, 158–59. Julio Guerrero, born 1862, was a lawyer and founder of the *Revista de Jurisprudencia.* He published a book of poems, *Cantigas y rapsodias* (Mexico City: Botas, 1920).

41 Guerrero, *La genesis del Crimen,* 46–53.

42 Angel de Campo, *Ocios y apuntes y La rumba* (Mexico City: Porrúa, 1976), 276.

43 Gamboa, *Santa,* 96, 302. For a similar perspective on prostitution, see Mariano Azuela's early text, "Impresiones de un estudiante," in *Obras completas,* 3 vols. (Mexico City: Fondo de Cultura Económica, 1958), 2:1026–28.

44 Gamboa, *Santa,* 69, 291. Gamboa not only echoed foreign ideas, but also expressed the "typically Porfirian . . . ingrained sense of class segregation that persisted in spite (and probably also because) of a long-standing history of carnal relations between upper-class men and lower-class women." Buffington, *Criminal and Citizen,* chap. 4.

45 De Campo, *Ocios y apuntes y La rumba,* 298.

46 Gamboa, *Diario de Federico Gamboa,* 160–61; Federico Gamboa, *La llaga* (Mexico City: Eusebio Gómez de la Puente, 1922, [1913]), 54–55, 49.

47 Heriberto Frías, "Crónicas desde la cárcel," *Historias* 11 (Oct.–Dec. 1985): 47–71. In 1905, approximately 4,400 inmates crowded Belem, including men, women, and minors (*La Voz de México,* 8 Oct. 1897, p. 3; Charles F. Lummis, *The Awakening of a Nation: Mexico of To-day* [New York: Harper and Bros., 1899], 63–64).

48 Macedo, *La criminalidad,* 34; *Gaceta de Policía* 1:20 (11 Mar. 1906): 2–3; Gamboa, *La llaga,* 38; Fernández Ortigoza, *Identificación científica de los reos,* 18–20. For the rules of internal discipline and marriages between inmates, see Roumagnac, *Los criminales,* 88, 136, 126–27; and Frías, "Crónicas desde la cárcel," 47–71. For commerce, see *La Voz de México,* 14 Oct. 1897, p. 3. A fuller discussion appears in chapter 8 below.

49 *Diario del Hogar,* 23 Nov. 1907, p. 1; ibid., 19 Nov. 1907, p. 1. This criticism of prisons developed together with the modern ideas about the prison as the main instrument of punishment, Michel Foucault, *Discipline and Punish: The Birth of the Prison* (New York: Vintage, 1979), 265.

50 Francisco Martínez Baca and Manuel Vergara, *Estudios de Antropología Criminal: Memoria que por disposición del Superior gobierno del Estado de Puebla presentan . . .* (Puebla: Benjamín Lara, 1892), 5. See also Fernández Ortigoza, *Identificación científica de los reos.*

51 Roumagnac, *Los criminales,* 68; Roumagnac, *Crimenes sexuales y pasionales,* 1:11, 24; see also vol. 2, *Matadores de mujeres.*

52 Roumagnac, *Los criminales,* 69–72.

53 Ibid., 287, 256–57, 376–82; he continued the dictionary in 1923, Carlos Roumagnac, *Elementos de policía científica. Obra de texto para la Escuela Científica de Policía de México* (Mexico City: Botas, 1923).

54 Gamboa, *La llaga,* 58, 36. For an example of the language that prompted Gamboa's complaints, see *El Diablito Bromista,* 10 Oct. 1907, p. 3.

55 Roumagnac, *Crimenes sexuales,* 1:5.

56 Leps, *Apprehending the Criminal,* 44, 55.

57 For an overview of the emergence of the discipline, see David Garland, "Of Crimes and Criminals: The Development of Criminology in Britain," in Maguire et al., eds., *The Oxford Handbook of Criminology* (New York: Clarendon Press, 1994), 17–68. Urueta approached Ferri in Italy. He sent articles to *La Revista Moderna* of Mexico dealing with the theories of Ferri; Margarita Urueta, *Jesús Urueta: la historia de un gran desamor* (Mexico City: Stylo, 1964), 32–33, 36–37. Bibliophile Genaro García acquired French translations of the Italian masters and other influential treaties in his personal library. García's collection was later bought along with the rest of his library by the University of Texas at Austin.

58 For the eclecticism of criminology and its Victorian context, see Peter Gay, *The Cultivation of Hatred: The Bourgeois Experience, Victoria to Freud* (New York: Norton, 1993), 151–59; Leps, *Apprehending the Criminal,* 35–36. For the accumulative method of gathering evidence, see Cesare Lombroso, *Delitti di libidine,* 2d ed. (Torino: Fratelli Bocca, 1886).

59 Cesare Lombroso, *L'Homme Criminel. Criminel Né. Fou Moral. Epileptique. Criminel Fou. Criminel d'Occasion. Criminel par Passion. Etude Anthropologuique ent Psychiatrique,* 2d ed. (Paris: Félix Alcan, 1895), vi. Cesare Lombroso (1836–1909) established an initial taxonomy of criminal types (born, occasional, emotional). Closely related to Lombroso's school of thought, Enrico Ferri (1856–1929) linked criminology with positivist sociology and proposed a manifold study of the causes of crime: anthropological, physical, and social. He attacked traditional notions of penal responsibility and refined Lombroso's classification, explaining criminals as the product of multiple internal and external influences. Raffaelle Garofalo (1852–1934) was also known for his studies about the juridical applications of criminology, Bernaldo de Quiros, *Modern Theories of Criminality* (Boston: Little, Brown and Company, 1912), 3, 6–7, 13, 16, 19–22.

60 Pick, "The Faces of Anarchy: Lombroso and the Politics of Criminal Science in Post-Unification Italy," *History Workshop* 23 (Spring 1986): 62–63, 65.

61 Justo Sierra, ed., *México, su evolución social: síntesis de la historia política, de la organización administrativa y militar y del estado económico de la federación mexicana; de sus adelantamientos en el orden intelectual; de su estructura territorial y del desarrollo de su población y de los medios de comunicación nacionales y internacionales; de sus conquistas en el campo industrial, agrícola, minero, mercantil, etc., etc. Inventario monumental que resume en trabajos magistrales los*

grandes progresos de la nación en el siglo XIX (Mexico City: Ballescá, 1900), vol. 1, chap. 8. Hale, *Transformation of Liberalism,* 140–41, chap. 7. For the efforts, not always succesful, to achieve academic respectability in Latin America, see Rosa del Olmo, *América Latina y su criminología* (Mexico City: Siglo Veintinuno, 1981); Luis Marco del Pont, *Grandes corrientes de la criminología: Los delitos de cuello blanco (o de los poderosos)* (Córdoba, Argentina: Editorial Dimas, 1984). The lack of institutional support also affected European and U.S. criminology until the 1960s. Leps, *Apprehending the Criminal,* 38.

62 José Angel Ceniceros, *Tres estudios de criminología* (Mexico City: Cuadernos Criminalia, 1941), 50–51; del Olmo, *América Latina y su criminología,* 136, dates these discussions in 1889; see also Roumagnac, *Los criminales,* 32.

63 Carlos Díaz Infante, "Estudios penales. La sociología criminal," *Revista de Legislación y Jurisprudencia* 12 (Jan.–June 1897): 191–206; and J. Zacrewsky, "Algunas consideraciones sobre el Congreso de Ginebra," ibid.: 511–25; *El Foro* 50:1 (4 Jan. 1898): 1; ibid., 50:15 (25 Jan. 1898): 1.

64 Bernaldo de Quiros, *Modern Theories,* 120–21; also Ceniceros, *Tres Estudios de Criminología,* 52–53.

65 Rafael de Zayas Enríquez, *Fisiología del crimen: Estudio jurídico-sociológico* (Veracruz: Impr. de Rafael de Zayas, 1885). For a fuller discussion on early criminology, see Buffington, *Criminal and Citizen,* chaps. 1 and 2; Martínez Baca and Vergara, *Estudios de Antropología Criminal,* 2, 9; Roumagnac, *Los criminales,* 13–14; Macedo, *La criminalidad,* 37; Gamboa, *La llaga,* 186; L. G. Rubin, "Los dos grandes males," *El Bien Social,* 15 May 1900, p. 1; and Lara y Pardo, *La prostitución en México,* vii–viii.

66 On the dilemma of penal responsibility and psychiatric diagnosis, see Alexandre Lacassagne, *Vacher l'eventreur et les crimes sadiques* (Lyon: Stork, 1899), 5, 8; Enrico Ferri, *La Sociologie Criminelle,* 3d. ed. (Paris: Arthur Rousseau, 1893 [1881]), 100; Robert A. Nye, *Crime, Madness, and Politics in Modern France: The Medical Concept of National Decline* (Princeton; NJ: Princeton University Press, 1984), 194–96.

67 Roumagnac, *Los criminales,* 32.

68 *San Lunes,* 4 Sept. 1907, p. 3; *La Guacamaya,* 29 Sept. 1902, p. 3; ibid., 21 Nov. 1907; *El Hijo del Fandango,* 21 Oct. 1901, p. 3. Although the label "liberal" can be applied to a great variety of tendencies, I will use it here to refer to those that appealed to the values of nineteenth-century Mexican liberalism—against the Díaz regime's technocratic leanings and its conciliatory policies toward the Catholic church.

69 María Elena Díaz, "The Satiric Penny Press for Workers in Mexico, 1900–1910: A Case Study in the Politicization of Popular Culture," *Journal of Latin American Studies* 22 (1990): 507–8.

70 *La Voz de México,* 9 Sept. 1897, p. 2; ibid., 3 Sept. 1897, p. 2; Sánchez Santos, *El Alcoholismo en la República Mexicana,* 92; Adame Goddard, *El pensamiento político,* 219–20, 206; *El Heraldo, Diario Católico,* 19 Jan. 1890, p. 2.

71 *El Periquillo Sarniento,* 28 Dec. 1902, p. 1, 4.

72 Macedo, *La criminalidad,* 29.

73 *Diario del Hogar,* 19 Nov. 1907, p. 1.

74 Ibid., 30 June 1905, p. 2. Lara y Pardo referred to the "epidemics" of suicides and abductions as having no other explanation than imitation, Lara y Pardo, *La prostitución en México,* 118–19; Gabriel Tarde, *La philosophie pénale* (Lyon-Paris: A. Stork–G. Masson, 1890), 410. For examples of Mexican uses of contagion, see Roumagnac, *Los criminales,* 59–60; Junta General del Ramo de Pulques, *Dictámen que presenta,* 12–13; José Almaraz, "Regímenes penitenciarios," in *Memoria del Primer Congreso Nacional Penitenciario celebrado en la Ciudad de México del 24 de noviembre al 3 de diciembre de 1932, convocado por la Dirección Antialcohólica* (Mexico City: Talleres Gráficos de la Nación, 1935), 83.

75 Lara y Pardo, *La prostitución en México,* 120–21; Ponce, *El Alcoholismo en México,* 10–11; Roumagnac, *Los criminales,* 14, 11; Junta General del Ramo de Pulques, *Dictámen que presenta la comisión,* 12–13. "La enseñanza contra el alcoholismo," *El Bien Social* 18:21 (12 Feb. 1906): 157–58.

76 Sánchez Santos, *El Alcoholismo en la República Mexicana,* 17–24. For the moral effects of prostitution, see Lara y Pardo, *La prostitución en México,* 108–9. Degeneration caused by alcohol appeared in the first generation as depravity and proneness to excesses, in the fourth generation as stupidity and sterility, eventually leading to the extinction of the family. Román Ramírez, *Resúmen de medicina legal y ciencias conexas para uso de los estudiantes de las escuelas de derecho* (Mexico City: Tip. de Fomento, 1901), 164, 183; *Gaceta de Policía* 1:33 (24 June 1906): 8.

77 Roumagnac, *Los criminales,* 9–10.

78 Sánchez Santos, *El Alcoholismo en la República Mexicana,* 28–29.

79 Martínez Baca and Vergara, *Estudios de antropología criminal,* 11. See also José P. Saldaña, "Prólogo," in ibid., ix: "All Indians are thieves," regardless of where they live.

80 Sánchez Santos, *El Alcoholismo en la República Mexicana,* 27, 55.

81 "Sobre el número y clase de presos," 34; Ponce, *El Alcoholismo en México,* 99, 100–101; *La Voz de México,* 30 Sept. 1897, p. 2.

82 Roumagnac, *Los criminales,* 15–27, 59–60.

83 Ibid., 50–53; Guerrero, *La génesis del crimen,* ix–x.

84 "Sobre el número y clase de presos," 35; Guerrero, *La génesis del crimen,* 153–54, 235–36, 254; Gamboa, *La llaga,* 397; Roumagnac, *Los criminales,* 27–31,

7–8, quotes in this regard Constancio Bernaldo de Quirós, *Criminología de los delitos de sangre en España,* and Gabriel Tarde, *La Criminalité comparée,* the source of the statement that "el pueblo mexicano en el pueblo más criminal del mundo." The implications of criminology for Mexican racialized nationalism are analyzed in depth in Buffington, *Criminal and Citizen.*

85 See Ferri, *La Sociologie Criminelle,* 22; Lombroso, *L'Homme Criminel,* 3rd section. One comment on the Chinese encyclopedia classification of animals is Michel Foucault, *The Order of Things: An Archeology of Human Sciences* (New York: Pantheon Books, 1971).

86 Manuel González de Cosío, *Memoria que presenta al Congreso de la Unión el General . . . Secretario de Estado y del Despacho de Gobernación* (Mexico City: Imprenta del Gobierno Federal, 1900), 855. Macedo's classification was the basis for the government's statistical division of the Federal District population into "First," "Second," and "Third" classes, *Boletín Mensual de Estadística del Distrito Federal* 8:11 (Nov. 1908): 18–19. See also Macedo, *La criminalidad,* 6, 10; Hale, *Transformation of Liberalism,* 216n; Buffington, *Criminal and Citizen,* chap. 4.

87 Guerrero, *La génesis del crimen,* 111, 157–58, 167, 158–82.

88 These considerations determined the building of the new penitentiary in the distant eastern plains of the city, "Memoria sobre la Penitenciaría, presentada por el ingeniero José María Romero" [1882], in *Boletín del Archivo General de La Nación: La Penitenciaría de México* 5:4 (1981–82): 40–41. Miguel Macedo, "Discurso pronunciado en la ceremonia inaugural," in *ibid.,* 18. See also Macedo, *La criminalidad,* 6, 10.

89 Porfirian prison reform discourse was influential with respect to revolutionary constitutional ideas about the penitentiary system, although it was limited by the political concern about excessive centralization and past abuses. Buffington, *Criminal and Citizen,* chap. 4. Lombroso, Ferri, and Garofalo continue to excersise a great influence on Mexican judges. Personal communication, Ana Gamboa de Trejo and Salvador Martínez Martínez, Xalapa, Veracruz, 1998. Revisions of positivist criminology and the increasing influence of psychiatry and the social sciences are reflected, for example, by the works of Matilde Rodríguez Cabo and, more recently, Sergio García Ramírez and Elena Azaola Garrido.

90 Guerrero, *La génesis del crimen,* 356, 316–17.

II THE PRACTICES

1 See "A note on Mexican Statistics of Crime" preceding the tables.

2 Unless otherwise noted, I will be referring here to the database results. Only

12 (4 percent) of the 275 accused whose age was available were under sixteen years. For the overrepresentation of males among criminals see John Braithwaite, *Crime, Shame and Reintegration* (New York: Cambridge University Press, 1989), 44–45. See chapter 1 for the data on Mexico City's population.

3 Official statistics show that the literacy rate of suspects was lower than that of the population. In 1900, 41 percent of the population of the city knew how to read, but only 16 percent of those sentenced did. The difference narrowed but was still clear after the Revolution: 58 percent and 40 percent, respectively, in 1921. Dirección General de Estadística, *División territorial de la República Mexicana, Censo y división territorial del Distrito Federal, verificado en 1900* (Mexico City: Secretaría de Fomento, 1901), 67–95, 11; Departamento de la Estadística Nacional, *Censo general de habitantes, 30 de noviembre de 1921, Distrito Federal* (Mexico City: Talleres Gráficos de la Nación, 1925–28), 32. Between 1871 and 1885, the percentage of literate convicts was 24. Dirección General de Estadística, *Estadística del ramo criminal en la república mexicana que comprende un periodo de quince años, de 1871 a 1885* (Mexico City: Secretaría de Fomento, 1890).

4 *Estadísticas históricas de México* (Mexico City: INEGI, 1994); Dirección General de Estadística, *Censo general de la República Mexicana verificado el 20 de octubre de 1895* (Mexico City: Secretaría de Fomento, 1897–1899). Single men were more likely to commit crimes in most societies. See Eric A. Johnson, *Urbanization and Crime: Germany 1871–1914* (New York: Cambridge University Press, 1995), 200; Braithwaite, *Crime, Shame and Reintegration,* 46. Between 1871 and 1885, a total of 35 percent of sentenced suspects were married, while in 1895, statistics showed that 43 percent of the population sixteen years or older was married in Mexico City. Dirección General de Estadística, *Estadística del ramo criminal.*

5 AJ, 1027237, Battery, 1920.

6 Dirección General de Estadística, *División territorial de la República Mexicana,* 67–95, 11; Departamento de la Estadística Nacional, *Censo general de habitantes, 30 de noviembre de 1921,* 32. Artisans were 12 to 13 percent of those sentenced between 1871 and 1885, Dirección General de Estadística, *Estadística del ramo criminal.*

4 HONOR AND VIOLENT CRIME

1 AJ, 19334, Homicide, 1924.

2 The personal data provided by battery and homicide suspects are very similar to those of suspects in general, described in the introduction to part II above. The proportion of males was slightly higher among suspects of vio-

lent crime (82 percent against 80 percent in the database); fewer (3.4 percent) are listed as artisans, and the percentage of journeymen (14 percent against 8 in the database) and shoemakers (9 and 5 percent, respectively) was higher.

3 Lyman L. Johnson, "Changing Arrest Patterns in Three Argentine Cities: Buenos Aires, Santa Fe, and Tucumán, 1900–1930," in Lyman L. Johnson, ed., *The Problem of Order in Changing Societies: Essays on Crime and Policing in Argentina and Uruguay, 1750–1940* (Albuquerque: University of New Mexico Press, 1990), 136. Between 1900 and 1904, the homicide convictions rate in the Seine department in France was 2.01 per 100,000; in Berlin in 1905–1909, the rate was 2.75. Howard Zehr, *Crime and the Development of Modern Society: Patterns of Criminality in Nineteenth Century Germany and France* (London: Croom Helm, 1976), 118. The rate in Rome in 1900–1909 was 8 per 100,000, Daniele Boschi, "Homicide and Knife Fighting in Rome, 1845–1914," in Spierenburg, ed., *Men and Violence*, 132–33.

4 Pablo Piccato, "Politics and the Technology of Honor: Dueling in Turn-of-the-Century Mexico," *Journal of Social History* 33:2 (Winter 1999): 331–54; on the internalization of honor as a right, see Frank Henderson Stewart, *Honor* (Chicago: University of Chicago Press, 1994), 47–48, 51, 145–46. For the colonial concern about *honra* and the focus on the family and female virtue see Patricia Seed, *To Love, Honor, and Obey in Colonial Mexico: Conflicts over Marriage Choice, 1574–1821* (Stanford, CA: Stanford University Press, 1992), 63; Alexandra Parma Cook and Noble David Cook, *Good Faith and Truthful Ignorance: A Case of Transatlantic Bigamy* (Durham, NC: Duke University Press, 1991); Ann Twinam, "The Negotiation of Honor: Elites, Sexuality, and Illegitimacy in Eighteenth-Century Spanish America," in *The Faces of Honor: Sex, Shame, and Violence in Colonial Latin America*, Lyman L. Johnson and Sonya Lipsett-Rivera, eds. (Alburquerque: University of New Mexico Press, 1998); Sueann Caulfield, *In Defense of Honor: Sexual Morality, Modernity, and Nation in Early-Twentieth-Century Brazil* (Durham, NC: Duke University Press, 2000); for a study in the modern period, see Ana María Alonso, *Thread of Blood, Colonialism, Revolution, and Gender on Mexico's Northern Frontier* (Tucson: University of Arizona Press, 1995).

5 Julian A. Pitt-Rivers, "Honour and Social Status," in Jean Peristiany, ed., *Honour and Shame: The Values of Mediterranean Society* (London: Weidenfeld and Nicolson, 1965), 21, 29. See also Stewart, *Honor*, 12. For honor as the gendered structure of public reputation and its centrality in the conjunction of bourgeois public and private behaviors, see Kenneth S. Greenberg, *Honor and Slavery: Lies, Duels, Noses, Masks, Dressing as a Woman, Gifts, Strangers,*

Death, Humanitarianism, Slave Rebellions, The Pro-Slavery Argument, Baseball, Hunting, and Gambling in the Old South (Princeton, NJ: Princeton University Press, 1996); Robert A. Nye, *Masculinity and Male Codes of Honor in Modern France* (New York: Oxford University Press, 1993); William M. Reddy, *The Invisible Code: Honor and Sentiment in Postrevolutionary France, 1814–1848* (Berkeley: University of California Press, 1997).

6 Following Bourdieu, I define "rule" as "a scheme (or principle) immanent in practice, which should be called implicit rather than unconscious." Pierre Bourdieu, *Outline of a Theory of Practice*, trans. by Richard Nice (Cambridge, UK: Cambridge University Press, 1998), 27, 61. The "point of honour is a permanent disposition, embedded in the agents' very bodies in the form of mental dispositions, schemes of perception and thought." Ibid., 15, 11.

7 For the need to study honor as a relative category, shared by diverse groups in society, see Twinam, "The Negotiation of Honor," and Lyman L. Johnson, "Dangerous Words, Provocative Gestures, and Violent Acts: The Disputed Hierarchies of Plebeian Life in Colonial Buenos Aires," in *The Faces of Honor*. On "popular duels," see Pieter Spierenburg, ed., *Men and Violence: Gender, Honor, and Rituals in Modern Europe and America* (Columbus: Ohio University Press, 1998). For the need to disassemble honor into its smaller components, such as hospitality, respect, and honesty, see David Gilmore, "Introduction: The Shame of Dishonor," in Gilmore, ed., *Honor and Shame and the Unity of the Mediterranean* (Washington: American Anthropological Association, 1987), 3; Michael Herzfeld, "'As in Your Own House': Hospitality, Ethnography, and the Stereotype of Mediterranean Society," in Gilmore, ed., *Honor and Shame*, 75, 87–88. For an analysis focused on "true manhood" as a "stressed or embattled quality . . . an inner insecurity that needs dramatic proof," see David Gilmore, *Manhood in the Making: Cultural Concepts of Masculinity* (New Haven, CT: Yale University Press, 1990), 17.

8 CP 1871, 511.

9 CP 1871, 518, 519, 527, 529. Other aggravating circumstances referred to situations in which one of the contenders had an unfair advantage due to his or her greater physical strength, use of weapons, help from third parties, or to the position of the victim. CP 1871, 517.

10 Two-thirds of the regular sentence would be used in this case against the suspect who started the quarrel, and one-half against the one who was provoked. CP 1871, 527, 502; CP 1929, 1023; CP 1931, 502. Shorter sentences for battery in a fight in CP 1929, 949 and CP 1931, 297.

11 CP 1871, 502. *Golpes* were classified in the 1929 Code as "crimes concerning honor," along with defamation and insults—both classified by the 1871 code as "crimes against reputation." CP 1871, 517.

12 CP 1871, 531, 534, 535, 544, 555. See also CP 1929, 956; CP 1931, 294.

13 CP 1871, 821, 127. The 1929 Code increased the sentence for castration to twelve years (CP 1929, 955). The 1931 Code did not have a specific article concerning castration, but article 292 gave ten years of prison to the author of a wound that caused "loss of sexual abilities." On battery commited by a descendant, CP 1871, 127.

14 CP 1871, 34, 39, 402. The exception of responsibility in the defense of honor was maintained in CP 1929, 45, 56, 59; CP 1931, 15.

15 AJ, 19321, Homicide, 1923. See also AJ, 18516, Homicide, 1926.

16 Antonio Tovar, *Código nacional mexicano del duelo por el coronel de caballería . . .* (Mexico City: Imprenta Lit. y Encuadernación de Ireneo Paz, 1891), 13–15.

17 Tovar, *Código nacional.* Tovar's code followed the lines of the European codes by the Count of Chateauvillard and the Marquis of Cariñana. See also Vicente E. Manero, *Apuntes sobre el duelo* (Mexico City: Nichols, 1884); Gonzalo A. Esteva, *El duelo a espada y a pistola* (Mexico City: Tip. de Gonzalo A. Esteva, 1878); *Código del duelo, traducido, arreglado y anotado por Joaquin Larralde y Anselmo Alfaro* (Mexico City: Ireneo Paz, 1886). For a translation of Chateauvillard's code, see *Código del Duelo observado en Francia, según el conde de Chatauvillard,* trans. Aristides Simonpietri (Ponce, Puerto Rico: Tipografía El Comercio, 1887). Other available codes were *Código del honor en España formulado por el Marqués de Cabriñana* (Barcelona: Librería de Feliu y Susanna, 1900), and Pietro Lanzilli, *Código del honor para América Latina* (Guatemala: Tipografía Nacional, 1898).

18 CP 1871, 54–56. See Piccato, "Politics." I did not find trials for duels among judicial records, nor a single case cited by statistics after 1885; although some duelists might have been prosecuted for homicide or battery. Between 1871 and 1885, there were 32 convictions for dueling. Dirección General de Estadística, *Estadística del ramo criminal en la República Mexicana que comprende un periodo de quince años, de 1871 a 1885* (México, Secretaría de Fomento, 1890). Antonio Escudero discusses 78 duels between 1850 and 1929 in *El duelo en México: Recopilación de los desafíos habidos en nuestra República, precedidos de la historia de la esgrima en México y de los duelos más famosos verificados en el mundo desde los juicios de Dios hasta nuestros días* (Mexico City: Mundial, 1936).

19 CP 1871, 597, 561, 600, 587; CP 1929, 1076, 1079, 1065, 1066, 1067.

20 Miguel Macedo, *La criminalidad en México: Medios de combatirla* (Mexico City: Secretaría de Fomento, 1897), 13, 20.

21 "Defectos de nuestro pueblo: Los que no se rajan," *El Bien Social,* 15 Mar. 1901, pp. 178–79.

22 Junta General del Ramo de Pulques, *Dictámen que presenta la comisión nom-*

brada por la . . . al señor Gobernador del Distrito (Mexico City: Tipografía Artística, 1896), 12–13. 9.

23 Federico Gamboa, *La llaga* (Mexico City: Eusebio Gómez de la Puente, 1922 [1913]), 397. The notion of a Mexican "subculture of poverty," characterized by violence and machismo, was advanced by Oscar Lewis, *The Children of Sánchez. Autobiography of a Mexican Family* (New York: Random House, 1961), xxiv, 38, 57. For an example of similar assessments from the point of view of the sociology of deviance (in Mexico "the use of violence is taken for granted and homicide is a common form of death" and there prevails "a fatalistic expectation of violence and death"), see Marvin E. Wolfgang and Franco Ferracuti, *The Subculture of Violence* (London: Tavistock Publishers, 1967), 280; but see Albert K. Cohen and James F. Short, Jr., "Research in Delinquent Subcultures," *Journal of Social Issues* 14:3 (1958): 20–37; Matthew C. Gutmann, "Los hijos de Lewis: la sensibilidad antropológica y el caso de los pobres machos," *Alteridades* 4:7 (1994): 9–19.

24 From 1927 to 1935, one fifth of those arrested for battery were drunk at the moment of committal. Norman S. Hayner, "Criminogenic zones in Mexico City," *American Sociological Review* 11:4 (Aug. 1946): 436; see also Alfonso Quiroz Cuarón et al., *Tendencia y ritmo de la criminalidad en México* (Mexico City: Instituto de Investigaciones Estadísticas, 1939); Trinidad Sánchez Santos, *El Alcoholismo en la República Mexicana: Discurso pronunciado en la sesión solemne que celebraron las Sociedades Científicas y Literarias de La Nación, el día 5 de junio de 1896 y en el salón de sesiones de la Cámara de Diputados* (Mexico City: Imprenta del Sagrado Corazón de Jesus, 1897).

25 See *El Imparcial,* 29 Jan. 1906, p. 1; *El Foro,* 14:28 (9 Feb. 1895): 110; Antonio Saborit, "Nueve semanas en otro lugar: el viaje a México de Stephen Crane," *Historias* 6 (Apr.–July 1984): 3–17; AGN, SJ, 713, 614; "Por las típicas cuestiones de nuestros hombres de la clase ínfima, riñieron ayer en el bario de Romita, Esteban Mejía y J. Jesús Ortiz," *El Imparcial,* 7 Jan. 1906, p. 3; Antonio García Cubas, *El libro de mis recuerdos: Narraciones históricas, anecdóticas y de costumbres mexicanas anteriores al actual estado social, ilustradas con más de trescientos fotograbados* (Mexico City: Editorial Porrúa, 1986 [1904]), 220–21. For similar explanations, see Jean-Charles Sournia, *A History of Alcoholism,* trans. N. Hindley and G. Stanton (Oxford: Basil Blackwell, 1990), 102–7, but see 175.

26 James Greenberg, *Blood Ties: Life and Violence in Rural Mexico* (Tucson: University of Arizona Press, 1989), 153. For William Taylor, alcohol consumption took place within the context of communal beliefs and practices that determined the use of violence. William B. Taylor, *Drinking, Homicide, and Rebellion in Colonial Mexican Villages* (Stanford, CA: Stanford University

Press, 1989), 71–72. For an examination of the effect of intoxication on violent behavior, see Jeffrey Fagan, "Intoxication and Aggression," in Michael Tonry and James Q. Wilson, eds., *Drugs and Crime* (Chicago: University of Chicago Press, 1990), 241–320.

27 AJ, 434206, Battery, 1903; AJ, 1074687, Battery, 1915. Manuel Baleriano, by contrast, tried to prove that he was not drunk when he committed battery, reasoning that "he remembers everything perfectly." AJ, 1027222, Battery, 1920.

28 AJ, 18515, Battery, 1925.

29 AJ, 1027249, Battery, 1920.

30 AJ, 18489, Battery, 1922; Secretaría de Justicia, Comisión Revisora del Código Penal, *Trabajos de revisión del Código Penal: Proyecto de reformas y exposición de motivos,* 4 vols. (Mexico City: Tip. de la Oficina Impresora de Estampillas, 1912), 1: 15, 26, 33, 36, 176–77, 240–45; AGN, SJ, 713, 614.

31 The 1871 Penal Code established that offenders who did not cause a life-threatening wound would be sentenced to arrest between eight days and two months. In 1884, a reform reduced the minimum term to two days, CP 1871, 527.

32 For the penalties against rural bandits, see Paul J. Vanderwood, *Disorder and Progress: Bandits, Police and Mexican Development,* 2d. ed. (Wilmington, DE: Scholarly Resources, 1992), 89. For contemporary social constructions of "the violent crime problem," see Michael Levi, "Violent Crime," in Mike Maguire, Rod Morgan, and Robert Reiner, eds., *The Oxford Handbook of Criminology* (Oxford: Clarendon Press, 1994), 297–99.

33 *El Imparcial,* 1 May 1897, p. 2. For a wounded man who hides from the police for fear of the Juarez Hospital, see *El Imparcial,* 1 Apr. 1897, p. 2. For a case involving the arrest, without evidence of a fight, of two wounded persons, and the dismissal of charges after both suspects claimed that they were too drunk to know what they had done, see AJ, 19381, Battery, 1926; see also AJ, 781394, Battery, 1901. For a wounded man arrested, AJ, 430153, Battery, 1904. For a case of a death due to lack of medical attention at a police station, see *El Universal,* 6 June 1930, 2d. sec., p. 1. For a wounded suspect who denied that her wounds were caused in a fight, see AJ, 596562, Battery, 1908. For a victim whose deposition was taken minutes before her death, see *Nueva Era,* 9 Aug. 1911, p. 7. The Juárez Hospital also housed the morgue, Carlos Roumagnac, *Crimenes sexuales,* vol. 1 of *Crimenes sexuales y pasionales: Estudios de psicología morbosa* (Mexico City: Librería de Bouret, 1906), 136. Beggars and lepers were also detained at the hospital, ASSA, EA, Dormitorios Públicos, 1, 6; AGN, GPR, 41, 16, fol. 24. For a 1913 inspection denouncing poor conditions and overcrowding at the Juárez Hospital, see AGN, GPR, 38, 22,

n.d. For an example of judges' failure to press charges, see Ignacio Rosales to City Council, 14 Apr. 1919, AHA, Justicia, Cárcel Municipal, 2707, 1. For arrests performed in the middle of "a big scandal" see AJ, 518298, Fight and battery, 1907.

34 The judge could not contest the ruling. AJ, 18516, Homicide, 1926. For other controversial acquittals, see Demetrio Sodi, *El jurado en México: Estudios sobre el jurado popular* (Mexico City: Secretaría de Fomento, 1909), 41–44, 120–21; *El Universal,* 7 Aug. 1929, p. 3; AJ, 1051492, Homicide, 1921. During the colonial period in Buenos Aires, plebeian actors in civil and criminal cases also avoided the use of the word *honor.* Johnson, "Dangerous Words, Provocative Gestures, and Violent Acts," 148.

35 Not a literal translation. The expression used by Torres was "*le pelaban la verga.*" AJ, 19377, Battery, 1931; *El Universal,* 1 Feb. 1917, p. 9.

36 AJ, 1074681, Theft, 1915.

37 AJ, 705337, Fraud, 1911.

38 See Julian A. Pitt-Rivers, "Honor," in David L. Sills, ed., *International Encyclopedia of the Social Sciences* (New York: Macmillan, 1968), 6:503.

39 *Nueva Era,* 11 Aug. 1911, p. 2. At a dance, Gumersindo Herrera, Soberino Vega, and J. Féliz Martínez "started a quarrel which, by common agreement, they interrupted in the ball room to go outside." *El Universal,* 7 Feb. 1917, p. 6. See also AJ, 1027237, Battery, 1920; AJ, 1027234, Battery, 1920.

40 There were no witnesses to the event (or at least none willing to testify), and the García brothers could not be convicted despite a lengthy investigation. AJ, 1024574, Homicide, 1900. For a victim who refused to name her attacker see *El Universal,* 3 Feb. 1917, p. 8. For a similar case, involving mother and daughter, see AHA, Justicia Comisarías, 2717, 17. For a case in which both the victim and the accused changed their statements in order to have the case dismissed, see AJ, 781394, Battery, 1901.

41 AJ, 518298, Fight and battery, 1907. For a similar avoidance of police intervention see John Charles Chasteen, "Violence for Show: Knife Duelling on a Nineteenth-Century Cattle Frontier," in Lyman Johnson, ed., *The Problem of Order in Changing Societies* (Albuquerque: University of New Mexico Press, 1990), 56; Greenberg, *Blood Ties,* 196–97.

42 *El Universal,* 1 Oct. 1920, p. 6. A similar case, in AJ, 1067899, Battery, 1919.

43 AJ, 453715, Battery, 1904. For a case in which the accused verbally attacked the witness who called the police, see AJ, 1067905, Battery and attacks to authority, 1922.

44 AJ, 434206, Battery, 1903. See also *El Universal,* 26 Dec. 1916, p. 6; AJ, 19331, Battery, Homicide, 1924. On suicides, *El Imparcial,* 9 Jan. 1906, p. 3; ibid., 25 Sept. 1897, p. 3. On vocabulary, see AJ, 1027242, Battery, 1920.

45 Alonso Rodríguez Miramón, *Requisitoria pronunciada por el Agente del Ministerio Público . . . en la vista en jurado de la causa instruida contra Francisco Guerrero (a) Antonio el Chalequero y contra José Montoya, por robos, violaciones, heridas y homicidios perpetrados del año de 1881 a julio de 1888* (Mexico City: Antigua imprenta y librería de Murguía, 1891), 10, 32–33.

46 Carlos Roumagnac, *Matadores de mujeres,* vol. 2 of *Crímenes Sexuales y Pasionales* (Mexico City: Librería de Bouret, 1910), 81–96.

47 Carlos Roumagnac, *Los criminales en México: Ensayo de psicología criminal. Seguido de dos casos de hermafrodismo observado por los señores doctores Ricardo Egea . . . Ignacio Ocampo* (Mexico City: Tipografía El Fénix, 1912 [1904]), 112.

48 Ibid., 126, 376–82; Arnulfo Trejo, *Diccionario Etimológico Latinoamericano del Léxico de la Delincuencia* (Mexico City: UTEHA, 1968).

49 Shortly before her confrontation with Esperanza Gutiérrez, Villa asked a friend "how deep into the human body the blade of her knife needed to sink in order to cause death." *El Foro* 50:67 (14 Apr. 1898): 267.

50 Trejo, *Diccionario Etimológico,* 91; *El Imparcial,* 25 Sept. 1897, p. 3; Roumagnac, *Los criminales,* 272. See AJ, 430153, Battery, 1904; AJ, 19381, Battery, 1926. For a list of weapons confiscated by the police in 1919 see AHA, Gobernación, 1112, 123; ibid., 1112, 119; ibid., 1114, 190.

51 Roumagnac, *Los criminales,* 79–81. But compare with the stylized technique and prestige of knife fighting in the Rio de la Plata region. Richard W. Slatta, *Gauchos and the Vanishing Frontier* (Lincoln: University of Nebraska Press, 1983), 118; Thomas Holloway, *Policing Rio de Janeiro* (Stanford, CA: Stanford University Press, 1993), 40; Chasteen, "Violence for Show," 52; Jorge Luis Borges, *Evaristo Carriego* in *Obras Completas: 1923–1949* (Barcelona: Emecé Editores, 1989 [1930]), 128.

52 *El Imparcial,* 3 July 1908, p. 1.

53 Trejo, *Diccionario Etimológico,* 95; AJ, 1024574, Homicide, 1900. For examples of street fights, see *El Imparcial,* 1 Sept. 1906, p. 3. For the meaning of attacks to the face in France and the antebellum South, see Ruth Harris, "Melodrama, Hysteria and Feminine Crimes of Passion in the Fin-de-Siècle," *History Workshop* 25 (Spring 1988): 56; Greenberg, *Honor and Slavery,* 15. See also Pitt-Rivers, "Honour and Social Status," 25; among nineteenth-century German students, facial scars were a desirable sign of virility. Peter Gay, *The Cultivation of Hatred. The Bourgeois Experience, Victoria to Freud* (New York: Norton, 1993), chaps. 1 and 2.

54 Calderón's mother and wife named several suspects, but no one was convicted of the crime. AJ, 19337, Homicide, 1924. For a similar use of knives, see Boschi, "Homicide and Knife Fighting in Rome," 147. On scars as criminal

antecedents, see Demetrio Sodi, *El jurado en México: Estudios sobre el jurado popular* (Mexico City: Secretaría de Fomento, 1909), 149–50.

55 *El Universal,* 3 Feb. 1917, p. 8. In a meaningful reversal of this rule, José María Gatica cut his common-law wife Luisa Filio in her buttocks because she allowed a younger man to court her. *El Universal,* 2 Feb. 1917, p. 4.

56 Roumagnac, *Los criminales,* 167, 169.

57 *El Foro* 14:7 (10 Jan. 1895): 27.

58 *El Foro* 14:4 (5 Jan. 1895): 15–16.

59 *Código del duelo, traducido, arreglado y anotado por Joaquin Larralde y Anselmo Alfaro* (Mexico City: Ireneo Paz, 1886), 8; Juan María Rodríguez, *El duelo. Estudio filosófico Moral por. . . .* (Mexico City: Tipografía Mexicana, 1869), 26; Escudero, *El duelo en México,* 36, 37. On women's weakness, see Francisco Serralde, *El crimen de Santa Julia. Defensa gráfica que, sirviéndose de signos físicos encontrados en los cuerpos de las víctimas del crimen, presenta . . . defensor del coronel Timoteo Andrade* (Mexico City: F. P. Hoeck, 1899), 15.

60 In 12 of the 21 battery cases in the database in which a woman was accused, another woman was also accused or was the victim. In only 7 of these 21 cases was a man a victim. By contrast, of the 83 battery cases in which a man was accused, 27 had women as victims, but 53 had men as victims or co-accused. Ministerio Público del Distrito y Territorios Federales, *Cuadros estadísticos e informes,* 1900. The database presents a smaller participation of women: of 142 accused of battery and homicide in the examined cases, 24 (16 percent) were female.

61 AGN, SJ, 891, 3940; AJ, 1027247, Battery, 1920; AJ, 518295, Battery, 1906; AJ, 1027226, Battery, 1920. See also *El Universal,* 10 Dec. 1916, p. 4. Bites were also a feature of fights between women, ibid., 1 Feb. 1917, p. 9. For knives, see ibid., 13 Jan. 1917, p. 8. For similar cases, see ibid., 10 Dec. 1916, p. 4; ibid., 23 Dec. 1916, p. 6.

62 Roumagnac, *Los criminales,* 108–11; Robert Buffington and Pablo Piccato, "Tales of Two Women: The Narrative Construal of Porfirian Reality," *The Americas* 55:3 (Jan. 1999): 391–424.

63 *El Imparcial,* 12 Jan. 1906, p. 4.

64 Heliodoro was sentenced to a minimum of two years and eight months. Casimiro was also declared guilty, but he was released because he had already served his sentence. AJ, 596565, Battery, 1909.

65 AJ, 1027244, Battery, 1920. "El Raton" told his friend Mauro Becerril that he was going to stab him once for each cent he refused to pay at the *pulquería.* Only one stab was necessary to kill Becerril. *El Imparcial,* 10 Jan. 1900, p. 2.

66 AJ, 492115, Battery, 1905. See also AJ, 430153, Battery, 1904.

67 Between 1916 and 1920, of those sentenced for battery, 11.79 percent were merchants, second only to domestic workers, who were 14.44 percent. Procuraduría General de Justicia del Distrito y Territorios Federales, Sección de Estadística, *Estadística de la penalidad habida en los juzgados del fuero común del Distrito y territorios federales durante los años de 1916 a 1920* (Mexico City: Talleres Gráficos de la Nación, 1923).

68 Sordo survived and Pérez was sentenced to two years and four months of prison. AJ, 596551, Battery, 1909. For the use of guns, see AJ, 434207, Battery, 1903. For another case in which all involved were Spaniards, see AJ, 781371, Battery, 1913. For the importance of the audience for violence in Buenos Aires, see Lyman L. Johnson, "Dangerous Words, Provocative Gestures," 148–49.

69 AHA, BE, 1331, 41, fol. 1. For Hayner, "crimes against the person usually involve people from the same neighborhood—acquaintances, friends or relatives." Hayner, "Criminogenic Zones," 433.

70 *Excélsior,* 4 Oct. 1929, 2d. sec., p. 1.

71 Quote from AJ, 1027222, Battery, 1920. Lewis, *The Children of Sánchez,* 73. See also AJ, 434207, Battery, 1903.

72 AJ, 1024574, Homicide, 1900.

73 AJ, 18516, Homicide, 1926. See also AJ, 18515, Battery, 1925.

74 Gutmann has noted that the use of guns in male fights in contemporary Mexico City is socially condemned as dangerous and rural behavior. Matthew Gutmann, *The Meaning of Macho: Being a Man in Mexico City* (Los Angeles: University of California Press, 1996), 202–3n. For a similar disrupting effect of guns, see Greenberg, *Blood Ties,* 152.

75 In the 1930s and 1940s, according to Alfonso Quiroz Cuarón, 26 percent of all murders in the country were committed with guns. Quiroz Cuarón, *La Criminalidad en la República Mexicana* (Mexico City: UNAM, 1958), 41.

76 AHA, Gobernación, 1110, 43, and ibid., 1110, 44; *El Universal,* 5 Feb. 1917, p. 5; Francisco Ramírez Plancarte, *La ciudad de México durante la revolución constitucionalista* (Mexico City: Botas, 1941), 70. The prices of Colt and Smith and Wesson pistols in pawn shops decreased, while they became more common. Marie Eileen Francois, "When Pawnshops Talk: Popular Credit and Material Culture in Mexico City, 1775–1916" (Ph.D. diss., University of Arizona, 1998), 289, 328–29.

77 AHA, Gobernación, 1115, 391.

78 *El Universal,* 3 Oct. 1923, p. 1; *Excélsior,* 17 Dec. 1921, p. 4; José P. Saldaña, *Crónicas históricas* (Monterrey: N.p., 1982), 3:125; *Excélsior,* 13 Nov. 1924, p. 1; *El Universal,* 3 Oct. 1923, p. 1. See Pablo Piccato, "El parlamentarismo

desde la Cámara de Diputados, 1912–1921: Entre la opinión pública y los grupos de choque," in Pablo Piccato, ed., *El Poder Legislativo en las Décadas Revolucionarias* (Mexico City: Instituto Nacional de Estudios Históricos de la Revolución Mexicana, 1997).

79 See AGN, SJ, 894, 4578.

80 *El Universal,* 2 Oct. 1916, p. 1.

81 Alfonso Taracena, *La verdadera revolución mexicana* (Mexico City: Jus, 1960), 5:214.

82 For attacks by strangers, *El Universal,* 2 Jan. 1917, p. 6; ibid., 3 Jan. 1917, p. 5. Criminal courts to City Council, various dates, AHA, Gobernación, 1115, 371; *El Universal,* 1 Feb. 1917, p. 3; *Estadísticas históricas de México* (Mexico City: INEGI, 1994); AE 1938; AE 1940.

83 See above chap. 1, note 23.

84 Pitt-Rivers, "Honour and Social Status," 61, 65. Lewis, *The Children of Sánchez,* for example, focused on a vecindad at Tepito, although Lewis's informants stressed that "criminals" had left Tepito some time ago, ibid., 146.

85 For the inability of historians to grasp the importance of shame, see Reddy, *The Invisible Code,* 13–15. For shame in the contemporary world, see John Braithwaite, "Shame and Modernity," *The British Journal of Criminology* 33:1 (Winter 1993): 2. Kristin Ruggiero has noted the increasing value of family honor in late-nineteenth-century Buenos Aires. Kristin Ruggiero, "Honor, Maternity, and the Disciplining of Women: Infanticide in Late Nineteenth-Century Buenos Aires," *Hispanic American Historical Review* 72:3 (1992): 361, quote from 357.

86 "There is one thing / that nobody will regret / in this world: / to have been brave." Jorge Luis Borges, *Obra poética* (Madrid: Alianza, 1972), 282.

5 VIOLENCE AGAINST WOMEN

1 Gaceta de Policía 1:2, 19 Oct. 1905, pp. 7–10; ibid., 1:19, 4 Mar. 1906, pp. 6–7. For other press perspectives on this crime see Elisa Speckman, "Crimen y castigo: Legislación penal, interpretaciones de la criminalidad y administración de justicia: Ciudad de México 1872–1910" (Ph.D. diss., El Colegio de México, Mexico City, 1999), part 2, chap. 5.

2 By "family" I will refer not only to the nuclear family but also to the extended families that integrated relatives of three generations, structured by kinship but also by the proximity of relatives and friends. They afforded moral and economic support to their members. See Larissa Adler Lomnitz and Marisol Pérez Lizaur, *Una familia de la élite mexicana. Parentesco, clase y cultura 1820–1980* (Mexico City: Alianza, 1993). For the need to look at male violence

on women in the same historical context as male-against-male violence, see Pamela Haag, "The 'Ill-Use of a Wife:' Patterns of Working-Class Violence in Domestic and Public New York City, 1860–1880," *Journal of Social History* 25:3 (Summer 1992): 449.

3 *Excélsior,* 10 Oct. 1929, 2d sec., 1. See also *El Imparcial,* 23 Jan. 1906, p. 1; ibid., 16 Aug. 1912, p. 1. For the construction of crimes of passion as an interaction between "weak" female offenders and judicial and penitentiary institutions, see Ruth Harris, "Melodrama, Hysteria and Feminine Crimes of Passion in the Fin-de-Siècle," *History Workshop* 25 (Spring 1988): 31–63.

4 *El Imparcial,* 10 Sept. 1913, p. 1; see also *El Universal,* 17 Oct. 1916, p. 1.

5 Junta General del Ramo de Pulques, *Dictámen que presenta la comisión nombrada por la . . . al señor Gobernador del Distrito* (Mexico City: Tipografía Artística, 1896), 12–13; see also *Gaceta de Policía* 1:14, 28 Jan. 1906, p. 2.

6 Cesare Lombroso, *Crime its Causes and Remedies,* trans. by Henry P. Horton (Boston: Little, Brown and Company, 1918), 256; Cesare Lombroso, *Delitti di libidine,* 2d ed. (Torino: Fratelli Bocca, 1886), 20.

7 Carlos Roumagnac, *Crimenes sexuales,* vol. 1 of *Crimenes sexuales y pasionales: Estudios de psicología morbosa* (Mexico City: Librería de Bouret, 1906), 85n. Carlos Roumagnac, *Matadores de mujeres,* vol. 2 of *Crimenes sexuales y pasionales* (Mexico City: Librería de Bouret, 1910), 221, 258. I have tried to avoid Roumagnac's interpretations about the internal motivations of the criminals he interviewed, focusing instead on the detailed anecdotal information he provides. For a critical view of Roumagnac's studies, see Robert Buffington, *Criminal and Citizen in Modern Mexico* (Lincoln: University of Nebraska, 1999), chaps. 2 and 3.

8 *El Heraldo: Diario Católico,* 1 Jan. 1890, p. 3; "Sobre el número y clase de presos que debe alojar la Penitenciaría de México, Proyecto de Penitenciaría del Distrito Federal, Junta formada por el gob. Ramón Fernández" [1882], *Boletín del Archivo General de La Nación: La Penitenciaría de México* 5:4 (Oct. 1981–Mar. 1982): 34; Miguel Macedo, *La criminalidad en México: Medios de combatirla* (Mexico City: Secretaría de Fomento, 1897), 11; *Gaceta de Policía* 2:52 (18 Nov. 1906): 8.

9 *El Imparcial,* 13 Sept. 1897, p. 1. A criticism of abusive women in *Gaceta de Policía* 1:34 (1 July 1906): 11. For a satiric poem, see *Don Cucufate* 1:7 (10 Sept. 1906): 4; see also *La Voz de México,* 16 Oct. 1897, p. 3.

10 Roumagnac, *Matadores de mujeres,* 81; *El Demócrata,* 20 Oct. 1914, p. 1. See also *El Imparcial,* 4 May 1914, p. 5; *El Heraldo: Diario Católico,* 19 Jan. 1890, p. 3; *El Imparcial,* 8 May 1914, p. 1.

11 *Gaceta de Policía* 1:19 (4 Mar. 1906): 6–7; Roumagnac, *Matadores de mujeres,* 97.

12 CP 1871, 821; Macedo, *La criminalidad en México,* 14–15; AGN, SJ, 892, 3963; *La Voz de México,* 12 Jan. 1906, p. 1.

13 CP 1871, 63. See also Speckman, "Crimen y castigo," part 3.

14 CP 1871, 821. For a similar pattern in France and Argentina, see Harris, "Melodrama, Hysteria and Feminine Crimes of Passion," 35; Kristin Ruggiero, "Wives on 'Deposit': Internment and the Preservation of Husband's Honor in Late Nineteenth-Century Buenos Aires," *Journal of Family History* 17:3 (1992): 253–70; William M. Reddy, *The Invisible Code: Honor and Sentiment in Postrevolutionary France, 1814–1848* (Berkeley: University of California Press, 1997), 70.

15 Luis Lara y Pardo, *La prostitución en México* (Mexico City: Bouret, 1908), 75–76.

16 AJ, 1074702, Homicide, 1915.

17 Carlos Roumagnac, *Los criminales en México: Ensayo de psicología criminal. Seguido de dos casos de hermafrodismo observado por los señores doctores Ricardo Egea . . . Ignacio Ocampo* (Mexico City: Tipografía El Fénix, 1912 [1904]), 146.

18 M. Guadalupe G. also killed her pimp because she found him with another prostitute. Roumagnac, *Los criminales,* 152, 162. See the case of Prisciliana Cortéz, who slit her lover's throat because she found him with another woman, *El Universal,* 17 Feb. 1917, p. 8.

19 Roumagnac, *Matadores de mujeres,* 97–107.

20 For female sacrifice and male irresponsibility as part of conjugal relations structured by the extended family in a contemporary Mexico City barrio, see Larissa Adler de Lomnitz, *Cómo sobreviven los marginados* (Mexico City: Siglo Veintiuno, 1975), 100–101, 103. For a study of networks of support focused on the household, and thus stressing locality and poverty as factors of violence, see Mercedes González de la Rocha, *The Resources of Poverty: Women and Survival in a Mexican City* (Cambridge, UK: Blackwell, 1994).

21 *Excélsior,* 11 Oct. 1929, p. 5; Roumagnac, *Los criminales,* 282; Julio Guerrero, *La génesis del crimen en México: estudio de psiquiatría social* (Paris: Viuda de Bouret, 1901), 111, 157–58. For similar concerns among Catholics, see Manuel Ceballos, *El Catolicismo social: Un tercero en discordia. Rerum Novarum, la "cuestión social" y la movilización de los católicos mexicanos (1891–1911)* (Mexico City: El Colegio de México, 1991), 149–50. In 1895, in Mexico City 43 percent of the population aged sixteen years or older was married; for the country as a whole, the percentage was 48. *Estadísticas históricas de México* (Mexico City: INEGI, 1994); Dirección General de Estadística, *Censo general de la República Mexicana verificado el 20 de octubre de 1895* (Mexico City: Secretaría de Fomento, 1897–1899). For the late colonial period, see Steve

Stern, *The Secret History of Gender: Women, Men, and Power in Late Colonial Mexico* (Chapel Hill: University of North Carolina Press, 1995), 253–69.

22 AJ, 1074688, Theft, 1915.

23 See for example, AHA, Justicia Negocios Diversos, 2730, 370–15. Between 1871 and 1885 there were seven convictions for bigamy. Dirección General de Estadística, *Estadística del ramo criminal en la República Mexicana que comprende un periodo de quince años, de 1871 a 1885* (Mexico City: Secretaría de Fomento, 1890). I found no other mention of the offense in statistics.

24 AJ, 1027222, Battery, 1920. See also AJ, 434207, Battery, 1903.

25 AJ, 1067902, Battery and Theft, 1921. For the conflicts between wives and mothers-in-law in these circumstances, see Ann Varley, "Women and the Home in Mexican Family Law," in Elizabeth Dore and Maxine Molyneux, eds., *Hidden Histories of Gender and the State in Latin America* (Durham, NC: Duke University Press, 2000), 238–61.

26 AJ, 1024574, Homicide, 1900; *El Heraldo: Diario Católico,* 1 Jan. 1890, p. 3. Lomnitz observes that the frequency of common-law marriages in her sample of contemporary Mexico City's urban poor (18 percent) does not imply the instability of relationships. Couples could marry after several years of consensual cohabitation. Lomnitz, *Cómo sobreviven los marginados,* 104–5.

27 AJ, 596562, Battery, 1908. Alberta Rodríguez was sentenced to thirteen months of prison, and Matilde Sánchez to nineteenth months. See also AJ 1027221, Battery, 1920. For the Tarasquillo Street murder, see Robert Buffington and Pablo Piccato, "Tales of Two Women: The Narrative Construal of Porfirian Reality," *The Americas* 55:3 (Jan. 1999): 391–424.

28 Roumagnac, *Matadores de mujeres,* 81–96.

29 Roumagnac, *Los criminales,* 253–58.

30 Roumagnac, *Matadores de mujeres,* 61, 76.

31 *El Universal,* 9 Dec. 1916, p. 8.

32 Viscaya was not accused of battery, but received a sentence of nine months of prison for resisting arrest. AJ, 1067905, Battery and attacks to authority, 1922. See also AJ, 1027239, Battery, 1920.

33 AGN, SJ, 892, 3961. On concierges, see AJ, 434207, Battery, 1903.

34 Roumagnac, *Matadores de mujeres,* 97–107.

35 "Poor Arnulfo Villegas / His time has arrived / On Wednesday morning / He was sent to the other life // Carlota Mauri, gentlemen, / Was the reason, it is clear: / She was so pretentious / That Arnulfo had to kill her // If only she'd told him / A lie, that she was indeed / Ready to marry him / The tragedy would not have been / Villegas, with unbridled craze / Two shots gave her / And when she was dead / Still caressed her, ferocious and insane. // The verdict of justice / Was 'Capital Punishment' / Which he received in

Belem / Unable to do otherwise // His wife, doña L. B. / As well as his little daughter / Both cry profusely / For the incredible misfortune. // See how expensive / The love of women can be / For those who are married / Already, and go about those things // Men, take stock / Of this very sad ending / And contain your insanity / To avoid such an early death // Don't be so terribly jealous / Don't love with such fury / Because that was the cause / Of inevitable melancholy // Don't give yourselves so much / To any woman / Because they are, always / The cause of your ruin." "Reflexiones después del fusilamiento," in Roumagnac, *Matadores de mujeres.*

36 See Alonso Rodríguez Miramón, *Requisitoria pronunciada por el Agente del Ministerio Público . . . en la vista en jurado de la causa instruida contra Francisco Guerrero (a) Antonio el Chalequero y contra José Montoya, por robos, violaciones, heridas y homicidios perpetrados del año de 1881 a julio de 1888* (Mexico City: Antigua imprenta y librería de Murguía, 1891), 7–9; Roumagnac, *Crimenes sexuales,* 1:91–92. For further discussion on the criminological implications of this case, see Pablo Piccato, "El Chalequero, or 'the Mexican Jack the Ripper': The Meanings of Sexual Violence in Turn-of-the-Century Mexico City," *Hispanic American Historical Review* (forthcoming).

37 *El siglo diez y nueve,* 16 Dec. 1890, p. 2; see also *La Voz de México,* 20 July 1888, p. 3; Roumagnac, *Crimenes sexuales,* 93; idem, *Matadores de mujeres,* 224; Judith Walkowitz, *City of Dreadful Delight: Narratives of Sexual Danger in Late-Victorian London* (Chicago: University of Chicago Press, 1992), 2, 4, 196, 210.

38 On medical reports on Guerrero's sanity in his first murder trial, see *El Siglo Diez y Nueve,* 17 Dec. 1890, p. 2. See CP 1871, 42; Roumagnac, *Matadores de mujeres,* 182–93, 221–26, 233–36. On criminal taxonomies, see Enrico Ferri, *La Sociologie Criminelle,* 3d. ed. (Paris: Arthur Rousseau, 1893 [1881]), 80–98, 120–28.

39 Rodríguez Miramón, *Requisitoria,* 10–11. For rape as a crime against property and persons, see Anna Clark, *Women's Silence, Men's Violence: Sexual Assault in England 1770–1845* (London: Pandora, 1987), 39.

40 Roumagnac, *Matadores de mujeres,* 201, 207, 216; ibid., *Crimenes sexuales,* 91–99; Rodríguez Miramón, *Requisitoria,* 10–40; Guillermo Colín Sánchez, *Así habla la delincuencia y otros más . . . ,* 2d. ed. (Mexico City: Porrúa, 1991); Itzel Delgado, "Prostitución, sífilis y moralidad sexual en la ciudad de México a fines del siglo XIX" (B.A. thesis, Escuela Nacional de Antropología e Historia, 1993), 153–54, 65, 72, 60. The jury also found him guilty of rape, battery, and theft. Roumagnac, *Crimenes sexuales,* 97; Rodríguez Miramón, *Requisitoria,* 14. In 1909, Guerrero still denied all the murders he was blamed for except that of Gallardo. Roumagnac, *Matadores de mujeres,* 206.

41 AJ, 55375, Abduction, 1908.

42 Roumagnac, *Crimenes sexuales,* 1:28.

43 AJ, 1051597, Statutory rape, 1921.

44 AJ, 19351, Rape and theft, 1925; AJ, 553759, Abduction, 1908; AJ, 781387, Battery and rape, 1913.

45 AJ, 1067903, Statutory rape, 1921; AJ, 781387, Battery and rape, 1913; AJ, 781394, Battery, 1901.

46 AJ, 518259, Corruption of minors, 1906.

47 *El Imparcial,* 1 Apr. 1897, p. 2.

48 On rape, CP 1871, 795, 797. The 1929 Code maintained the same penalties but instead of establishing fourteen years as the divide, it used the category of "pubescent," CP 1929, 862. In the 1931 Code, the punishment was up to six years if the victim was pubescent and up to twelve years if the victim was below the age of puberty, CP 1931, 265. On statutory rape, CP 1871, 793, 794. The 1929 Penal Code reduced the penalties to three years if the victim was "below the age of puberty" and one year if she was "pubescent." Intercourse without violence was not punished if the woman was older than eighteen. CP 1929, 858. The 1931 Penal Code punished statutory rape with three years. CP 1931, 262, 263. On abduction, CP 1871, 808, 809, 812, 799, 800, 801, 813. The 1929 and 1931 codes maintained these provisions. The 1929 Code established a maximum sentence of five years for abduction (ten if the offender did not inform about the location of the victim), and the 1931 Code a maximum of six years. CP 1929, 869, 870, 871, 873; CP 1931, 267, 268, 269, 270.

49 AJ, 1067903, Statutory rape, 1921. See also AJ, 19329, Statutory rape, 1924, in which the lack of physical evidence and the failure of the victim to ask for help were the judge's arguments to change the case from rape to statutory rape, and later to dismiss the case for lack of evidence.

50 AJ, 1051597, Statutory rape, 1921. See also AJ, 518279, Statutory rape, 1906. The victim, fourteen-year-old Catarina Hernández, was knocked to the ground and forcefully penetrated by the suspect, but he promised to marry her and she delayed in accusing him.

51 AJ, 1067903, Statutory rape, 1921.

52 See, for example, AJ, 596568, Statutory rape, 1908.

53 AJ, 781387, Battery, rape, 1913.

54 AJ, 19393, Abduction, 1927.

55 *Excélsior,* 17 Oct. 1929, 2d. sec., p. 1.

56 CP 1871, 62.

57 AJ, 553759, Abduction, 1908.

58 AJ, 781387, Battery, rape, 1913.

59 See AJ, 596555, Abduction and statutory rape, 1909. The accused had been

arrested before for the same reason and also released after negotiating with the victim's brother.

60 AJ, 596569, Abduction and statutory rape, 1909. See also AJ, 1074707, Abduction, 1915.

61 AJ, 18514, Abduction, 1925.

62 AJ, 596569, Abduction and statutory rape, 1909. See also AJ, 596553, Abduction, 1909. The victim, María de la Luz García, worked in a factory and declared that she willingly had intercourse with the accused, forcing her mother to drop the charges.

63 AJ, 518259, Corruption of minors, 1906.

64 AJ, 596568, Statutory rape, 1908. That was not the end of the negotiation. Raquel changed her testimony in front of the judge and accused the suspect, Gabriel Uriarte, of statutory rape. He replied that she was changing her story "because her family advised her to do so, probably to get money from him." The accusation was finally withdrawn. For other cases of parents' accusation against boyfriends, contrary to daughters' will, see AJ, 596552, Abduction and statutory rape, 1909; AJ, 596564, Breaking and entering, 1909; AJ, 19393, Abduction, 1927; AJ, 518283, Abduction and statutory rape, 1906.

65 AJ, 596559, Kidnapping, 1909.

66 AJ, 553759, Abduction, 1908.

67 AJ, 430168, Abduction, 1904.

68 Silvia Marina Arrom, *The Women of Mexico City, 1790–1857* (Stanford, CA: Stanford University Press, 1985), 237, 249. See Varley, "Women and the Home," and Mary Kay Vaughan, "Modernizing Patriarchy: State Policies, Rural Households, and Women in Mexico, 1930–1940," in the same volume, 194–214. (See tables 12 and 13 in the appendix.)

69 *Excélsior,* 11 Oct. 1929, p. 5.

70 *El Universal,* 3 June 1930, p. 3. On female participation in the civil war, Gabriela Cano, "*Soldaderas* and *Coronelas,*" in Michael S. Werner, ed., *Encyclopedia of Mexico: History, Society and Culture* (Chicago: Fitzroy Dearborn Publishers, 1997), 2:1357–60.

71 See descriptions of jury trials in *El Universal,* 4 Oct. 1923, 2d. sec., p. 1; *La Voz de México,* 12 Jan. 1906, p. 1. See the cases defended by Querido Moheno in the 1920s: Querido Moheno, *Procesos Célebres. Nidia Camargo. Discurso en defensa de la acusada* (Mexico City: Botas, 1925); idem, *Mis últimos discursos* (Mexico City: Botas, 1923). Similar arguments were used in France, see Harris, "Melodrama, Hysteria and Feminine Crimes of Passion," 31.

72 *Excélsior,* 11 Oct. 1929, p. 5, echoing Julio Guerrero's discussion of "la señora decente" (analyzed in chapter 3); Guerrero, *La génesis,* 167, 158–82.

73 Studies that examine the meanings of female and sexual honor in Latin

America also point to the complex relationship between this aspect of honor and dominant views on women's access to reputation and autonomy. See Sueann Caulfield, *In Defense of Honor: Sexual Morality, Modernity, and Nation in Early-Twentieth-Century Brazil* (Durham, NC: Duke University Press, 2000); Stern, *The Secret History;* Kristin Ruggiero, "Wives on 'Deposit,'" 260; Susan Midgen Socolow, "Women and Crime: Buenos Aires, 1757–97," in Lyman L. Johnson, ed., *The Problem of Order in Changing Societies: Essays on Crime and Policing in Argentina and Uruguay, 1750–1940* (Albuquerque: University of New Mexico Press, 1990).

6 MONEY, CRIME, AND SOCIAL REACTIONS TO LARCENY

1 Ethel B. Tweedie, *Mexico as I Saw It* (London: Hurst and Blackett, 1901), 223–24. Prolific travel writer and feminist, Tweedie (1860–1940) also wrote *The Maker of Modern Mexico: Porfirio Díaz* (London and New York: John Lane, 1906).

2 Miguel Macedo, *La criminalidad en México: Medios de combatirla* (Mexico City: Secretaría de Fomento, 1897), 12. For examples of petty theft, see *El Imparcial,* 2 Jan. 1900, p. 3; AGN, SJ, 892, 4173. See also Ilán Semo, "La ciudad tentacular: notas sobre el centralismo en el siglo XX," in Isabel Tovar de Arechederra and Magdalena Mas, eds., *Macrópolis mexicana* (Mexico City: Universidad Iberoamericana-Consejo Nacional para la Cultura y las Artes-DDF, 1994), 49.

3 But see Michael Charles Scardaville, "Crime and the Urban Poor: Mexico City in the Late Colonial Period" (Ph.D. diss., University of Florida, 1977); Gabriel J. Haslip, *Crime and Punishment in Late Colonial Mexico City, 1692–1810* (Albuquerque: University of New Mexico Press, 1999); for the case of urban Brazil, see Boris Fausto, *Crime e cotidiano: A criminalidade em São Paulo, Brazil: 1880–1924* (São Paulo, Brazil: Brasiliense, 1984). On the political character of banditry, relating it to cultural and institutional conditions, besides mere resistance, see Paul J. Vanderwood, *Disorder and Progress: Bandits, Police and Mexican Development,* 2d. ed. (Wilmington, DE: Scholarly Resources, 1992); Alan Knight, *The Mexican Revolution* (Lincoln: University of Nebraska Press, 1990), 2:392–406; Gilbert M. Joseph, "On the Trail of Latin American Bandits: A Reexamination of Peasant Resistance," in Jaime E. Rodríguez, ed., *Patterns of Contention in Mexican History* (Irvine: University of California Press, 1992), 293–336. For the formulation of bandits as "pre-political" rebels, see Eric Hobsbawm, *Primitive Rebels: Studies in Archaic Forms of Social Movement in the 19th and 20th Centuries* (New York:

Norton, 1959), 6. For approaches to theft see John D. Rogers, "Theories of Crime and Development: An Historical Perspective," *The Journal of Development Studies* 25:3 (Apr. 1989): 314–28; James C. Scott, "Everyday Forms of Peasant Resistance," in James C. Scott and Benedict J. Tria Kerkvliet, eds., *Everyday Forms of Peasant Resistance in South-East Asia* (London: Frank Cass, 1986), 5–6; idem, *Weapons of the Weak: Everyday Forms of Peasant Resistance* (New Haven, CT: Yale University Press, 1985), 267.

4 Rodney D. Anderson, *Outcasts in Their Own Land: Mexican Industrial Workers, 1906–1911* (DeKalb: Northern Illinois University Press, 1976), 27.

5 Stephen Haber, *Industria y subdesarrollo: La industrialización de México, 1890–1940* (Mexico City: Alianza Editorial, 1992), 43–45. The national population in 1895 was 12,634,427.

6 Carlos Illades, *Hacia la república del trabajo: La organización artesanal en la ciudad de México, 1853–1876* (Mexico City: El Colegio de México–Universidad Autónoma Metropolitana, 1996), 42.

7 The amount of circulating currency in Mexico in 1880–81 was 25 million pesos; in 1910–11 it reached 310 million. In the Federal District, sales amounted to 124.31 pesos per inhabitant, while in the country as a whole they were 23.57 pesos. Fernando Rosenzweig, "El desarrollo económico de México de 1877 a 1911," *Secuencia* 12 (Sept.–Dec. 1988): 160, 167. The First Monetary Census, compiled in 1903, established that in the Federal District there were 34 pesos in coins of gold, silver, and copper per inhabitant; for the country as a whole, the amount was 5. Even when considering only the cash held by private individuals, the amount of money per capita in Mexico City was greater than that in the country as a whole: 9 cents in the capital and 6 cents in the country. AE 1902, 246–47. I owe this reference to Edward Beatty.

8 François-Xavier Guerra, *México: Del Antiguo Régimen a la Revolución* (Mexico City: Fondo de Cultura Económica, 1988), 2:233–35; John H. Coatsworth, "Producción de alimentos durante el Porfiriato," in *Los orígenes del atraso: Nueve ensayos de historia económica de México en los siglos XVIII y XIX* (Mexico City: Alianza Editorial, 1990), 177; see also Anderson, *Outcasts in Their Own Land,* 68. Despite a recovery by the very end of the Porfiriato, real wages decreased between 1898 and 1911. Rosenzweig, "El desarrollo económico," 184. Wholesale prices in Mexico City between 1886 and 1935 show a steady increase during the Porfiriato, in contrast to a downward tendency after the Revolution. *Estadísticas históricas de México* (Mexico City: INEGI, 1994). According to William Schell, the conversion from silver to the gold standard in 1905 created a "severe currency shortage," causing "a greater hardship on the poor and working classes than did infla-

tion." William Schell, Jr., "Money as a Commodity: Mexico's Conversion to the Gold Standard, 1905," *Mexican Studies/Estudios Mexicanos* 12:1 (Winter 1996): 80, 83.

9 The general trend during the years 1913–20 was one of decreasing production, devaluation, and lowering of living standards. Alan Knight, "The Working Class and the Mexican Revolution: c. 1900–1920," *Journal of Latin American Studies* 16 (1984): 72. See also Knight, *The Mexican Revolution,* 2:409; José A. Bátiz, *Historia del papel moneda en México* (Mexico City: Banamex, 1984), 87; Nacional Financiera, *50 años de Revolución Mexicana en cifras* (Mexico City: Cultura, 1963), 115.

10 In 1929, the Monte de Piedad granted more than 600,000 loans (as compared with its previous yearly average of less than 500,000), and reached 1.5 million in 1933. Moisés González Navarro, *La pobreza en México,* 228–29, 157. *Memoria del ayuntamiento de 1901,* 2:39–41. For a study of pawning in Mexico City, see Marie Eileen Francois, "When Pawnshops Talk: Popular Credit and Material Culture in Mexico City, 1775–1916" (Ph.D. diss., University of Arizona, 1998), 234, 69, and chap. 5. On the reception of stolen goods at pawn shops, see José Daniel Nations to Minister of the Interior, 4 Dec. 1912, AGN, GPR, 66, 14. For the small-scale economy of the urban poor, see Brian Roberts, *Cities of Peasants: The Political Economy of Urbanization in the Third World* (London: Sage, 1978), 109–10, 128, 141–44.

11 For descriptions of theft and poverty in the late colonial period, see José Joaquín Fernández de Lizardi, *El Periquillo Sarniento* (Madrid: Editora Nacional, 1976). Writers on the historical trends of theft in Europe disagree on the way in which economic factors impacted crime rates. Although the correlation between economic indicators (such as food prices) and theft rates might be a useful explanatory device, studies have not arrived at a consensus regarding the multiple historical and cultural factors (dietary uses, availability of money) that mediate that correlation. Specific types of theft might increase or decrease according to their economic viability—i.e., according to the ease of pawning and the likelihood of being caught. See Howard Zehr, *Crime and the Development of Modern Society: Patterns of Criminality in Nineteenth Century Germany and France* (London: Croom Helm, 1976), 80–81, 46, 52–55. Although Eric A. Johnson rejects Zehr's broad linking of modernization and crime rates, he agrees that "the relationships between economic conditions and property offenses are far stronger than those between economic conditions and other types of offenses." Eric A. Johnson, *Urbanization and Crime: Germany 1871–1914* (New York: Cambridge University Press, 1995), 140; see also idem, "The Crime Rate: Longitudinal and Periodic Trends in Nineteenth- and Twentieth-

Century German Criminality, from Vormärz to Late Weimar," in Richard J. Evans, ed., *The German Underworld: Deviants and Outcasts in German History* (New York: Routledge, 1988), 181.

12 See table 2 for arrest totals. Between 1916 and 1920, theft produced an average of 22.67 percent of those sentenced each year in the Federal District. Procuraduría General de Justicia del Distrito y Territorios Federales, Sección de Estadística, *Estadística de la Penalidad habida en los juzgados del fuero común del Distrito y territorios federales durante los años de 1916 a 1920* (Mexico City: Talleres Gráficos de la Nación, 1923).

13 Alfonso Quiroz Cuarón et al., *Tendencia y ritmo de la criminalidad en México* (Mexico City: Instituto de Investigaciones Estadísticas, 1939); James W. Wilkie, *The Mexican Revolution: Federal Expenditure and Social Change Since 1910* (Berkeley-Los Angeles: University of California Press, 1967), 38; for an increase of theft in the years before the Revolution based on police data, see Laurence John Rohlfes, "Police and Penal Correction in Mexico City, 1876–1911: A Study of Order and Progress in Porfirian Mexico" (Ph.D. diss., Tulane University, 1983), 168, 245.

14 For perceptions of an increase before the Revolution, see *La Voz de México,* 18 Jan. 1890, p. 2; *Gaceta de Policía* 1:2, 19 Oct. 1905, p. 3; Carlos Roumagnac, *Los criminales en México: Ensayo de psicología criminal. Seguido de dos casos de hermafrodismo observado por los señores doctores Ricardo Egea . . . Ignacio Ocampo* (Mexico City: Tipografía El Fénix, 1912 [1904]), 373; *El Hijo del Ahuizote,* 17 Jan. 1897, p. 39; *El Imparcial,* 4 Jan. 1897, p. 2; *La Voz de México,* 29 Jan. 1890, p. 2. Miguel Macedo, *La criminalidad en México: Medios de combatirla* (Mexico City: Secretaría de Fomento, 1897), 23, 4. For perceptions of increase during the revolutionary decade, see Venustiano Carranza, address to Congress, *Diario de los Debates de la Cámara de Diputados,* 27th Congress, 1:9 (15 Apr. 1917), 13; *El Demócrata,* 12 Oct. 1914, p. 1; Francisco Ramírez Plancarte, *La ciudad de México durante la revolución constitucionalista* (Mexico City: Botas, 1941), chaps. 12 to 20. After 1920, see Manuel I. Fierro, "Algunas consideraciones sobre esta publicación," in *Estadística de la penalidad,* 3; Casimiro Cueto, "Consideraciones generales y apuntes para la crítica, estadística de la criminalidad habida en el Distrito Federal durante el año de 1922," *Boletín de la Sociedad Mexicana de Geografía y Estadística* 5:12 (1928): 38. The space devoted by the daily press to police news decreased noticeably during the early 1920s, but the tendency changed again toward the end of the decade.

15 See table 10; Rohlfes, "Police and Penal Correction," 153–56. See chapter 7 for a discussion of these campaigns. In 1895, for example, 38,577 persons were arrested in Mexico City for different crimes, but only 16,795 were for-

mally charged in court, the rest being dealt with by the government of the Federal District. AE 1896. In 1930, 90,564 persons were "conducted to the police" in the Federal District but only 11,208 were formally charged of any offense. Quiroz Cuarón, *Tendencia y ritmo;* AE 1938.

16 Julio Guerrero, *La génesis del crimen en México: estudio de psiquiatría social* (Paris: Viuda de Bouret, 1901), 137. Similar words used in *El Universal,* 5 July 1930, 2d. sec., p. 1.

17 "Sobre el número y clase de presos que debe alojar la Penitenciaría de México," *Boletín del Archivo General de La Nación: La Penitenciaría de México* 5:4 (1981–82): 33, 36.

18 AGN, FIM, 70. Several letters in this folder echo Hernández's arguments.

19 See AJ, 705331, Theft, 1911.

20 AGN, SJ, 894, 4578. See also the case of Juan Tavera. He was arrested by his supervisor when he was pawning some stolen tools from a construction site in 1913. AGN, SJ, 894, 4610.

21 Cruz and Díaz were formally accused, but there is no conclusion in the file. Rosario N. was not arrested. AJ, 1074688, Theft, 1915. Pino González sold for 700 pesos stolen cars that had cost him 400. AJ, 23196, Criminal association and robbery, 1930. Nicolasa Martínez pawned a 25-peso diamond ring for 2 pesos, according to the receipt found in her house by the police. The owner of the ring declared its value was 150 pesos. AJ, 434208, Theft, 1903.

22 AJ, 1067904, Theft, 1920.

23 For a precise chronology, see Jorge H. Jiménez Muñoz, *La traza del poder: Historia de la política y los negocios urbanos en el Distrito Federal desde sus orígenes a la desaparición del Ayuntamiento (1824–1928)* (Mexico City: Codex, 1993), 129. For a discussion of the 1915 crisis, see Ariel Rodríguez Kuri, "Desabasto, hambre y respuesta política, 1915," in Carlos Illades and Ariel Rodríguez Kuri, eds., *Instituciones y ciudad: Ocho estudios históricos sobre la ciudad de México* (Mexico City: FP-Sones-Uníos, 2000).

24 Ramírez Plancarte, *La ciudad,* 348.

25 "Carta abierta al Licenciado D. Francisco Carvajal" [Aug. 1914], n.p, leaflet, MPP. Another similar leaflet warned that the defense of the city could cause robberies and looting by the city's poorer classes. Waldo D. Orozco and G. Lecuona, "Comité Paz," 3 Aug. 1914, n.p, leaflet, MPP. In mid-1912, basic provisions such as beans, meat, sugar, and charcoal were already scarce and expensive, *La Nación,* 16 July 1912, pp. 1, 3; Ramírez Plancarte, *La ciudad,* 225. For rumors of a Zapatista "invasion" in 1912, see *La Nación,* 2 Sept. 1912, pp. 1–2. Trade routes and water facilities south of the capital were important sources of supplies for the Zapatistas. John Womack Jr., *Zapata and the Mexican Revolution* (New York: Vintage, 1970), 248, 266–67.

26 *El Universal,* 26 Nov. 1916, p. 3; Ramírez Plancarte, *La ciudad,* 223; *La Convención,* 20 Feb. 1915, p. 4.

27 *El Demócrata,* 24 Sept. 1914, p. 1.

28 AJ, 1074705, Theft, 1915.

29 Bátiz, *Historia del papel moneda,* 59.

30 Ramírez Plancarte, *La ciudad,* 238, 70; Government of the Federal District to City Council, 4 Dec. 1914, AHA, PG, 3645, 1734. See also *La Convención,* 20 Feb. 1915, p. 4. On a gendarme enlisted to avoid Huerta's *leva,* see Lamberto García to Minister of Justice, 17 Oct. 14, AGN, SJ, 893, 4392.

31 Ramírez Plancarte, *La ciudad,* 550. For a civilian killed by a soldier without reason, AJ, 1074679, Homicide, 1915. On confiscations by revolutionary armies, see Martín Luis Guzmán, *El Aguila y la Serpiente,* in *Obras Completas* (Mexico City: Fondo de Cultura Económica, 1984), 1:379. On a shooting rampage after a bar brawl, see *La Convención,* 7 May 1915, p. 1. On excessive force used to arrest civilians, AJ, 1074685, Homicide, 1915.

32 AGN, SJ, 891, 3686. For a gendarme wounded by a woman during a food riot in 1915 and for reports of gendarmes deserting, see AHA, PG, 3645, 1761, AHA, PPP, 3664, 3. For soldiers released on orders of officers, see AJ, 1027242, Battery, 1920. The order could come from Carranza himself, Secretary of the First Chief to Ministry of the Interior, 28 Aug. 1916. AGN, GPR, 71, 68, fol. 1. On a mob releasing prisoners from a police station, Juez Cuarto. Auxiliar to Jefe Sección de Justicia, Secretaría de Justicia, 26 Nov. 1914, AHA, Justicia juzgados correccionales, 2759, 4. For examples of military and revolutionaries attacking gendarmes, see Francisco J. Sánchez to President Porfirio Díaz, Tacubaya, 15 Feb. 1911, APD, 36, 2834–5; AJ, 1074696, Battery, 1915; Cesar López de Lara, governor of the Federal District, to Venustiano Carranza, 19 Sept. 1916, Archivo Venustiano Carranza, Condumex, Mexico City, 95, 10790; for similar cases in 1917 and 1918, see AHA, PPP, 3664, 2; Comandancia de la gendarmería de a pie to Presidente Municipal, 22 Mar. 1918; AHA, PG, 3646, 1786; *El Universal,* 12 Jan. 1918, p. 1. For Carrancista forces taking police weapons, see AHA, PG, 3645, 1734.

33 This description is based on Irineo Paz's newspaper *La Patria,* politically favorable to the demonstration but critical of its "reprehensible" sides. *La Patria,* 25 May 1911, p. 3; ibid., 26 May 1911, p. 3. See John Robert Lear, "Workers, *Vecinos,* and Citizens: The Revolution in Mexico City, 1909–1917" (Ph.D. diss., University of California at Berkeley, 1993), chap. 8. For a demonstration in demand of food and the authorities' reaction, see *La Convención,* 20 Feb. 1915, p. 4.

34 AHA, PG, 3645, 1761.

35 See Samuel Brunk, "'The Sad Situation of Civilians and Soldiers': The Ban-

ditry of Zapatismo in the Mexican Revolution," *American Historical Review* 101:2 (Apr. 1996).

36 AJ, 1024566, Theft, 1915.

37 Gabriela Cano, "*Soldaderas* and *Coronelas*," in Michael S. Werner, ed., *Encyclopedia of Mexico: History, Society and Culture* (Chicago: Fitzroy Dearborn Publishers, 1997), 2:1357–60.

38 AJ, 1074681, Theft, 1915. The trial was full of irregularities—as were most conducted that year. Only one of the eighteen cases examined for 1915 concluded with a sentence. For another judge who refused to apply a long sentence against a thief, see AGN, SJ, 894, 4610. For peaceful actions, see *La Convención,* 25 June 1915, pp. 1, 4; Ramírez Plancarte, *La ciudad,* 254, 314–15.

39 Alfonso Taracena, *La verdadera revolución mexicana* (Mexico City: Jus, 1960), 4:34.

40 *La Convención,* 25 June 1915, pp. 1, 4; Taracena, *La verdadera,* 4:214–16, 225–26, 43; John Mason Hart, *Anarchism and the Mexican Working Class, 1860–1931* (Austin: University of Texas Press, 1978), chap. 9, pp. 130, 150–55. For complaints, in December 1916, by Compañía de Luz workers and other public employees about receiving part of their pay in coins and the rest in bonds, see *El Universal,* 3 Dec. 1916, p. 1; ibid., 7 Dec. 1916, p. 1.

41 Taracena, *La verdadera,* 4:47, 107–8.

42 The measure did not stop the depreciation of the peso, Taracena, *La verdadera,* 4:149, 166–67, 191–92; for a description of monetary chaos, see Knight, *The Mexican Revolution,* 2:407–10. In January 1916, Zapata accused the Carrancista government of being a "money forger" that stole from the poor with its systematic devaluation of the currency. Taracena, *La verdadera,* 5:40; *Discusión de la credencial del diputado don Luis Cabrera y documentos justificativos* (Mexico City: Imp. Cámara de Diputados, 1917); Fernando Alejandro Vázquez Pando and Arturo Sotomayor Jiménez, "El derecho monetario en México de 1864 a febrero de 1917," in Beatriz Bernal, ed., *Memoria del IV Congreso de Historia del Derecho en México (1986)* (Mexico City: UNAM, 1988), 1063.

43 AGN, SJ, 891, 3906. According to William Schell, counterfeiting became more important after the monetary reform of 1905 as "an urban form of social banditry, of resistance to a program of state hegemony by both counterfeiters and 'victims' " who accepted obviously fake coins in order to maintain business. Schell, "Money as a Commodity," 84. It is difficult to see, however, how counterfeiters (whose activities, which certainly had victims, were successful only if hidden from public view), could manage to appropriate and express any political position or become popular. For coinage shortage and use of tokens in the late eighteenth century, see Richard L. Garner, *Eco-*

nomic Growth and Change in Bourbon Mexico (Gainesville: University Press of Florida, 1993), 243–44.

44 AJ, 1074715, Insults to authority, 1915. The 1897 regulation of police established that gendarmes had to see that merchants accepted the currency used by customers. "Reglamento de las obligaciones del gendarme" [1897], Art. 57 in Manuel González de Cosío, *Memoria que presenta al Congreso de la Unión el General . . . Secretario de Estado y del Despacho de Gobernación* (Mexico City: Imprenta del Gobierno Federal, 1900), 765. See on the Reservada investigations, AGN, SJ, 891, 3939.

45 *La Nación,* 20 July 1912, p. 2; CP 1871, 683, 670, 675. The 1929 Penal Code reduced the penalties for forging coins (one to five years plus fine), returned to the original rule of six coins in the possession of the suspect, and reduced the penalty for falsifying paper money to eight years plus fine. CP 1929, 655, 659, 668. The 1931 Penal Code maintained these guidelines, setting the penalty for coin forgery from six months to five years, and eight years for forging paper money. CP 1931, 234, 238.

46 Taracena, *La verdadera,* 4:53, 77; for other executions, *El Demócrata,* 17 Aug. 1915, p. 4.

47 *El Imparcial,* 18 Jan. 1900, p. 2. See also *La Nación,* 20 July 1912, p. 2.

48 *El Universal,* 3 Oct. 1916, p. 1; AGN, SJ, 891, 3939.

49 A workshop discovered in 1914 used a coffee pot, a hammer, a file, and a toothbrush. AGN, SJ, 891, 3939.

50 *Gaceta de Policía* 1:29, 27 May 1906, p. 2.

51 *El Imparcial,* 4 July 1908, 8; *El Diablito Bromista,* 9:6, 18 Aug. 1907, p. 1; for the use of *cartones* see Bátiz, *Historia del papel moneda,* 87; Carlos Roumagnac, *Elementos de policía científica: Obra de texto para la Escuela Científica de Policía de México* (Mexico City: Botas, 1923).

52 AGN, SJ, 892, 4171. Iglesias was sentenced to two years. AGN, SJ, 868, 8469. A similar defense was used by Gerónimo Acosta and José Monzón in Morelia, Mich., in 1919, AGN, SJ, 891, 3906; AGN, SJ, 892, 3977; *El Imparcial,* 13 Jan. 1900, p. 3.

53 AJ, 1074681, Theft, 1915. See Ramírez Plancarte, *La ciudad,* 348. For an official accusation against Spanish intermediaries, see AHA, Gobierno del Distrito, Rastros, 1786, 67. On new attitudes about theft, see *El Demócrata,* 22 Nov. 1915, p. 2; *La Convención,* 25 June 1915, pp. 1, 4; Mariano Azuela, *Los caciques,* in Antonio Castro Leal, ed., *La novela de la Revolución Mexicana* (Mexico City: Aguilar–Secretaría de Educación Pública, 1988 [1917]), 1:132 and part 1, chap. 9; ibid., *Los de abajo* [1916], Castro Leal, ed., *La novela de la Revolución Mexicana,* 1:84 and part 2, chap. 14.

54 *El Demócrata,* 12 Oct. 1914, p. 1. Ramírez Plancarte, *La ciudad,* chap. 12

to 20. In August 1914, Constitutionalist troops executed two "well-known thieves," as an example of the strict official attitude toward criminals. Taracena, *La verdadera,* 2:343. In June, 1915, two thieves captured by Zapatista forces in the capital were publicly executed by instructions of commander Amador Salazar. *La Convención,* 2 June 1915, pp. 1–2. See also Emiliano Zapata, "Circular," Brioso y Candiani Collection, Benson Latin American Collection, University of Texas at Austin, leaflet.

55 In 19 of the 52 cases of theft where address information is available, one or more of the accused lived no more than a few blocks away from the victim. Twenty-six of 97 theft suspects lived in the zone where the theft took place. In several others, victims and offenders were otherwise related.

56 AJ, 281, 596570, Theft, 1909.

57 AJ, 1074686, Theft, 1915; AJ, 1067904, Theft, 1920.

58 In 1900, 17.30 percent of those accused of theft were younger than eighteen, compared to 12.30 percent of those accused of battery. *Cuadros estadísticos e informe del Procurador de Justicia,* 1900 (Mexico City: La Europea, 1903).

59 See Norman S. Hayner, "Criminogenic zones in Mexico City," *American Sociological Review* 11:4 (Aug. 1946): 436; Elena Azaola Garrido, *La institución correccional en México: Una mirada extraviada* (Mexico City: Siglo Veintiuno, 1990), 64–65. For the formulation of laws and institutions addressed at juvenile offenders, see ibid., 45–58. Although young offenders could be sent to correctional schools during the Porfiriato, many were also incarcerated in Belem and other jails; ad hoc correctional courts and regulations were established by the late 1920s. The limits of the new institutions are described in Luis Buñuel's 1950 film *Los olvidados.*

60 *El Universal,* 3 Feb. 1917, p. 8.

61 AJ, 1027226, Battery, 1920. Concierges were usually women: 1,431 as opposed to 994 men. Dirección General de Estadística, *Censo General de la República Mexicana verificado el 20 de octubre de 1895* (Mexico City: Secretaría de Fomento, 1898). Seven of the eight *porteros* of the database were witnesses to different crimes.

62 AJ, 19353, Theft, 1925. There is no sentence in this case. See also AJ, 1074683, Theft, 1915. Hernández's case in AJ, 1074694, Theft, 1915.

63 Despite some weaknesses in his account, Torres was released because he claimed to having bought the sarape at the Tepito market. AJ, 19360, Theft, 1925. See also AJ, 781370, Theft, 1913.

64 AJ, 705334, Theft, 1912. See AJ, 19325, Battery, 1923. Judges focused on the violent offense that prompted arrests: only three cases in the database were labeled "Battery and theft."

65 AJ, 18517, Theft, 1926. Ramos was found guilty. Pérez's case in AJ, 1074693, Theft, 1915. The file does not include a sentence.

66 For the police mediating a dispute, see AJ, 19367, Fraud, 1925. The costs of taking legal actions, even if Mexican laws did not charge expenses to the offended party, effectively discouraged people from going to the police. The same consideration seems to have resulted in fewer prosecutions in early modern Europe, and the use of extrajudicial settlements. In England, the tendency had decreased markedly by the nineteenth century, due to the professionalization of the police and magistracy, V. A. C. Gatrell, "The Decline of Theft and Violence in Victorian and Edwardian England," in *Crime and the Law: The Social History of Crime in Western Europe since 1500,* ed. V. A. C. Gatrell, Bruce Lenman, and Geoffrey Parker (London: Europa Publications, 1980), 244; Bruce Lenman and Geoffrey Parker, "The State, the Community and the Criminal Law in Early Modern Europe," in *Crime and the Law,* 19, 22.

67 This became clearer after the Revolution. Articles 17, 21, and 103 of the 1917 Constitution established that prosecution could be pursued only by the judiciary. This theoretically prevented victims from actively intervening in judicial proceedings. Instituto de Investigaciones Jurídicas, *Diccionario jurídico mexicano* (Mexico City: Porrúa-UNAM, 1987), 1:39.

68 The 1929 Code established a sentence from one to three years for theft occurring in these circumstances, but not in addition to the sanction established based on the value of the stolen object. The 1931 code established that sentences based on the value of the stolen good would be increased up to three years when these circumstances occurred. PC 1929, 1131; PC 1931, 381. In eighteenth-century tobacco factories, workers saw the use of small quantities of tobacco and paper as a "nonmonetary perquisite." Susan Deans-Smith, "The Working Poor and the Eighteenth-Century Colonial State: Gender, Public Order, and Work Discipline," in William H. Beezley, Cheryl English Martin, and William E. French, eds., *Rituals of Rule, Rituals of Resistance* (Wilmington, DE: Scholarly Resources, 1994): 57–58. See also Illades, *Hacia la República del Trabajo,* 66. For the interaction of coercion and "imperfect" market forces in the colonial workplace, see Richard J. Salvucci, *Textiles and Capitalism in Mexico: An Economic History of the Obrajes, 1539–1840* (Princeton, NJ: Princeton University Press, 1987), 114–15. On criminalization of customary taking, see Peter Linebaugh, *The London Hanged: Crime and Civil Society in the Eighteenth Century* (Cambridge, UK: Cambridge University Press, 1992).

69 The charges were later dismissed. AJ, 19343, Theft, 1924. Fifteen of the ac-

cused in the database were domestic workers, nine of them for theft. As witnesses, they were thirteen, eight of them in cases of theft. On the mix of work and private life, Morgan, "Proletarians, Politicos, and Patriarchs," 151; William E. French, *A Peaceful and Working People: Manners, Morals and Class Formation in Northern Mexico* (Albuquerque: University of New Mexico Press, 1996).

70 Guerrero, *La génesis del crimen,* 168.

71 Six days after the arrest, Mariana and her mother were discharged for lack of evidence. Ten days later, however, Vázquez was still asking the judge for her daughter to be released from the general jail, where she had been sent instead of the correctional school. AJ, 1074713, Theft, 1915.

72 *Colección de leyes y disposiciones gubernativas municipales y de policía vigentes en el Distrito Federal formada por acuerdo del C. gobernador Lic. Carlos Rivas* (Mexico City: Imprenta y Litografía de Ireneo Paz, 1884), 2:249–51; Rohlfes, "Police and Penal Correction," 79.

73 Luis Lara y Pardo, *La prostitución en México* (Mexico City: Bouret, 1908), 111–12; *El Universal,* 5 Jan. 1917, p. 5; *El Universal,* 22 Jan. 1918, p. 3.

74 Guerrero, *La génesis del crimen,* 170–71. Three of the ten domestic workers who appear as victims in the database suffered sexual abuse. For some employers' concern about the sexual life of their domestic employees, see AJ, 596551, Battery, 1909, discussed in chapter 4.

75 AJ, 596563, Theft, 1908. Five days after being fired from her previous job, Teodora Rodríguez asked for a job at Luis S. Viramontes' house. The first day of work she fled with money and jewels, but she was captured. Although she denied ever having worked at Viramontes' house, she was sentenced to two years and one month of prison. AJ, 705334, Theft, 1912. On hiring practices, AJ, 434208, Theft, 1903; Guerrero, *La génesis del crimen,* 170; *El Universal,* 13 Jan. 1917, p. 7.

76 AJ, 19375, Theft, 1925. See the same situation in AJ, 781309, Theft, 1914. The accused took a six-peso pin to pay for six months of work owed to her and was sentenced to two years and fifteen days of prison.

77 AJ, 1856, Theft, 1929. There is no sentence in the file. See also AJ, 430146, Theft, 1904.

78 *Diario del Hogar,* 17 Sept. 1906, p. 1.

79 Guerrero, *La génesis del crimen,* 167. See also *El Universal,* 5 Jan. 1917.

80 AHA, Justicia Juzgados Correccionales, 2759, 1.

81 Anderson, *Outcasts in Their Own Land,* 46, 106–7, 70–73; Illades, *Hacia la República del Trabajo,* 54. For the paternalistic practices among employers before the Revolution, see Alan Knight, "The Working Class and the Mexi-

can Revolution, c. 1900–1920," *Journal of Latin American Studies* 16 (1984): 51–79, cit. p. 59.

82 AHA, Gobierno del Distrito, Rastros, 1785, 10; ibid., 17. For reports of illegal commerce, see ibid., 1785; for the stealing of blood, ibid., 1786, 63; for the use of falsified seals, ibid., 1785, 10; for a complaint against Spanish intermediaries, ibid., 1786, 67.

83 The owner of the hardware booth confirmed that the belt Mireles was selling was not the one that had been stolen, and the suspect was released. AJ, 1074683, Theft, 1915.

84 AJ, 430147, Theft, 1904.

85 For the mobility of workers see Haber, *Industria y Subdesarrollo,* 52; Guerra, *México,* 1:338, 356.

86 E. P. Thompson, "The Moral Economy of the English Crowd in the Eighteenth Century," *Past and Present* 50 (1971): 78.

87 Ricardo Salvatore and Carlos Aguirre, "The Birth of the Penitentiary in Latin America: Towards an Interpretive Social History of Prisons," in Salvatore and Aguirre, eds., *The Birth of the Penitentiary in Latin America* (Austin: Texas University Press, 1996). For the use of prisons to establish industrial disciplines, see Dario Melossi and Massimo Pavarini, *Cárcel y fábrica: Los orígenes del sistema penitenciario (siglos XVI–XIX)* (Mexico City: Siglo Veintiuno, 1980). For a more specific analysis of money and labor relations among railway and mining workers during the Porfirian period, see Jonathan C. Brown, "Foreign and Native-Born Workers in Porfirian Mexico," *American Historical Review* 98:3 (June 1993): 786–818, particularly 795.

88 Labor historiography in Latin America has not explored workers' reluctance to be unfairly labeled as criminals. In this regard, Mexico City bosses diverged from the developmentalist ideals of employers in Hidalgo del Parral, who hoped to turn "a new, and feared, floating population of rural and urban workers into patriotic citizens and peaceful, hardworking, and suitably motivated workers." French, *Peaceful and Working People,* 63.

7 THE INVENTION OF *RATEROS*

1 Antonio A. de Medina y Ormaechea, *Las colonias de rateros* (Mexico City: Imprenta del Gobierno en el Ex-Arzobispado, 1895), 30–31.

2 *El Imparcial,* 1 July 1897, p. 1; Miguel Macedo, *La criminalidad en México: Medios de combatirla* (Mexico City: Secretaría de Fomento, 1897), 35–36.

3 The 1737 Spanish *Diccionario de autoridades* defined *ratero* as "the thief who

steals things of little value, or from the pouch." The origin of the word, according to the same *Diccionario* is found in the *germanía* ("thieves' slang") where *rata* means *faltriquera* (pocket). The contemporary *Diccionario de la lengua española* defines *ratero* as an adjective for the thief who "steals with skill and caution things of small value." Although *ratero* does not seem to come from *rata* or *ratón,* the association was commonly made in Mexican language. In its classic definition, the word *ratero* connotes lowliness: the *Diccionario de autoridades* defines *ratero* as "the thing that crawls on the ground," as *rastrero,* and adds the metaphorical meaning of "lowly in his thoughts and deeds, or vile and despicable thing." Real Academia Española, *Diccionario de autoridades* (Madrid: Gredos, 1963 [1737]); Real Academia Española, *Diccionario de la lengua española,* 21st ed. (Madrid: Real Academia Española, 1992).

4 AJ, 18493, Theft, 1922; AJ, 1074705, Theft, 1915.

5 *Nueva Era,* 21 Aug. 1911, p. 3; *La Voz de México,* 29 Jan. 1890, p. 2; Trinidad Sánchez Santos, *El alcoholismo en la República Mexicana: Discurso pronunciado en la sesión solemne que celebraron las Sociedades Científicas y Literarias de la Nación, el día 5 de junio de 1896 y en el salón de sesiones de la Cámara de Diputados* (Mexico City: Imprenta del Sagrado Corazón de Jesus, 1897), 28.

6 Julio Guerrero, *La génesis del crimen en México: estudio de psiquiatría social* (Paris: Viuda de Bouret, 1901), 137.

7 Medina y Ormaechea, *Las colonias,* 30–31.

8 *El Universal,* 13 Oct. 1916, p. 4.

9 Two days later, the newspaper announced that the chief of police had followed its advice. *El Universal,* 21 Dec. 1916, p. 1; ibid., 23 Dec. 1916, p. 1.

10 Junta General del Ramo de Pulques, *Dictámen que presenta la comisión nombrada por la . . . al señor Gobernador del Distrito* (Mexico City: Tipografía Artística, 1896), 14–15; *El Imparcial,* 1 Apr. 1897, p. 2.

11 *El Imparcial,* 10 Jan. 1897, p.1.

12 *México y sus alrededores. Guía para los viajeros escrita por un mexicano. Cuidado con los rateros* (Mexico City: Tip. Luis B. Casa, 1895), 15.

13 AJ, 19368, Theft, 1925; see also AJ, 23196, Criminal association and robbery, 1930.

14 Santamaría's *Diccionario de mejicanismos* defines *rateril* ("related to the ratero") and *raterismo* ("habit of being a ratero; art of the ratero"). Francisco J. Santamaría, *Diccionario de mejicanismos* (Mexico City: Porrúa, 1974). This usage also appears in other Latin American countries. Francisco J. Santamaría, *Diccionario General de Americanismos* (Mexico City: Pedro Robredo, 1942), 3:16. In Argentina *raterear* means "steal things of little value with skill and subtlety." Diego Abad de Santillán, *Diccionario de Argenti-*

nismos de Ayer y Hoy (Buenos Aires: Tipográfica Editora Argentina, 1976), 804. The Real Academia dictionary includes "ratero," "ratería," and "ratear." *Diccionario de la lengua española.* The word entered the standard Spanish of lawyers. "Ratería" is defined as a small theft carried out with caution. Rafael de Pina and Rafael de Pina Vara, *Diccionario de derecho,* 12th ed. (Mexico City: Porrúa, 1983), 413.

15 *El Hijo del Ahuizote,* 17 Jan. 1897, p. 39.

16 *El Universal,* 10 Oct. 1923, p. 6.

17 AGN, GPR, 117, 2.

18 The police arrested more than forty suspects, and twenty-four remained in jail after the first investigations. *Excélsior,* 11 Oct. 1929, 2d sec., p. 1.

19 CP 1871, 368. The offense was consummated "the moment the thief has in his hands the stolen thing; even when it is taken away from him before he takes it elsewhere or abandons it." CP 1871, 370.

20 A 1900 internal memorandum acknowledged that, in spite of the recent reforms to the penitentiary system, "theft has not decreased as expected." The solution, added the memorandum, was to force judges to adhere strictly to guidelines regarding punishment of recidivism. AGN, SJ, 372, 364. According to positivist criminology, the dangerousness of a criminal justified his or her removal from society, even if he or she had not committed a crime. Enrico Ferri, *La Sociologie Criminelle,* 3d ed. (Paris: Arthur Rousseau, 1893 [1881]), chap. 2. On penalties, see CP 1871, 376, 388, 400, 404.

21 Manuel González de Cosío, *Memoria que presenta al Congreso de la Unión el General . . . Secretario de Estado y del Despacho de Gobernación* (Mexico City: Imprenta del Gobierno Federal, 1900), 85, 891; "Sobre el número y clase de presos que debe alojar la Penitenciaría de México," *Boletín del Archivo General de La Nación: La Penitenciaría de México* 5:4 (1981–82): 36.

22 Medina y Ormaechea, *Las colonias,* 30–31; Antonio Ramos Pedrueza, *La ley penal en México de 1810 a 1910* (Mexico City: Díaz de León, 1911), 17. The same wording was used in the Reglamento General de Establecimientos Penales del Distrito Federal, decreed in September 14, 1900, Article 8. González de Cosío, *Memoria,* 843.

23 AGN, SJ, 372, 364. For the 1903 reform, CP, 1871, 376.

24 See Teresa Lozano Armendares, *La criminalidad en la ciudad de México: 1800–1821* (Mexico City: Universidad Nacional Autónoma de México, 1987), 98–99; Colin MacLachlan, *La justicia criminal del Siglo XVIII en México: Un estudio sobre el Tribunal de la Acordada* (Mexico City: SepSetentas, 1976), 131. For a personal example of transportation, and its negligible effects, see "Causa formada de oficio de la Real Justicia á Don Santiago Balvas por vago y mal entretenido," Puebla, 1817. Edmundo O'Gorman Collection, Benson

Latin American Collection, University of Texas at Austin. For service in the army, see Christon I. Archer, "To Serve the King: Military Recruitment in Late Colonial Mexico," *Hispanic American Historical Review* 55:2 (1975): 239; idem, *El ejército en el México borbónico, 1760–1810* (Mexico City: Fondo de Cultura Económica, 1983), 288; José Angel Ceniceros at the Primer Congreso Criminológico y Penitenciario, *El Universal,* 18 Oct. 1923, p. 1. During the Porfiriato, convicted thieves were transferred to the Ministry of War's authority, which turned them over to the military commanders. Government of the Federal District to Ministry of Justice, 11 June 1904, AGN, SJ, 468, 406. After 1911, enlistment offered prisoners a good prospect for a sentence abbreviated by desertion. For enlistment of inmates, see Vicente Fuentes to President Victoriano Huerta, Cárcel General, 14 Mar. 1914, AGN, SJ, 894, 4554.

25 John Kenneth Turner, *Barbarous Mexico* (Chicago: Charles H. Kerr, 1910), 107, 75; Jacinto Barrera Bassols, *El caso Villavicencio: Violencia y poder en el porfiriato* (Mexico City: Alfaguara, 1997), chaps. 12–15. On plantations and forced labor, see Armando Bartra, *El México bárbaro: Plantaciones y monterías del sureste durante el porfiriato* (Mexico City: El Atajo Ediciones, 1996). See also Laurence John Rohlfes, "Police and Penal Correction in Mexico City, 1876–1911: A Study of Order and Progress in Porfirian Mexico" (Ph.D. diss., Tulane University, 1983), 155.

26 Ramos Pedrueza, *La Ley Penal,* 12, 17.

27 Proposal by Alberto Lombardo in Secretaría de Justicia, Comisión Revisora del Código Penal, *Trabajos de revisión del Código Penal: Proyecto de reformas y exposición de motivos* (Mexico City: Tip. de la Oficina Impresora de Estampillas, 1912), 1:48, 4:414–15, 428; *El Imparcial,* 31 July 1908, p. 1.

28 Medina y Ormaechea, *Las colonias,* 1. In Peru, by contrast, penitentiary authorities could defend the use of flogging by arguing that it was already used in the army and the household. Carlos Aguirre, "The Lima Penitentiary and the Modernization of Criminal Justice in Nineteenth-Century Peru," in Ricardo Salvatore and Carlos Aguirre, eds., *The Birth of the Penitentiary in Latin America* (Austin: Texas University Press, 1996), 65. For a synthesis of the discussions and projects of transportation, see Rohlfes, "Police and Penal Correction," chap. 6. For the British case in the late eighteenth century, see John Hirst, "The Australian Experience: The Convict Colony," in Norval Morris and David J. Rothman, eds., *The Oxford History of the Prison: The Practice of Punishment in Western Society* (New York: Oxford University Press, 1995), 264.

29 These proposals were not divorced from the author's interests. In 1881, Antonio and Carlos de Medina y Ormaechea had proposed the establish-

ment of a penitentiary system based on the building of penitentiaries underwritten by their Compañía Constructora de Penitenciarías en la República Mexicana. Antonio A. de Medina y Ormaechea and Carlos A. de Medina y Ormaechea, *Proyecto para el establecimiento del régimen penitenciario en la República Mexicana* (Mexico City: Imprenta del Gobierno, en Palacio, 1881), 23.

30 Guerrero, *La génesis del crimen,* 155; *Gaceta de Policía* 1:26 (6 May 1906): 9.

31 *Trabajos de revisión,* 4:428. See *El Universal,* 27 June 1930, p. 1; *El Universal,* 30 June 1930, p. 3.

32 *El Imparcial,* 12 Oct. 1897, p. 2.

33 *Gaceta de Policía* 1:19 (4 Mar. 1906): 2; see also *La Nación,* 28 July 1912, p. 6.

34 *El Demócrata,* 25 Sept. 1914, p. 1.

35 AJ, 781373, Theft, 1914.

36 AHA, PPP, 3664, 3.

37 *Nueva Era,* 15 Aug. 1911, pp. 1–2.

38 Francisco Ramírez Plancarte, *La ciudad de México durante la revolución constitucionalista* (Mexico City: Botas, 1941), 553.

39 *El Universal,* 21 Dec. 1916, p. 1.

40 *Diario de los Debates de la Cámara de Diputados,* 27th Congress, 1:9 (15 Apr. 1917), 13; *El Universal,* 21 Dec. 1916, p. 1.

41 AHA, PPP, 3664 and 3665; *El Universal,* 25 Jan. 1918, p. 1. AHA, PPP, 3664, 1. The penalty against vagrants was up to eleven months of arrest and a fine of up to five hundred pesos. CP 1871, 855. Alberto Jiménez to President of City Council, 30 Nov. 1917, AHA, Vagos y rateros, 4140, 14; AHA, Vagos y rateros, 4157, 1. On nineteenth-century practices, see Salvador Rueda Smithers, *El diablo de Semana Santa: El discurso político y el orden social en la ciudad de México en 1850* (Mexico City: INAH, 1991), 72.

42 *El Universal,* 14 Dec. 1916, p. 3. For a suspect sent to the islands in 1919 without a trial, see Paulina Paredes to Minister of the Interior, 27 July 1921, AGN, GPR, 117, 6.

43 AHA, Vagos y rateros, 4157–60.

44 *El Universal,* 14 Oct. 1920, p. 9.

45 See Beneficencia Pública del Distrito Federal, *La mendicidad en México* (Mexico City: Departamento de Acción Educativa, Eficiencia y Catastros Sociales, 1931); AHA, Sección Asistencial, Serie Asilados y Mendigos; José Angel Ceniceros, *El nuevo código penal de 1931, en relación con los de 1871 y 1929* (Mexico City: Botas, 1931), 32–33.

46 *El Universal,* 1 Oct. 1920, p. 1; ibid., 14 Oct. 1920, p. 3, 9; ibid., 12 Oct. 1920, p. 12; ibid., 13 Oct. 1920, p. 1.

47 *El Universal,* 27 Oct. 1920, p. 1; AGN, POC, 122-D2-P-7; clipping from *El*

Universal, 10 Jan. 1922, AGN, POC, 307-P-12; ibid., 407-P-15; ibid., 122-D2-P-7.

48 *El Universal,* 1–22 May 1925, AGN, POC, 121-G-I-4. In August 1929, a group of 133 "rateros and degenerates" was sent to the Islas Marías penal colony. *El Universal,* 3 Aug. 1929, 2d sec., p. 1. For the transportation of political prisoners in 1931, see ASSA, SP, Sección Salubridad del Distrito Federal, 29, 7; José Revueltas, *Los muros de agua* (Mexico City: Ediciones Era, 1978). For the success of appeals against banishment, see *El Universal,* 28 June 1930, p. 1. On Cárdenas, Hector Madrid Muliá, "La política contra la delincuencia en el periodo del general Lázaro Cárdenas (1934–1940)," *Revista mexicana de justicia* 3:9 (July–Sept. 1991): 99.

49 Ramos Pedrueza, *La ley penal,* 17.

50 *Excélsior,* 10 Oct. 1929, 2d sec., p. 1. On appeals, *El Foro* 49:80 (23 Oct. 1897): 3; *El Imparcial,* 10 Dec. 1897, p. 2; *El Universal,* 27 June 1930, p. 1. The trip itself was very hard, and life in the islands particularly difficult. A first-hand experience in Revueltas, *Los muros de agua.*

51 *Ratero* was not part of the lingo of Mexican criminals. According to Roumagnac, the words for thief and ratero were "rupante" and "riño" respectively. Carlos Roumagnac, *Los criminales en México: Ensayo de psicología criminal. Seguido de dos casos de hermafrodismo observado por los señores doctores Ricardo Egea . . . Ignacio Ocampo* (Mexico City: Tipografía El Fénix, 1912 [1904]), 126. According to Trejo, "rata" and "ratón" are preferred to *ratero* in the slang of Mexican delinquency, among other words like "cacle," "caco," "carrancista" or "carranclán," "rupa" or "rupante," and "talón." Arnulfo Trejo, *Diccionario Etimológico Latinoamericano del Léxico de la Delincuencia* (Mexico City: UTEHA, 1968), 18. A 1987 dictionary of crime did not include the word *ratero,* but listed "rata," "ratón," and "ratoncito" with the meaning of thief or ratero. Guillermo Colín Sánchez, *Así habla la delincuencia y otros más . . .* (Mexico City: Porrúa, 1991), 172. As in Victorian England, these "professional criminals" were a minority, but they had a large impact on public perceptions of crime and the police's social function. Clive Emsley, *Crime and Society in England, 1750–1900,* 2d ed. (London: Longman, 1996), 175. In modern England and the United States, professional criminals are defined as felons engaged in organized activities. Dick Hobbs notes the shared culture of market and workplace activities, entrepreneurship, geographical concentration in cities, and taste for conspicuous consumption. Dick Hobbs, "Professional and Organized Crime in Britain," in Mike Maguire, Rod Morgan, and Robert Reiner, eds., *The Oxford Handbook of Criminology* (New York: Clarendon Press, 1994), 441–68, esp. 447–49. As in Mexico, violence is also a trait of professional criminals. According to Hobbs, "To

establish and maintain a niche in the contemporary marketplace, violence is a key resource." Ibid., 460. See also Neal Shover, *Great Pretenders: Pursuits and Careers of Persistent Thieves* (Boulder: Westview Press, 1996).

52 *El Demócrata,* 20 Dec. 1915, p. 6; ibid., 13 Dec. 1915, p. 1. For studies on the gang, see Constancio Bernaldo de Quiros, *El bandolerismo en España y en México* (Mexico City: Editorial Jurídica Mexicana, 1959), 391; Juan Mérigo, *La banda del automóvil gris y yo!* (Mexico City: N.p., 1959); *La Convención,* 20 Jan. 1915, p. 4.

53 *El Demócrata,* 20 Dec. 1915, p. 2, 6.

54 *El Imparcial,* 7 Sept. 1897, p. 3.

55 Ibid., 7 May 1914, p. 1.

56 Alvaro Matute, "Salud, familia y moral social (1917–1920)," *Históricas* 31 (1991): 34. According to *El Demócrata,* the way in which the Gray Automobile Gang operated resembled the famous "Apaches" of Paris. *El Demócrata,* 13 Dec. 1915, p. 1; ibid., 20 Dec. 1915, p. 1.

57 *El Universal,* 9 May 1925, p. 3. For the suspected emergence of a "maffia" of foreigners in the colonia de La Bolsa, *El Universal,* 9 Oct. 1920, p. 9; foreigners blamed for high crime in *El Universal,* 9 May 1925, p. 3. For accusations about stealing and deceiving of Mexican women by foreigners, "Patriota Anónimo" to Minister of the Interior, 1931, AGN, DGG, 2.014(29)10, c. 2, exp. 27. "Foreign anarchists" were arrested in 1897, *La Voz de México,* 3 Aug. 1897. Foreigners were linked to illegal gambling, *El Imparcial,* 1 July 1912, p. 1–2. In 1905, 70 of 258 registered prostitutes were foreign. Luis Lara y Pardo, *La prostitución en México* (Mexico City: Bouret, 1908), 49–50. In Mexico City, however, foreigners only made for a very small fraction of the population. They were only 8 of the 282 suspects in the database and 18 among the 197 victims.

58 *La Nación,* 30 July 1912, p. 6.

59 Martín Luis Guzmán, *El Aguila y la Serpiente,* in *Obras Completas* (Mexico City: Fondo de Cultura Económica, 1984), 1:482–83.

60 *El Universal,* 13 May 1925, 2d sec., p. 1; see also *La Nación,* 30 July 1912, p. 6; AJ, 23196, Criminal association and robbery, 1930; *Excélsior,* 1 Oct. 1929, p. 1.

61 Alfonso Taracena, *La verdadera revolución mexicana* (Mexico City: Jus, 1960), 4: 64, 55; Mérigo, *La banda del automóvil gris,* 6. But see *El Demócrata,* 20 Dec. 1915, p. 6. See Knight, *The Mexican Revolution,* 2:404–6.

62 Mérigo, *La banda del automóvil gris,* 175–76; Taracena, *La verdadera,* 4:77, 97, 109–10, 118, 5:65–82; Bernaldo de Quiros, *El bandolerismo,* 292, 395; *El Demócrata,* 13 Dec. 1915, p. 1; ibid., 20 Dec. 1915, p. 1. The device used by Granda and Mercadante was also utilized by other prisoners expecting to obtain favors: González received in 1916 a letter from two inmates of the

penitentiary, offering to inform about a bounty of jewels. Carlos Acosta and Carlos Martínez to Pablo González [1916]. Gral. Pablo González Archives, University of Texas at Austin, microfilm, roll 3.

63 Guzmán, *Obras completas,* 2:568–74; John Womack Jr., *Zapata and the Mexican Revolution* (New York: Vintage, 1970), 322–26.

64 Aurelio de los Reyes, *Medio siglo de cine mexicano: 1896–1847* (Mexico City: Trillas, 1988), 80; Cándido Aguilar to Pablo González, Veracruz, 8 June 1915, Gral. Pablo González Archives, microfilm, roll 3. According to Taracena, González proposed another Constitutionalist office to share the profits of a search warrant, Taracena, *La verdadera,* 4:72–73.

65 Guzmán, *El Aguila y la Serpiente,* 1:380. The Constitutionalists were also called "Con sus uñas listas" in "Entusiasta despedida a los ladrones Carranza, Nerón y sus fariseos," leaflet, n.d., and "La Cucaracha (Canción dedicada al Iscariote barbón)," leaflet, n.d. MPP. For other examples, see Ramírez Plancarte, *La ciudad,* 223–24, 245; "Los dos bandoleros (Parodia de una fábula conocida)," leaflet, n.d., MPP.

66 Mérigo, apparently the only high-ranking revolutionary formally accused in connection with the gang, claims that González had the case's records disappeared. Mérigo, *La banda del automóvil gris,* 169. For a defense of González's reputation, see Pablo González, *Centinela fiel del constitucionalismo* (Saltillo: Textos de Cultura Historiográfica, 1971). Constitutionalist troops under González's command in the oil-producing zones were also prone to corruption and robbery. Jonathan C. Brown, *Oil and Revolution in Mexico* (Berkeley: University of California Press, 1993), 203–10. Taracena, *La verdadera,* 5:98–09; For corruption among revolutionary leaders, see José Vasconcelos, *La tormenta: Segunda parte del Ulises criollo* (Mexico City: Jus, 1983), 10–11.

67 *El Demócrata,* 23 Sept. 1914, p. 1; several rateros were also apprehended in these days, some of them wearing fine police uniforms, ibid., 25 Sept. 1914, p. 1; *El Universal,* 15 Feb. 1917, p. 3. In 1916, bandits in San Angel and Tlalpan committed different offenses while pretending to be Zapatista revolutionaries. Significantly, the source is Carrancista *El Demócrata,* 7 Oct. 1916, p. 1. The use of fake search warrants also appeared in a 1918 case of a robbery at a jewelry store, by six men "properly dressed." *El Universal,* 11 Jan. 1918, p. 1. Military men engaging in robberies in 1920 in El Universal, 11 Oct. 1920, 12; ibid., 5 Jan. 1917, p. 4. The Ministry of War requested police authorities to report whether or not military personnel arrested by the police were wearing their uniforms at the time of arrest. Oficial Mayor de Gobernación del Ayuntamiento to Inspector General de Policía, 18 Mar. 1922, AHA, Gobernación, 1115, 379.

68 AJ, 1074699, Theft, 1915.

69 Several prisoners to Minister Creel, 15 Aug. 1910, AGN, SJ, 714, 674.

70 This time, Jaramillo was sentenced to two years and six months and Hernández to thirty days of arrest. AJ, 705332, Battery, 1912. For a *ratero conocido*'s long list of short inarcerations, see Teresa García vda. de Bringas to Minister of the Interior, 21 June 1921 and Inspector General de Policía to Minister of the Interior, 28 June 1921, AGN, GPR, 117, 4. Anselmo Cejudo and Pedro Camarillo were "specialists in stealing curtains from windows." Cejudo was sent to Belem jail forty-three times for the same offense, and both men had been sent twice to the Valle Nacional penal colony. *El Imparcial,* 4 Jan. 1900, p. 1. See also Carlos Roumagnac, *La estadística criminal en México* (Mexico City: García Cubas, 1907), 14; *El Universal,* 30 June 1930, p. 3; Macedo, *La criminalidad,* 23; Ramos Pedrueza, *La ley penal,* 14; Moisés González Navarro, *El Porfiriato: La vida social,* vol. 4 of *Historia Moderna de México* (Mexico City: Hermes, 1957), 427. According to the press, rateros and cruzadoras avoided the use of photography for identification purposes by changing their facial expression at the moment of being photographed in Belem. *Gaceta de Policía* 1:17 (18 Feb. 1906): 2. In 1905, the Ministry of Justice asked judges to request information from police chiefs to find out about the recidivism of theft suspects. AGN, SJ, 515, 603; also AGN, SJ, 680, A. The 1923 Criminological Congress proposed that short prison terms be used less frequently. The idea, formulated by Miguel Macedo's committee for the reform of the penal code, was adopted by the 1931 Code. Article 90 established that *condena condicional* could be granted to first-time offenders sentenced to less than two years, who demonstrated good behavior, "honest means of living," and paid a deposit determined by the judge. *El Universal,* 16 Oct. 1923, p. 1; ibid., 18 Oct. 1923, p. 9; CP 1931, 90; José Angel Ceniceros, *Tres estudios de criminología* (Mexico City: Cuadernos Criminalia, 1941), 116–17.

71 CP 1871, p. 34. Similar words in Medina y Ormaechea, *Proyecto para el establecimiento,* 12.

72 Roumagnac, *Los criminales,* 310–11. Juvenile offenders lived among adults in Belem prison; González de Cosío, *Memoria,* 82–83; *El Imparcial,* 26 May 14, p. 7; Dr. Alberto Lozano Garza, "El problema de los niños dentro de las prisiones," in *Memoria del Primer Congreso nacional Penitenciario celebrado e la Ciudad de México del 24 de noviembre al 3 de diciembre de 1932, convocado por la Dirección Antialcohólica* (Mexico City: Talleres Gráficos de la Nación, 1935), 263.

73 Mérigo, *La banda del automóvil gris,* 11; AJ, 23196, Criminal association and robbery, 1930. For "differential association" among inmates, see John Braithwaite, *Crime, Shame and Reintegration* (New York: Cambridge University Press, 1989), 37n.

74 Mérigo, *La banda del automóvil gris,* 1. It took Huertista authorities several months to make a list of the 938 prisoners escaped. AGN, SJ, 838, 1311.

75 *La Nación,* 20 July 1912, p. 2; Roumagnac, *Los criminales,* 324–25.

76 *El Universal,* 2 Oct. 1923, 2d sec., p. 1; AJ, 23196, Criminal association and robbery, 1930; AGN, PG, 1931/2, 2245.

77 Téllez argued that in his work, selling lottery tickets downtown, "he usually has in his hands bills for one or two hundred pesos . . . which demonstrates that people trust him and has a way of making a living and thus [he] would not steal." AJ, 19368, Theft, 1925. See also AJ, 1074681, Theft, 1915; AJ, 23196, Criminal association and robbery, 1930; AJ, 1027237, Battery, 1920; for leniency denied to a confessed thief, AJ, 18517, Theft, 1926. On descriptions, see AJ, 1074699, Theft, 1915. A victim in 1921 described two offenders: one had regular features and "wears blue demin overalls, a jacket of the same kind and color, sometimes he wears black shoes and sometimes he is barefoot." AJ, 18483, Battery, 1921. Other suspects were simply described as "poorly dressed" (AJ, 1074693, Theft, 1915) or "dresses poorly like all shoeshiners" (AJ, 1067904, Theft, 1920) or "without remembering further details" (AJ, 1067900, Theft, 1919).

78 *El Imparcial,* 12 Oct. 1897, p. 2; Governor of the Federal District to Minister of Justice, 19 Oct. 1911, AGN, SJ, 749, 873; *El Universal,* 27 June 1930, p. 1.

79 *El Universal,* 17 Oct. 1920, 2d sec., p. 1. In 1900, there were 2,303 cases of simple theft, against 61 cases of theft accompanied with the use or threat of physical violence. See also Rohlfes, "Police and Penal Correction," 245. Statistics suggest that theft was decreasingly violent in the capital. In the 1871–85 period, 7.94 percent of sentences for theft in the Federal District were for theft with violence; in 1900, the percentage was 2.27. Dirección General de Estadística, *Estadística del ramo criminal en la República Mexicana que comprende un periodo de quince años, de 1871 a 1885* (Mexico City: Secretaría de Fomento, 1890); *Cuadros estadísticos e informe del Procurador de Justicia concernientes a la criminalidad en el Distrito Federal y territorios* (Mexico City: Ministerio Público del Distrito y Territorios Federales, 1900). It is difficult to compare, in this regard, prerevolutionary statistics with those published since 1920 because the categories for classification varied. For a similar development in Brazil, see Boris Fausto, *Crime e cotidiano: a criminalidade em São Paulo, 1880–1924* (São Paulo, Brazil: Brasiliense, 1984), 127, 134–35.

80 *El Universal,* 6 Oct. 1920, p. 12. For more cases of violent theft, perceived as a new crime "wave," see *El Universal,* 10 Oct. 1923, p. 6.

81 In July 23, 1931, a court formed by three judges sentenced the suspects. Pineda was sentenced to 18 years; Rojas to 16 years; Manuel Castillo to 14 years; Antonio Martínez to 14 years; Leonor Jiménez to 10 years, and Pino

González to 6 years. All of the sentences could be increased by half at the discretion of penitentiary authorities, and all were accompanied by fines ranging from 667 to 2,000 pesos. The Federal District's high court reduced all the sentences by three years on appeal. AJ, 23196, Criminal association and robbery, 1930.

82 See Barrera Bassols, *El caso Villavicencio.* A confusing episode, in which a man suspected of attempting to assassinate Porfirio Díaz was killed by a mob, caused the arrest of several police officers and the suicide of the police chief. *Hijo del Ahuizote,* 26 Sept. 1897; ibid., 28 Nov. 1897, p. 738; see also *Nueva Era,* 15 Aug. 1911, pp. 1–2.

83 AJ, 1027222, Battery, 1920; see also *El Universal,* 6 June 1930, 2d sec., p. 1.

84 AJ, 1051501, Battery, 1922.

85 Obregón to Gasca, 4 May 1922. AGN, POC, 407-P-15. For Obregón's involvement in police reform, ibid., 104-S-5; for a purge of the police in 1921, ibid., 122-D2-P-4; in 1922, ibid., 122-D2-P-13; and in 1923, ibid., 122-D2-P-14. On militarization, see ibid., 122-D2-P-6 and ibid., 122-D2-P-11. For increased resources assigned to the capital's police under Obregón, see ibid., 121-D5-D-1; ibid., 121-D5-P-8; ibid., 122-D2-P-2; ibid., 121-D5-G-22; on the establishment of mounted police, see ibid., 121-D5-G-22; ibid., 121-W-D-2; on the distribution of new guns, see *Excélsior,* 22 Nov. 1921, 2d sec., p. 1.

86 AJ, 19367, Fraud, 1925. On corruption at police stations in the early 1920s, see AHA, Justicia comisarías, 2717, 15; AHA, Gobernación, 1112, 124bis, n.d.

87 Visitador de Juzgados to Governor of the Federal District, 1 July 1919, AHA, Justicia comisarías, 2717, 11; O. Medellín Ostos to President Alvaro Obregón, 20 Dec. 1922, AGN, POC, 121-D5-P-3; *Excélsior,* 24 Nov. 1921, 2d sec., p. 1. On robberies committed by police agents, M. Blanco to President Pascual Ortiz Rubio, Aug. 1931, AGN, Fondo Presidente Pascual Ortiz Rubio, 1931/217, 5659.

88 For an opinion supporting a secret political police, see Carlos Magaña to President Francisco I. Madero, 8 Nov. 1911, AGN, FIM, 60, 226, fol. 1. For the need to reorganize the police, see *El Universal,* 14 Oct. 1920, p. 9. For the "secret budget" for the judicial police between 1923 and 1928 and hirings of more agents, see AGN, POC, 121-P4-G-1; ibid., 121-P4-P-12; ibid., 121-G-I-3.

89 González to President Obregón, 4 Apr. 1922. AGN, POC, 307-14-16. For an expose of police corruption, see *Excélsior,* 24 Nov. 1921, 2d sec., p. 1; AGN, POC, 307-P-12.

90 Inspector General de Policía to President Alvaro Obregón, 9 Aug. 1924, AGN, POC, 104-P-106; Obregón to Gasca and Almada, 4 May 1922. AGN, POC, 122-D2-P-7; Obregón to Gasca, 16 Nov. 1921. AGN, POC, 605-P-6.

91 Cristóbal Trápaga to Ministry of the Interior, 24 Oct. 1933, AGN, DGG, 2.014(29)22, c.2, exp. 15; Federal District officials, however, opposed new authorizations because some of the members of detective agencies "discredited the police." Octavio B. Barona to Minister of the Interior, 10 Feb. 1934, ibid. The advertisement in *El Universal,* 8 May 1925, 2d sec., p. 5. On the issuance of identifications, *El Universal,* 7 June 1930, p. 1. See also AJ, 1067900, Theft, 1919; Enrique Jiménez to Minister of the Interior, 28 July 1934, AGN, DGG, 2.014(29)27, c.2, exp. 10.

8 PENAL EXPERIENCE IN MEXICO CITY

1 Carlos Roumagnac, *Los criminales en México: Ensayo de psicología criminal. Seguido de dos casos de hermafrodismo observado por los señores doctores Ricardo Egea . . . Ignacio Ocampo* (Mexico City: Tipografía El Fénix, 1912 [1904]), 145, 212, 156, 262, 203, 129–30, 236.

2 Sergio García Ramírez, "Introducción," in Carmen Castañeda García, *Prevención y readaptación social en México (1926–1979)* (Mexico City: Instituto Nacional de Ciencias Penales, 1979). See also idem, *El final de Lecumberri: Reflexiones sobre la prisión* (Mexico City: Porrúa, 1979); on the transfer of prisoners to the penitentiary, see Antonio Padilla Arroyo, "Criminalidad, cárceles y sistema penitenciario en México, 1876–1910" (Ph.D. diss., El Colegio de México, 1995). For a legal history of penitentiary institutions, see Raúl Carrancá y Rivas, *Derecho penitenciario: Cárceles y penas en México* (Mexico City: Porrúa, 1896); Antonio Ramos Pedrueza, *La ley penal en México de 1810 a 1910* (Mexico City: Díaz de León, 1911); Robert Buffington, *Criminal and Citizen in Modern Mexico* (Lincoln: University of Nebraska Press, 1999), chaps. 4 and 5. A cultural and historical approach to the sociology of punishment in David Garland, *Punishment and Modern Society: A Study in Social Theory* (Chicago: University of Chicago Press, 1990), 28.

3 Elena Azaola Garrido and Cristina José Yacamán, *Las mujeres olvidadas: Un estudio sobre la situación actual de las cárceles de mujeres en la República Mexicana* (Mexico City: El Colegio de México, 1996); Luis de la Barreda Solórzano, *Justicia penal y derechos humanos* (Mexico City: Porrúa, 1997), 218–22.

4 For popular culture and state in Mexico, see Gilbert Joseph and Daniel Nugent, eds., *Everyday Forms of State Formation: Revolution and the Negotiation of Rule in Modern Mexico* (Durham, NC: Duke University Press, 1994), esp. Joseph and Nugent, "Popular Culture and State Formation in Revolutionary Mexico," 3–23. For the interaction of science and policies and the public sphere as an historical process. See Jürgen Habermas, *Ciencia y técnica como "ideología"* (Mexico City: Rei, 1993), 75–78; idem, *The Structural*

Transformation of the Public Sphere: An Inquiry into a Category of Bourgeois Society, trans. Thomas Burger (Cambridge, MA: MIT Press, 1991).

5 Alfonso Teja Zabre, "Exposición de motivos," in *Código penal para el Distrito y Territorios Federales y para toda la República en Materia de Fuero Federal* (Mexico City: Botas, 1938), 29. For complaints of late payments to judicial and prison employees, AGN, POC, 811-R-82; AGN, PG, 1932/2, 2258; APD, 36, 2576; AGN, SJ, 714, 675; ibid., 600, 949. The percentage of the federal budget spent in the administration of justice decreased after 1912. Gustavo F. Aguilar, *Los presupuestos mexicanos desde los tiempos de la colonia hasta nuestros días* (Mexico City: N.p., 1946); *Estadísticas económicas del porfiriato: Fuerza de trabajo y actividad por sectores* (Mexico City: El Colegio de México, n.d.). For judges' and police corruption, see *El Universal,* 19 Jan. 1918, p. 1; AHA, PG, 3645, 1777; AHA, Justicia comisarías, 2717, 15; AGN, POC, 307-P-12; Guillermo Mellado, *Belén por dentro y por fuera* (Mexico City: Cuadernos Criminalia, 1959), 170–75. The 1910 census counted 1,631 men and 3 women with "judicial" jobs in the capital—more than a fourth of the national total. Dirección de Estadística, *Censo de 1910* (Mexico City: Secretaría de Fomento, 1911); Miguel Macedo received five thousand pesos for his participation in the commission that reviewed the penal code, Miguel Macedo to Minister of Justice, 14 June 1912, AGN, SJ, 790, 1079; José Angel Ceniceros became assistant attorney general after his participation on the committee that drafted the 1931 Code, José Angel Ceniceros, *Un discurso sobre el código penal de 1931: Bosquejo de una sociología de la delincuencia* (Mexico City: Editorial La Justicia, 1977), 26.

6 Sergio García Ramírez, "Pena y prisión: Los tiempos de Lecumberri," in *Lecumberri: Un palacio lleno de historia* (Mexico City: Secretaría de Gobernación, 1994), 71–84; Clementina Díaz y de Ovando, "La Ciudad de México en el amanecer del siglo XX (inauguración de la Penitenciaría)," in ibid., 11–41; *Boletín del Archivo General de La Nación: La Penitenciaría de México* 5:4 (1981–82). Díaz's remarks in Mellado, *Belén por dentro,* 16. An 1897 decree established that the Belem jail was to be jointly supported by the federal government and the city council. Manuel González de Cosío, *Memoria que presenta al Congreso de la Unión el General . . . Secretario de Estado y del Despacho de Gobernación* (Mexico City: Imprenta del Gobierno Federal, 1900), 83, 837. See also Carrancá y Rivas, *Derecho penitenciario,* 440; Ramos Pedrueza, *La ley penal,* 12; Cámara de Diputados, *Diario de los debates de la Cámara de Diputados: Decimaoctava Legislatura Constitucional* (Mexico City: Imprenta de "El Partido Liberal," 1896), 28.

7 Buffington, *Criminal and Citizen;* see also Rebollar's cite in ibid., 97. For the design and construction of the penitentiary, see Elisa García Barragán,

"El Palacio de Lecumberri y su contexto arquitectónico," in *Lecumberri: Un palacio lleno de historia,* 45–67. Prisoners began to occupy the penitentiary in 1897. *El Imparcial,* 1 Aug. 1897, p. 2.

8 Secretaría de Justicia, Comisión Revisora del Código Penal, *Trabajos de revisión del Código Penal: Proyecto de reformas y exposición de motivos,* 4 vols. (Mexico City: Tip. de la Oficina Impresora de Estampillas, 1912), 1:1; Miguel Macedo to Minister of Justice, 14 June 1912, AGN, SJ, 790, 1079. For a similar project to gather opinions about the Código de Procedimientos Penales undertaken by Maderista authorities, see memorandum Ministry of Justice, 3 Dec. 1912, ibid., 790, 1062. For a brief chronology of the committee, see Celestino Porte Petit Candaudap, *Apuntamientos de la parte general de derecho penal* (Mexico City: Porrúa, 1991), 47–48.

9 *Trabajos de revisión,* 1:265–67; for a discussion of penal reforms up to the 1931 Code, see Robert Buffington, *Criminal and Citizen,* chap. 5.

10 Consejo Ejecutivo de los Estados Unidos Mexicanos, "Ley General sobre la Administración de la Justicia," Cuernavaca, 1 and 18 Dec. 1915, Archivo Genaro Amezcua, Centro de Estudios Históricos Condumex, Mexico City, vol. 3, fol. 216–22. A contest for the writing of a new penal code was convoked in June 1915, but the law of December 1915 did not make any reference to it, *La Convención,* 1 June 1915, p. 12. On the Zapatista legislative project, Arturo Warman, "The Political Project of Zapatismo," in Friedrich Katz, ed., *Riot, Rebellion, and Revolution: Rural Social Conflict in Mexico* (Princeton, NJ: Princeton, University Press, 1988); but see Samuel Brunk, " 'The Sad Situation of Civilians and Soldiers': The Banditry of Zapatismo in the Mexican Revolution," *American Historical Review* 101:2 (Apr. 1996): 345.

11 *El Pueblo,* 1 Jan. 1915, p. 3. *El Universal* hailed the reestablishment of courts in the Federal District as a step toward prompt and fair justice and against the legalistic style of old judges. *El Universal,* 1 Oct. 1916, p. 1; ibid., 9 Oct 1916, p. 3. On decrees see *El Demócrata,* 15 Sept. 1914, p. 1; ibid., 20 Sept. 1914, p. 1.

12 Speech of Carranza, 17 Apr. 1917, *Diario de los Debates de la Cámara de Diputados,* 27th Congress, 1:9, pp. 10–23.

13 *Diario de los Debates del Congreso Constituyente* (Mexico City: INEHRM, 1960), 2:74; for the Carrancista proposal and its arguments, see ibid., 1:506, 931; for the federalist arguments, see ibid., 1:941. See also Buffington, *Criminal and Citizen,* chap. 5.

14 Gobierno del Distrito Federal, *Primer Congreso Criminológico y Penitenciario Mexicano* (Mexico City: Tip. Escuela Correccional Tlalpan, 1923), 3. For the chronicles of the Congress, see *El Universal,* 12–21 Oct. 1923. Several of the presenters also participated in the 1932 Primer Congreso Nacional

Penitenciario en 1932, *Memoria del Primer Congreso Nacional Penitenciario celebrado en la Ciudad de México del 24 de noviembre al 3 de diciembre de 1932, convocado por la Dirección Antialcohólica* (Mexico City: Talleres Gráficos de la Nación), 1935.

15 José Almaraz, *Exposición de motivos del Código Penal promulgado el 15 de diciembre de 1929* (Mexico City: N.p., 1931), 12; Porte Petit Candaudap, *Apuntamientos,* 48. A positivist penal code, drafted by Enrico Ferri in Italy for Mussolini in 1921, was available to provide direct inspiration. José Angel Ceniceros, *Tres estudios de criminología* (Mexico City: Cuadernos Criminalia, 1941), 57.

16 The entire chapter on probation, with minor corrections, was adopted from Macedo's commission proposal. José Angel Ceniceros, *El nuevo código penal de 1931, en relación con los de 1871 y 1929* (Mexico City: Botas, 1931), 32.

17 Almaraz, *Exposición de motivos,* 114, 12, 18, 100–101; CP 1929, 64, 203, 204.

18 Porte Petit Candaudap, *Apuntamientos,* 41–42. According to José Angel Ceniceros, the technical knowledge available in Mexico was not enough to assess the dangerousness of individual suspects. Ceniceros, *El nuevo código penal,* 10–12, 17. On the change of vocabulary, "sanción" instead of "pena" and "segregación" instead of "prisión," see AGN, PG, 2/432, 9597; Porte Petit Candaudap, *Apuntamientos,* 48–49. In February 1929, the Ministry of the Interior had invited government officials, scholars, and journalists to discuss the new penal code, but the discussions did not reach a wide audience. AGN, PG, 2/430, 2697.

19 Ceniceros, *El nuevo código penal,* 37–39.

20 Ibid., 26; Procurador General de Justicia of the Federal District to the press, AGN, PG, 2/432, 14108; *Excélsior,* 20 Oct. 1929, p. 1; ibid., 26 Oct. 1929, p. 1.

21 Porte Petit Candaudap, *Apuntamientos,* 49; Ceniceros, *El nuevo código penal,* 97–99.

22 *El Nacional,* 8 May 1931, p. 1; Teja Zabre, "Exposición de motivos," 13–14; Ceniceros, *Tres estudios,* 87.

23 Teja Zabre, "Exposición de motivos," 33–38. Lombardo Toledano's statement in *El Universal,* 18 Oct. 1923, p. 1. The 1929 Code excluded from penal responsibility "those who, without using deceit or violent means, appropriate once the food strictly necessary to satisfy their momentary need of nourishment." CP 1929, 45. Article 379 of the 1931 Code stated: "There will be no punishment against those whom, without using deceit or violent means, appropriate once the objects strictly necessary to satisfy their momentary personal or family needs." See also Porte Petit Candaudap, *Apuntamientos,* 447–55.

24 Hector Madrid Muliá, "La política contra la delincuencia en el periodo

del general Lázaro Cárdenas (1934–1940)," *Revista Mexicana de Justicia* 3:9 (July–Sept., 1991): 88.

25 Cf. Carlos Aguirre, "The Lima Penitentiary and the Modernization of Criminal Justice in Nineteenth-Century Peru," in Salvatore and Aguirre, eds., *The Birth of the Penitentiary,* 62; Michael Ignatieff, *A Just Measure of Pain: The Penitentiary in the Industrial Revolution* (London: Penguin, 1978).

26 Joaquín García Icazbalceta, *Informe sobre los establecimientos de beneficencia y corrección de esta capital; su estado actual; noticia de sus fondos; reformas que desde luego necesitan y plan general de su arreglo presentado por José María Andrade* (Mexico City: Moderna Librería Religiosa, 1907), 71.

27 *Trabajos de revisión,* 1:73; *Gaceta de Policía* 1:20 (3 Nov. 1906): 2–3; Federico Gamboa, *La llaga* (Mexico City: Eusebio Gómez de la Puente, 1922 [1913]), 38; Miguel Macedo, *La criminalidad en México: Medios de combatirla* (Mexico City: Secretaría de Fomento, 1897), 34.

28 *La Voz de México,* 23 Jan. 1890, p. 2.

29 *Diario del Hogar,* 19 Nov. 1907, p. 1. Heriberto Frías, "Crónicas desde la cárcel," *Historias* 11 (Oct.–Dec. 1985): 51–54. Porfirio Díaz reported to Congress the break of an epidemic of typhus in the municipal jail in 1896. *Diario de los Debates . . . Decimaoctava Legislatura,* 27–28. See also AJ, 518263, Battery, 1906; *El Imparcial,* 19 Jan. 1900, p. 1; "Informe del inspector sanitario del Cuartel No. 7," in Consejo Superior de Salubridad, *Memoria* (Mexico City: N.p., 1905), 249. On improvements in 1886, see José Ceballos, *Memoria presentada al C. Lic Manuel Romero Rubio Secretario de Estado y del Despacho de Gobernación por el . . . Gobernador del Distrito Federal y que comprende los años de 1886 y 1887* (Mexico City: Eduardo Dublán, 1888), 140; and before the inauguration of the penitentiary, including the purchase of new lots, González de Cosío, *Memoria,* 83; *Gaceta de Policía* 1:2 (19 Oct. 1905): 6–7. The Belem jail was established in 1862, during Maximilian's empire. It replaced the jail of the colonial Tribunal de la Acordada, considered too close to the city's center. The federal government ceded to the city council the building of the former Colegio de Belem, a seventeenth-century convent for women, and the jail was established in January 22, 1863. It was first called Cárcel Nacional. In 1887 it was renamed Cárcel Municipal, when the city government took charge of it. In 1900, after the official inauguration of the penitentiary, it became the Cárcel General del Distrito. In addition to Belem, each municipality of the Federal District had a jail, and there was a military prison in Tlatelolco. In 1886, the Cárcel de Detenidos, until then located downtown, was integrated into Belem's building. Miguel Macedo, "El Municipio: Los establecimientos penales. La asistencia pública," in Justo Sierra, ed., *México, su evolución social: síntesis de la historia política, de la orga-*

nización administrativa y militar y del estado económico de la federación mexicana; de sus adelantamientos en el orden intelectual; de su estructura territorial y del desarrollo de su población y de los medios de comunicación nacionales y internacionales; de sus conquistas en el campo industrial, agrícola, minero, mercantil, etc., etc. Inventario monumental que resume en trabajos magistrales los grandes progresos de la nación en el siglo XIX (Mexico City: Ballescá, 1900), 1:698–99; García Icazbalceta, *Informe,* 65–66; Ceballos, *Memoria,* 140. Belem continued operating until the early thirties, when it was demolished to build a public school, the Centro Escolar México. See AGN, GPR, 81, 4; Luis Vázquez and Julio Baz to City Council, 27 July 1917, AHA, Justicia juzgados, 2745, 1. Turning the jail into a school was probably José Vasconcelos's idea. Obregón had granted the lot and buildings of the Belem jail to the Ministry of Education. AGN, POC, 241-E-B-4; García Ramírez, "Pena y Prisión," 78.

30 *Gaceta de Policía* 1:39 (12 Aug. 1906): 8.

31 García Icazbalceta, *Informe,* 68–69; Ceballos, *Memoria,* 142–46; *Gaceta de Policía* 1:39 (12 Aug. 1906): 8; *Nueva Era,* 15 Aug. 1911, p. 2; a 1904 visitor, however, counted 2,939. AGN, SJ, 516, 757. See also Minister of the Interior to Minister of Justice, 28 Aug. 1912, ibid., 789, 872; *Memoria del Primer Congreso Nacional Penitenciario.*

32 *Diario del Hogar,* 24 June 1905, p. 2; Roumagnac, *Los criminales,* 215–16, 123, 210, 306.

33 Mellado, *Belén por dentro,* 56–57; "Reglamento General de Establecimientos Penales del Distrito Federal," 14 Sept. 1900, articles 61 to 67, in González de Cosío, *Memoria,* 849. Authorities acknowledged deficiency in food supplies in 1922 by allowing prisoners to receive additional food from relatives. Obregón decided to give each prisoner the amount of federal contributions destined to their food so they could buy it independently. AGN, POC, 811-R-82; Ma. Jesús Marín to President Francisco I. Madero, 15 Nov. 1911, AGN, FIM, 70; *La Voz de México* 14 Oct. 1897, p. 3.

34 González de Cosío, *Memoria,* 846–47; *La Voz de México,* 25 Jan. 1890, p. 3; Roumagnac, *Los criminales,* 191; *Diario del Hogar,* 23 Nov. 1907, p. 1; CP 1871, p. 264.

35 González de Cosío, *Memoria,* 855.

36 Roumagnac, *Los criminales,* 228; Ceballos, *Memoria,* 146; *La Voz de México,* 8 Oct. 1897, p. 3.

37 Roumagnac, *Los criminales,* 246. Girls worked in the kitchen of the hospice for the poor, while inmates from Belem went to the correctional prison to cook for juvenile inmates. García Icazbalceta, *Informe,* 162, 21, 30. See also Roumagnac, *Los criminales,* 113, 219; González de Cosío, *Memoria,* 864–65, 848. In 1863 there were no workshops. García Icazbalceta, *Informe,* 70. The

1871 Penal Code mandated inmates' work and allowed them to accumulate some savings or to support their families after the prison deducted a percentage from the sale of their manufactures. Ceballos, *Memoria,* 142, 145.

38 Roumagnac, *Los criminales,* 215–18, 220n, 357–62. The official version of the failed escape in Ceballos, *Memoria,* 147; González de Cosío, *Memoria,* 866; AJ, 518258, Fraud, 1906.

39 Letter to Dr. don Rafael Silva, Department of Health, Belem jail, 26 Jan. 1931, ASSA, SP, Sección Epidemiología, 56, 1; *Diario del Hogar,* 3 June 1905, p. 2, Emilio Helgero to President Francisco I. Madero,14 Nov. 1911, AGN, FIM, 60, 242; members of the Federación de Sindicatos Obreros del Distrito Federal to President Plutarco Elías Calles, 18 Feb. 1925, AGN, POC, 707-P-27; Manuel Rivas to President Alvaro Obregón, 5 Apr. 1921, ibid., 307-14-16; Sebastián Hidalgo to Minister of Justice, 11 Jan. 1914, AGN, SJ, 892, 4165. The problem of food and prisoners' complaints forced a visit to the municipal jail, in October 1920, in which a fraud involved the preparation of food was discovered. Marcos González to Porfirio Díaz, Cárcel General, 27 Feb. 1911, APD, 36, 3820.

40 On delays in proceedings for absence of court employees, Ignacio Rosales to City Council, 14 Apr. 1919, AHA, Justicia, Cárcel Municipal, 2707, 1; AJ, 1027237, Battery, 1920. On the "constant" delays of courts to issue sentences, sometimes up to a year, see "Anteproyecto del Lic. Jesús M. Aguilar para capítulos VI y VII, titulo XI, libro III del Código Penal," [1911] AGN, SJ, 749, 780; see also visit of a judge from the Tribunal Superior de Justicia del Distrito Federal to Belem jail, 21 June 1904, ibid., 470, 697; ibid., 516, 757; and "Proyecto a la Comisión de Justicia del Ayuntamiento, por licenciados Vázquez y Bas," [1917], AHA, Justicia juzgados, 2745, 1. For prisoners' complaints, see Minister of Justice to Attorney General, 6 Nov. 1909, AGN, SJ, 683, 817; Mellado, *Belén por dentro,* 167–76.

41 AJ, 596561, Theft, 1908. See also *El Imparcial,* 20 Jan. 1900, p. 3; AJ, 1027234, Battery, 1920; AJ, 1027244, Battery, 1920; Flores also appointed two other defenders, and was acquitted of murder. AJ, 1051492, Homicide, 1921; Arroyo de Anda to Minister of Justice, 8 Apr. 1904, AGN, SJ, 481, 793; AJ, 518268, Fraud, 1906; Pedro Ruíz Ramírez to President Alvaro Obregón, 15 Dec. 1922, AGN, POC, 811-B-18; José M. Lozano and Manuel Zamora to Minister of Justice, 4 July 1902, AGN, SJ, 436, 1949.

42 AGN, SJ, 894, 4578; AJ, 1067901, Theft, 1922; AJ, 596570, Theft, 1909; AGN, SJ, 891, 3930; Police Inspectors to City Council, 23 Dec. 1920, AHA, Justicia comisarías, 2717, 17.

43 Governor of the Federal District to Minister of Justice, 19 Oct. 1911, AGN, SJ, 749, 873; *El Imparcial,* 4 Jan. 1897, p. 4; García Ramírez, *El final de Lecum-*

berri, 141; AJ, 19325, Battery, 1923; Sixth Correctional Judge to Minister of Justice, 27 Oct. 1910, AGN, SJ, 716, 895; José B. Robles to governor of the Federal District, 7 Oct. 1929; Juan Sandoval et al. to President Porfirio Díaz, 30 Apr. 1910, ibid., 714, 673.

44 Agustin Ulibarri et al. to President Porfirio Díaz, 1 Dec. 1900, AGN, SJ, 382, 1450. For a similar letter, see Cirilo Noveno et al. to President Díaz, 9 Aug. 1910, ibid., 714, 672.

45 See Pablo Sánchez Hurtado and José López Trejo to President Francisco I. Madero, 5 Oct. 1912 and Felipe Lugo to President Madero, 3 Dec. 1911, both in AGN, FIM, 70, 354.

46 Francisco P. Díaz to President Porfirio Díaz, 11 Feb. 1911, APD, 36, 3299.

47 Bonifacio y Tomás Ordóñez to President Francisco I. Madero, 25 Nov. 1911, AGN, FIM, 70; several prisoners to Minister Creel, 15 Aug. 1910, AGN, SJ, 714, 674.

48 Cirilo Noveno et al. to President Porfirio Díaz, 9 Aug. 1910. AGN, SJ, 714, 672. Similar reasonings in Miguel Torres to President Francisco I. Madero, 7 Nov. 1911, AGN, FIM, 70; Juan Sandoval et al. to President Díaz, 30 Apr. 1910, AGN, SJ, 714, 673. See also Atanasio Pacheco to President Victoriano Huerta, n.d., and to Venustiano Carranza, 18 July 1914; ibid., 892, 4165; Martiniano Nerey to President Huerta, Belem Jail, 30 July 1914; ibid., 894, 4558.

49 González de Cosío, *Memoria,* 847–48.

50 Guadalupe Cuéllar to President Victoriano Huerta, 26 Mar. 1914, AGN, SJ, 892, 3992; Eva Rojo and others to President Francisco I. Madero, 7 Apr. 1912, AGN, FIM, 70, 123; ibid., 70, 5; Vicente Fuentes to President Huerta, Cárcel General, 14 Mar. 1914, AGN, SJ, 894, 4554; ibid., 891, 3930. For requests to enter the army, see Minister of Justice to Minister of the Interior, 17 July 1913, AGN, GPR, 121, 4; ibid., 118, 3. Sebastián Hidalgo was taken by the leva to Mexico City and then sent to Islas Marías because he was not fit for service in the army. Hidalgo to President Huerta, 11 Jan. 1914, AGN, SJ, 892, 4165. On the escape, see Agustina Carrillo to President Huerta, 12 Jan. 1914, ibid., 891, 3940; Agustín Arroyo de Anda to Minister of Justice, 26 Feb. 1913, ibid., 838, 1311.

51 Pioquinto Gómez and 37 others to President Alvaro Obregón, 29 Oct. 1922, AGN, POC, 213-B-12.

52 Emiliano Helguero to President Francisco I. Madero, 14 Nov. 1911, AGN, FIM, 60, 242; Sino Hernández Serrano and others to President Alvaro Obregón, 21 Sept. 1921, AGN, POC, 811-I-10; Pablo A. Palacio, Antonio B. Esqueda, Cecilio Castillo, Leonardo Aguilar to President Obregón, 5 Nov. 1924, ibid., 731-I-10; Antonio Martínez García and others to President Pas-

cual Ortiz Rubio, 20 Mar. 1931, AGN, PG, 1931/2, 2245; Jerónimo Vázquez to Secretary of the President, 17 Aug. 1925, AGN, POC, 101-R2-D-2. For the scribes, called *evangelistas,* in Belem, see Mellado, *Belén por dentro,* 65.

53 Two prisoners' organizations existed, according to Hector Madrid, during Abelardo Rodríguez's presidency (1932–1934), the Asociación Pro-Presos de la República Mexicana and the Unión General de Reclusos del País. Madrid Muliá, "La política contra la delincuencia en el periodo del general Lázaro Cárdenas," 87–88, 98. For the union's statutes, see Pedro Ruíz Ramírez et al. to President Alvaro Obregón, 15 Dec. 1922 and President Obregón to Pedro Ruiz Ramírez, 10 Jan. 1923. AGN, POC, 811-B-18. Also ibid., 811-I-2; Unión Penitenciaria Pro Indulto to President Plutarco Elías Calles [1924], ibid., 731-I-10; Secretary of Unión Penitenciaria, A. Antunes, to President Obregón, México D.F., 6 Oct. 1924, ibid., 731-I-10.

54 President Alvaro Obregón to Minister of the Interior, 14 Sept. 1921, AGN, POC, 121-G-R-1; ibid., 811-I-10. Also in 1924, see Enrique Cumplido and Joaquín Becerra to President Obregón, 30 Sept. 1924, ibid., 731-I-10; President Obregón to governor of the Federal District, 16 May 1921, ibid., 122-D2-P-12. For the distribution of new clothes and shoes to inmates, see President Obregón to Director of Department of General Provisions, 4 Sept. 1922, ibid., 121-D4-D-1; also ibid., 121-D5-P-10. García Ramírez, *El final de Lecumberri;* matrimonial visits were recommended by the 1923 Criminological Congress with the support of the governor of the Federal District, *El Universal,* 18 Oct. 1923, p. 1.

55 On resistance, see James C. Scott, *Weapons of the Weak: Everyday Forms of Peasant Resistance* (New Haven, CT: Yale University Press, 1985); on its applicability to the Mexican Revolution, see Alan Knight, "Weapons and Arches in the Mexican Revolutionary Landscape," 24–68.

CONCLUSIONS

1 For a theory of crime centered around the impact of community reaction to crime, see John Braithwaite, *Crime, Shame and Reintegration* (New York: Cambridge University Press, 1989), chap. 1; he defines stigmatization as "shaming that is disintegrative . . . [which] divides the community by creating a class of outcasts," ibid., 55.

2 Oscar Lewis, *Anthropological Essays* (New York: Random House, 1970), 58, 424, 439.

3 In 1994, an average of 442 crimes per day were reported. The average number for the first weeks of 1996 was 655. *La Jornada,* 14 Jan. 1996. The number

of arrests per day in March 1997 was 664. Yet, a 1998 poll revealed that 82 percent of incidents were not reported to the police. *La Jornada,* 6 Aug. 1998. For the reform of police bodies, see *La Jornada,* 31 Mar. 1997.

4 For an example of the persistence of traditional attitudes about women and rape, see the case of Claudia Rodríguez, convicted for the murder of a man who was sexually assaulting her. She was released after one year thanks to the pressure of public opinion. *La Jornada,* 12 Feb. 1997. For recent reviews of judicial and police practices, see Human Rights Watch, "Abuso y desamparo: Tortura, desaparición forzada y ejecución extrajudicial en México," internet document (http://www.hrw.org/spanish/reports/mexico99/index.htm), January 1999; John Cross, "The Great Rip-off: 'Commercial Plazas,' Street Vendors and the 'System,'" internet document (http://www.openair.org/alerts/cross.html), 24 Dec. 1995.

5 For the law against organized crime that authorizes law-enforcement agencies to record telephone conversations and to use seized property with greater freedom, see Ley Federal Contra La Delincuencia Organizada, 28 Nov. 1996. For the federal government's signs of support for the death penalty, see *La Jornada,* 17 Aug. 1998.

6 One of these elite squads, the "Jaguares," was disbanded in 1997 after several of their leaders were involved in the killing of seven young men from the colonia Buenos Aires, a few blocks from the author's home in 1995. On police practices, Daniel Gerdts, *Paper protection: Human rights violations and the Mexican criminal justice system. A report of the Minnesota Lawyers International Human Rights Committee* (Minneapolis, MN: The Committee, 1990).

APPENDIX: STATISTICS OF CRIME

1 Carlos Roumagnac, *La estadística criminal en México* (Mexico City: García Cubas, 1907), 19, 10–15. Mexican statistics, critics claimed, failed to account for recidivism and the delay of the processes. Ignacio Fernandez Ortigoza, *Identificación científica de los reos: Memoria escrita por . . .* (Mexico City: Sagrado Corazón de Jesús, 1892), 8; Miguel Macedo, *La criminalidad en México: Medios de combatirla* (Mexico City: Secretaría de Fomento, 1897), 23; Antonio Ramos Pedrueza, *La Ley Penal en México, de 1810 a 1910* (México: Tip. Vda. de Díaz de León, 1911), 14. For Mexican perspectives on statistics of crime, see above chapter 3, note 6. Twentieth-century trends are presented and examined in Ira Beltrán and Pablo Piccato, "Crimen en el siglo XX: Fragmentos de análisis sobre la evidencia cuantitativa," in Ariel Rodríguez Kuri and Sergio Tamayo, eds., *Ciudad de México: Los últimos cien años, los próximos cien años* (Mexico City: UAM, 2001).

2 Moises González Navarro, *El Porfiriato: La vida social,* vol. 4 of *Historia moderna de México* (Mexico City: Hermes, 1957), 427; V. A. C. Gatrell, Bruce Lenman, and Geoffrey Parker, "Introduction," in Gatrell, Lenman, and Parker, eds., *Crime and the Law: The Social History of Crime in Western Europe since 1500* (London: Europa Publications, 1980), 9; V. A. C. Gatrell, "The Decline of Theft and Violence in Victorian and Edwardian England," in *Crime and the Law,* 243–51; Eric H. Monkkonen, *The Dangerous Class: Crime and Poverty in Columbus, Ohio, 1860–1885* (Cambridge, MA: Harvard University Press, 1975), 67–68, 57; Howard Zehr, *Crime and the Development of Modern Society. Patterns of Criminality in Nineteenth Century Germany and France* (London: Croom Helm, 1976), 15, 17–18. For criticisms of the use of statistics in positivist criminology, see Ian Taylor, Paul Walton, and Jack Young, *The New Criminology: For a Social Theory of Deviance* (London: Routledge & Kegan Paul, 1973), 11, 14, 37. A recent review of long-term statistical data in Eric A. Johnson and Eric H. Monkkonen, eds., *The Civilization of Crime: Violence in Town and Country since the Middle Ages* (Urbana: University of Illinois Press, 1996).

3 *El Universal,* 3 Oct. 1924, 2d sec, pp. 1–7; *Excélsior,* 7 Sept. 1925, 2d sec., p. 6. For the disparity between police arrests and judicial cases of theft, see chapter 6, note 19.

4 *Cuadros estadísticos e informe del Procurador de Justicia concernientes a la criminalidad en el Distrito Federal y territorios* (Mexico City: Ministerio Público del Distrito y Territorios Federales, 1904), 2; ibid., 1906.

5 For conflicting practices when arresting suspects, see *El Imparcial,* 1 Apr. 1897, p. 4; ibid., 12 Oct. 1897, p. 2; *El Universal,* 3 Oct. 1924, 2d sec, pp. 1–7. Laurence John Rohlfes, "Police and Penal Correction in Mexico City, 1876–1911: A Study of Order and Progress in Porfirian Mexico" (Ph.D. diss., Tulane University, 1983), 154–61. On the delay of trials, see Demetrio Sodi, *El jurado en México: Estudios sobre el jurado popular* (Mexico City: Secretaría de Fomento, 1909), 100–101; *Diario del Hogar,* 19 Nov. 1907, p. 1. After the Revolution, there were several changes in the structure of the judiciary and penal systems, see Manuel I. Fierro, "Algunas consideraciones sobre esta publicación," in Procuradoría General de Justicia del Distrito y Territorio Federales, *Estadística de la penalidad habida en los juzgados del fuero común del Distrito y territorios federales durante los años de 1916 a 1920* (Mexico City: Talleres Gráficos de la Nación, 1923), 1–2; *El progreso de México: Estudio económico estadístico del Departamento de la Estadística Nacional* (Mexico City: Diario Oficial, 1924), 8–9; Ramos Pedrueza, *La ley penal en México,* 12; "Circular no. 54 del Gobierno Constitucionalista de México, 3 de enero de 1917," *Boletín del Archivo General de La Nación,* 1:3 (Oct.–Dec. 1977), 44; "La esta-

dística como elemento de cultura," *Boletín del Departamento de la Estadística Nacional* 2:2 (Aug. 1924), 21. For institutional conflicts after the Revolution, see Alfonso Quiroz Cuarón et al., *Tendencia y ritmo de la criminalidad en México* (Mexico City: Instituto de Investigaciones Estadísticas, 1939), 46.

6 Fierro, "Algunas consideraciones," 3; AE 1938; Quiroz, *Tendencia y ritmo,* 104–5.

7 Monkkonnen, *The Dangerous Class,* 43; Gatrell, Lenman, and Parker, "Introduction," 9.

8 *Estadísticas históricas de México* (Mexico City: INEGI, 1994); *Estadísticas económicas del porfiriato: Fuerza de trabajo y actividad por sectores* (Mexico City: El Colegio de México, n.d.); Gustavo F. Aguilar, *Los presupuestos mexicanos desde los tiempos de la colonia hasta nuestros días* (Mexico City: N.p., 1946), 140–47.

9 A similar conclusion to criticisms about the historical use of statistics can be found in Gatrell, "The Decline," 249.

Bibliography

ARCHIVAL SOURCES

Archivo Genaro Amezcua, Centro de Estudios Históricos Condumex, Mexico City

Archivo General de la Nación, Mexico City

- Alvaro Obregón-Plutarco Elías Calles
- Dirección General de Gobierno
- Gobernación Período Revolucionario
- Emilio Portes Gil
- Francisco I. Madero
- Pascual Ortiz Rubio
- Secretaría de Justicia
- Secretaría de Gobernación

Archivo Histórico del Antiguo Ayuntamiento, Mexico City

- Bebidas Embriagantes
- Gobernación
- Gobierno del Distrito
- Justicia
- Justicia Comisarías
- Justicia Juzgados
- Justicia Juzgados Correccionales
- Justicia Negocios Diversos
- Policía en General
- Policía Presos Penitenciaría
- Sección Asistencial
- Vagos y Rateros

Archivo del Tribunal Superior de Justicia del Distrito Federal, Reclusorio Sur, Mexico City

Archivo Porfirio Díaz, Universidad Iberoamericana, Mexico City

Archivo Histórico de la Secretaría de Salud, Mexico City

Beneficencia Pública

Establecimientos Asistenciales

Salubridad Pública

Archivo Venustiano Carranza, Centro de Estudios Históricos Condumex, Mexico City

Fototeca Nacional, Fondo Casasola, Pachuca, Hidalgo

Mexican Political Parties Propaganda, Benson Latin American Collection, University of Texas at Austin, Austin, Texas

PERIODICALS

El Alacrán

El Anti-Reeleccionista

Anuario Estadístico de la República Mexicana (published irregularly by Secretaría de Fomento before 1910 and by Talleres Gráficos de la Nación afterward)

Arrebol Social, Organo de la Gran Liga de Carpinteros de los Estados Unidos Mexicanos

El Ahuizotito

El Bien Social

Boletín Mensual de Estadística del Distrito Federal

Boletín del Departamento de la Estadística Nacional

El Charrito

La Convención

El Demócrata

Don Cucufate

Diario del Hogar

Diario de los Debates de la Cámara de Diputados

El Diablito Bromista

Estadística Nacional

Excélsior

Gaceta de Policía

La Guacamaya

El Foro

El Heraldo: Diario Católico

El Hijo del Ahuizote

El Hijo del Fandango
El Imparcial
La Jornada
El Monitor Republicano
El Mero Mero Petatero
La Nación
El Nacional
Nueva Era
El País
La Patria
El Periquillo Sarniento
Regeneración Social: Periódico mensual (Mérida)
Reforma
El Siglo Diez y Nueve
La Tribuna
El Universal
La Voz de México
San Lunes

PRIMARY PUBLICATIONS

Almaraz, José. *Exposición de motivos del Código Penal promulgado el 15 de diciembre de 1929*. Mexico City: N.p., 1931.

———. "Regímenes penitenciarios." In *Memoria del Primer Congreso Nacional Penitenciario celebrado en la Ciudad de México del 24 de noviembre el 3 de diciembre de 1932, convocado por la Dirección Antialcohólica*. Mexico City: Talleres Gráficos de la Nación, 1935.

Alvarado, Salvador. *La Reconstrucción de México: Un mensaje a los pueblos de América*. Reprint. México: Fondo de Cultura Económica-INEHRM, 1985 [1919].

Ayuntamiento Constitucional de México. *Argumentos contra la iniciativa presidencial por eliminar el ayuntamiento de la ciudad de México. Envían presidente municipal L. L. Hernández y regidor encargado de la secretaría general J. Prieto Laurens*. Mexico City: Imprenta Francesa, 1919.

Azuela, Mariano. "Impresiones de un estudiante." In *Obras completas*. 3 vols. Mexico City: Fondo de Cultura Económica, 1958.

———. *Los caciques*. In *La novela de la Revolución Mexicana*, vol. 1, edited by Antonio Castro Leal. Mexico City: Aguilar–Secretaría de Educación Pública, 1988 [1917].

———. *Los de abajo*. In *La novela de la Revolución Mexicana*, vol. 1, edited by

Antonio Castro Leal. Mexico City: Aguilar–Secretaría de Educación Pública, 1988 [1916].
Barrera Lavalle, Francisco. "Apuntes para la historia de la estadística en México." *Boletín de la Sociedad Mexicana de Geografía y Estadística de la República Mexicana* 5:4 (1910).
Beneficencia Pública del Distrito Federal. *La mendicidad en México.* Mexico City: Departamento de Acción Educativa, Eficiencia y Catastros Sociales, 1931.
Bórquez, Djed. *Crónica del Constituyente.* Mexico City: Talleres Gráficos de la Nación, 1967.
Cámara de Diputados. *Diario de los debates de la Cámara de Diputados: Decimaoctava Legislatura Constitucional.* Mexico City: Imprenta de "El Partido Liberal," 1896.
Ceniceros, José Angel. *Un discurso sobre el código penal de 1931: Bosquejo de una sociología de la delincuencia.* Mexico City: Editorial La Justicia, 1977.
———. *El nuevo código penal de 1931, en relación con los de 1871 y 1929.* Mexico City: Botas, 1931.
———. *Tres estudios de criminología: El Código Penal Mexicano. La escuela Positiva y su influencia en la legislación penal Mexicana. Los sustitutivos de las penas cortas de privación de la libertad.* Mexico City: Cuadernos Criminalia, 1941.
Código del duelo observado en Francia, según el conde de Chatauvillard. Translated by Aristides Simonpietri. Ponce, Puerto Rico: Tipografía el Comercio, 1887.
Código del duelo, traducido, arreglado y auotado por Joaquin Larralde y Anselmo Alfaro. Mexico City: Ireneo Paz, 1886.
Código del honor en España formulado por el Marqués de Cabriñana. Barcelona: Librería de Felice y Susanna, 1900.
Código penal para el Distrito y territorios federales y para toda la república en materia de fuero federal [1931]. Mexico City: Botas, 1938.
Código penal para el Distrito y territorios federales [1929]. Mexico City: Talleres Gráficos de la Nación, 1929.
Colección de leyes y disposiciones gubernativas municipales y de policía vigentes en el Distrito Federal formada por acuerdo del C. gobernador Lic. Carlos Rivas. Mexico City: Imprenta y Litografía de Ireneo Paz, 1884.
Consejo Superior de Salubridad. *Memoria de los trabajos ejecutados en el . . . en el año de 1904.* Mexico City: 1905.
Cossío, José Lorenzo. "Algunas noticias sobre las colonias de esta capital." *Boletín de la Sociedad Mexicana de Geografía y Estadística* 47:1. (September 1937).

Crimenes célebres desde el Chalequero hasta Gallegos: La delincuencia en México. Mexico City: El Gráfico, 1932.

Crónicas y debates de las sesiones de la Soberana Convención Revolucionaria, edited by Florencio Barrera Fuentes. Mexico City: INEHRM, 1964.

Cueto, Casimiro. "Consideraciones generales y apuntes para la crítica, estadística de la criminalidad habida en el Distrito Federal durante el año de 1922." *Boletín de la Sociedad Mexicana de Geografía y Estadística* 5:12 (1928).

de Campo, Angel. *Ocios y apuntes y La rumba.* Mexico City: Porrúa, 1976.

Departamento de la Estadística Nacional. *Censo de población, 15 de mayo de 1930.* Mexico City: Talleres Gráficos de la Nación, 1934.

Departamento de la Estadística Nacional. *Censo general de habitantes, 30 de noviembre de 1921, Distrito Federal.* Mexico City: Talleres Gráficos de la Nación Departamento de la Estadística, 1925–28.

Diario de los Debates del Congreso Constituyente. Mexico City: INEHRM, 1960.

Díaz Infante, Carlos. "Estudios penales. La sociología criminal." *Revista de Legislación y Jurisprudencia* 12 (January–June 1897): 191–206.

Dirección General de Estadística. *Censo general de la República Mexicana verificado el 20 de octubre de 1895.* Mexico City: Secretaría de Fomento, 1897–99.

Dirección General de Estadística. *Censo general de la República Mexicana verificado el 28 de octubre de 1900.* Mexico City: Secretaría de Fomento, 1901–1907.

Dirección General de Estadísticas. *División territorial de la República Mexicana, Censo y división territorial del Distrito Federal, verificado en 1900.* Mexico City: Secretaría de Fomento, 1901.

Dirección General de Estadística. *Estadística del ramo criminal en la República Mexicana que comprende un periodo de quince años, de 1871 a 1885.* Mexico City: Secretaría de Fomento, 1890.

Discusión de la credencial del diputado don Luis Cabrera y documentos justificativos. Mexico City: Imp. Cámara de Diputados, 1917.

Documentos relativos a la nomenclatura de calles y numeración de casas de la ciudad de México. Mexico City: La Europea, 1904.

El progreso de México: Estudio económico estadístico del Departamento de la Estadística Nacional. Mexico City: Diario Oficial, 1924.

Escudero, Angel. *El duelo en México: Recopilación de los desafíos habidos en nuestra República, precedidos de la historia de la esgrima en México y de los duelos más famosos verificados en el mundo desde los juicios de Dios hasta nuestros días.* Mexico City: Mundial, 1936.

Estadística Gráfica: Progreso de los Estados Unidos Mexicanos. Mexico City: Empresa de Ilustraciones, 1896.

Esteva, Gonzalo A. *El duelo a espada y a pistola.* Mexico City: Tip. de Gonzalo A. Esteva, 1878.

Fernández de Lizardi, José Joaquín. *El Periquillo Sarniento,* edited by L. Sainz de Medrano. Madrid: Editora Nacional, 1976.

Fernández Ortigoza, Ignacio. *Identificación científica de los reos: Memoria escrita por....* Mexico City: Sagrado Corazón de Jesús, 1892.

Ferri, Enrico. *La Sociologie Criminelle.* 3d ed. Paris: Arthur Rousseau, 1893 [1881].

Fierro, Manuel I. "Algunas consideraciones sobre esta publicación." In Procuraduría General de Justicia del Distrito y Territorios Federales. *Estadística de la penalidad habida en los juzgados del fuero común del Distrito y territorios federales durante los años de 1916 a 1920.* Mexico City: Talleres Gráficos de la Nación, 1923.

Flores Magón, Ricardo. *Regeneración: 1900–1918. La corriente más radical de la revolución mexicana de 1910 a través de su periódico de combate,* edited by Armando Bartra. Mexico City: ERA, 1977.

Frías, Heriberto. "Crónicas desde la cárcel." *Historias* 11 (October–December 1985): 47–71.

Gamboa, Federico. *Diario de Federico Gamboa, 1892–1939.* Mexico City: Siglo Veintiuno, 1977.

———. *La llaga.* Mexico City: Eusebio Gómez de la Puente, 1922 [1913].

———. *Santa.* Mexico City: Eusebio Gómez de la Puente, 1922 [1903].

García Cubas, Antonio. *El libro de mis recuerdos: Narraciones históricas, anecdóticas y de costumbres mexicanas anteriores al actual estado social, ilustradas con más de trescientos fotograbados.* Mexico City: Editorial Porrúa, 1986 [1904].

———. *Plano topográfico de la ciudad de México formado por el ingeniero Antonio García Cubas con las nuevas calles abiertas hasta la fecha y los ferrocarriles.* Mexico City: Antigua librería de M. Murguía, 1886.

García Icazbalceta, Joaquín. *Informe sobre los establecimientos de beneficencia y corrección de esta capital; su estado actual; noticia de sus fondos; reformas que desde luego necesitan y plan general de su arreglo presentado por José María Andrade.* Mexico City: Moderna Librería Religiosa, 1907.

Garza y Melo, Trinidad de la. *Apuntes para la estadística criminal del Estado de Nuevo-León.* Monterrey: Imprenta del Gobierno, 1870.

González, Pablo. *Centinela fiel del constitucionalismo.* Saltillo: Textos de Cultura Historiográfica, 1971.

González de Cosío, Manuel. *Memoria que presenta al Congreso de la Unión el General... Secretario de Estado y del Despacho de Gobernación.* Mexico City: Imprenta del Gobierno Federal, 1900.

Guerrero, Julio. *La génesis del crimen en México: estudio de psiquiatría social.* Paris: Viuda de Bouret, 1901.

Gutiérrez Nájera, Manuel. *La novela del tranvía y otros cuentos.* Mexico City: Secretaría de Educación Pública, 1984.

Guzmán, Martín Luis. *El Aguila y la Serpiente* in *Obras Completas.* Mexico City: Fondo de Cultura Económica, 1984.

———. *Obras Completas.* Mexico City: Fondo de Cultura Económica, 1984.

Historia de la Cámara de Diputados de la XXVI Legislatura Federal. Vol. 2, *La Revolución tiene la palabra: Actas del "Diario de los Debates" de la Cámara de Diputados, del 2 de Septiembre al 11 de Octubre de 1912.* Mexico City: INEHRM, 1962.

Junta General del Ramo de Pulques. *Dictámen que presenta la comisión nombrada por la . . . al señor Gobernador del Distrito: Impugnando el vulgar error de que el consumo de esta bebida nacional es causa de la criminalidad en México, y en el que se exponen las razones legales con que se combaten las medidas restrictivas que atacan la libertad de este comercio.* Mexico City: Tipografía Artística, 1896.

Lacassagne, Alexandre. *Vacher l'eventreur et les crimes sadiques.* Lyon: Stork, 1899.

Lara y Pardo, Luis. *La prostitución en México.* Mexico City: Viuda de Bouret, 1908.

Lauzilli, Pietro. *Código del honor para América Latina.* Guatemala: Tipografía Nacional, 1898.

Lombroso, Cesare. *Crime: Its causes and remedies.* Translated by Henry P. Horton. Boston: Little, Brown, and Company, 1918.

———. *Delitti di libidine.* 2d ed. Torino: Fratelli Bocca, 1886.

———. *L'Homme Criminel. Criminel Né. Fou Moral. Epileptique. Criminel Fou. Criminel d'Occasion. Criminel par Passion. Etude Anthropologuique ent Psychiatrique.* 2d ed. Paris: Félix Alcan, 1895.

Lummis, Charles F. *The Awakening of a Nation: Mexico of To-day.* New York: Harper and Bros., 1899.

Macedo, Miguel. "Discurso pronunciado en la ceremonia inaugural" (1900). *Boletín del Archivo General de la Nación: La penitenciaría de México,* 5:4 (1981–82).

———. "El Municipio: Los establecimientos penales. La asistencia pública." In *México, Su evolución social.* Mexico City: Ballescá, 1900.

———. *La criminalidad en México: Medios de combatirla.* Mexico City: Secretaría de Fomento, 1897.

Manero, Vicente E. *Apuntes sobre el duelo.* Mexico City: Nichols, 1884.

Marroqui, José María. *La ciudad de México. Contiene: El origen de los nombres de muchas de sus calles y plazas, del de varios establecimientos públicos y privados, y no pocas noticias curiosas y entretenidas.* Mexico City: La Europea, 1900.

Martínez Baca, Francisco. *Los tatuajes: estudio psicológico y médico-legal en delincuentes y militares.* Puebla: Oficina Impresora del Timbre, 1899.

Martínez Baca, Francisco, and Manuel Vergara. *Estudios de Antropología Criminal: Memoria que por disposición del Superior gobierno del Estado de Puebla presentan . . . .* Puebla: Benjamín Lara, 1892.

Martínez de Castro, Antonio. *Código penal para el Distrito Federal y Territorio de la Baja-California sobre delitos del fuero común y para toda la República Mexicana sobre delitos contra la Federación. Edición correcta, sacada de la oficial, precedida de la Exposición de motivos dirigida al Supremo Gobierno por el C. Lic. . . . Presidente de la comisión encargada de formar el Código.* Veracruz and Puebla: La Ilustración, 1891.

Medina y Ormaechea, Antonio A. de, and Carlos A. de Medina y Ormaechea. *Proyecto para el establecimiento del régimen penitenciario en la República Mexicana.* Mexico City: Imprenta del Gobierno, en Palacio, 1881.

Medina y Ormaechea, Antonio A. de. *Las colonias de rateros.* Mexico City: Imprenta del Gobierno en el Ex-Arzobispado, 1895.

———. *México ante los congresos internacionales penitenciarios.* Mexico City: Secretaría de Fomento, 1892.

Mellado, Guillermo. *Belén por dentro y por fuera.* Mexico City: Cuadernos Criminalia, 1959.

Memoria del Ayuntamiento de 1901. 2 vols. Mexico City: La Europea, 1902.

Memoria del Primer Congreso Nacional Penitenciario celebrado en la Ciudad de México del 24 de noviembre al 3 de diciembre de 1932, convocado por la Dirección Antialcohólica. Mexico City: Talleres Gráficos de la Nación, 1935.

Mérigo, Juan. *La banda del automóvil gris y yo!* Mexico City: N.p., 1959.

México y sus alrededores. Guía para los viajeros escrita por un Mexicano. Cuidado con los rateros. Mexico City: Tip. Luis B. Casa, 1895.

Ministerio Público del Distrito y Territorios Federales. *Cuadros estadísticos e informe del Procurador de Justicia concernientes a la criminalidad en el Distrito Federal y territorios.* Mexico City: Ministerio Público del Distrito y Territorios Federales, 1900–1909.

Moheno, Querido. *¿Hacia dónde vamos? Bosquejo de un cuadro de instituciones políticas adecuadas al pueblo mexicano.* Mexico City: I. Lara, 1908.

———. *Mis últimos discursos.* Mexico City: Botas, 1923.

———. *Procesos Célebres: Nidia Camargo. Discurso en defensa de la acusada.* Mexico City: Botas, 1925.

Plano oficial de la Ciudad de México. Edición especial para el Consejo Superior de

Gobierno del Distrito Federal, con motivo de la reunión del X Congreso Geológico Internacional. N.p.: 1906.

Ponce, Fernando. *El Alcoholismo en México.* Mexico City: Antigua Imprenta de Murguía, 1911.

Posada, José Guadalupe. *José Guadalupe Posada: Ilustrador de la vida mexicana.* Mexico City: Fondo Editorial de la Plástica Mexicana, 1963.

Prida, Ramón. *La criminalidad en México.* Mexico City: Soc. Mexicana de Geografía y Estadística, 1933.

Procuraduría General de Justicia del Distrito y Territorios Federales, Sección de Estadística. *Estadística de la penalidad habida en los juzgados del fuero común del Distrito y territorios federales durante los años de 1916 a 1920.* Mexico City: Talleres Gráficos de la Nación, 1923.

Ramírez Plancarte, Francisco. *La ciudad de México durante la revolución constitucionalista.* Mexico City: Botas, 1941.

Ramírez, Román. *Resúmen de medicina legal y ciencias conexas para uso de los estudiantes de las escuelas de derecho.* Mexico City: Tip. de Fomento, 1901.

Ramos Pedrueza, Antonio. *La ley penal en México de 1810 a 1910.* Mexico City: Díaz de León, 1911.

Revueltas, José. *Los muros de agua.* Mexico City: Ediciones Era, 1978.

Rodríguez Miramón, Alonso. *Requisitoria pronunciada por el Agente del Ministerio Público . . . en la vista en jurado de la causa instruida contra Francisco Guerrero (a) Antonio el Chalequero y contra José Montoya, por robos, violaciones, heridas y homicidios perpetrados del año de 1881 a julio de 1888.* Mexico City: Antigua imprenta y librería de Murguía, 1891.

Roumagnac, Carlos. *Los criminales en México: Ensayo de psicología criminal. Seguido de dos casos de hermafrodismo observado por los señores doctores Ricardo Egea . . . Ignacio Ocampo.* Mexico City: Tipografía El Fénix, 1912 [1904].

———. *Crimenes sexuales y pasionales: Estudios de psicología morbosa.* Vol. 1, *Crimenes sexuales,* and vol. 2, *Matadores de mujeres.* Mexico City: Librería de Bouret, 1906, 1910.

———. *Elementos de policía científica: Obra de texto para la Escuela Científica de Policía de México.* Mexico City: Botas, 1923.

———. *La estadística criminal en México.* Mexico City: García Cubas, 1907.

Saldaña, José P. *Crónicas históricas.* 5 vols. Monterrey: N.p., 1982.

Sánchez Santos, Trinidad. *El alcoholismo en la República Mexicana: Discurso pronunciado en la sesión solemne que celebraron las Sociedades Científicas y Literarias de la Nación, el día 5 de junio de 1896 y en el salón de sesiones de la Cámara de Diputados.* Mexico City: Imprenta del Sagrado Corazón de Jesus, 1897.

Secretaría de Justicia, Comisión Revisora del Código Penal. *Trabajos de revisión del Código Penal: Proyecto de reformas y exposición de motivos.* 4 vols. Mexico City: Tip. de la Oficina Impresora de Estampillas, 1912.

Serralde, Francisco. *El crimen de Santa Julia. Defensa gráfica que, sirviéndose de signos físicos encontrados en los cuerpos de las víctimas del crimen, presenta . . . , defensor del coronel Timoteo Andrade.* Mexico City: F. P. Hoeck, 1899.

Sesto, Julio. *México de Porfirio Díaz (hombres y cosas). Estudios sobre el desenvolvimiento general de la República Mexicana. Observaciones hechas en el terreno oficial y en el particular.* 2d ed. Valencia: Sempere y Compañía, 1910.

Sierra, Justo, ed. *México, su evolución social: síntesis de la historia política, de la organización administrativa y militar y del estado económico de la federación mexicana; de sus adelantamientos en el orden intelectual; de su estructura territorial y del desarrollo de su población y de los medios de comunicación nacionales y internacionales; de sus conquistas en el campo industrial, agrícola, minero, mercantil, etc., etc. Inventario monumental que resume en trabajos magistrales los grandes progresos de la nación en el siglo XIX.* 2 vols. Mexico City: Ballescá, 1900.

Smith, Eaton. *Flying Visits to the City of Mexico and the Pacific Coast.* Liverpool: Henry Young and Sons, 1903.

Sodi, Demetrio. *El Jurado en México: Estudios sobre el jurado popular.* Mexico City: Secretaría de Fomento, 1909.

Tablada, José Juan. *La feria de la vida.* Mexico City: Consejo Nacional para la Cultura y las Artes, 1991 [1937].

Tarde, Gabriel. *La philosophie pénale.* Lyon-Paris: A. Stork–G. Masson, 1890.

Teja Zabre, Alfonso. "Exposición de motivos." In *Código penal para el Distrito y Territorios Federales y para toda la República en Materia de Fuero Federal.* Mexico City: Botas, 1938.

Tovar, Antonio. *Código nacional mexicano del duelo.* Mexico City: Imprenta Lit. y Encuadernación de Ireneo Paz, 1891.

Turner, John Kenneth. *Barbarous Mexico.* Chicago: Charles H. Kerr, 1910.

Tweedie, Ethel B. *Mexico as I Saw It.* London: Hurst and Blackett, 1901.

Urueta, Margarita. *Jesús Urueta: la historia de un gran desamor.* Mexico City: Stylo, 1964.

Vasconcelos, José. *La tormenta: Segunda parte del Ulises criollo.* Mexico City: Jus, 1983.

Zayas Enríquez, Rafael de. *Fisiología del crimen: Estudio jurídico-sociológico.* Veracruz: Impr. de Rafael de Zayas, 1885.

SECONDARY SOURCES

Abad de Santillán, Diego. *Diccionario de Argentinismos de Ayer y Hoy.* Buenos Aires: Tipográfica Editora Argentina, 1976.

Adame Goddard, Jorge. *El pensamiento político y social de los católicos mexicanos, 1867–1914.* Mexico City: Universidad Nacional Autónoma de México, 1980.

Aguilar, Gustavo F. *Los presupuestos mexicanos desde los tiempos de la colonia hasta nuestros días.* Mexico City: N.p., 1946.

Aguirre, Carlos. "The Lima Penitentiary and the Modernization of Criminal Justice in Nineteenth-Century Peru." In *The Birth of the Penitentiary in Latin America,* edited by Ricardo Salvatore and Carlos Aguirre. Austin: Texas University Press, 1996.

Alba, Francisco. "Evolución de la Población: Realizaciones y Retos." In *México a fines de siglo,* edited by José Joaquín Blanco and José Woldenberg. Mexico City: Fondo de Cultura Económica, 1993: 1:130–51.

Alonso, Ana María. *Thread of Blood, Colonialism, Revolution, and Gender on Mexico's Northern Frontier.* Tucson: University of Arizona Press, 1995.

Ampudia M., José Enrique. "La penitenciaría de México (1882–1911)." *Boletín de Archivo General de la Nación: La Penitenciaría de México* 5:4 (1981–82): 5–8.

Anderson, Benedict. *Imagined Communities.* New York–London: Verso, 1983.

Anderson, Rodney D. *Outcasts in Their Own Land: Mexican Industrial Workers, 1906–1911.* DeKalb: Northern Illinois University Press, 1976.

Archer, Christon. *El ejército en el México borbónico, 1760–1810.* Mexico City: Fondo de Cultura Económica, 1983.

———. "To Serve the King: Military Recruitment in Late Colonial Mexico." *Hispanic American Historical Review* 55, no. 2 (1975): 226–50.

Armus, Diego. "La ciudad higiénica entre Europa y Latinoamerica." In *Mundialización de la ciencia y cultura nacional,* edited by Antonio Lafuente. Madrid: Doce Calles, 1993.

Arrom, Silvia Marina. *The Women of Mexico City, 1790–1857.* Stanford, CA: Stanford University Press, 1985.

Avila Méndez, Agustín. "Mapa serie barrios de la ciudad de México 1811 y 1882." In Alejandra Moreno Toscano et al., *Investigaciones sobre la historia de la ciudad de México (I).* Mexico City: INAH, 1974: 155–81.

Azaola Garrido, Elena. *La institución correccional en México: Una mirada extraviada.* Mexico City: Siglo Veintiuno, 1990.

Azaola Garrido, Elena, and Cristina José Yacamán. *Las mujeres olvidadas: Un estudio sobre la situación actual de las cárceles de mujeres en la República Mexicana.* Mexico City: El Colegio de México, 1996.

Baratta, Alessandro. *Criminología crítica y crítica del derecho penal,* translated by Alvaro Búnster. Mexico City: Siglo Veintiuno, 1986.

Barrera Bassols, Jacinto. *El caso Villavicencio: Violencia y poder en el porfiriato.* Mexico City: Alfaguara, 1997.

Bartra, Armando. *El México bárbaro: Plantaciones y monterías del sureste durante el porfiriato.* Mexico City: El Atajo Ediciones, 1996.

Bataillon, Claude, "México, ciudad mestiza." *Ciencias Políticas* 35:1 (1964): 161–84.

Bátiz, José A. *Historia del papel moneda en México.* Mexico City: Banamex, 1984.

Beattie, J. M. *Crime and the Courts in England, 1660–1800.* Princeton, NJ: Princeton University Press, 1986.

Becker, Howard S. *Outsiders: Studies in the Sociology of Deviance.* New York: Free Press, 1963.

Beezley, William H. *Judas at the Jockey Club and Other Episodes of Porfirian Mexico.* Lincoln: University of Nebraska Press, 1987.

———. "The Porfirian Smart Set Anticipates Thorstein Veblen in Guadalajara." In *Rituals of Rule, Rituals of Resistance: Public Celebrations and Popular Culture in Mexico,* edited by William H. Beezley et al. Wilmington, DE: Scholarly Resources, 1994.

Beezley, William H., Cheryl English Martin, and William E. French, eds. *Rituals of Rule, Rituals of Resistance.* Wilmington, DE: Scholarly Resources, 1994.

Beltrán, Ira, and Pablo Piccato. "Crimen en el siglo XX: Fragmentos de análisis sobre la evidencia cuantitativa." In *Ciudad de México: Los últimos cien años, los próximos cien años,* edited by Ariel Rodriguez Kuri and Sergio Tamayo. Mexico City: UAM, 2001.

Bernaldo de Quirós, Constancio. *El bandolerismo en España y en México.* Mexico City: Editorial Jurídica Mexicana, 1959.

———. *Modern Theories of Criminality.* Boston: Little, Brown and Company, 1912.

Blackbourn, David, and Geoff Eley. *The Peculiarities of German History: Bourgeois Society and Politics in Nineteenth-Century Germany.* Oxford: Oxford University Press, 1984.

Boletín del Archivo General de la Nación: La Penitenciaría de México. 5:4 (October 1981–March 1982).

Borges, Dain. "'Puffy, Ugly, Slothful and Inert': Degeneration in Brazilian Social Thought, 1880–1940." *Journal of Latin American Studies* 23 (1993): 235–56.

Borges, Jorge Luis. *Evaristo Carriego.* In *Obras Completas: 1923–1949*. Barcelona: Emecé Editores, 1989 [1930].

———. *Obra poética.* Madrid: Alianza, 1972.

Boschi, Daniele. "Homicide and Knife Fighting in Rome, 1845–1914." In *Men and Violence: Gender, Honor, and Rituals in Modern Europe and America,* edited by Pieter Spierenburg. Columbus: Ohio University Press, 1998.

Bourdieu, Pierre. *Outline of a Theory of Practice.* Trans. Richard Nice. Cambridge, UK: Cambridge University Press, 1998.

Braithwaite, John. *Crime, Shame and Reintegration.* New York: Cambridge University Press, 1989.

———. "Shame and Modernity." *The British Journal of Criminology* 33:1 (Winter 1993): 1–18.

Brown, Jonathan C. "Foreign and Native-Born Workers in Porfirian Mexico." *American Historical Review* 98:3 (June 1993): 786–818.

———. *Oil and Revolution in Mexico.* Berkeley: University of California Press, 1993.

Brunk, Samuel. " 'The Sad Situation of Civilians and Soldiers': The Banditry of Zapatismo in the Mexican Revolution." *American Historical Review* 101:2 (April 1996): 331–54.

Buffington, Robert. *Criminal and Citizen in Modern Mexico.* Lincoln: University of Nebraska Press, 1999.

———. "Forging the Fatherland: Criminality and Citizenship in Modern Mexico." Ph.D. dissertation, University of Arizona, 1994.

Buffington, Robert, and Pablo Piccato. "Tales of Two Women: The Narrative Construal of Porfirian Reality." *The Americas* 55:3 (January 1999): 391–424.

Caimari, Lila. "Psychiatrists, Criminals, and Bureaucrats: The Production of Scientific Biographies in the Argentine Penitentiary System (1907–1945)." In *Argentina on the Couch,* edited by Mariano Plotkin. Albuquerque: New Mexico University Press, forthcoming.

Camarena, Mario. "El tranvía en época de cambio." *Historias* 27 (October–March 1992): 141–46.

Cano, Gabriela. "*Soldaderas* and *Coronelas.*" In *Encyclopedia of Mexico: History, Society and Culture,* edited by Michael S. Werner, 2:1357–60. Chicago: Fitzroy Dearborn Publishers, 1997.

Carrancá y Rivas, Raúl. *Derecho penitenciario: Cárceles y penas en México.* Mexico City: Porrúa, 1896.

Castillo, Alberto del. "Entre la moralización y el sensacionalismo: Prensa, poder y criminalidad a finales del siglo XIX en la Ciudad de México." In *Hábitos, Normas y Escándalo: Prensa, criminalidad y drogas durante el porfiriato tardío,* edited by Ricardo Pérez Montfort. Mexico City: Ciesas-Plaza y Valdés, 1997.

Castro Leal, Antonio. "Introducción." In *La novela de la Revolución Mexicana,* vol. 1, edited by Antonio Castro Leal. México: Aguilar–Secretaría de Educación Pública, 1988.

Caulfield, Sueann. *In Defense of Honor: Sexual Morality, Modernity, and Nation in Early-Twentieth-Century Brazil.* Durham, NC: Duke University Press, 2000.

Ceballos, Manuel. *El Catolicismo social: Un tercero en discordia. Rerum Novarum, la "cuestión social" y la movilización de los católicos mexicanos (1891–1911).* Mexico City: El Colegio de México, 1991.

Certeau, Michel de. *The Practice of Everyday Life.* Translated by Steven Rendall. Berkeley: University of California Press, 1984.

Chasteen, John Charles. "Violence for Show: Knife Duelling on a Nineteenth-Century Cattle Frontier." In *The Problem of Order in Changing Societies: Essays on Crime and Policing in Argentina and Uruguay, 1750–1940,* edited by Lyman L. Johnson. Albuquerque: University of New Mexico Press, 1990.

Clark, Anna. *Women's Silence, Men's Violence: Sexual Assault in England 1770–1845.* London: Pandora, 1987.

Coatsworth, John H. *Los orígenes del atraso: Nueve ensayos de historia económica de México en los siglos XVIII y XIX.* Mexico City: Alianza Editorial, 1990.

Cohen, Albert K. *Delinquent Boys: The Culture of the Gang.* New York: Free Press, 1955.

Cohen, Albert K., and James F. Short Jr. "Research in Delinquent Subcultures." *Journal of Social Issues* 14:3 (1958): 20–37.

Colín Sánchez, Guillermo. *Así habla la delincuencia y otros más . . . .* Mexico City: Porrúa, 1991.

Cordova, Arnaldo. *La ideología de la Revolución Mexicana. La formación del nuevo régimen.* Mexico City: ERA, 1973.

Cosío Villegas, Daniel. *Historia moderna de México.* Vol. 8, *El porfiriato: Vida política interior.* Mexico City: Hermes, 1972.

Cruz Barrera, Nydia E. "El despliege del castigo: Las penitenciarías porfirianas en México." Manuscript.

Darnton, Robert. *The Great Cat Massacre and Other Episodes in French Cultural History.* New York: Vintage Books, 1984.

Dávalos, Marcela. "La salud, el agua y los habitantes de la ciudad de México. Fines del siglo XVIII y principios del XIX." In *La ciudad de México en la primera mitad del siglo XIX,* edited by Regina Hernández Franyuti. Mexico City: Instituto Mora, 1994.

Davies, Keith A. "Tendencias demográficas urbanas durante el siglo XIX en México." *Historia Mexicana* 21:3 (January–March 1972): 481–524.

Deans-Smith, Susan. "The Working Poor and the Eighteenth-Century Colonial State: Gender, Public Order, and Work Discipline." In *Rituals of Rule, Rituals of Resistance,* edited by William H. Beezley, Cheryl English Eartin, and William E. French. Wilmington, DE: Scholarly Resources, 1994.

de la Barreda Solórzano, Luis. *Justicia pena y derechos humanos.* Mexico City: Porrúa: 1997.

Delgado, Itzel. "Prostitución, sífilis y moralidad sexual in la ciudad de México a fines del siglo XIX." B.A. thesis, Escuela Nacional de Antropología e Historia, 1993.

del Olmo, Rosa. *América Latina y su criminología.* Mexico City: Siglo Veintiuno, 1981.

de los Reyes, Aurelio. *Medio siglo de cine mexicano: 1896–1847.* Mexico City: Trillas, 1988.

Díaz, María Elena. "The Satiric Penny Press for Workers in Mexico, 1900–1910: A Case Study in the Politicization of Popular Culture." *Journal of Latin American Studies* 22 (1990): 497–520.

Díaz y de Ovando, Clementina. "La Ciudad de México en el amanecer del siglo XX (inauguración de la Penitenciaría)." In *Lecumberri: un palacio lleno de historia.* Mexico City: Secretaría de Gobernación, 1994.

Diego-Fernández, Salvador. *La ciudad de Méjico a fines del siglo XIX.* Mexico City: N.p., 1937.

Dirks, Nicholas B., Geoff Eley, and Sherry B. Ortner. "Introduction." In *Culture/Power/History: A Reader in Contemporary Social Theory,* edited by Nicholas B. Dirks, Geoff Eley, and Sherry B. Ortner. Princeton, NJ: Princeton University Press, 1994.

Di Tella, Torcuato. "The Dangerous Classes in Early Nineteenth Century Mexico." *Journal of Latin American Studies* 5 (1973): 79–105.

Eckstein, Susan. *The Poverty of Revolution: The State and the Urban Poor in Mexico.* Princeton, N.J.: Princeton University Press, 1977.

Eguiarte Sakar, Estela. "Los jardines en México y la idea de la ciudad decimonónica." *Historias* 27 (October–March 1992): 129–38.

Emsley, Clive. *Crime and Society in England, 1750–1900.* 2d ed. London: Longman, 1996.

Erikson, Kai T. "Notes on the Sociology of Deviance." *Social Problems* 9:4 (Spring 1962): 307–14.

———. *Wayward Puritans: A Study in the Sociology of Deviance.* New York: John Wiley, 1966.

Estadísticas históricas de México. Mexico City: INEGI, 1994.

Estadísticas sociales del porfiriato, 1877–1910. Mexico City: Dirección General de Estadística, 1956.

Fagan, Jeffrey. "Intoxication and Aggression." In *Drugs and Crime,* edited by Michael Tonry and James Q. Wilson. Chicago: University of Chicago Press, 1990.

Farriss, Nancy. *Maya Society under Colonial Rule: The Collective Enterprise of Survival.* Princeton, NJ: Princeton University Press, 1992.

Fausto, Boris. *Crime e cotidiano: a criminalidade em Sao Paulo, 1880–1924.* Sao Paulo, Brazil: Brasiliense, 1984.

Foucault, Michel. *La arqueología del saber.* Mexico City: Siglo Veintiuno, 1979.

———. *Discipline and Punish: The Birth of the Prison.* Translated by Alan Sheridan. New York: Vintage, 1979.

———. *The Order of Things: An Archeology of Human Sciences.* New York: Pantheon Books, 1971.

———. "Politics and the Study of Discourse." In *The Foucault Effect: Studies in Governmentality with Two Lectures and Interview with Michel Foucault,* edited by Graham Burchell, Colin Gordon, and Peter Miller. Chicago: University of Chicago Press, 1991.

Franco, Jean. *Plotting Women: Gender and Representation in Mexico.* New York: Columbia University Press, 1988.

Francois, Marie Eileen. "When Pawnshops Talk: Popular Credit and Material Culture in Mexico City, 1775–1916." Ph.D. dissertation, University of Arizona, 1998.

Frayling, Christopher. "The House that Jack Built: Some Stereotypes of the Rapist in the History of Popular Culture." In *Rape,* edited by Sylvana Tomaselli and Roy Porter. Oxford: Basil Blackwell, 1986.

French, William E. *A Peaceful and Working People: Manners, Morals and Class Formation in Northern Mexico.* Albuquerque: University of Mexico Press, 1996.

———. "Peaceful and Working People: The Inculcation of the Capitalist Work Ethic in a Mexican Mining District (Hidalgo del Parral, Chihuahua, 1880–1920)." Ph.D. Dissertation, University of Texas at Austin, 1990.

———. "*Progreso Forzado:* Workers and the Inculcation of the Capitalist Work Ethic in the Parral Mining District." In *Rituals of Rule, Rituals of Resistance: Public Celebrations and Popular Culture in Mexico,* edited by William H. Beezley et al., 191–212. Wilmington, DE: Scholarly Resources, 1994.

Friederich, Paul. *Agrarian Revolt in a Mexican Village.* Englewood Cliffs, NJ: Prentice Hall, 1970.

García Barragán, Elisa. "El Palacio de Lecumberri y su contexto arquitectónico." In *Lecumberri: Un palacio lleno de historia*. Mexico City: Secretaría de Governación, 1994.

García Ramírez, Sergio. *El final de Lecumberri: Reflexiones sobre la prisión*. Mexico City: Porrua, 1979.

———. "Introducción." In Carmen Castañeda García, *Prevención y readaptación social en México (1926–1979)*. Mexico City: Instituto Nacional de Ciencias Penales, 1979.

———. "Pena y prisión: Los tiempos de Lecumberri." In *Lecumberri: Un palacio lleno de historia*. Mexico City: Secretaría de Gobernación, 1994.

Garland, David. "Of Crimes and Criminals: The Development of Criminology in Britain." In *The Oxford Handbook of Criminology*, edited by Mike Maguire, Rod Morgan, and Robert Reiner. New York: Clarendon Press, 1994.

———. *Punishment and Modern Society: A Study in Social Theory*. Chicago: University of Chicago Press, 1990.

———. *Punishment and Welfare: A History of Penal Strategies*. Aldershot, Hants, UK: Gower Publishing Company, 1985.

Garner, Richard L. *Economic Growth and Change in Bourbon Mexico*. Gainesville: University Press of Florida, 1993.

Gatrell, V. A. C. "The Decline of Theft and Violence in Victorian and Edwardian England." In *Crime and the Law: The Social History of Crime in Western Europe since 1500*, edited by V. A. C. Gatrell, Bruce Lenman, and Geoffrey Parker. London: Europa Publications, 1980.

Gay, Peter. *The Cultivation of Hatred: The Bourgeois Experience, Victoria to Freud*. New York: Norton, 1993.

Gerdts, Daniel. *Paper protection: Human rights violations and the Mexican criminal justice system. A report of the Minnesota Lawyers International Human Rights Committee*. Minneapolis, MN: The Committee, 1990.

Gibson, Charles. *The Aztecs under Spanish Rule: A History of the Indians of the Valley of Mexico, 1519–1810*. Stanford, CA: Stanford University Press, 1964.

Gilmore, David. "Introduction: The Shame of Dishonor." In *Honor and Shame and the Unity of the Mediterranean*, edited by David Gilmore.

———. *Manhood in the Making: Cultural Concepts of Masculinity*. New Haven, CT: Yale University Press, 1990.

González de la Rocha, Mercedes. *The Resources of Poverty: Women and Survival in a Mexican City*. Cambridge, UK: Blackwell, 1994.

González Navarro, Moisés. *Historia Moderna de México*. Vol. 4, *El Porfiriato: La vida social*. Mexico City: Hermes, 1957.

———. *La pobreza en México*. Mexico City: El Colegio de México, 1995.

Greenberg, James. *Blood Ties: Life and Violence in Rural Mexico.* Tucson: University of Arizona Press, 1989.

Greenberg, Kenneth S. *Honor and Slavery: Lies, Duels, Noses, Masks, Dressing as a Woman, Gifts, Strangers, Death, Humanitarianism, Slave Rebellions, The Pro-Slavery Argument, Baseball, Hunting, and Gambling in the Old South.* Princeton, NJ: Princeton University Press, 1996.

Gruzinski, Serge. *La colonización de lo imaginario: Sociedades indígenas y occidentalización en el México español, siglos XVI–XVIII.* Mexico City: Fondo de Cultura Económica, 1991.

Guedea, Virginia. "México en 1812: Control político y bebidas prohibidas." *Estudios de historia moderna y contemporánea de México* 8 (1980): 23–64.

Guerra, François-Xavier. *México: Del Antiguo Régimen a la Revolución.* Mexico City: Fondo de Cultura Económica, 1988.

Guerrero Guerrero, Raúl. *El pulque.* Mexico City: Joaquín Mortiz, 1986.

Gutmann, Matthew C. "Los hijos de Lewis: la sensibilidad antropológica y el caso de los pobres machos." *Alteridades* 4:7 (1994): 9–19.

———. *The Meaning of Macho: Being a Man in Mexico City.* Los Angeles: University of California Press, 1996.

Guy, Donna. *Sex and Danger in Buenos Aires: Prostitution, Family, and Nation in Argentina.* Lincoln: University of Nebraska Press, 1991.

Haag, Pamela. "The 'Ill-Use of a Wife': Patterns of Working-Class Violence in Domestic and Public New York City, 1860–1880." *Journal of Social History* 25:3 (1992): 447–77.

Haber, Stephen. *Industria y subdesarrollo: La industrialización de México, 1890–1940.* Mexico City: Alianza Editorial, 1992.

Habermas, Jürgen. *Ciencia y técnica como "ideología."* Mexico City: Rei, 1993.

———. *The Structural Transformation of the Public Sphere: An Inquiry into a Category of Bourgeois Society,* trans. Thomas Burger. Cambridge, MA: MIT Press, 1991.

Hale, Charles A. *The Transformation of Liberalism in Late Nineteenth-Century Mexico.* Princeton, NJ: Princeton University Press, 1989.

Harris, Ruth. "Melodrama, Hysteria and Feminine Crimes of Passion in the Fin-de-Siècle." *History Workshop* 25 (Spring 1988): 31–63.

Hart, John Mason. *Anarchism and the Mexican Working Class, 1860–1931.* Austin: University of Texas Press, 1978.

Haslip, Gabriel J. *Crime and Punishment in Late Colonial Mexico City, 1692–1810.* Albuquerque: University of New Mexico Press, 1999.

Hay, Douglas. "Property, Authority and the Criminal Law." In *Albion's Fatal Tree: Crime and Society in Eighteenth-Century England,* edited by Douglas Hay et al. New York: Pantheon Books, 1975.

Hayner, Norman S. "Criminogenic zones in Mexico City." *American Sociological Review* 11:4 (August 1946): 428–38.

Herzfeld, Michael. "'As in Your Own House': Hospitality, Ethnography, and the Stereotype of Mediterranean Society." In *Honor and Shame and the Unity of the Mediterranean,* edited by David Gilmore. Washington: American Anthropological Association, 1987.

Hirst, John. "The Australian Experience: The Convict Colony." In *The Oxford History of the Prison. The Practice of Punishment in Western Society,* edited by Norval Morris and David J. Rothman. New York: Oxford University Press, 1995.

Hoberman, Louisa Schell, and Susan Migden Socolow, eds. *Cities and Society in Colonial Latin America.* Albuquerque: University of New Mexico Press, 1986.

Hobsbawm, Eric. *Primitive Rebels: Studies in Archaic Forms of Social Movement in the 19th and 20th Centuries.* New York: Norton, 1959.

Holloway, Thomas. *Policing Rio de Janeiro.* Stanford, CA: Stanford University Press, 1993.

Hunt, Lynn. *The New Cultural History.* Berkeley: University of California Press, 1989.

Ignatieff, Michael. *A Just Measure of Pain: The Penitentiary in the Industrial Revolution.* London: Penguin, 1978.

Illades, Carlos. *Hacia la república del trabajo. La organización artesanal en la ciudad de México, 1853–1876.* Mexico City: El Colegio de México–Universidad Autónoma Metropolitana, 1996.

Instituto de Investigaciones Jurídicas. *Diccionario jurídico mexicano.* Mexico City: Porrúa-UNAM, 1987.

International Encyclopedia of the Social Sciences, edited by David L. Sills. New York: Macmillan, 1968.

Jiménez Muñoz, Jorge H. *La traza del poder: Historia de la política y los negocios urbanos en el Distrito Federal desde sus orígenes a la desaparición del Ayuntamiento (1824–1928).* Mexico City: Codex, 1993.

Johns, Michael. *The City of Mexico in the Age of Díaz.* Austin: University of Texas Press, 1997.

Johnson, Eric A. "The Crime Rate: Longitudinal and Periodic Trends in Nineteenth- and Twentieth-Century German Criminality, from Vormärz to Late Weimar." In *The German Underworld: Deviants and Outcasts in German History,* edited by Richard J. Evans. New York: Routledge, 1988.

———. *Urbanization and Crime: Germany 1871–1914.* New York: Cambridge University Press, 1995.

Johnson, Eric A., and Eric H. Monkkonen, eds. *The Civilization of Crime:*

Violence in Town and Country since the Middle Ages. Urbana: University of Illinois Press, 1996.

Johnson, Lyman L. "Changing Arrest Patterns in Three Argentine Cities: Buenos Aires, Santa Fe, and Tucumán, 1900–1930." In *The Problem of Order in Changing Societies: Essays on Crime and Policing in Argentina and Uruguay, 1750–1940,* edited by Lyman L. Johnson. Albuquerque: University of New Mexico Press, 1990.

———. "Dangerous Words, Provocative Gestures, and Violent Acts: The Disputed Hierarchies of Plebeian Life in Colonial Buenos Aires." In *The Faces of Honor: Sex, Shame, and Violence in Colonial Latin America.* Edited by Lyman L. Johnson and Sonya Lipsett-Rivera. Albuquerque: University of New Mexico Press, 1998.

Johnson, Lyman L., ed. *The Problem of Order in Changing Societies: Essays in Crime and Policing in Argentina and Uruguay, 1750–1919.* Albuquerque: University of New Mexico Press, 1990.

Johnson, Lyman L., and Sonya Lipsett-Rivera, eds. *The Faces of Honor: Sex, Shame, and Violence in Colonial Latin America.* Albuquerque: University of New Mexico Press, 1998.

Jones, Gareth Stedman. "The Determinist Fix: Some Obstacles to the Further Development of the Linguisic Approach to History in the 1990s." *History Workshop Journal* 46 (1996): 19–35.

Joseph, Gilbert M. "On the Trail of Latin American Bandits: A Reexamination of Peasant Resistance." In *Patterns of Contention in Mexican History,* edited by Jaime E. Rodríguez. Irvine: University of California Press, 1992.

Joseph, Gilbert M., and Daniel Nugent, eds. *Everyday Forms of State Formation: Revolution and the Negotiation of Rule in Modern Mexico.* Durham, NC: Duke University Press, 1994.

Knight, Alan. *The Mexican Revolution.* Lincoln: University of Nebraska Press, 1990.

———. "Racism, Revolution and Indigenismo: Mexico, 1910–1940." In *The Idea of Race in Latin America, 1870–1940,* edited by Richard Graham. Austin: University of Texas Press, 1990.

———. "Revolutionary Project, Recalcitrant People: Mexico, 1910–40." In *The Revolutionary Process in Mexico: Essays on Political and Social Change, 1880–1940,* edited by Jaime O. Rodríguez. Irvine: University of California Press, 1990.

———. "Weapons and Arches in the Mexican Revolutionary Landscape." In *Everyday Forms of State Formation: Revolution and the Negotiation of Rule in*

Modern Mexico, edited by Gilbert Joseph and Daniel Nugent. Durham, NC: Duke University Press, 1994.

———. "The Working Class and the Mexican Revolution: c. 1900–1920." *Journal of Latin American Studies* 16 (1984): 51–79.

Lau, Ana, and Carmen Ramos, eds. *Mujeres y Revolución, 1900–1917.* Mexico City: Instituto Nacional de Estudios Históricos de la Revolución Mexicana, 1993.

Lauderdale-Graham, Sandra. *House and Street: The Domestic World of Servants and Masters in Nineteenth-Century Rio de Janeiro.* Austin: University of Texas Press, 1992.

Leal, Juan Felipe and Mario Huacuja Rountree. *Economía y sistema de haciendas en México: La hacienda pulquera en el cambio: Siglos XVIII, XIX y XX.* Mexico City: Ediciones Era, 1982.

Lear, John Robert. "Mexico City: Space and Class in the Porfirian Capital, 1884–1910." *Journal of Urban History* 22:4 (May 1996): 444–92.

———. "Workers, *Vecinos* and Citizens: The Revolution in Mexico City, 1909–1917." Ph.D. dissertation, University of California at Berkeley, 1993.

Lenman, Bruce, and Geoffrey Parker. "The State, the Community, and the Criminal Law in Early Modern Europe." In *Crime and the Law: The Social History of Crime in Western Europe since 1500,* edited by V.A.C. Gatrell, Bruce Lenman, and Geoffrey Parker. London: Europa Publications, 1980.

Leps, Marie-Christine. *Apprehending the Criminal: The Production of Deviance in Nineteenth-Century Discourse.* Durham, NC: Duke University Press, 1992.

Levi, Michael. "Violent Crime." In *The Oxford Handbook of Criminology,* edited by Mike Maguire, Rod Morgan, and Robert Reiner. Oxford: Clarendon Press, 1994.

Lewis, Oscar. *Anthropological Essays.* New York: Random House, 1970.

———. *The Children of Sánchez: Autobiography of a Mexican Family.* New York: Random House, 1961.

Lira, Andrés. *Comunidades indígenas frente a la ciudad de México: Tenochtitlan y Tlatelolco, sus pueblos y barrios, 1812–1919.* Mexico City: El Colegio de México, 1995.

Linebaugh, Peter. *The London Hanged: Crime and Civil Society in the Eighteenth Century.* Cambridge, UK: Cambridge University Press, 1992.

Lomnitz, Larissa A. *Cómo sobreviven los marginados.* Mexico City: Siglo Veintiuno, 1975.

Lomnitz, Larissa A., and Marisol Pérez Lizaur. *Una familia de la élite mexicana: Parentesco, clase y cultura 1820–1980.* Mexico City: Alianza, 1993.

Lozano Armendares, Teresa. *La criminalidad en la ciudad de México: 1800–1821.* Mexico City: Universidad Nacional Autónoma de México, 1987.

Lüdtke, Alf. "Introduction: What Is the History of Everyday Life and Who Are Its Practitioners?" In *The History of Everyday Life: Reconstructing Historical Experiences and Ways of Life,* edited by Alf Lüdtke, translated by William Templer. Princeton, NJ: Princeton University Press, 1995.

Mac Gregor Campuzano, Javier. "Historiografía sobre criminalidad y sistema penitenciario." *Secuencia: Revista de historia y ciencias sociales* 22 (1992): 221–57.

MacLachlan, Colin. *La justicia criminal del Siglo XVIII en México: Un estudio sobre el Tribunal de la Acordada.* Mexico City: SepSetentas, 1976.

Madrid Muliá, Hector. "La política contra la delincuencia en el periodo del general Lázaro Cárdenas (1934–1940)." *Revista mexicana de justicia* 3:9 (July–September 1991): 83–101.

Maguire, Mike, Rod Morgan, and Robert Reiner, eds. *The Oxford Handbook of Criminology.* New York: Clarendon Press, 1994.

Mallon, Florencia. *The Defense of Community in Peru's Central Highlands: Peasant Struggle and Capitalist Transition, 1860–1940.* Princeton, NJ: Princeton University Press, 1983.

Marco del Pont, Luis. *Grandes corrientes de la criminología: Los delitos de cuello blanco (o de los poderosos).* Córdoba, Argentina: Editorial Dimas, 1984.

Matute, Alvaro. "Salud, familia y moral social (1917–1920)." *Históricas* 31 (1991): 25–34.

McCreery, James. "'This Life of Misery and Shame': Female Prostitution in Guatemala City, 1880–1920." *Journal of Latin American Studies* 18 (November 1986): 333–53.

Melossi, Dario, and Massimo Pavarini. *Cárcel y fábrica: Los orígenes del sistema penitenciario (siglos XVI–XIX).* Mexico City: Siglo Veintiuno, 1980.

Menéndez, Eduardo. *Morir de alcohol: saber y hegemonía médica.* Mexico City: Alianza-CNCA, 1990.

Meyer, Jean. "La ciudad de México, ex de los palacios." In *La reconstrucción económica,* vol. 10 of *Historia de la Revolución Mexicana.* Mexico City: El Colegio de México, 1977.

Monkkonen, Eric H. *The Dangerous Class: Crime and Poverty in Columbus, Ohio, 1860–1885.* Cambridge, MA: Harvard University Press, 1975.

Morales, María Dolores. "La expansión de la ciudad de México en el siglo XIX: el caso de los fraccionamientos." In *Investigaciones sobre la historia de la ciudad de México,* edited by Alejandra Moreno Toscano et al. Mexico City: INAH, 1974.

Morgan, Tony. "Proletarians, Politicos, and Patriarchs: The Use and Abuse of Cultural Customs in Early Industrialization of Mexico City, 1880–1910." In *Rituals of Rule, Rituals of Resistance: Public Celebrations and Popular Culture in Mexico,* edited by William H. Beezley et al. Wilmington, DE: Scholarly Resources, 1994.

Muir, Edward, and Guido Ruggiero. "Introduction: The Crime of History." In *History from Crime,* edited by Muir and Ruggiero. Baltimore: John Hopkins University Press, 1994.

Nacif Mina, Jorge. "Policía y seguridad pública en la ciudad de México, 1770–1848." In *La ciudad de México en la primera mitad del siglo XIX,* edited by Regina Hernández Franyuti. Mexico City: Instituto Mora, 1994.

Nacional Financiera. *50 años de Revolución Mexicana en cifras.* Mexico City: Cultura, 1963.

Nye, Robert A. *Crime, Madness, and Politics in Modern France: The Medical Concept of National Decline.* Princeton, NJ: Princeton University Press, 1984.

———. *Masculinity and Male Codes of Honor in Modern France.* New York: Oxford University Press, 1993.

Pacheco, José Emilio. "Nota preliminar." In *Diario de Federico Gamboa, 1892–1939.* Mexico City: Siglo Veintiuno, 1977.

Padilla Arroyo, Antonio. "Criminalidad, cárceles y sistema penitenciario en México, 1876–1910." Ph.D. dissertation, El Colegio de México, 1995.

Pani, Alberto J. *La higiene en México.* Mexico City: Ballescá, 1916.

Parma Cook, Alexandra, and Noble David Cook. *Good Faith and Truthful Ignorance: A Case of Transatlantic Bigamy.* Durham, NC: Duke University Press, 1991.

Piccato, Pablo. "El chalequero, or 'The Mexican Jack the Ripper': The Meanings of Sexual Violence in Turn-of-the-Century Mexico City." *Hispanic American Historical Review* 81, nos. 3–4 (2001).

———. "El parlamentarismo desde la Cámara de Diputados, 1912–1921: Entre la opinión pública y los grupos de choque." In *El Poder Legislativo en las Décadas Revolucionarias,* edited by Pablo Piccato. Mexico City: Instituto Nacional de Estudios Históricos de la Revolución Mexicana, 1997.

———. " 'El Paso de Venus por el disco del Sol': Criminality and Alcoholism in the Late Porfiriato." *Mexican Studies/Estudios Mexicanos* 11:2 (Summer 1995): 203–41.

———. "Politics and the Technology of Honor: Dueling in Turn-of-the-Century Mexico." *Journal of Social History* 33, no. 2 (Winter 1999): 331–54.

Pick, Daniel. "The Faces of Anarchy: Lombroso and the Politics of Criminal Science in Post-Unification Italy." *History Workshop* 23 (Spring 1986): 61–85.

Pina, Rafael de, and Rafael de Pina Vara. *Diccionario de derecho.* 12th ed. Mexico City: Porrúa, 1983.

Pitt-Rivers, Julian A. "Honor." In *International Encyclopedia of the Social Sciences,* edited by David L. Sills. New York: Macmillan, 1968.

———. "Honour and Social Status." In *Honour and Shame: The Values of Mediterranean Society,* edited by Jean Peristiany. London: Weidenfeld and Nicolson, 1965.

Porte Petit Candaudap, Celestino. *Apuntamientos de la parte general de derecho penal.* Mexico City: Porrúa, 1991.

Quiroz Cuarón, Alfonso. *La Criminalidad en la República Mexicana.* Mexico City: UNAM, 1958.

Quiroz Cuarón, Alfonso, et al. *Tendencia y ritmo de la criminalidad en México.* Mexico City: Instituto de Investigaciones Estadísticas, 1939.

Rago, Margareth. *Os Prazeres da Noite: Prostituição e Codigos da Sexualidade Feminina em São Paulo, 1890–1930.* Rio de Janeiro: Paz e Terra, 1991.

Real Academia Española. *Diccionario de autoridades.* Reprint. Madrid: Gredos, 1963 [1737].

———. *Diccionario de la lengua española.* 21st ed. Madrid: Real Academia Española, 1992.

Reddy, William M. *The Invisible Code: Honor and Sentiment in Postrevolutionary France, 1814–1848.* Berkeley: University of California Press, 1997.

———. *The Rise of Market Culture: The Textile Trade and French Society, 1750–1900.* Cambridge, UK: Cambridge University Press, 1984.

Reyes Domínguez, Guadalupe, and Ana Rosas Mantecón. *Los usos de la identidad barrial: una mirada antropológica a la lucha por la vivienda: Tepito 1970–1984.* Mexico City: Universidad Autónoma Metropolitana, Unidad Iztapalapa, 1993.

Riguzzi, Paolo. "México próspero: las dimensiones de la imagen nacional en el porfiriato." *Historias* 20 (April–September 1988): 137–57.

Rivera Garza, Cristina. "The Masters of the Streets: Bodies, Power and Modernity in Mexico, 1867–1930." Ph.D. dissertation, University of Houston, 1995.

Roberts, Brian. *Cities of Peasants: The Political Economy of Urbanization in the Third World.* London: Sage, 1978.

Rodríguez, Juan María. *El duelo Estudio Filosófico moral por. . . .* Mexico City: Tipografía Mexicana, 1869.

Rodríguez, Julia. "Encoding the Criminal: Criminology and the Science of 'Social Defense' in Modernizing Argentina (1880–1921)." Ph.D. dissertation, Columbia University, 1999.

Rodríguez, Miguel. *Los tranviarios y el anarquismo en México (1920–1925).* Puebla: Universidad Autónoma de Puebla, 1980.

Rodríguez Kuri, Ariel. "Desabasto, hambre y respuesta política, 1915." In

Instituciones y ciudad: Ocho estudios históricos sobre la ciudad de México. Mexico City: FP-Sones-Uníos, 2000.

———. *La experiencia olvidada. El ayuntamiento de México: política y administración, 1876–1912.* Mexico City: El Colegio de México, 1996.

Rodríguez Piña, Jaime. "Las vecindades en 1811: Tipología." In Alejandra Moreno Toscano et al., *Investigaciones sobre la historia de la ciudad de México (II).* Mexico City: INAH, 1976.

Rogers, John D. "Theories of Crime and Development: An Historical Perspective." *The Journal of Development Studies* 25:3 (April 1989): 312–28.

Rohlfes, Laurence John. "Police and Penal Correction in Mexico City, 1876–1911: A Study of Order and Progress in Porfirian Mexico." Ph.D. dissertation, Tulane University, 1983.

Rosenthal, Anton. "The Arrival of the Electric Streetcar and the Conflict over Progress in Early Twentieth-Century Montevideo." *Journal of Latin American Studies* 27 (1995): 319–41.

Rosenzweig, Fernando. "El desarrollo económico de México de 1877 a 1911." *Secuencia* 12 (September–December 1988): 151–90.

Rothman, David J. *The Discovery of the Asylum: Social Order and Disorder in the New Republic.* Boston: Little, Brown and Company, 1971.

Rueda Smithers, Salvador. *El diablo de Semana Santa: El discurso político y el orden social en la ciudad de México en 1850.* Mexico City: INAH, 1991.

Ruggiero, Kristin. "Honor, Maternity, and the Disciplining of Women: Infanticide in Late Nineteenth-Century Buenos Aires." *Hispanic American Historical Review* 72:3 (1992): 353–73.

———. "Wives on 'Deposit': Internment and the Preservation of Husband's Honor in Late Nineteenth-Century Buenos Aires." *Journal of Family History* 17:3 (1992): 253–70.

Ruiz Harrell, Rafael. *Criminalidad y mal gobierno.* Mexico City: Sansores y Aljure, 1998.

Saborit, Antonio. "Nueve semanas en otro lugar: el viaje a México de Stephen Crane." *Historias* 6 (April–July 1984): 3–17.

Salvatore, Ricardo, and Carlos Aguirre. "The Birth of the Penitentiary in Latin America: Towards an Interpretive Social History of Prisons." In *The Birth of the Penitentiary in Latin America,* edited by Salvatore and Aguirre. Austin: Texas University Press, 1996.

Salvatore, Ricardo, and Carlos Aguirre, eds. *The Birth of the Penitentiary in Latin America.* Austin: Texas University Press, 1996.

Salvucci, Richard J. *Textiles and Capitalism in Mexico: An Economic History of the Obrajes, 1539–1840.* Princeton, NJ: Princeton University Press, 1987.

Santamaría, Fransisco J. *Diccionario General de Americanismos.* Mexico City: Pedro Robredo, 1942.

———. *Diccionario de mejicanismos.* Mexico City: Porrúa, 1974.

Scardaville, Michael Charles. "Crime and the Urban Poor: Mexico City in the Late Colonial Period." Ph.D. disseration, University of Florida, 1977.

Schell, Jr., William. "Money as a Commodity: Mexico's Conversion to the Gold Standard, 1905." *Mexican Studies/Estudios Mexicanos* 12:1 (Winter 1996): 67–89.

Scobie, James R. *Buenos Aires: From Plaza to Suburb, 1870–1910.* New York: Oxford University Press, 1974.

Scott, James C. *Domination and the Arts of Resistance: Hidden Transcripts.* New Haven, CT: Yale University Press, 1990.

———. "Everyday Forms of Peasant Resistance." In *Everyday Forms of Peasant Resistance in South-East Asia,* edited by James C. Scott and Benedict J. Tria Kerkvliet. London: Frank Cass, 1986.

———. *Weapons of the Weak: Everyday Forms of Peasant Resistance.* New Haven, CT: Yale University Press, 1985.

Scott, Joan Wallach. *Gender and the Politics of History.* New York: Columbia University Press, 1988.

Scott, Rebecca. *Slave Emancipation in Cuba: The Transition to Free Labor, 1860–1899.* Princeton, NJ: Princeton University Press, 1985.

Seed, Patricia. *To Love, Honor, and Obey in Colonial Mexico: Conflicts over Marriage Choice, 1574–1821.* Stanford, CA: Stanford University Press, 1992.

Semo, Ilán. "La ciudad tentacular: notas sobre el centralismo en el siglo XX." In *Macrópolis mexicana,* edited by Isabel Tovar de Arechederra and Magdalena Mas. Mexico City: Universidad Iberoamericana–Consejo Nacional para la Cultura y las Artes–DDF, 1994.

Shover, Neal. *Great Pretenders: Pursuits and Careers of Persistent Thieves.* Boulder: Westview Press, 1996.

Slatta, Richard W. *Gauchos and the Vanishing Frontier.* Lincoln: University of Nebraska Press, 1983.

Socolow, Susan Midgen. "Women and Crime: Buenos Aires, 1757–97." In *The Problem of Order in Changing Societies: Essays on Crime and Policing in Argentina and Uruguay, 1750–1940,* edited by Lyman L. Johnson. Albuquerque: University of New Mexico Press, 1990.

Sodi, Carlos Franco. *Don Juan Delincuente y otros ensayos.* Mexico City: Botas, 1951.

Sournia, Jean-Charles. *A History of Alcoholism,* trans. N. Hindley and G. Stanton. Oxford: Basil Blackwell, 1990.

Speckman, Elisa. "Crimen y castigo: Legislación penal, interpretaciones de la criminalidad y administración de justicia: Ciudad de México 1872–1910." Ph.D. dissertation, El Colegio de México, Mexico City, 1999.

Spierenburg, Pieter, ed. *Men and Violence: Gender, Honor, and Rituals in Modern Europe and America.* Columbus: Ohio University Press, 1998.

Staples, Anne. "Policía y Buen Gobierno: Municipal Efforts to Regulate Public Behavior, 1821–1910." In *Rituals of Rule, Rituals of Resistance: Public Celebrations and Popular Culture in Mexico,* edited by William H. Beezley et al. Wilmington, DE: Scholarly Resources, 1994.

Stepan, Nancy Leys. *"The Hour of Eugenics": Race, Gender and Nation in Latin America.* Ithaca, NY: Cornell University Press, 1991.

Stern, Steve. *The Secret History of Gender: Women, Men, and Power in Late Colonial Mexico.* Chapel Hill: University of North Carolina Press, 1995.

Stern, Steve, ed. *Resistance, Rebellion and Consciousness in the Andean Peasant World. 18th to 20th Centuries.* Madison: University of Wisconsin Press, 1987.

Stewart, Frank Henderson. *Honor.* Chicago: Chicago University Press, 1994.

Taracena, Alfonso. *La verdadera revolución mexicana.* 18 vols. Mexico City: Jus, 1960.

Taylor, Ian, Paul Walton, and Jack Young. *The New Criminology: For a Social Theory of Deviance.* London: Routledge and Kegan Paul, 1973.

Taylor, William B. "Between Global Process and Local Knowledge: An Inquiry into Early Latin American Social History, 1500–1900." In *Reliving the Past: The Worlds of Social History,* edited by Olivier Zunz. Chapel Hill: University of North Carolina Press, 1985: 115–90.

———. *Drinking, Homicide, and Rebellion in Colonial Mexican Villages.* Stanford, CA: Stanford University Press, 1989.

Tenenbaum, Barbara A. "Streetwise History: The Paseo de la Reforma and the Porfirian State, 1876–1910." In *Rituals of Rule, Rituals of Resistance: Public Celebrations and Popular Culture in Mexico,* edited by William H. Beezley et al. Wilmington, DE: Scholarly Resources, 1994.

Tenorio, Mauricio. *Mexico at the World's Fairs: Crafting a Modern Nation.* Los Angeles: University of California Press, 1996.

———. "1910 Mexico City: Space and Nation in the City of the *Centenario.*" *Journal of Latin American Studies* 28 (1996): 75–104.

Thompson, E. P. "The Moral Economy of the English Crowd in the Eighteenth Century." *Past and Present* 50 (1971): 76–136.

Trejo, Arnulfo. *Diccionario Etimológico Latinoamericano del Léxico de la Delincuencia.* Mexico City: UTEHA, 1968.

Twinam, Ann. "The Negotiation of Honor: Elites, Sexuality, and Illegitimacy in Eighteenth-Century Spanish America." In *The Faces of Honor: Sex, Shame, and Violence in Colonial Latin America,* edited by Lyman L. Johnson and

Sonya Lipsett-Rivera. Alburquerque: University of New Mexico Press, 1998.

Van Young, Eric. "Islands in the Storm: Quiet Cities and Violent Countrysides in the Mexican Independence Era." *Past and Present* 118 (1988): 130–55.

Vanderwood, Paul J. *Disorder and Progress: Bandits, Police and Mexican Development.* 2d ed. Wilmington, DE: Scholarly Resources, 1992.

Varley, Ann. "Women and the Home in Mexican Family Law." In *Hidden Histories of Gender and the State in Latin America,* edited by Elizabeth Dore and Maxine Molyneux. Durham, NC: Duke University Press, 2000.

Vaughan, Mary Kay. "Modernizing Patriarchy: State Policies, Rural Households, and Women in Mexico, 1930–1940." In *Hidden Histories of Gender and the State in Latin America,* edited by Elizabeth Dore and Maxine Molyneux. Durham, NC: Duke University Press, 2000.

Vázquez Pando, Fernando Alejandro, and Arturo Sotomayor Jiménez. "El derecho monetario en México de 1864 a febrero de 1917." In *Memoria del IV Congreso de Historia del Derecho en México (1986),* edited by Beatriz Bernal. Mexico City: UNAM, 1988: 1043–116.

Vidrio, Manuel. "El transporte en la Ciudad de México en el siglo XIX." In *Atlas de la ciudad de México.* Mexico City: Departamento del Distrito Federal–Colegio de México, 1987.

Viqueira Albán, Juan Pedro. *¿Relajados o reprimidos?: Diversiones públicas y vida social en la ciudad de México durante el siglo de las luces.* Mexico City: Fondo de Cultura Económica, 1987.

Voekel, Pamela. "Peeing on the Palace: Bodily Resistance to Borboun Reforms." University of Texas at Austin, manuscript.

Walkowitz, Judith. *City of Dreadful Delight: Narratives of Sexual Danger in Late-Victorian London.* Chicago: University of Chicago Press, 1992.

Warman, Arturo. "The Political Project of Zapatismo." In *Riot, Rebellion, and Revolution: Rural Social Conflict in Mexico,* edited by Friedrich Katz. Princeton, NJ: Princeton University Press, 1988.

Wells, Allen, and Gilbert M. Joseph. "Modernizing Visions, *Chilango* Blueprints, and Provincial Growing Pains: Mérida at the Turn of the Century." *Mexican Studies/Estudios Mexicanos* 8:2 (Summer 1992): 167–216.

Wilkie, James W. *The Mexican Revolution: Federal Expenditure and Social Change Since 1910.* Berkeley-Los Angeles: University of California Press, 1967.

Wolf, Eric R. *Peasant Wars of the Twentieth Century.* New York: Harper and Row, 1969.

Wolfgang, Marvin E., and Franco Ferracuti. *The Subculture of Violence.* London: Tavistock Publishers, 1967.

Womack Jr., John. *Zapata and the Mexican Revolution.* New York: Vintage, 1970.

Wuthnow, Robert. *Communities of Discourse: Ideology and Social Structure in the Reformation, the Enlightenment and European Socialism.* Cambridge, MA: Harvard University Press, 1989.

Zea, Leopoldo. *El positivismo y la circunstancia mexicana.* Mexico City: FCE-SEP, 1985.

Zedner, Lucia. *Women, Crime, and Custody in Victorian England.* Oxford: Clarendon Press, 1991.

Zehr, Howard. *Crime and the Development of Modern Society: Patterns of Criminality in Nineteenth Century Germany and France.* London: Croom Helm, 1976.

Zimmermann, Eduardo A. "Racial Ideas and Social Reform: Argentina, 1890–1916." *Hispanic American Historical Review* 72, no. 1 (1992): 23–46.

Index

Pablo Piccato is Assistant Professor in the Department of History at Columbia University. He is the author of various articles and books, including (with Ricardo Pérez Montfort and Alberto del Castillo) *Hábitos, Normas y Escándalo: Prensa, Criminalidad y Drogas Durante el Porfiriato Tardío* (1997) and *Congreso y revolución: El parlamentarismo en la XXVI Legislatura* (1990).

Library of Congress Cataloging-in-Publication Data
Piccato, Pablo.
City of suspects : crime in Mexico City, 1900–1931 /
Pablo Piccato.
p. cm.
Includes bibliographical references.
ISBN 0-8223-2750-3 (cloth : alk. paper)
ISBN 0-8223-2747-3 (pbk. : alk. paper)
1. Crime—Mexico—Mexico city. 2. Criminals—Mexico—Mexico city. 3. Working class—Mexico—Mexico city.
4. Poor—Mexico—Mexico city. I. Title: Crime in Mexico City, 1900–1931. II. Title.
HV6815.M4 P53 2001
364.972′53—dc21 2001023943